Rave Culture and Religion

Rave Culture and Religion explores the role of the technocultural rave in the spiritual life of contemporary youth. Documenting the sociocultural and religious parameters of rave and post-rave phenomena at various locations around the globe, scholars of contemporary religion, dance ethnologists, sociologists and other cultural observers unravel this significant youth cultural practice.

The collection provides insights on developments in post-traditional religiosity (especially 'New Age' and 'Neo-Paganism') through studies of rave's gnostic narratives of ascensionism and re-enchantment, explorations of the embodied spirituality and millennialist predispositions of dance culture, and investigations of transnational digital-art countercultures manifesting at geographic locations as diverse as Goa, India, north-eastern New South Wales, Australia and Nevada's Burning Man Festival. Contributors examine raving as a new religious or revitalization movement; a powerful locus of sacrifice and transgression; a lived bodily experience; a practice comparable with world entheogenic rituals; and as evidencing a new Orientalism. A range of technospiritual developments are explored, including:

- DJ techniques of liminality and the ritual process of the dance floor
- techno-primitivism and the sampling of the exotic 'Other'
- the influence of gospel music and the Baptist church on garage music
- psychedelic trance, ecology and millennialism
- psychoactive substance use and neural tuning.

Rave Culture and Religion will be essential reading for advanced students and academics in the fields of sociology, cultural studies and religious studies.

Graham St John is Postdoctoral Research Fellow in the Centre for Critical and Cultural Studies at the University of Queensland, where he is working on a critical ethnography of the Australian techno-tribal movement, and researching new youth countercultures and unofficial strategies of reconciliation. He recently edited *FreeNRG: Notes from the Edge of the Dance Floor* (2001).

Routledge Advances in Sociology

This series aims to present cutting-edge developments and debates within the field of sociology. It will provide a broad range of case studies and the latest theoretical perspectives, while covering a variety of topics, theories and issues from around the world. It is not confined to any particular school of thought.

Rave Culture and Religion

Edited by Graham St John

 Routledge
Taylor & Francis Group

LONDON AND NEW YORK

First published 2004
by Routledge
2 Park Square, Milton Park, Abingdon, Oxon, OX14 4RN

Simultaneously published in the USA and Canada
by Routledge
270 Madison Ave, New York NY 10016

Routledge is an imprint of the Taylor & Francis Group

Transferred to Digital Printing 2009

Typeset in Baskerville by Taylor & Francis Books Ltd

British Library Cataloguing in Publication Data
A catalogue record for this book is available from the British Library

Library of Congress Cataloging in Publication Data
A catalog record for this book has been requested

ISBN10: 0–415–31449–6 (hbk)
ISBN10: 0–415–55250–8 (pbk)

ISBN13: 978–0–415–31449–7 (hbk)
ISBN13: 978–0–415–55250–9 (pbk)

Publisher's Note
The publisher has gone to great lengths to ensure the quality of this reprint
but points out that some imperfections in the original may be apparent.

Contents

Illustrations

Plates

Contributors

Anthony D'Andrea is a PhD candidate in Anthropology at the University of Chicago. Having lived in Brazil, India, Spain and the USA, his publications on alternative spiritualities and lifestyles reflect his current research interests in globalization, subjectivity and emancipation.

Erik Davis is a San Francisco-based writer and author of *TechGnosis: Myth, Magic and Mysticism in the Age of Information*. Besides serving as a contributing writer for *Wired*, Erik has published articles in numerous magazines and journals, including *BookForum* and *The Village Voice*. Recent books that include his essays include *Sound Unbound, Zig Zag Zen: Buddhism and Psychedelics* and *Prefiguring Cyberculture*. Erik has lectured internationally on topics relating to cyberculture, electronic music and spirituality in the postmodern world, and some of his work can be accessed at http://www.techgnosis.com. He is currently writing a history of California spirituality.

Gina Andrea Fatone is a Faculty Fellow in Music at the University of California, Santa Cruz, currently examining the cross-cultural use of oral mnemonics in the learning of instrumental music. She was inspired to explore the implications of *gamelan* in the San Francisco rave scene after performing with Gamelan Anak Swarasanti at a rave in the Sierras in 1997. Gina's research interests include the psychology of music learning and transmission, vocalization and gesture, and musical memory.

François Gauthier is a PhD student, research staff and lecturer at the *Sciences des religions* (Religious Studies) department of the Université du Québec à Montréal (UQÀM), where he specializes in issues regarding religion and its contemporary economy outside traditional institutions. He is the author of a master's thesis as well as articles on rave and techno culture and has co-directed a multidisciplinary project whose works are compiled in *Techn-oritualités: religiosité rave* (in *Religiologiques*, No. 24, fall 2001: http://www.religiologiques.uqam.ca/no24/24index.html). His present research expands to include manifestations of festal contestation in youth culture and the alter-globalization movement.

Morgan Gerard is a freelance journalist completing his PhD dissertation in Social Anthropology at the University of Toronto on ritual and performance in underground dance music. His research interests include popular music and performance, the Canadian music industry and the role of discographies in constructing local histories.

Robert V. Kozinets is an Assistant Professor of Marketing at Northwestern University's Kellogg School of Management. A marketer and anthropologist by training, he has consulted with over 500 companies. His research encompasses high-technology consumption, communities (online and off), entertainment, brand management, consumer activism and themed retail. He has written and published articles on retro brands, Wal-Mart, online coffee connoisseurs, ESPN Zone, *Star Trek*, and the Burning Man Festival for journals such as the *Journal of Consumer Research*, the *Journal of Marketing*, the *Journal of Marketing Research* and the *Journal of Retailing*.

James Landau is a graduate of the University of Colorado at Boulder. His research interests include technologies of the body, discourses of the rave, literature of epistemological uncertainty, psychoanalysis, and theories of the imagination. He is currently working towards his Masters in English Literature at New York University.

Ciaran O'Hagan is a PhD candidate at South Bank University, London, researching dance music, drug use and the information needs of London's underground trance and techno and UK garage scenes. Ciaran's understanding of drug consumption stems from his own experience consuming dance music as a participant, promoter and later as a DJ. During the early 1990s he became a dance outreach worker, providing drugs information at many London events and enabling access to numerous scenes.

Tim Olaveson is a PhD candidate at the University of Ottawa. His areas of specialty are the anthropology of religion, ritual studies, the anthropology of experience, and consciousness studies. He has published articles and book chapters on ritual theory, the rave/party experience in central Canada and the future of electronic music cultures.

Hillegonda C. Rietveld is Senior Lecturer at South Bank University, London. Her main research interest is underground dance club culture, its music and its mediation. She has published widely in the field, including *This Is Our House: House Music, Cultural Spaces and Technologies* (Ashgate, 1998).

Douglas Rushkoff is the author of 10 books about media, values and culture, translated into over 20 languages, including *Media Virus, Ecstasy Club* and *Coercion*, winner of the Marshall McLuhan Award for best media book. His latest, *Nothing Sacred: The Truth About Judaism*, looks at religion's participatory roots and subsequent distortions. He teaches at New York University.

Graham St John has published widely in the fields of anthropology, cultural, youth and religious studies, and recently edited *FreeNRG: Notes from the Edge of the Dance Floor* (Altona: Common Ground, 2001). In 2003 he took up a Postdoctoral Research Fellowship in the Centre for Critical and Cultural Studies at the University of Queensland, where he is working on a critical ethnography of the Australian techno-tribal movement, researching new youth countercultures and unofficial strategies of reconciliation.

Arun Saldanha graduated in Communication Studies at the Free University of Brussels in 1997, where he subsequently spent three years as a Teaching Assistant. Since 2000 he has conducted doctoral research at the Department of Geography, Open University, UK. His research interests include music, globalization, feminism, postcolonial studies and poststructuralism.

John F. Sherry, Jr, is Professor of Marketing at the Kellogg School, and is an anthropologist who studies both the sociocultural and symbolic dimensions of consumption and the cultural ecology of marketing. He is a Fellow of the American Anthropological Association, as well as the Society for Applied Anthropology. He is a past President of the Association for Consumer Research and a former Associate Editor of the *Journal of Consumer Research*. He enjoys wandering the world as a researcher, teacher and consultant.

Melanie Takahashi is a PhD candidate in the Department of Classics and Religious Studies at the University of Ottawa. Her research interests include the anthropology of religion, ritual and altered states of consciousness, and contemporary youth movements. She is currently conducting research on the DJ as technoshaman phenomenon and the causal relationship between the techniques of the DJ and the precise nature of the experiences had by ravers.

Des Tramacchi is a PhD candidate in the Department of Studies in Religion at the University of Queensland. His research interests include the religious use of psychoactive substances, ecstatic dance cultures and the anthropology of consciousness. He is currently investigating pharmacological cultures and social attitudes toward them.

Foreword

Never trust a writer to chronicle a movement.

Those of us filing early dispatches from the temporary autonomous zones later known as raves really thought we were just observing the scene – well, participating in the way that all journalists since Hunter S. Thompson have had to acknowledge their own presence at the fringe of the story, but not really engaging in the event as one of *them*, those kids who really think something is happening beyond a bunch of people dancing on drugs.

Right. *You* try going to a rave as a spectator and see what happens.

For me, it all began while I was researching a book on early cyberculture. Around 1990, the entirety of California's emerging digital society seemed to be summed up by a single image: the fractal. I'd see the paisley-like geometry on Grateful Dead tickets, in new reports out of UC Santa Cruz about systems theory, on the T-shirts of kids also wearing cryptic smiles, in books on chaos maths and on the computer screens of virtual-reality programmers at Sun. These depictions of non-linear math equations – equations that cycle almost infinitely rather than finding 'solutions' as we commonly think of them – embodied a new way of looking at the world.

As we were all to learn, the fractal is a self-similar universe. Zoom in on one level, and you find a shape strikingly similar but not exactly the same as one on a higher level, and so on. The fractal is a conceptual leap, inhabiting the space between formerly discrete dimensions. In the process, it allows us to measure the very rough surfaces of reality – rocks, forests, clouds and the weather – more accurately and satisfactorily than the idealistic but altogether limited linear approximations we'd been using since the ancient Greeks. The fractal heralded a new way of looking at the world – of experiencing it – and of understanding that every tiny detail reflected, in some small way, the entirety of the system.

That's why when an anonymous skate kid on the Lower Haight happened to hand me a tiny swatch of paper with a fractal stamped on one side, I was compelled to turn it over and try to decrypt the little map on the other. By about two the next morning, having found the mysterious location (apparently an abandoned whorehouse in Oakland), I also discovered the true meaning of the fractal.

See, I was a writer – on assignment from New York, with a real advance. That gave me the perfect excuse to play the part of participant-observer. To stand on the fringe, watch the crazy kids on E drinking their smart drinks, playing with brain machines and dancing under lasers to the 120 bpm bleep tracks. Cool. I'd happened upon an update of the Acid Test, an environment designed to induce altered states of consciousness.

I didn't take it so very seriously, though, until I began talking with the organizers. As the first journalist on this particular scene, I got the royal treatment. This was before the rave movement and most of the rest of America became a media circus. There were still a few pockets like this one, and grunge, that remained relatively undiscovered country. But, unlike grunge, the kids making raves in America wanted to be discovered. They believed that they had created a hybrid of countercultural agenda and mainstream hype. It was a delicate balance, but the main idea was to make love trendy.

And all you had to do to 'get it' was show up, maybe pop an E, and dance with the beautiful boys and girls. That's right – dance with everyone, not a partner. It wasn't about scoring; it was about group organism. Like a slam-dance or mosh pit, but without the slamming. Just the groove. And the smiles. If everything went right – and usually everything went right – there'd be a moment, or maybe even a whole hour – when it just clicked into place. All the individual dancers would experience themselves as this single, coordinated being. A creature with a thousand arms and eyes, making love with itself and reaching back as far as creation and forward to the very end of time. They became a living fractal, feeding back on itself – sometimes quite literally with video cameras, projectors and screens – right through to infinity. And, as Peter Pan, the first fairytale raver, told us, 'beyond'.

Evolution was no longer competition, it was a team sport. Fuelled by music, chemicals, motion and, most of all, empathy. We were navigating a course through hyperspace to the attractor at the end of history.

Did I say 'we'? Of course I mean 'they'. For I was determined to remain on the fringe. One foot in, so I'd know what I was writing about, but one foot out, so I'd maintain my journalistic integrity. Or so I thought.

For what was I really hanging on to by keeping one foot off the dance floor at all times? Perspective? What did that matter when the view from inside the fractal is no less objective? All perspectives are arbitrary. Besides, how could I write about what this thing called 'rave' really looks like if I didn't know how the group sees itself? After all, that's the whole point of this exercise, right? To create group consciousness and group perspective?

No, I wasn't maintaining journalistic integrity at all, I told myself. I was just afraid. Of what? The intimacy. Losing myself to the sea of, well, love. Breaking the boundaries that helped me maintain the illusion that I am me, Douglas, the separate person from you. From them.

So, as I'm sure you've guessed by now, I went in. Well, why the fuck not? It was contagious, alive, welcoming and so very *very* seductive. It was a lust that I felt, plain and simple. Not for a sexual union, but to merge with this creature and all its many component people.

They got me. Or should I say *it* got me. And then I was it.

And I dutifully wrote my books about what I found out: there's a bunch of people dancing to a new kind of music, but it isn't just dancing because what they've discovered is that they've learned how to make God. Add a few bracketing devices so it doesn't look like I necessarily believe they can do what they think they're doing, and call it a day.

There was no way for me to emerge from the experience of rave, however, without becoming both its chronicler and its propagandist. This is your brain on journalism; this is your brain after being dipped into the rave phenomenon. My work of that period is probably more valuable as an example of what people wrote like when they were experiencing the rave reality than what may have actually happened. Or what it was really about. After I was done with my 'non-fiction' book about this culture, I wrote a fictitious novel that was entirely more accurate.

That's why this volume strikes me as so important. The contributors to this book have taken the time and exercised the discipline necessary to put rave in its proper historical and social context as a religious movement. I may have some problems with the word religion, because it sounds so organized and institutional, while rave has always been such a spontaneous and emergent phenomenon. But there are certainly some formulas involved in making a rave happen, and a pretty common set of reactions to the experience.

If it really is a religion, then I suppose rave is over in some respects. For once it can be catalogued and comprehended is it still a spiritual experience capable of breaking the boundaries between self and everything else? Perhaps not.

But beware. You don't have to be on E, or even in a club, to be infected by the very viral thought structures and emotional responses generated by a rave gathering. After all, a rave doesn't happen in space, but in time – stretching well into the past and into the future. We knew back then that we were speaking to others through our movements. Maybe those others were you.

Indeed, the raves on pages ahead of you are still occurring, and no matter how removed you think you might be from their effects, the logic of the fractal may just come to include you, too.

Douglas Rushkoff
New York, March 2003

Acknowledgements

The compilation of this collection was motivated by extended morning sessions with fellow liminars on dance floors and adjacent environs in the southeast of Australia. The book, and the editor's own contributions in particular, became the progeny of this 'community of feeling', and was made manifest with the assistance of various midwives.

Discussions and exchanges with contributors to the collection assisted in its production. Communications with François Gauthier, Hillegonda C. Rietveld, Des Tramacchi, Robert Kozinets and Erik Davis proved particularly stimulating and helpful at various times and I would like to thank them. My gratitude is also extended to Douglas Rushkoff for writing the foreword, and Saskia Folk, the Drop Bass Network, Alexander Browne, Martin Reddy, Steven Wishman and Caroline Hayeur (http://www.agencestockphoto.com/rituelfestif), for permitting the reproduction of quality image material. I would also like to thank Hillegonda C. Rietveld for permitting the use of the cover image to her book *This Is Our House*, taken circa 1990 by Tod Fath at the Hacienda, Manchester, UK.

For a wide range of assistance with leads, links, contacts, sources and ideas throughout the volume's production, I doff my cap to Henry Kielarowski (Apollo), Fraser Clark, Wolfgang Sterneck, Jason Keehn (Cinnamon Twist), Dave Green, Adam Fish, Linda Rightmire, Douglas Fraser, Mark Dery, George McKay, Paul Chambers, David Voas, Mathew Guest, Neil Elliot, Robin Cooke, Eugene ENRG, Mari Kundalini, Rak Razam, Ray Castle, Rolf Bjerkhamn, Monikat (Unchained Reaction) and Torsten (from Liquid Crystal Vision). As usual, Kurt Svendsen and Richard Martin were more than accommodating with various (sometimes outlandish) requests. Finally, the project would not have been achievable without the support and understanding of my favourite party girl, Jackie.

Introduction

Graham St John

Dance parties have transmuted the role that organised religion once had to lift us onto the sacramental and supramental plane.

(Ray Castle, in ENRG 2001: 169)

From African priests to Korean shamans, there was and still is the belief that dance and music can open communication with intangible powers and produce tangible benefits for the communities involved: self-knowledge; fuller understanding of the natural world; good health; and a sense of belonging to a supportive group in an often dark and hostile but ultimately understandable universe.

(Apollo 2001: issue 34)

David danced and sang before God and we're just bringing it back with a funkier beat.[1]

On the other side of nihilism new formations are emerging, this time exploiting the faultlines in the cultural landscape by slipping through the gaps. Ecstatic dance offers one such line of flight. Dance culture exploits the power of music to build a future on the desolate terrain of the present.

(Hemment 1996: 26)

In early December 2002, several thousand psychedelic trance enthusiasts journeyed to Lindhurst in the South Australian outback where, in the calm of a weeklong sonic onslaught, they witnessed a total solar eclipse. With precedents like the Solipse festivals in Hungary and Zambia, Outback Eclipse attracted young electronic dance music habitués from dozens of nations. Contemporary global events like Solipse, Portugal's Boom, Japan's Solstice23 and Australia's Exodus Cybertribal Festival draw inspiration from epic beach parties at the former Portuguese colony of Goa (India) and Moontribe's Full Moon gatherings in the Mojave Desert near Los Angeles. While diverse themselves, these events represent a mere snapshot of the moving panorama of that which came to be known as *rave*:[2] from the celebration of celestial events at remote locations to electro-salvation at metropolitan massives; from temporary Arcadias flourishing in converted warehouses, to transformational rituals like those facilitated by

Philadelphia's Gaian Mind, to the brand-name liminality of super-clubs like London's Ministry of Sound; from huge corporate-sponsored extravaganzas like Tribal Gathering (where tens of thousands may congregate), to 'megatribal' gatherings like Earthdream, a 'technomadic' carnival held annually in Central Australia and destined to culminate on 21 December 2012 in accordance with the Mayan Sacred Calendar; from the gospel-inspired exhilaration of house and garage, to the Afrofuturism of jungle and Detroit techno, to techno-pagan doofs held in outdoor locations featuring ceremonial art installations and revived 'ancestral rituals'; from Earthdance, a Free Tibet movement fundraiser transpiring in over 100 cities in 70 countries simultaneously with a synchronized global cybercast, to Christian ecumenical raves like Sheffield's notorious 'Rave Mass' or Matthew Fox's Techno Cosmic Mass in California.[3] Electronic dance music culture is a truly heterogeneous global phenomenon, motivating new spiritualities and indicating the persistence of religiosity amongst contemporary youth.

Despite its hybridization throughout the 1990s, the dance party rave – involving masses of young people dancing all night to a syncopated electronic rhythm mixed by DJs – maintains rapturous popularity in the West, developing diasporic tendrils from Ibiza to London, West Coast USA to Goa, India, Japan to South Africa, Brazil to Australia, and tourist enclaves from Thailand to Madagascar. Commonly accorded effects ranging from personal 'healing' or replenishment to transformations on social, cultural or political scales, rave – from clubland to outdoor doof, to technomadic festival – is a hyper-crucible of contemporary youth spirituality. Thus the question motivating this volume: what exactly is the role of the technocultural rave in the spiritual life of contemporary youth?

Emerging in London in 1988, and subsequently exported around the world, rave has proliferated and mutated alongside associated music and body technologies. Its primary theatre of action was and remains the dance floor, a kinaesthetic maelstrom inflected by diverse sonic currents and technological developments influencing that which has been generically dubbed 'house', 'electronica' and 'techno'. Throughout the 1990s rave grew prevalent in the experience of urban youth as vast numbers attached primary significance to raving. With the combined stimulus of electronic musics, psychotropic lighting, chemical alterants and all-night dancing, young novices and experienced habitués transcended the mundane in converted warehouses, wilderness areas, beaches, deserts and streets. Decked out in esoteric accessories, ultra violet (UV)-reactive clothing, personalized icons and an array of assimilated 'religious' glossolalia, their ecstatic experiences moved multitudes to draw on a plenitude of traditional interpretative religious frameworks – Hindu, Buddhist, Christian, pagan, Australian Aboriginal, mystical, etc. – often refracted through lenses taken up by generational forebears themselves heir to frameworks inadequate for communicating their own revelations.

Such communications are fraught with the dilemmas not unfamiliar to earlier generations of youth, for there exists a curious tension between contraries within the culture of rave. The desire to disseminate event-derived revelations, to mount the 'rave-o-lution', competes with a desire to remain hidden, covert, cultic even. For many, the orthodox rave is, and should remain, underground, with the location of parties communicated by word of mouth and on subtle flyers distributed through local channels. Efforts to maintain a 'tribal' identity, an 'underground sociality' (Maffesoli 1996), through commitment to genre (e.g. jungle, psytrance, gabba, garage, ragga, two step, etc.) and to the almost universal envelope-pushing esoterica. Simon Reynolds (1998: xvii) identifies as *hardcore*, evidence a refusal, an aloofness, an invisibility thought to hold back the long entwined arms of state administrations and corporate entertainment industries – which have made significant advances in regulating and assimilating this culture. Yet, while with acid house 'a whole subculture attempts to vanish' (Melechi 1993: 38), others rupture this logic of disappearance, desiring to inject the 'meme' into the parent culture, to share the conspiracy, converting, through various channels, the 'hundredth monkey'. While tacticians of dance undertake to transform values without seeking to attract attention to themselves, for cultural luminaries disappearance and secrecy cultivate paranoia and panic, thwarting the critical mass pursued.

Rave enjoys a direct inheritance from disco and house developments in the post-Stonewall gay communities of New York City (NYC) and Chicago in the 1970s and 1980s. As Apollo (Henry Kielarowski) postulates in his intimate history of house, *House Music 101*, it was in this period in NYC that an oppressed subculture consisting of a fair proportion of African-Americans and Latinos gave birth to house music and modern electronic dance culture. Deriving from gospel, soul and funk, as well as Latino salsa, house is said to be the music 'of both sin and salvation', an attempt to 'reconcile body and soul' which, in its current manifestations, retains 'that yearning we all have to celebrate the spirit through the body' (Apollo 2001: issue 3). Significantly, house evolved at a time when it was widely anticipated by its adherents that it would abolish all 'the soul sickness of the world – racism, bigotry, poverty, Puritanism, war – and establish a new order based on peace and love' (*ibid.*). The anthem was sampled and remixed in time for the much-mythologized 'second summer of love' (late 1980s), and at the beginning of the 21st century post-rave maintains a millennialist charge.

Members of the rave milieu hold shares in ecstatic 'communities of feeling', both clandestine and over the counter. A popular vehicle of hope, compassion and expectancy – surely amplified at a time when a millennium closes and another begins – rave holds a conspiratorial optimism perhaps best characterized by zippie Fraser Clark's widely promoted 'pronoia', a term coined by Electronic Frontier Foundation co-founder and Grateful Dead lyricist John Perry Barlow as 'the suspicion the Universe is conspiring on your behalf'.[4] Assembled from cyber, digital and chemical technologies, rave is believed to be the foundation for a culture democratic, empathogenic, cyborgian and sublime – its culture a determined flight, with varying degrees of success, from pop, rock and club realms where the dancing body is an object of media, state (and male) surveillance. While indebted to the 1960s, which saw the mass production and distribution of new technologies of transformation (especially LSD) and multimedia excursions like Kesey's Trips Festival (San Francisco, January 1966), the empathetic character distinctive to rave has been largely activated by the 'love drug' MDMA, or 'ecstasy' – an entheogenic 'body technology' regarded as something of a 'utopiate' infiltrating house club culture through 1970s and 1980s gay and mixed club scenes, psycho-therapeutic circles and new spiritual formations in the US (Eisner 1994; Beck and Rosenbaum 1994). In his comprehensive treatment of dance culture, *Energy Flash*,[5] Reynolds suggests that 'E' was early exalted as 'the remedy for alienation caused by an atomised society', with rave evolving 'into a self-conscious science of intensifying MDMA's sensations' (1998: xxii, xxvi).

Despite commercial encroachment and state regulatory controls, through Chicago house and with the advent of acid house (in the late 1980s, UK) a utopic strain has nourished the hybrid rave experience and remains at the centre of its self-promotion – a utopianism expressed in the pop-mantra PLUR (peace, love, unity, respect), the 'Four Pillars of House Community' adapted from comments attributed to DJ Frankie Bones at a Brooklyn Storm Rave in 1992 (Fritz 1999: 203–4). Post-rave promoters have successfully endorsed raving as a possibility engine for the self; a nocturnal utopia upon which rave-tourists disembark from their everyday lives; an antinomian otherworld within which event-inhabitants are licensed to perform their other selves; a sacred topos where dance-initiates and habitués (re)connect with co-liminars, nature and the cosmos. Many commentators celebrate the non-Christian religiosity of dance 'ritual', dubbing it, as does chaos art designer Gregory Sams (1997), the 'new church'. Optimistic or nostalgic, embracing pre- or post-Christian communions, post-rave pundits champion the 'shamanic' states of consciousness engendered or 'trance' states triggered by the new ritual.

The rhythmic soundscapes of electronic dance music genres are thought to inherit the sensuous ritualism, percussive techniques and chanting employed by non-Western cultures and throughout history for spiritual advancement. As house is compared favourably with the Cult of Oro in pre-Christian Polynesia, the Hopi Indian Snake Dance and Yoruba trance (Apollo 2001: issue 33), and raving with Sufi dancing or the Kirtan dancing of Hare Krishnas (Fritz 1999), the new church is, as Jimi Fritz claims in his *Rave Culture: An Insider's Overview*, 'non-denominational' – with the 'trance states' serving 'a more personal journey through the dancer's own psyche that can ultimately prove to be…rewarding for spiritual or psychological growth' (Fritz 1999: 79). While rave's trance dance is rarely culturally encoded and incorporated into everyday life in a fashion that may characterize the experience of the Yoruba, having caught the eye of 'post-modern theologians', the new 'mass' has been embraced for ecumenical purposes, a circumstance exemplified by the monthly Techno Cosmic Mass in Oakland, California, where the Episcopal priest and director of the University of Creation Spirituality, Matthew Fox, adopts electronic music, multimedia, trance dancing and rap to revitalize the Judeo-Christian Mass, to reawaken 'a sense of the sacred'.[6]

Extolled as a source of growth, union, salvation or the sacred, raving is thus exalted as a site of becoming. Driven by post-1960s millenarianism, many have laboured to disclose a 'revolutionary' culture holding the potential 'to ultimately change the course of human consciousness' (Fritz 1999: 38). With rave, class, ethnicity, gender and other social distinctions were imagined to dissipate. Thus, according to one baton-wielding commentator: 'We are the visionaries, and it is our job to slowly change society. There was a women's movement, a sexual revolution, and many other giant steps taken by previous generations. It is now time for the next revolution' (Pete, in Saunders *et al.* 2000: 175). In the euphoric head-rush of post-apartheid South Africa, David Dei and Jesse Stagg (n.d.) wrote that 'fascism dissolves before the resistance of the rave generation' and the 'love virus' said to be infecting South African youth in the early 1990s. Offering a blueprint for social change, trailblazing a path to the promised land, the 'Mass', 'movement' or 'rave nation' elicited by these authors, practitioners and spokespeople is even thought to seed 'a new form of liberation theology' (Hill 1999: 97). Sampling 'brotherhood' and 'heart chakras', rave evangelists communicate their conversion experiences. Amidst a rich vein of reports, Fritz communicates his first rave (at the age of 40):

> I had walked into a different world...without judgement or fear...I was in a sea of six hundred radiant souls putting into practice five thousand years of religious and philosophical hypothesis. Beyond the conceptual world of ideas and dogma this was a direct experience of tribal spirituality practiced by our ancestors...my experience that night changed my life for the better.
>
> (Fritz 1999: 5–6)

Subsequent to his revelation, Fritz went forth to deliver the word.

Other commentary, including that rising to the surface of the global media-scape and evident in the serial moralizing of Christian teen fiction (cf. LaHaye and DeMoss 2001), questions the meaning and morals of rave/dance culture, challenging the quality of the 'communion', the purpose of the 'ritual' and the substance of this youth 'movement'. Gauging the range of responses to youth *ekstasis*, the collective expression amongst contemporary youth of that which for Reynolds smells like 'Dionysian spirit', is a curious project. For establishment reaction, evident for example in the notorious RAVE (or Reducing Americans' Vulnerability to Ecstasy) Bill in the United States,[7] reveals a trenchant fear of youth transcendence – as authorities, suspicious of bodily pleasure, conflate dance with moral corruption. Yet the prospect is also received with discomfort and even treated with contempt by an academic tradition inheriting the scepticism of Birmingham's Centre for Contemporary and Cultural Studies, for whom neo-Marxist-oriented youth cultural 'resistance' was primary. By and large, youth cultural studies has unsatisfactorily addressed both dance – dismissed as a retreat from (masculine) resistance – and non-traditional youth religiosity. From the jazz, rock, purist perspective, dance maintains a 'seductive' force, thought to 'weaken critical faculties by encouraging us to respond to music in ways which involve neither contemplation nor respect' (Straw 2001: 159). Disciplinary paradigms populated by secular humanists too often baulk at the prospect of young (especially white) people corporealizing utopian dreams, entering alternate states of consciousness and communicating with the sacred (with or without the assistance of psychoactives). This is probably, in part, due to the way rational sociological models cannot possibly circumscribe that which Rudolf Otto named the '*mysterium tremendum*', the religious experience which he indicated 'may burst in sudden eruption up from the depths of the soul with spasms and convulsions, or lead to the strongest excitements, to intoxicated frenzy, to transport, and to ecstasy' (1959: 27).

Furthermore, the significance of that which the anthropologist of cultural performance Victor Turner dubbed the realm of the 'subjunctive mood' – a world of 'wish, desire, possibility or hypothesis' (Turner 1982: 83) – has been routinely overlooked or misapprehended by practitioners of youth cultural studies. Ludic spaces are too often cast as 'frivolous' and 'inconsequential'. Although recent dance ethnographies conducted on clubbing (Malbon 1999; Pini 2001) provide exceptions, the highly valued, unpredictable and potentially transcendent alterities licensed are often dismissed as irrational and mere 'pretence' as emic *play* is consigned to the devalued territory of 'make-believe' or 'fantasy' (Handelman 1990: 70). While an apparent depthless 'hyperreality' transpires (see Redhead 1993), the 'fantasy of liberation' (Melechi 1993: 37) thought to characterize rave demonstrates continuity with the ineffectual 'rituals of resistance' thought to underline earlier youth 'subcultures'.

Questioning rave's millennialism, some commentators challenge the ostensible levelling of social relations of the liberatory rave (e.g. McRobbie 1994: 170; Thornton 1995; Saldanha 2002). Others, like Douglas Rushkoff (1999), have lamented the compromising of rave's 'Sabbath'-like holy day by corporate interests and politics. Others still, usually health researchers, have highlighted the risks to youth posed by ecstasy, often having neglected to report that much of what passes for 'ecstasy' is substituted (often cut with aspirin, caffeine, methamphetamine or other dangerous substances), with national prohibitionary classifications and the intransigent dismissal of harm-minimization strategies unnecessarily compromising public health and increasing risks for the uneducated. The title of one publication, *The Love Drug: Marching to the Beat of Ecstasy* (Cohen 1998), calls up an image of innocent youth seduced by an insipid robopharmacological pied piper. For Reynolds (1998), a dystopic comedown from chemical nirvana suggests that the living dream may have turned nightmare – with raving mutating from a 'paradise regained' to a 'psychic malaise'. With the excessive and routinized use of adulterated ecstasy (and increased polydrug abuse – e.g. mixing with 'crystal meth' and other 'obliviates') 'scenes lose their idyllic lustre and become a soul-destroying grind' (Reynolds 1998: xxxi; see also Push and Silcott 2000: ch. 13). And, together with genre fragmentation, the plunge into rave's dark side has precipitated a 'seeping away of meaning, the loss of a collective sense of going somewhere' (Reynolds 1997: 102).

What is the religious experience of rave? Is it confined to the appropriation of religious resources and iconography, such as the ironized Christian motifs of Drop Bass Network's 'Jesus Raves', held in Racine, Wisconsin in June 2002? Is rave just one more cultural sphere in tension with established practices and public policy 'using religion' to symbolize 'ultimate meaning, infinite power, supreme indignation and sublime compassion'? (Beckford 1989: 172). Does spiritual rhetoric serve to establish subcultural capital within youth milieus? Or does rave contextualize phenomenal religious experiences? Does it conform to Bauman's perceived devolution or 'relocation' of religious experience as 'the product of a life devoted to the art of consumer self-indulgence' (Bauman 1998: 70) or assist in delivering youth from a legion of maladies and stresses, offering meaning, purpose and hope to those whose playground may otherwise be confined to the parameters of Playstation II? A religious experience or a total leisure concept? Should we thus give credence to the experiences of its adherents as genuinely liberating or transcendent? Does rave assist in the provision of assurance in the face of pain, suffering and mortality, providing answers to life's mysteries, or is this a contemporary realm for 'psychedelic theophanies' where, as Huston Smith (1976: 155) warned, one more readily finds an addiction to acquiring 'the religious experience' above commitment to 'the religious life'?

Furthermore, what is rave's ritual character? Is it a rite of passage – and, if so, what is its level and quality of efficacy? What is its telos? Is it a ritual of communion, a mass 'return' to a 'womb' which sees co-inhabitants secure in a nutrient-rich and numinous pre-separation stage, or an *anomic* post-partum 'dead-zone' catering for escapist desires and tragic careers in over-expenditure? An 'oceanic experience' (Malbon 1999) or a kind of prolonged youth suicide? Does post-rave more closely approximate a church, Disney World, or a 'detention camp for youth' (Reynolds 1998: 424)? Has the cyber-chemical-millenarianism which flourished under the roof of the original acid house been domesticated – the rapture contained and smothered in regulated and commodified leisure sites? Or has its technospiritual fervour been smuggled away into furtive temporary autonomous zones where it percolates still?

Perhaps the inquiry should be less about religion *per se* than spirituality. After all, as Heelas has stated, in the de-traditionalized present 'people have what they *take* to be "spiritual" experiences without having to hold religious *beliefs*' (1998: 5). The current volume holds that something substantial is at work in dance culture. Rave culture has certainly not been impervious to niche marketing, consumer pressure and brand loyalties, and it would not be inaccurate to articulate contemporary formations as part of the 'meta-experiential goods and services' industry run by today's peak-experience providers (Bauman 1998). Yet, as a temporary respite from the cycle of living-through-buying at the heart of possessive materialism, as a community largely for and by youth, rave and its progeny are potent sites of *being together*. And this, together with an understanding of the commitments undertaken by young people to defend their community from those who would imperil or undermine it, should provide us with a subject worthy of our contemplation.

Book outline

The collection is divided into four parts. The first, 'Techno culture spirituality', deciphers trends within the fast developments and vast detritus of rave culture. In the road-mapping of a spiritual practice and the fashioning of a teleology, a purpose, a commitment, the dance millennium draws upon a vast repertoire of theistic and communitarian principles. In Chapter 1, 'The difference engine: liberation and the rave imaginary', the editor initiates a comprehensive investigation of rave's religiosity, exploring the vast psycho-cultural terrain of the rave imaginary. Attending to primary narratives (ascensionist and re-enchantment) and soteriological functions, I explore the liberatory configuration of rave, charting the gnostic and salvific themes implicit in its culture and illuminating contemporary youth participation in key developments (e.g. New Age and Neo-Pagan) of post-traditional religiosity. While dancescapes are often reported to be utopic experiences perhaps best translated – in the language of Victor Turner – as a techno-'communitas' (a theme cropping up regularly throughout the volume), they are complex utopic sites, often appearing rather heterotopic in character. Elective 'disappearance' into carnivalesque zones facilitating sustained experimentation with subjectivity and community enables the modification of self and society, but it does so in a hyper-liminal context.

As a techno-communion, dance culture constitutes an interfacing of technology and humans, a core theme taken up by Hillegonda C. Rietveld in Chapter 2, 'Ephemeral spirit: sacrificial cyborg and communal soul'. Undertaking an exploration of techno (trance) and house developments in the history of electronic music, Rietveld concludes that, as an 'interface spirituality', post-rave is the 'spiritual rite of the post-industrial cyborg'. Both this and the previous chapter are partially informed by Erik Davis's *Techgnosis* (1998). While the former makes a not always clear division of the posthumanist (spirituality) from the revivalist (sacrality) trajectories of techno, Rietveld makes a corresponding distinction between a cyborgian techno spirit and a gospel-influenced (and thus embodied and ensouled) house community – an analysis informed by the sexual politics of electronic music: where males become more devoted to a machine aesthetic, females are engaged in the scene's human relational experience. Sacrifice is another key theme common to both opening chapters. While in the earlier contribution individual commitment to underground ('DIY') events forges community identification and may facilitate redemption, in the latter an adaptation of Georges Bataille's concept of sacrifice informs Rietveld's observation of the dancer losing self to the music, to the machine, thereby assisting transition to a cyborg-like subjectivity in a period of information-technology-induced identity crisis.

The theme of self-sacrifice assists our passage to Part II, 'Dance, rapture and communion', which investigates the primary activity of raving, dance. In Chapter 3, 'Rapturous ruptures: the "instituant" religious experience of rave', François Gauthier draws on seminal French theory to explicate how rave's primary activity constitutes a religious experience. As he explains, the strong and growing 'effervescence of rave in contemporary youth culture', illustrates thriving religiosity in fragmented and non-institutional forms. In conjunction with an application of French anthropologist and theorist of contemporary religion Roger Bastide, which assists in the transcription of raving as 'savage trance' in a period where 'truth and meaning must come from and be judged on the scale of *experience*', Gauthier draws upon a depth reading of Bataille to regard rave as an exemplary manifestation of the 'damned', 'blasted' or 'accursed share' of contemporary humanity. Focusing on its tendency towards excess and communion, rave is perceived as a cultural resurgence of the festive, an eternal present 'brewing up mythologies of an elsewhere' which provides 'new avenues for experiences of the sacred in an atomized society'. Committed to a 'logic of sacrificial consumption', rupturing the profane, becoming 'other' or 'feral' to rock spectaculars and 'domesticated' leisure practices and facilitating a transgression most readily observable in the abandon of *dance* or 'trance', rave hastens that which Bastide calls an 'instituant' religious experience.

Curiously, the savage religion of the 'instituant' experience parallels performance ethnographer Victor Turner's concept of 'spontaneous communitas', itself indexing a primary moment, an apocalypse of subjectivity. Like the instituant, communitas often catalyses normative social configurations, which themselves stimulate unstructured, or 'anti-structural' paroxysms. Indeed, Turner's work has become seminal to rave culture studies. Such is demonstrated in Chapter 4, ' "Connectedness" and the rave experience: rave as new religious movement?' Drawing upon an ethnographic study of the central Canadian rave scene, Tim Olaveson pays tribute to the utility of Turner and Émile Durkheim, whose equivalent approaches to public paroxysms – as 'communitas' and 'effervescence' – offer conceptual value in the systematic exploration of a core attribute of raving – 'connectedness'. Olaveson proposes that rave's techniques and practices of connectedness demonstrate instances of 'syncretic ritualizing' (Grimes) which, in their creative spontaneity, their 'vibe' (a theme arising elsewhere in the volume – Chapter 7–10), constitute a likely source of contemporary cultural revitalization. Thus, his discussion also raises the possibility of understanding rave as a new religious movement, adaptive to the apparent meaninglessness of consumer culture – a prospect tentatively embraced since global rave is hardly a 'movement' or 'cult' with a central body of teachings or a single charismatic leader. While Olaveson holds 'connectedness' to be a phenomenological experience involving an embodied condition, it is James Landau who attends to the corporeal experience of raving, in Chapter 5. With the assistance of traditional philosophies of depth, in 'The flesh of raving: Merleau-Ponty and the "experience" of ecstasy' Landau describes the lived, bodily experience of ravers' self/other boundary dissolution. Deleuze and Guattari's Body-without-Organs (BwO) and the Lacanian Real are found wanting. But, with its emphasis on reversibility, ambiguity and interconnectedness, with its non-dualistic 'ontology of the flesh', Maurice Merleau-Ponty's phenomenology is cast as a useful model for understanding the apparent contradiction in the ecstatic rave experience: the claim that participants feel simultaneously 'dissolved within *and* separate from the universe'. Such is possible since the body possesses 'innate knowledge' of its simultaneous unity with the world and its alterity from it – its 'difference-within-identity'.

Any study of electronic music culture, especially with relation to the sense of community, abandonment and transcendence occasioned on the dance floor, would be incomplete without attention to the significance of psychoactive substances or 'entheogens' – a non-pejorative non-ethnocentric term recommended by Ott (1993) to indicate shamanistic substances. While Landau laudably avoids a 'neurodeterministic reduction of ecstasy to MDMA', we cannot ignore the role of substances like MDMA, LSD or other entheogens in dance. In 'Entheogenic dance ecstasis: cross-cultural contexts' (Chapter 6), Des Tramacchi explores the broad parallels existing between non-Western community-oriented entheogenic rituals and psychedelic dance parties. Drawing on ethnographic descriptions of peyote use among the Mexican Huichol, *yajé* (*ayahuasca*) sessions among the Barasana of Colombia and *eboka* by Bwiti cult members among the Fang and Metsogo of Gabon, Tramacchi discerns that their common structural elements are also prominent features of 'bush parties', or 'doofs', found flourishing in northern New South Wales and southeast Queensland, Australia. Though LSD may be the most common psychoactive at doofs, MDMA or 'E' is clearly the most prevalent dance drug. Yet, while this may be the case, in Chapter 7, 'The "natural high": altered states, flashbacks and neural tuning at raves', Melanie Takahashi indicates that most participants in her central Canadian research emphasized that, contrary to much of the literature, substance use is not as central to their experience. While the limitation or discontinuance of psychoactive consumption is reported among 'a growing category of rave participants', psychoactives remain significant since, as Takahashi observes, initial exposure to MDMA in particular can stimulate permanent changes in the central nervous system ('neural tuning'), enabling the 'natural' approximation of alternative states of consciousness at subsequent raves given the presence of specific triggering devices within the dance environment.

The discussion of neural tuning propels us toward the role of music in dance cultures and its purported transformative function, and thus towards Part III, 'Music: the techniques of sound and ecstasy'. While practitioners and scholars of dance culture wax lyrical about the 'ritual' or 'shamanic' character of rave, as Morgan Gerard points out there has generally been a dearth of analysis explaining such ritual. Drawing on his ethnography of Toronto's Turbo Niteclub, in Chapter 8, 'Selecting ritual: DJs, dancers and liminality in underground dance music', Gerard offers a meta-processual interpretation of the rave/club experience, which in the totality of the electronic music performance, dancing participants and their ongoing interaction is a complex liminal environment. Heavily indebted to Victor Turner, Gerard thus understands the complicated interactive performance context of the underground rave/club as something of a unique 'ritual process'. Departing from the lack of interest in the music and dance of youth ritual displayed by earlier theorists of youth culture, the rave/club is described as an arena of youth transformation made possible by the spatialization and performance of music, and thought dependent upon the way participants 'negotiate liminality' throughout the course of events. Depending on their 'ritual knowledge', for dancers each DJ mix may replay, and eventually accelerate, the phases of van Gennep's rites of passage, effecting belonging in a dance-floor community.

From Canadian tech-house and techno to UK garage. In Chapter 9, 'Sounds of the London Underground: gospel music and Baptist worship in the UK garage scene', Ciaran O'Hagan traces the way African-American patterns of worship have influenced developments within UK garage. In a discussion of repressive legislation, south London's Sunday scene and pirate radio, O'Hagan indicates how gospel-inspired house music in the United States and procedures within the Baptist church have informed the musical structure and style of delivery particular to this scene. Indeed, the tactics and role of the UK garage MC possess an apparent equivalence to that of the Baptist preacher – employing call-response techniques and fostering belonging and communion.

If, as Gerard suspects (echoing Turner), 'retribalisation is well underway', it has been arguably most visible in San Francisco. Through discussion of the performances of a Santa Cruz-based Balinese *gamelan* group (Gamelan Anak Swarasanti) at raves within the Bay Area, in Chapter 10, '*Gamelan*, techno-primitivism and the San Francisco rave scene', Gina Andrea Fatone indicates two significant features of this development: first, that it highlights parallels in the trance-inducing structure of techno and traditional *gamelan* music – though, as Fatone infers, research on the character of altered states of consciousness in electronic music culture requires further exploration; and, second, in furtherance to a discussion initiated in this volume by St John (on re-enchantment, Chapter 1) and Gerard (the perceived 'primitive numinosity' of dance), the appropriation of *gamelan* evidences rave's nostalgia for the 'primitive' and reverence for hi-technology, a juxtaposition revealing a 'techno-primitivism' whereby the *gamelan* ensemble, not unlike the didjeridu and other homogenized 'ethnic' and exotic instruments, becomes 'a tool of authentication' for youth facing 'the threat of ever increasing mechanization'.

The subsumption of the 'primitive' in events transpiring in the 'technocultural present' enables our negotiation to the final part, 'Global tribes: the technomadic counterculture', which covers the countercultural proclivities of a globalized psychedelic trance culture: its neotribalism, ecologism, revivalism, principle sites of pilgrimage, and its role in the formation of a digital art religion in possession of an idealistic, utopic and 'resistant' character open to challenge. In Chapter 11, 'Techno millennium: dance, ecology and future primitives', the editor documents the significance of ecologism for an emergent dance movement. The chapter documents the patterns by which awareness of an accelerating environmental crisis has shaped neo-tribes and new rituals forming in global centres. It documents how, throughout the 1990s, a creative synthesis of new technologies and reconstructed pre-industrial religiosity characterized the interventions of several thinkers, artists and spokesmen whose millenarian ideas circulate within trance culture. From London to San Francisco, a 'cyber-tribal' youth network – whose events are often claimed to occasion an ethical relationship, or reconciliation, with the Earth – emerged within a period of optimism and revitalization fed by cyber and digital developments. The Mediterranean island of Ibiza (Spain) and the former Portuguese colony of Goa (India) are principal exotic locations in the evolution of this global counterculture. Based on ethnography undertaken at these sites, in Chapter 12, 'Global nomads: techno and New Age as transnational countercultures in Ibiza and Goa', Anthony D'Andrea explores the convergence of techno-culture and self-expressive (New Age) spirituality in the formation of 'nomadic subjects' whose technological adaptation, transpersonal rituals, 'erotico-aesthetics' and transgressions, whose 'limit experiences' (Foucault), are said to be composed within a 'globalizing digital art-religion'. Investigating an emergent 'techno' movement possessing strong New Age influences, D'Andrea maps the new nomadic sites of self- and community experimentation – a global 'utopian underground' exiting the nation-state, transgressing major moralities and challenging the dominant institutions constitutive of the modern subject.

As D'Andrea conveys, nomads with post-national identities gravitated to Goa – which became the exotic beachhead of trance-dance and digital-tribalism. Something of the 'post-sexual' lifestyle of D'Andrea's global freak is sighted in Chapter 13 by Erik Davis, whose 'Hedonic tantra: golden Goa's trance transmission' circumscribes the significance of trance, an intrinsic component of the non-genital pleasures of 'spiritual hedonism'. In a first-person journey into the psychedelic heart of Goan trance (based on a report from his visit there in 1993), Davis draws a parallel between Deleuze and Guattari's BwO and Hindu tantric procedure, implying the continuity of psychedelic trance dance with the latter. Effecting a transmutation of cosmic energy, or *shakti*, of sexual energy into 'rarer and more potent elixirs', trance harbours an 'alchemical dynamic' for the bohemian and psychedelic subcultures of rave. This at least approximates the received wisdom of those whose anti-authoritarian practices and techniques – mystical, provisional, cobbled together, ambivalent and often incoherent – have formed, in the 'freak colony' of Goa, something of an 'anti-traditional tradition' transmitted to current and future generations of post-Goa spiritualists. Nevertheless, Davis became alarmed about the 'superficiality' of the Goan scene's relationship with India, with the egotism of DJs and the presence of those bearing a resemblance to a 'gnostic elite'. Such themes are taken up by Arun Saldanha, who argues in Chapter 14, 'Goa trance and trance in Goa: smooth striations', that mystical experiences and exclusionary politics are interdependent. Drawing on ethnography conducted on the practices of trance travellers in Anjuna, Goa, Saldanha illustrates the fiction of PLUR and challenges rave's status as a site of resistance, thus renovating the postructuralism of Deleuze and Guattari. Through a popular Deleuzo–Guattarian lens, the dance floor and its associated trance state are – by contrast to the 'striated', quantified and segregated spaces of capitalism, colonialism and the state – regarded as a 'smooth space' of non-subjectivity, of non-'faciality', a BwO. With the ethnographic revelation that 'power and desire, domination and resistance, regulation and freedom, discipline and trance, habit and transcendence' are not disentangled in the culture of rave, Saldanha concludes that raves do indeed reproduce the 'striations' of capitalism, state regulation, patriarchy, heterosexism, classism, nationalism and racism. Thus, while not seeking to empty rave of its spiritual dimensions, he takes issue with the perception that raves are exclusively 'smooth' and opposed to 'striation'. In isolating these shortcomings in the BwO, Saldanha effectively deals with the social consequences of the limitations in the BwO earlier noted by Landau – that its 'smoothness' does not account for the persistence of individual identity and distinctions.

Of all the emergent sites for the global freak, Nevada's annual Burning Man Festival – which, not unlike developments described in previous chapters (10 and 11), evolved from the countercultural hub of San Francisco – remains a most unique venue for the expression of New Age/techno religiosity. In Chapter 15, 'Dancing on common ground: exploring the sacred at Burning Man', Robert V. Kozinets and John F. Sherry, Jr, draw on their ethnography to discuss how Burning Man shares commonalities with rave and a range of other contemporary alternative cultural and new spiritual events invoking primitivist symbolism in the manifestation of techno-pagan ritual. Echoing other techno trance events delineated in previous chapters and embodying the enchantment-retrieving character of the rave imaginary outlined in Chapter 1, Kozinets and Sherry's ethnography of 'the burn' provides commentary on the conjoining of audio/cyber technologies and Neo-Pagan beliefs and sensibilities in the fashioning of postmodern ritual – therapeutic, 'tribal', transformative. The authors argue that the self-transformative capacity of such events is dependent upon the successful creation of sacred space, and the latter is achieved through temporary festive inversions manifesting in the *in situ* rules of no spectators, no authorities and no market.

The theme of dancing up the sacred in the contemporary period arises throughout this collection and goes to the heart of the rave phenomenon. Whether conceived as primal, futurist, tribal, global or some combination thereof, whether market-driven communitas or countercultural in orientation, new dance cultures are an important feature in the lives of contemporary youth. As the contributors to this collection demonstrate, electronic dance music culture contextualizes and fuels identity formation, inter-cultural understanding, resistance and belonging, despite evidence to the contrary. In a period of mass uncertainty and mounting crises, we cannot afford to underestimate the significance of this amorphous youth cultural presence.

Notes

1 http://www.thepipeline.org/clubworship/whatiscw.htm.
2 'Rave' is often used within this volume to denote a youth cultural sensibility that encompasses *both* the primary moment of rave (in the late 1980s, early 1990s) and its multifarious progeny. 'Post-rave' is sometimes used to designate a welter of cultural experiences and music events downstream from the moment of rave. Thus, far from denoting 'non-rave', 'post-rave' designates a quality of youth cultural experience that is firmly rooted in and indebted to rave.
3 From the late 1980s Sheffield's Anglican Nine O'clock Service constituted 'radical Christian discipleship' in a multimedia environment, later producing the 'theologically

experimental' and influential 'Planetary Mass' (Roberts 1999: 11; also see Howard 1996). For the Techno Cosmic Mass, see: http://www.technocosmicmass.org.

4   www.pronioa.net/def.html (accessed 16 October 2002).

5   Reynold's *Energy Flash: A Journey Through Rave Music and Dance Culture* (1998) was also published in the US as *Generation Ecstasy: Into the World of Techno and Rave Culture*.

6   http://www.technocosmicmass.org (accessed 16 November 2002).

7   This repressive Bill, though defeated in 2002, was successfully legislated in April 2003 when it re-emerged as the Illicit Drug Anti-Proliferation Act sponsored by Senator Biden, a component of 'Crack House' amendments attached to Senator Daschle's Justice Enhancement and Domestic Security Act of 2003. For more information, see http://epistolary.org/713.html (accessed 6 May 2003).

Bibliography

Apollo (Henry Kielarowski) (2001) 'House music 101', available online at http://www.livin-gart.com/raving/articles/housemusic101.htm (accessed 16 September 2002).

Bauman, Z. (1998) 'Postmodern religion?', in P. Heelas (ed.) *Religion, Modernity and Postmodernity*, Oxford: Blackwell.

Beck, J. and M. Rosenbaum (1994) *Pursuit of Ecstasy: The MDMA Experience*, Albany, NY: State University of New York Press.

Beckford, J. (1989) *Religion and Advanced Industrial Society*, London: Unwin Hyman.

Cohen, R. (1998) *The Love Drug: Marching to the Beat of Ecstasy*, New York: Hawarth Medical Press.

Cole, F. and M. Hannan (1997) 'Goa trance', *Perfect Beat* 3(3): 1–14.

Davis, E. (1998) *Techgnosis: Myth, Magic and Mysticism in the Age of Information*, New York: Three Rivers Press.

Dei, D. and J. Stagg (n.d.) ' "No easy rave to freedom" – the South African youth revolution', available online at http://hyperreal.org/raves/spirit/politics/South—African—Revolution.html (accessed 3 August 2002).

Eisner, B. (1994) [1989] *Ecstasy: The MDMA story*, Berkeley, CA: Ronin.

ENRG, E. (2001) 'Psychic sonics: tribadelic dance trance-formation', in G. St John (ed.) *FreeNRG: Notes from the Edge of the Dance Floor*, Altona: Common Ground.

Fritz, J. (1999) *Rave Culture: An Insider's Overview*, Canada: Smallfry Press.

Handelman, D. (1990) *Models and Mirrors: Towards an Anthropology of Public Events*, Cambridge: Cambridge University Press.

Heelas, P. (1998) 'Introduction: on differentiation and dedifferentiation', in P. Heelas (ed.) *Religion, Modernity and Postmodernity*, Oxford: Blackwell.

Hemment, D. (1996) 'E is for ekstasis', *New Formations* 31: 23–38.

Hill, D. (1999) 'Mobile anarchy: the house movement, shamanism and community', in T. Lyttle (ed.) *Psychedelics Reimagined*, New York: Autonomedia.

Howard, R. (1996) *The Rise and Fall of the Nine O'clock Service: A Cult Within the Church?*, London: Mowbray.

LaHaye, T. and B. DeMoss (2001) *All the Rave*, Nashville, TN: W Publishing Group.

McRobbie, A. (1994) *Postmodernism and Popular Culture*, London: Routledge.

Maffesoli, M. (1996) [1988] *The Time of the Tribes: The Decline of Individualism in Mass Society*, London: Sage.

Malbon, B. (1999) *Clubbing: Dancing, Ecstasy and Vitality*, London: Routledge.

Melechi, A. (1993) 'The ecstasy of disappearance', in Steve Redhead (ed.) *Rave Off: Politics and Deviance in Contemporary Youth Culture*, Aldershot: Avebury.

Ott, J. (1993) *Pharmacotheon: Entheogenic Drugs, Their Plant Sources and History*, Kennewick, WA: Natural Products Co.

Otto, R. (1959) *The Idea of the Holy*, London: Oxford University Press.

Pini, M. (2001) *Club Cultures and Female Subjectivity: The Move from Home to House*, Basingstoke, Hampshire: Palgrave.

Push and Silcott, M. (2000) *The Book of E: All About Ecstasy*, Omnibus Press.

Redhead, S. (1993) *Rave Off: Politics and Deviance in Contemporary Youth Culture*, Aldershot: Avebury.

Reynolds, S. (1997) 'Rave culture: living dream or living death?', in S. Redhead (ed.) *The Clubcultures Reader: Readings in Popular Cultural Studies*, Blackwell: Oxford

—— (1998) *Energy Flash: A Journey through Rave Music and Dance Culture*, London: Picador.

Roberts, P. (1999) *Alternative Worship in the Church of England*, Cambridge: Grove Books.

Rushkoff, D. (1999) 'Losing the plot: how utopia became big business', *THIS Magazine* November/December (unpaginated).

Saldanha, A. (2002) 'Music tourism and factions of bodies in Goa', *Tourist Studies* 2(1): 43–62.

Sams, G. (1997) *Uncommon Sense*, London: Chaos Works.

Saunders, N., A. Saunders and M. Pauli. (2000) *In Search of the Ultimate High: Spiritual Experience through Psychoactives*, London: Rider.

Smith, H. (1976) *Forgotten Truth: The Primordial Tradition*, New York: Harper & Row.

Straw, W. (2001) 'Dance music', in S. Frith, W. Straw and J. Street (eds) *The Cambridge Companion to Pop and Rock*, Cambridge: Cambridge University Press.

Thornton, S. (1995) *Club Cultures: Music, Media and Subcultural Capital*, Cambridge: Polity Press.

Turner, V. (1982) *From Ritual to Theatre: The Human Seriousness of Play*, New York: PAJP.

Part I
Techno culture spirituality

1 The difference engine

Liberation and the rave imaginary

Graham St John

[The] insurrectionary 'noise' or chaos of TAZs, uprisings, refusals and epiphanies...will release a hundred blooming flowers, a thousand, a million memes of resistance, of difference, of non-ordinary consciousness – the will to power as 'strangeness'.

(Bey 1995)

The last decade of the 20th century witnessed the growth of non-traditional desires for 'religious experience', for *liberation* in the sense Heelas (1998: 7) identified as the postmodern quest for personal freedoms, for *difference*, without seeking *essential*, or fundamental, difference. With a rich inheritance from earlier explorations, saturated with the tinctures of Eastern religion and Western psychotherapy, contemporary self-othering is textured by a farrago of beliefs and practices transparent in communications with the Otherworld, and in the transcendence devices of psychoactives, new technologies and consumer experiences agglomerated in public events – those 'privileged point[s] of penetration' (Handelman 1990: 9) and theatres for the performance of 'ultimate' or 'implicit' concerns (Bailey 1997: 9). In recent times, a growing corpus of work has introduced sites accommodating alternative spiritualities, gathering places for those 'hypersyncretic' seekers of self and enchantment that Sutcliffe calls a 'virtuosic avant-garde' (2000: 30). Mike Niman's *People of the Rainbow* (1997), Adrian Ivakhiv's *Claiming Sacred Ground* (2001) and Sarah Pike's *Earthly Bodies, Magic Selves* (2001a), for example, document the appearance of festivals and gatherings 'exemplifying the migration of religious meaning-making activities out of... temples and churches into otherspaces' (Pike 2001a: 5). Here the proliferating culture of rave and its expressive *otherspaces* will receive such attention.

Navigating a vast body of material and research, this chapter explores the significance of liberation and freedom in *the rave imaginary*, in the process offering signposts to the subsequent chapters. Rave demonstrates signs of that which Bozeman calls a 'technological millenarianism' pervading popular culture which, in nations like the United States, the United Kingdom, Japan, Canada and Australia, boils down to a faith in technological innovation to 'bring forth a better future beginning here and now' (1997: 155). Attending to the millennialist trope in post-rave, it is surmised that while commonly holding status as a portal to the utopic, as a means to the Millennium, it is hyper-millennial in character, possessing variant salvific trajectories. As a zone of outrageous difference, *a differ-ence engine*, the dance party is found to be a substantial node of indeterminacy for its inhabitants – providing youth with an uncertain passage experience typical of contemporary life.

The spiritual 'rave-o-lution'

Rave is no mere *event*, a temporal gathering of ravers. We would be unwise to overlook the global parameters of 'techno-tribalism' and its accelerating culture industry if our intention is a comprehensive investigation of rave's religiosity.[1] In digital art, screen-based animations and 3D projections, alongside computer-generated music itself; in the 'conceptechnics' of 'sonic fiction' (Eshun 1998) inscribed in voice samples, event themes, artist names and on flyers, CD covers and a labyrinth of websites; in proliferating CD-ROMS, novels, zines, street press, galleries, video texts and online discussion forums; in films and documen-taries; in fashion accessories from streetwear to ultra-violet-reactive art tapestries; in figureheads like Fraser Clark, Terence McKenna and Ray Castle. The whole chain inflects a congruent imaginary which, as we shall see, hosts an alternative or 'expressive spirituality'. By contrast to Christianity (which divides creator from created), in what Heelas (2000: 243) calls an expressive spirituality (typically manifest in 'New Age' and sometimes 'Neo-Paganism'), the divine Self serves as the font of authority, wisdom and judgement. With expressive spirituality, one is driven to:

> seek liberation from the contaminating effects of society and culture; seek genuine experience; seek to express all that one truly is as a spiritual being; and – for many – seek to experience and nurture all that is embedded within nature, beyond the reach of the artificial, the power games of the lower self, the destructive implementation of the technological.
>
> (Heelas 2000: 243)

Yet, as technology is essential to the cultural business of rave, and is integral to the quest for 'genuine experience', for vitality, wholeness and connection, for love, our approach must disassociate from that which would dismiss or abandon technologies or, indeed, psychotechnologies, as 'inauthentic'. Amplifying a *sampladelic* sensibility conveying a relativistic faith in the 'truth' of multiple paths, in options cut 'n' pasted in the ongoing process of identity formation, and in the conceptual architecture of events, digital and cyber technologies are accomplices to an expressive humanism. And, as ravers circulate amongst a growing milieu of spiritual seekers who 'select, synthesize and exchange amongst an increasing diversity of religious and secular options and perspectives' (Sutcliffe 1997: 105), rave becomes a provisional node in an emergent network of 'seeking'.

An unmistakable rapture resounds through rave's cultural accretion – its tech-nological assemblage long underwritten by an evidential *gnostic* drive. The rave 'techgnosis' manifests as a kind of 'occult mechanics' capable of liberating the self through esoteric gnosis: 'a mystical breakthrough of total liberation, an influx of knowing oneself to be part of the genuine godhead, of knowing oneself to be free' (Davis 1998: 94). In his *Techgnosis: Myth, Magic and Mysticism in the Age of Information* (1998), Erik Davis documents how the techno-liberationist flame, reignited throughout Western history, has conflagrated with the advent of the digital age. I suggest that the flame gutters yet glows in techno-rave, which is often felt to communicate, or potentiate, a profound sense of freedom, of recognition, often glossed as 'the gnosis'. With rave, this direct *familiarity* is associated with the collective experience of ecstatic dance. *Ekstasis* has often been considered to rupture gender-identity boundaries by liberating, or 'disarticulating', dominant feminine/masculine subjectivities (Gilbert and Pearson 1999: 104–5; see also Pini 2001), or more broadly, attending to Deleuze and Guattari's 'micropolitics of desire', through a sensuous intervention in the regulation of desire (Hemment 1996: 26–7; Jordan 1995) – processes which can be tracked through house music's gay underground (see Apollo 2001) to various post-rave trajectories. Yet, while rave licenses a carnal knowing evident in the night-long intimacy of the dance floor, the gnostic 'knowing' may be catalysed by an *ekstasis* which, as Hemment reminds us, citing Heidegger and not wanting to deny rave its 'hermeneutic depth', means 'a difference or a standing out from the surface of life's contingencies…[enabling] a more profound contemplation of being' (Hemment 1996: 23).

According to psychotherapist and rave proselytizer Richard Spurgeon, the 'quickening has begun'. But 'are you willing to become all you have the potential to be?' 'The truth is', he states, 'YOU, like Neo in *The Matrix*, are the One. Your very self is the doorway to the Infinite and the eternal'.[2] When Spurgeon moves on to postulate that rave is the space of 'awakening', that the edge of the dance floor is 'the edge of a vast remembering' upon which the physical earthly realm merges with the heavenly, and that to be a party to this experience amounts to *rapture*, he's articulating a strong gnostic theme. The theme of illumination is even stronger in a piece inspired by goings-on in the Arizona desert, and is worth quoting at length:

> Remember 2001 A Space Odyssey? When a tribe of Neanderthals woke up to the giant monolith planted in their midst? Raves remind me a lot of that scene. When I watch a group of sweaty dancers rest their heads on the metallic grill of a giant, black speaker and attach their trembling chests to the gaping mouth of a pulsating woofer, I instantly remember the same ape, 2 million years ago, touching, sniffing and kissing the unfamiliar and fascinating dark object. Raves are about our future. They inspire us to become aware of our selves, our surroundings and our humanity. They are about how we will come together as a species and how we will treat each other. They are about how we will communicate and express our thoughts and emotions to one another. We only need to remember that raves are NOT a way of life. They are a ritual. An exercise for the soul as well as the body. We need to realize that the monolith we climbed the night before was only there

to inspire us. We cannot take it to work with us for moral support and we cannot hide behind it to avoid life's strict requirements. We also need to accept that not everyone can, or wishes, to be a part of our ritual. We need to respect others for choosing different paths and not be disappointed if we are not accepted by them. Despite the overwhelming strength we draw from raving, we have to be the first to admit that we're no better than anyone else. If we are to promote peace, love, unity and respect we need to accept all others before we expect them to accept us.

(Ramy 1999)

In this extraordinary statement, rave is made synonymous with the black stone, the 'prima materia' or Philosopher's Stone which, in alchemical lore, is capable of transmuting humankind and which, according to interpretation (see Weidner 2000), inspired Stanley Kubrick's black monolith in *2001*. While Spurgeon's rhetoric may be obscure, and Ramy's statement relatively unknown, an awakening thesis reappears in the web-saturated 'Raver's Manifesto', where it is stated that 'in the heat, dampness, and darkness' of the womb-like party,

we came to accept that we are all equal. Not only to the darkness, and to ourselves, but to the very music slamming into us and passing through our souls: we are all equal. And somewhere around 35Hz we could feel the hand of God at our backs, pushing us forward, pushing us to push ourselves to strengthen our minds, our bodies, and our spirits. Pushing us to turn to the person beside us to join hands and uplift them by sharing the uncontrollable joy we felt from creating this magical bubble that can, for one evening, protect us from the horrors, atrocities, and pollution of the outside world. It is in that very instant, with these initial realizations that each of us was truly born.[3]

A dawning, a new beginning, rebirth? It seems pertinent to note at this juncture that the party is more than a pre-linguistic womb, that rave, as Pini (2001: 157) remarks, *speaks*, and that, while it is pregnant with possibility, what it communicates is not uniform or predictable, and that what is delivered may be mutant. It is also apparent that, if rave speaks, if it reveals information, then it often speaks in tongues evincing *bricolage à la carte* (Possamai 2002: 203), an effusion consistent with its syncretic digestion of existing symbol systems, philosophies and theologies. Nevertheless, while its message may be scrambled, postures and micro-narratives can be read from the texts, praxis and detritus of techno-rave youth culture, the gnosis transparent in moods decidedly *ascensionist* and/or *re-enchanting*.

Rave ascension

Rave is redolent with anticipation and promise. An assemblage of electronic, computer and audio-visual technologies that has descended amidst contemporary youth, techno-rave anticipates a posthumanist awakening. Remastering the inward turn of expressive spirituality, post-rave is pitched to potentiate the evolution of the self and, more broadly, human consciousness. According to Adrian Ivakhiv,

> [the] evolutionary potential of humanity is often modeled on the motif of 'ascension' to higher levels or dimensions of existence, and ascensionist literature makes frequent use of quasi-scientific language to describe the 'higher frequencies', 'vibrations', 'light quotients' and 'energy bodies', energy shifts and DNA changes, that are said to be associated with this epochal shift.
>
> (Ivakhiv 2001: 8)

From its emergence in the UK and subsequent export to North America and elsewhere, adopting out-of-body science futurisms like Fraser Clark's Megatripolitans (see Chapter 11), 'the Singularity', or promising a digitized dawning, rave culture – its literature, films, flyers, websites, etc. – is replete with ascensionism.

Nineties confidence in a tech-triggered consciousness evolution had a champion in Douglas Rushkoff, whose pop-anthropology of denizens of the early 1990s 'datasphere', *Cyberia: Life in the Trenches of Hyperspace* (1994), possessed the cartological premise of charting new youth cultures whose appropriation of cyber, chemical and audio-visual technologies was enabling them to 'explore unmapped realms of consciousness…to rechoose reality consciously and purposefully' (Rushkoff 1994: 19). In a gush of technophilia, Rushkoff observed that, in collusion with psychedelics, computers, chaos mathematics and feedback loops, the house/rave was facilitating 'the hardwiring of a global brain', an interconnected virtualized Otherworld: 'Cyberia'. Exemplifying the celebrated 'posthuman lift-off from biology, gravity and the twentieth century' Dery admonishes as a 'theology of the ejector seat' (1996: 17), in Cyberia, 'the age upon us now might take the form of categorical upscaling of the human experience onto uncharted, hyperdimensional turf' (*ibid.*: 18). As a strong cultural 'meme', itself resembling groupmind-like cyberspatial networks, such that dancing might be like surfing a transpersonal horizon, rave is heavily implicated in this 'cyberian paradigm'.

With an enthusiasm for 'designer reality', where humans 'alter their consciousness intentionally through technology' (Rushkoff 1994: 289), Rushkoff combines Extropian teleology with New Age 'Self-spirituality' (Heelas 1996) – a fusion redolent in a great deal of rave discourse and practice. Inheriting the idealism of the 1960s, the business acumen of the 1980s and adopting the techno-perfectionism of the 1990s, those operating within post-rave culture industries have sought to catalyse individuation through the rave machine. Guiding initiates along new paths of self-discovery, DJs are often heralded, or self-identify, as *shamanic* (Hutson 1999), a status earlier conferred upon disco and house legends like Larry Levan and Frankie Knuckles, or are perhaps more accurately *master drummers* who, as in Santeria, keep the beat for the dancers while always remaining sober, never possessed (Twist 1999: 107). The contemporary technicians of the self (including VJs and multimedia installation artists), manipulate an assemblage of 'psychotechnologies' (Ross 1992: 539–40), sampling art like that of visionary transformational artist Alex Grey, facilitating vision quests and self-revelations, opening crown chakras and portals to the transcendent, enabling collective consciousness. To take one example, for self-styled 'trancetheologian' Ray Castle, 'it's like psychic surgery': the party raises 'the kundalini serpent energy in the body's chakra system', and with the right setting and sonic progression 'you reach a crown-chakra-type unfolding' (Castle, in ENRG 2001: 161–2).

Breakbeat scientists and practitioners of the electronic healing arts apply that which Kodwo Eshun calls the 'science of sensory engineering' to harness the 'mythillogical principles' of sound, rhythm and vision technologies, repurposed to intensify sensations and abduct the Self to cosmic dimensions – propagating in a fashion 'new sensory lifeforms' (1998: 177, 185). And, as post-ravers testify to their apparent achievement of Zen-like states, familiarity with the Cosmic Christ, the release of anxieties, the generation of 'sympathetic resonance', and the channelling of energy to engender spiritual growth and healing (Hutson 2000), discourses of consciousness expansion, self-empowerment and metamorphosis pervade the rave imaginary. Castle again: 'The *dance cathexis* – a group cathartic psychodrama – on tribal, techno, beats, offers a potent *temenos* (sacred space) for reintegration of disconnected parts of the Self, which becomes a therapeutic *sonic homeopathy* of sorts' (Castle, in ENRG 2001: 164). In such text, post-rave appears consanguineous with the esoteric and therapeutic proclivities of alternative spiritual paradigms, remastering and amplifying the individualistic ethos of the latter. According to Sutcliffe (1998: 38), the inward turn of the New Age is a 'hermeneutic turn' where the Millennium no longer awaits external catastrophe – the Apocalypse – for 'the New Dispensation' follows the private apocalypse of self-realization.

Post-rave may be one among many lifestyle options, workshops, spaces, techniques sampled in the quest to maximize human potential. Indeed, psychedelic-oriented events themselves often possess the character of a spiritual supermarket or a festival of alternative religiosities. With its smorgasbord of modalities from West African drumming to Kinesiology and 'Trance Dance', the global event Earthdance, for instance, reconfigures the methods and constituency of the Healing Arts Festival and esoteric showcases like the Festival for Mind–Body–Spirit. Other events are known to mine the Mayan calendar or Hopi prophecy for signals of our coming transition to a new world, the birth of our 'higher selves', or a momentous merging of disparate 'tribes'. On a wider scale, programmed with a code of self-responsibility, and provided with a range of options, inhabitants of the global party sometimes referred to as 'electro' are incited to work their bodies, expand their minds and free their spirit. Impelled to upgrade their 'wetware' consciousness through aggregating electronic and computer hardware, downloading all the latest patches, post-rave lies somewhere between extreme sports and a cargo cult for cyborgs.

Post-ravers thus adopt electro-techniques of the Self, a slight variation of the 'technologies of the self' which Foucault identified as permitting individuals to effect 'a number of operations on their bodies and souls, thought, conduct and way of being, so as to transform themselves in order to attain a certain state of happiness, purity, wisdom, perfection or immortality' (Foucault 1988: 18; cited in Pini 2001: 144). New techniques of self-perfection possess varied currency in the techno milieu. Events with a typically Eastern inflection such as Earthdance, where workshops on Chi Kung, Pranic healing, Wushu and Reiki take place,[4] seem to enable participants to *Orient* themselves. Other cultural products like the techno documentary *Better Living Through Circuitry* – an update on the LSD-referenced 1960s slogan *Better Living Through Chemistry* (filched by several removes from the original DuPont slogan) – illustrate the posthuman edge thought obtainable with the assistance of electronic machines, or the 'futurhyth-machines' which, Eshun (1998: 104) explains, Detroit techno artists and other Afro-futurists have manipulated to 'technofy' themselves. The 'techniques' are transparent in documentaries like Ray Castle's Japo-futurist *Tokyo Techno Tribes* (2002) and futurist digital art installed at events, such as the body of work created by Melbourne mixed-media artist Deja Voodoo (Phil Woodman), which constitutes, he explains, 'a visual accelerator, an activation tool designed to trigger cellular memories…reigniting the DNA blueprint of the light body, enabling access to the higher vibration of the 5th dimension'.[5] Since the 'electronic enzymes' of digital music and visual art are potent when combined with other technologies of transformation, especially LSD, earlier preferences for 'better living' endure.

Comprised of the holistic body–mind–spirit, Self is, by itself, a 'technology' to be understood and harnessed. Those in the techno-rave milieu are reminded, as they are in Australia's Tranc.ition's *Global Eyes Yearbook 2002*, of their 'self-metaprogramming' capabilities, that they may empower themselves through gaining control of their 'inner and outer biotechnologies' (Phillips 2002: 23). Self-formatting through 'neurochemical prosthesis' (Hill 1999: 106) therefore remains critical to current chemical generations. In early 1990s London and San Francisco, 'smart bars' and 'nutrient cafes' dispensed cybertonics and nootropics (Rushkoff 1994: 131–48), and 'Virtuali Tea' rooms boasted brainwave synchronizers ('brain machines'). Musicians like System 7 developed music to 'manipulate brainwaves and entrain people' (as portrayed in the trance documentary *Liquid Crystal Vision*) and organizations like Visionary Music Inc. have implemented 'Energy Enhancement Environments'. While these 'consciousness technologies' (cf. Dery 1996: 57–8) are thought to improve memory and cognitive capabilities or assist conscious evolution, the most celebrated and far-reaching means of self-programming resided in inducing the euphoric sensation dubbed 'entactogenesis' (Push and Silcott 2000: 8) by actively triggering the release and inhibiting the re-uptake of serotonin – a mood-shaping neurotransmitter stimulated by the compound MDMA (ecstasy or 'E').[6]

With the MDMA 'family tree' of compounds granted subcultural legitimacy through work like Alexander and Anne Shulgin's *PIHKAL (or Phenethylamines I Have Known And Loved: A Chemical Love Story*, 1991) or Nicholas Saunders' oeuvre (including *E for Ecstasy* and *Ecstasy, Dance, Trance and Transformation*), and with therapeutic folk-lines traced through psychotechnologies like yoga, isolation tanks and meditation techniques, E is said to possess 'a quality of gnosis, of access to a wonderful secret' (Reynolds 1998: 410). Regarded by one therapist as 'penicillin for the psyche' (in Beck and Rosenbaum 1994: 89), MDMA is also thought comparable to Nepethe – the mythic drink of the ancient Greek Gods which induced a 'state of transcendent ecstasy [which] temporarily dispels our psychic darkness, filling us with the light that heals' (Eisner 1994: 137). Satisfying contemporary desires for instant self-actualization, for discount enlightenment, MDMA accelerates the arrival of perfection, quickens the knowing, enables 'neural tuning' (according to Takahashi, Chapter 7) and installs a dial-up connection to an advanced global consciousness which Rushkoff calls the 'Gaian neural net' (1994: 115). In this popular story, the techno-rave spiritual cyborg establishes contact with a neuro-digital network. Depending on your pill of choice, you might even crack the Matrix. Successful negotiation of the neo-network promises 'E-volution', a path, a way, a groove, a circuit with more than passing resemblance to the inner alchemical journey which, through all of its pitfalls and perils, promises bliss for the lonely avatar.

Return to the source

This fantasy of merging with something greater than one's self is detectable in a further cluster of narratives which emphasize enchantment or more pointedly, *re-enchantment*, through connection or reconnection to a source, to a sacred power. As the reconnection or remembering of the source implicit in such stories also catalyses self-perfection, the getting of wisdom, it is apparent that they too possess a gnostic trace. Yet, by comparison to the vectors of Cyberian *techgnosis* – replete with body-effacement and drives for self-immortality – the micro-narratives of 'return' suggest processes that, while not at all technophobic, are congruent with the recognition of a *chthonic* heritage. Inevitable crossovers notwithstanding, while ascensionism inclines toward New Edge cargo cult, re-enchantment implies a Romantic revivalism, variously disillusioned with modernity, patriarchy and institutional religion. It implies a pantheistic re-sacralization of the self and world. If there is a Millennium here, it appears more approximate to an Arcadian revival than an Extropian Golden Age. Those seeking the 'return' may be practitioners of magic, borrowers of traditional and indigenous iconographies, in possession of a desire to move closer to the sacred, to court the mysteries via clandestine dance and digital surrealism, to harmonize with the 'source'. Nature (often construed as the inner self), the female, the body, tradition, the indigene are here all homologically authentic and accorded hierophanic value – that is, are expressions of the sacred.

In expressing desires to reconnect with 'forgotten tribal roots', these narratives employ atavistic tropes. While this might explain the nostalgia manifested, for example, in the longing for earlier youth subcultural moments (hippy, punk, etc.) or earlier rave moments and locations (like the simulated Ibiza or Goa parties), raving is often promoted and perceived as a means of remembering a generalized heritage. The root source may be a long-lost vocabulary that has been stored in our bodies for millennia. According to Cinnamon Twist, summoning 'strange gestures, nonsensical mudras, twistings, kicks', these events may function to open humanity up to the 'bio-records of thousands of years of tribal and sacred dances, and untold aeons of primal animalic motion' (1999: 108). Reading French raves, Gaillot remarks on how they draw participants back to

> ancestral practices and customs, opening up a space to resonate with the echo of the bacchanalia and orgiastic delirium that have populated the margins of our history…. Dionysia of modern times [raves]…may in this sense be as old as man himself.
>
> (Gaillot 1999: 23)

While any rock concert, disco or club scene might be identified amongst such perennialism, anathematic to a space of wanton consumption and debauched revelry, narratives articulate the intentional reclaiming of pre-modern and non-Western ritual for its perceived efficacy. And in the process of reclaiming functional ritual, we observe the reclamation of putative traditions.

Thee Temple ov Psychick Youth founder Genesis P-Orridge claimed that acid house was 'going back to the roots of why music was invented: to reach ecstasy and visionary states, in a communal tribal celebration' (in Rietveld 1998a: 190). Such claims became the particular trademark of trance, or psychedelic trance, narratives, as evidenced by Goa trance veteran Goa Gil – whose goal was to redefine 'ancient tribal ritual for the 21st century' (in Cole and Hannan 1997: 5; and see Davis, Chapter 13) – or Ray Castle, who advocates the 'trib-adelic…sound sorcery' of 'theosophical trance' (ENRG 2001: 168). Chris Decker, who founded both London club and trance label Return to the Source (RTTS) and Earthdance is responsible for a much-sampled passage:

> The all night dance ritual is a memory that runs deep within us all; a memory that takes us back to a time when people had respect for our great mother earth and each other. Dancing was our rite of passage, our shamanic journey into altered states of reality where we embodied the Great Spirit and the magic of life…. At Return to the Source, it is our vision to bring back the dance ritual. A ritual is a sacred act with focused intention. We aim to create a modern day positive space, created with love where we can join as one tribe to journey deep into trance, just as our ancestors did.[7]

And this pagan sentiment was built under the roof of house – believed to be the principle conduit from Africa to rave. It has been suggested that venues like the Paradise Garage (New York) and the Warehouse (Chicago) occasioned the 'rebirth' of 'ancient, natural traditions of ecstatic dance' amongst a marginal African-American subculture, a 'liberation of the loins and soul through music and dance' (Apollo 2001: issue 34) later transmitted to rave and its progeny.

In expressing the desire for a new relationship to the natural world, rites performed also articulate a post-Christian return to something likened to the Eleusinian Mysteries. Indeed, preference for hallucinogenic substances like LSD – similar to the consciousness-altering substances thought to have been used in the Eleusinian initiation rites (Hofmann 1997) – generates resonance. For example, with each gathering including a ritual performance associated with a celebrated Oracle Card – like 'the Gypsy', 'In the Garden', 'the Senses' or 'the Elements' – the Pacific Northwest's Oracle Gatherings are dedicated to 'call[ing] upon new ritual experiences through dance based on the wisdom of our culture, creating: sacred space, transformational experiences, art with intent'.[8]

The strong revivalist sensibility in the rave imagination is consistent with the mood of cultural and spiritual recovery characteristic of Neo-Paganism. Inhabitants of post-rave are not so much heir to unchanged traditions, but are, as are many pagans and practitioners of Earthen spirituality, innovators, syncretists, sampling from existing traditions, cobbling together reinvented traditions and adopting new technologies in their veneration of nature. While many techno-pagan commentators allude to a generalized mythos of the 'tribal gathering' (see Fritz 1999: 171), some reconstructionists are informed by particular historical periods, cultural icons or regions, and others, more likely, work with a multiplicity of influences: e.g. Celticism, Druidry, Goddess Spirituality, Hinduism, the Mayan calendar, and perhaps fusing the ideas of Rupert Sheldrake, Buckminster Fuller and Terence McKenna. Ritual syncretism, for instance, is evident in RTTS, where 'a crystal symbolising cosmic energy is hung above [the dance floor]...spring water from Glastonbury is ritually sprinkled, and American Indian sage is burnt to cleanse the energy' (Saunders *et al.* 2000: 170). And the popular practice of remixing religious iconography, such as statues of the Buddha, Aboriginal didjeridus, images of Hindu deities and subverted Christian motifs, sometimes raises the ire of cultural authorities.[9]

Techno-pagans mount varied strategies of re-enchantment and re-sacralization. Eschewing rational materialist worldviews, they harness and exploit psychedelic, audio and computer technologies in preparation for what McKenna called a 'cosmic journey to the domain of Gaian Ideas' to be retrieved and fashioned into art 'in the struggle to save the world'.[10] Participating in what Davis (Chapter 13) deems 'spiritual hedonism', they sometimes form discrete techno-tribal outfits like Spiral Tribe, Moontribe or Cosmic Kidz, which practice a dissolution of human and nature, performer and audience, creator and created (see Green 2001), are sometimes accomplices to 'techno-primitivism' of the kind Fatone (Chapter 10) identifies in her research on the appropriation of a *gamalan* orchestra by elements within the San Francisco rave scene, and sometimes enter the global circuits of Fraser Clark's zippy 'Shamanarchy' (see Chapter 11), or that which D'Andrea (Chapter 12) calls a 'freak ethnoscape'. With such dimensions in mind, rave's fusion of 'ancestral wisdom and new science' has been manifested, for example, in the Australian-based Chaos Magick-informed Labyrinth installations developed by Orryelle Defenestrate-Bascule,[11] or even in new liturgical developments such as California's deconstructionist Techno Cosmic Mass which, according to Episcopalian priest and Mass founder Matthew Fox, integrates 'ecstatic live music, urban shamanism, multi-media imagery and eastern and indigenous spiritual elements' to build a new form of 'worship' and 'reawaken...the sacred'.[12]

The 'eternal return' of dance, of the 'Mass', supposes other layers of experience and narrative. As a return to 'the tacit *cogito*' from the Cartesian *cogito*, ecstasy is a flight to the foundation of consciousness (see Landau, Chapter 5). According to Castle, the reconnective therapy or 'psychodrama' of dance lies in its ability to revive 'a free-form play space, which we had as children' (ENRG 2001: 159). For Fox, to dance is to return to our origins, 'since we all expressed ourselves…in the womb by stretching our limbs, i.e. by dancing'.[13] In womb-like Warmth (the name of a San Francisco rave), where machine music predominates and low bass frequencies are said to resemble mother's heartbeat, the dance space facilitates the re-enlivening of 'the mystical child'. In this collective age regression, a prelapsarian Land of Oz (London rave, 1989) or Toon Town (the early San Francisco rave) is built, where the sucking of Chubba-Chupps, the wearing of fluffy animal rucksacks and hair in pigtails and the toting of super-soakers and bubble wands mark the intentional stripping away of worldly (adult) concerns and responsibilities. But Castle warns against squatting the womb, emphasizing the need to emerge at the light of a new day, to face the 'pain of having to become a separate entity' (ENRG 2001: 163–4). Here, in rave's quest to return, to remember that which is perceived to have been lost or forgotten (in either our collective heritage or personal development), we find the desire for ego-death, implying rebirth, a new awakening.

Techno-communitas and the body electric

While such micro-narratives are accentuated within the rave imaginary, a meta-narrative of *process*, the possibility of psycho-cultural (re)production, wrought by sheer indeterminacy, becomes apparent. And the possibility engine is the rave itself – *the party* – which has been variously identified as: synchronistic 'phase-locking' (Rushkoff 1994: 155–7); 'a desubjectified state of…rapture', a collective and singular body approximating Deleuze and Guattari's 'Body-without-Organs' (Jordan 1995: 129; see also Schütze 2001); a feeling of 'an indissoluble bond, of being one with the external world as a whole', which Malbon, drawing on Freud, calls an 'oceanic experience' (Malbon 1999: 107); a 'deconstructive *jouissance*' where the 'dissolution of certainty and identity is experienced as *pleasure*' (Gilbert and Pearson 1999: 181); or a festive continuity resembling the Bataillian sacrifice of individuality (Tramacchi 2001: 181; see also Chapters 2 and 3).[14] Yet, drawing on the work of ritual and performance theorist Victor Turner, the immediate dancescape can perhaps be most likened to a *techno-communitas*. The present explanation of the party's significance, and indeed that of post-rave culture, will be grounded in a renovation of Turner.

With recourse to Turner, the dance party is (as addressed in Chapters 4 and 8) a space of communal liminality, or *spontaneous communitas*. In the pan-human modality of communitas, esoteric knowledge and understanding is shared between neophytes, cultists, communards, pilgrims or tourists who experience a direct and immediate abandonment of socioculturally mediated divisions in 'a place that is no place, and a time that is no time' (Turner 1983: 103). The 'communitas spirit' resonates with millenarian and revitalization movements as it 'presses always to universality and ever-greater unity' (Turner 1983: 202). With names like Come-Unity, Utopia, Tribedelic, Oracle, Exodus, etc., dance party organizations labour to replicate the liminal experience of the 'tribal' neophyte, the 'cult' member, the hippy communard, the pagan 'ritual', the sacred pilgrimage, the epic quest or hunt. As subcultural 'VIPs' conspire to forge 'normative communitas' (see Chapter 8), the successful formulae for dancescapes from Earthdance to Tribal Gathering is enshrined.

In a parallel alluded to in Castle's *Tokyo Techno Tribes*, the party is something of an experiential equivalent to the Japanese *matsuri* – the Shinto festival of community renewal, purification and blessing, where under anti-structural conditions participants make public transit to a sensational realm of experience in which the usual conventions, demands and distinctions of daily life recede.[15] In his inspired insider's account, Fritz accumulates rich evidence of the resonant experience:

> With the rave experience, intellectual processes are overridden as you surrender to the music and experience a sense of brotherhood and camaraderie and a feeling of unification. You become connected on a molecular level to everyone and everything. All is well with the world.
>
> (Jane of Art, in Fritz 1999: 52)

Demonstrating that rave is not isolable as a Self-spirituality, not exclusively a 'cult of the individual', in such a zone dancers 'experience deep feelings of unlimited compassion and love for everyone around them.... For a few hours they are able to leave behind a world full of contradiction, conflict and confusion, and enter a universal realm where everyone is truly equal, a place where peace, love, unity and respect are the laws of the land' (Fritz 1999: 43, 172). The deep logic of such an experience is that it is simultaneously impermanent and perennial. While the party paroxysms are 'fleeting moments of intense interconnectedness' (Pini 2001: 167), they are recurrent in time and replicate in space. The cyclical, iterative, mutant reproduction of such ephemeral 'hypercommunities' (Kozinets 2002) is indicative of the universal function of liminality, which in the case of rave possesses an extraordinarily indeterminate telos.

Yet, while there are many possible outcomes, the idea of the rave-utopia is central to the imaginary. Commentators have highlighted the *disappearance* of a sense of both 'the other' and 'the self' (Rietveld 1998a: 194) within the process of dance. As the party makes possible a kind of collective ego-loss, a sense of communal singularity – a sensation of at-one-ness – is potentiated. Hemment explains:

> The disappearance into the singular field of the music is articulated within a general becoming-unlimited, by which the identities and hierarchies of the ego are abandoned as the dancer confronts the limits of pure possibility. At this point both self and others disappear together, releasing a profound

sense of unity.... In this collective moment bodies become one with the rhythm, each distinct gesture the fractal-expression of the singular sonic algorithm.

(Hemment 1996: 28)

For the raving habitué, nothing matters more than *being together* or, perhaps more accurately, being 'alone together' (Moore 1995: 207). As a 'seizure of presence', the experience is in concert with Hakim Bey, whose 'temporary autonomous zone' (TAZ) became a universal archetype of liberation eagerly adopted by the rave massive:

Are we who live in the present doomed never to experience autonomy, never to stand for one moment on a bit of land ruled only by freedom? Are we reduced either to nostalgia for the past or nostalgia for the future? Must we wait until the entire world is freed of political control before even one of us can claim to know freedom?

(Bey 1991: 98)

Not representing any greater 'Truth', rave came to answer Bey's call (and that of Blake, Fourier and Deleuze and Guattari, whose ideas he adapted) for the 'total liberation' of desire. In the rave,

one cannot help being struck by the primacy of the demand for a shared present, as if...in it were a whole epoch, ours, expressing an imperative not to give in to the future, some 'radiant future', rather to somehow be caught up by and in the present, lived or experienced collectively...the being-together exists only in the actuality of the dancing bodies, and is not based on any community of fact or appearance except the *fête* being shared at the moment.

(Gaillot 1999: 24–5)

The rave is a synaesthetic community wherein 'each dancer in the crowd becomes a medium transmitting sensory current' (Eshun 1998: 099). And it is organized through a Dionysian logic, which Maffesoli (1993, 1996) defines as a certain kind of sociality, sensuous, orgiastic and transgressive of imposed morality. Yet while young women, for instance, may feel like they are 'flirting with the crowd' (Jane, in Pini 2001: 164), the experience is not organized around sexual gratification. With attention cast towards rave's *jouissance*, recent commentators diverge markedly from Turner's comparatively sanitary sociality. Thus, for Gilbert and Pearson raves contextualize

waves of undifferentiated physical and emotional pleasure; a sense of immersion in a communal moment; wherein the parameters of one's individuality are broken down by the shared throbbing of the bass drum; an acute awareness of music in all its sensuality – its shimmering arpeggios, soaring string-washes, abrasive squelches, crackles and pops; an incessant movement forward, in all directions, nowhere; the bodily irresistibility of funk; the inspirational smiles of strangers; the awesome familiarity of friends; the child-like feeling of perfect safety at the edge of oblivion; a delicious surrender to cliché.

(Gilbert and Pearson 1999: 64)

Furthermore, as the 'community of feeling' is mediated through that which Schütze calls 'the techniques of auditory, visual, kinetic and chemical amplification' (2001: 162), *Dionysus needs Prometheus* (Gaillot 1999: 33; emphasis mine). As Reynolds points out, while Nietzche opposed science and technical knowledge to 'the orgiastic spirit of Dionysian art', in the techno-orgiasm 'the Dionysian paroxysm becomes part of the program, regularized, looped for infinity' (1998: 199–200). Machines have developed a special role in the development of 'body music' – which Eshun calls Afrodelic. When Gaillot suggests that 'Technica and Africa...are the two essential poles of techno' (1999: **35**), he acknowledges electro's simultaneous rootedness in the synthetic soul of Kraftwerk and in traditions of performance (blues and jazz clubs, soul, funk, disco, the Caribbean carnival) where body music is designed to be danced, not merely listened to, or watched, as in the European concert tradition (see Till 2000: 370).[16] For Eshun, contrary to a critical tradition which laments technology's disembodiment of the human, 'sound machines make you feel *more* intensely, along a broader band of the emotional spectra than ever before in the 20th Century'. Accordingly, 'the posthuman era is not one of disembodiment but the exact reverse: it's a *hyperembodiment*' (Eshun 1998: –**002**). With Afrodelica, '[y]ou are willingly mutated by intimate machines, abducted by audio into the populations of your bodies. Sound machines throw you onto the shores of the skin you're in. The hypersensual cyborg experiences herself as a galaxy of audiotactile sensations' (*ibid*.: –**001**).

Merging with a wider 'mind/body/spirit/technology assemblage' (Pini 2001: 169), ravers readily experience a 'release...from the rigid limitations of their sexually marked selves' (Pini 1997: 124–5).[17] With the accelerated 'erosion of the limits between the corporeal and the technological' (*ibid*.: 169), this is the eternal return of the cyborg, the return to the future, a journey into the transgressive space, pulsating sounds and immanent possibilities of the carnival. Yet, licensing digital miscegenation, post-rave constitutes a 'technophagic' upgrade on traditional carnivals which, like the Afro-Brazilian Bahian carnival, are deemed 'anthropophagic': an 'open process of dynamic incorporation in which identity is never fixed but always open to transmutations' (Schütze 2001: 160). A cyborgian context for Bakhtin's grotesque realism, never distant from Afrodelic influences, the techno-orgiasm appropriates a range of instruments to modulate 'normative modes of subjectivation and permit the experimentation of novel forms of subjectivity' (*ibid*.: 162).

The post-rave carnival contextualizes a millennialist implosion of the past/present/future – a collapse which opens up 'the fissure from which dancing bodies issue forth'. This is, according to Hemment, 'the moment of the present's differentiation from itself, the fracture between past and future that is the condition of creativity and change' (1996: 28). Thus, whether 'dancing like there's no tomorrow' or practising the art of 'making now last longer', there is a popular self-perception of the important role enacted, that the party is 'an epicenter from which to spread the positive and powerful vibrations generated...out into society at large' (Fritz 1999: 206). As a 'laboratory of the present', post-rave thus 'bears witness' (Gaillot 1999: 18–20) to that which, Fritz enthuses, is 'the largest popular cultural movement of the 20th century' (1999: 262).

Hyper-millennialism

We have found that while narratives of ascension, enchantment and various intertextualized permutations hold currency within the rave imaginary, the significance of the party is such that it constitutes a non-linear celebration of *presence* in which future/past, self/other, mind/body, male/female and human/technology distinctions undergo dissolution. Yet, while the immediate proclivities of rave potentiate spontaneous communitas, with raving we are remote from the kind of 'primordial communion' or 'primitive communism' often intended by the term 'tribal', which is commonly grifted on to denote the idyllic social relations associated with pre-modernity. Along with that which we might identify as the 'normative' domestic frameworks required by state authorities and corporate interests corralling youth into 'pleasure prisons' (Reynolds 1998: 424) mainstreaming, commodifying and segmenting the culture (Collin 1997; St John 2001a; Hollands 2002), a host of factors have been recognized as having jeopardized the ecstatic and empathetic techno-communitas, as having complicated and undermined the Millennium: an inveterate pharmacological dystopia (Reynolds 1997, 1998); a familiar sexual division of labour (Bradby 1993; McRobbie 1994: 170); participant anxieties and conflicts (Pini 2001: ch. 5); the phallocentric 'reglamorization of the dancefloor' (Gilbert and Pearson 1999: 176–8); elitism, exclusivity and 'coolness' (Thornton 1995); racism, cultural appropriation and a new imperialism (Hutnyk 2000: ch. 5; Chan 1998; Saldanha 1999, 2002; and Chapter 14 in this volume).

Rave's performative context complicates matters further. While seen to manifest principles of the traditional rite of passage experience which Turner saw refracted through 'the hall of mirrors' of contemporary culture (see Fatone 2001; and Chapter 8 in this volume), post-rave, as I have already indicated, is a journey possessing a performative quality perhaps more carnival than rite. As parties are carnivalesque stages for the performance of individual freedoms, for self-experimentation with the most intense sensations and most outrageous expressions of difference, from which a host of outcomes ensue, it may be wiser to suggest that, as theatres of expression, parties oscillate between difference and communion. As such, these sociocultural thresholds harbour an obdurate indeterminacy. Though precipitating states that may be likened to Confucianism's '*jen*' ('love, goodness, benevolence, humaneness and man-to-man-ness') or Zen Buddhism's '*prajna*' (intuition) – which Turner (1974: 283, 46) imagined might approximate the socio-liminal experience of communitas – with rave there is no collective Omega point, no guaranteed access to 'the Universal Mind'. While approximating that which Castle calls a '*chiros satori experience* (time outside of regular time), where one can gain a bright light bulb-like...illumination and understanding' (in ENRG 2001: 169), dance parties are a sea of sparkling and guttering flames.

While sometimes manifesting themselves as popular sympathetic magic – as in the 'critical mass'-like 'global prayer for peace' performed before live images of Gyoto monks at Earthdance, or in anti-fascist/racist celebrations like the World Peace Party in South Africa in 1991, or creative-resistance movements like Reclaim the Streets and Earthdream – it is not usual that post-rave events become 'platforms' for representation, or for 'resistance', as this is conventionally known. Nevertheless, while often cultural realms occasioning a 'politics of the moment' (Gilbert and Pearson 1999: 172) or fields of 'playful vitality' (Malbon 1999: 101), events dramatize ultimate concerns around which reveller-participants rally: freedom, self-growth, intercultural reconciliation, the environment, world peace. A party is no more a field of micro-politics than a carnival of narratives, no more utopia than a *heterotopia*, a concept which, in its application to large alternative gatherings and performance-art festivals like those at Stonehenge (Hetherington 2000), ConFest (St John 2001b) and Burning Man (Pike 2001b: 160), defines counterspatial 'laboratories' accommodating people, performances, language and objects, multitudinous and juxtaposed. This complex utopian model thus approximates the 'kaleidoscope conceptual space' of the TAZ, a project of 'indiscriminate syncretism', ' "broad-minded" enough to entertain more than two, or even six, impossible ideas "before breakfast" ' (Bey 1995).

As sites where multiple narratives intersect and compete, the post-rave event is a maelstrom of significations, contextualizing a conflagration of meanings. Thus, as Pini (2001: 54) argues, post-rave cannot be reduced to 'meaning structures' such as 'meaninglessness', a 'body-without-organs', 'escape' or 'autonomy'. Nor can it be adequately circumscribed through commitment to independent agenda or narrative: futurist, primitivist, pharmacological, gendered or otherwise. Thus, events indicate that while particular micro-narratives may rise to consciousness within the rave imaginary, they are intertextual.[18] Especially in its larger festive manifestations, the techno-rave becomes a dynamic community featuring a conurbation of zones, ramified narratives and a diverse constituency – a carnivalesque acceleration of the difference engine. Neither 'religious festivals' unifying 'worshippers' under divine Truth, nor indicative of a monolithic cultural movement, these are hyper-millenarian events where hybrid-utopias are (re)constructed from desirable futures and putative pasts, where multiple 'truths' may be accessed and performed, and from which many outcomes are possible.

Techno salvation

The title of Brewster and Broughton's history of the disc jockey, *Last Night a DJ Saved My Life*, may not be an altogether flippant reference to the liberatory character of the dance experience. Can dancing save your soul? Rescue the damned? Provide release? For members of contemporary Christian rave groups such as Club Worship in Philadelphia and Planet Jesus, a collection of DJs from Pennsylvania, such may not be far from the truth. According to Christian DJ Frankie Vibe, '[w]e're ministers on turntables...I can't make you believe, but I can make you dance yourself closer to God' (Sanders 2002). The dance-floor objective stated at www.christianraves.com imparts a serious mission: 'to come together and take back ground that Satan has stolen and perverted...[and] to win souls through the blood of Christ and give god praise and glory!'[19] While many examples of radical Christian discipleship do not share this charismatic evangelism, at Club Worship kids wear glowing cross-shaped necklaces and DJ Jon Carlson was reported to have read aloud from Isaiah 40: 'Even youths grow tired and weary/and young men stumble and fall/but those who hope in the Lord/will renew their strength' (Sanders 2002). It is little wonder that Christian alt.worshippers are assimilating elements of the rave imaginary. After all, the rave space possesses an ecstatic evangelistic atmosphere – a theme taken up by Hutson (2000: 39–40), who indicates that expressions of raw emotion, out-of-body experiences, hallucinations drawing the convert closer to God, and post-conversion healing characterize both rave and evangelical conversion in North America. Yet, the comparison can only be carried so far: PLUR is hardly theological scripture, evangelical Christians are not great exponents of cognitive liberty, and the separation of body and soul, so integral to the Judeo-Christian tradition, is anathema to rave.

While Hutson points out that with rave 'eternal Salvation is not at stake' (2000: 40), our attention should not, however, be diverted from observing the presence of salvific liberation, a profound sensation of being saved, of being released, within electronic dance music cultures. In his history of 1970s and 1980s dance clubs in New York City and Chicago (e.g. the Sanctuary – a converted Baptist church – the Paradise Garage and the Warehouse) Henry Kielarowski (a.k.a. Apollo) sheds light on dance culture's salvation and release through soulful/sensual communality refracted through house into the sensuous deluge of post-rave techno culture. For the gay and African-American/Latino community living with the threat of AIDS in the 1980s, dancing to house was a 'reaffirmation of life in the face of death and Puritan oppression' (Apollo 2001: issue 23). The music's essence can thus 'only be understood by telling the story of the creation of ecstasy out of agony.... Most of the men I danced with in the seventies died terrible deaths. I was one of a handful of dancers from that dance that survived' (Apollo 2001: issues 32 and 9). And, further, house music 'was born from the souls of all those boy dancers of the seventies who left us with their energy and love of music' (Apollo 2001: issue 9). In a period of deep uncertainty, self-loathing, guilt and despair not dissimilar to the process of deep intellectual questioning preceding Christian redemption, house music

> lifted our souls above the ruin [and] made the sexuality and the spirituality positive life-giving forces for us.... The house music came from people

...defiant in the face of death. People who were determined to celebrate sex
and spirit and create light in the darkness.

(Apollo 2001: issue 22)

With influences ranging from gospel to Hi NRG, electronic dance music was
thus born from the context of 'oppression, mortality connected to sexuality, and
the need for redemption and release through communal dance' (Apollo 2001:
issue 34).

Post-rave is remote from the ecclesiastical grip of faith detected in millenarian
movements promising 'an eternity of justice, bliss and glory in the light of God'
following the Second Coming (Weber 1999: 33), or the revival of a communitarian
Golden Age. Nevertheless, as dancers often report being changed, converted,
redeemed, 'born again', traces of millennialism, salvation, a longing for release are
detectable in the immediate and, as already indicated, indeterminate party.
Oftentimes such is over-determined by the imperatives of market forces, like huge
commercial operations such as Resurrection, where the 'release' of dollars for
tickets is promoted to ensure ascension. Othertimes events – like Toon Town's
'Psychedelic Apocalypse' held on New Year 1991/2 – resemble extreme-
psychedelic-sports parks. Conjured as 'a theme park for your brain' (Silcott 1999:
64), such events may evidence the 'new narcissism', where the 'prevailing passion'
is to live for the ecstatic moment (Lasch 1979: 5). In environments where young
people encounter addiction to a cocktail of 'religious experiences' amounting to
little more than psychedelic novelty rides, the atmosphere approximates that of
living the Apocalypse now, making the end of the world last longer. And if
burnout from excessive alterant use is risked at parties designed with the
Psychedelic Apocalypse cookie-cutter, perhaps in them we witness the possibility of
psychological Armageddon. In other events, the power of dance is harnessed for
the purpose of community development, as it is with spiritual dance communities
such as San Francisco's Sacred Dance Society, a 'non-profit religious organization'
for whom dancing is the core religious practice of its members, who aim to
convene a Council and Church of Sacred Dance in the Bay Area.[20] And in others
still, events possess a strong resonance of rapture, as with Spurgeon's neo-chiliastic
faith that 'Heaven is a rave on Earth'. Once, he states, 'we bridge the gap between
that which is "above" and that which is "below"...the Party can really begin'.[21]
Perhaps with its most infamous appearance in the annual Burning Man Festival –
where the blazing and exploding 'Man' sublimates the 'private apocalypse' sought
by a great many of the festival's population – 'the Party' may thus effect a Rapture
corresponding to the New Age 'eschatology' of self-realization.

Implying that raves, as extra-ordinary 'scenes', may be proto-religious sources
of 'salvation' for participants, Corsten (1999) begins to distinguish between two
types of salvation useful in the study of the global party: that raving may orchestrate a release *from* social routine or possess salvation values *in* itself. On the one
hand, 'these rituals liberate the individual from modern rational demands and
provide salvation; on the other, they offer experiences that may be interpreted as
values in themselves' (Corsten 1999: 27). On the one hand, they orchestrate a

freedom from everyday anxieties and relations – the nuclear family, your boss, TV, quotidian subjectivity. On the other, they contextualize a *freedom to* experiment with and explore new social and psychological territory. If we want to pursue extremes, the former mode of experience begins with the festal or party as *release valve*, paroxysms programmed to periodically revivify, wherein festival populations enjoy the state-sanctioned lifting of social taboos or the pleasures of corporate-sponsored utopia. At the other extreme, we have the party as crusade, staging the launch of proto-cultural 'memes' into the global system.

Yet there is more than one way to elucidate these modes of 'salvation'. Or at least they provide us with the opportunity to explain a range of experiences. We might initially suggest that they are implicit in the design of event providers. Increasingly subject to management by the 'new merchants of leisure' (Hannigan 1998: 7), clubs and large commercial raves are probable sites of the former experience. Literally getting 'out of it', ''avin it large' on weekend vacation, patrons are delivered from the world of classrooms and toil, politics and parents, to a state of *amnesia* (inspiration for the famous club by the same name in Ibiza). While it had been suggested that vacating day-to-day reality for the Living Dream where 'everything starts with an E' (Rietveld 1993: 43–4) indicated a kind of *tourism* whereby youth 'disaccumulate culture' to 'disappear' into 'the unculture of the hyperreal' (Melechi 1993: 37–8), today such disappearance can be carefully engineered within new 'branded playscapes' (Chatterton and Hollands 2002: 112), from super-clubs like London's Ministry of Sound to other night-time leisure corporations concentrated within the liminal zones of the post-industrial city (see Hobbs *et al.* 2000). Momentarily absconding from the demands and contingencies of 'growing up', dancing to the rhythm of chart music, big-label DJs, under the watchful gaze of bouncers and alcohol niche marketers, the clubbed inhabit a sanitized world of administered pleasure, regulated 'oceanic' experiences and 'E'-fuelled salvation, before 'transportation' home again – in Schechner's (1985: 125) sense of performers returning to their place of origin.

I do not want to suggest that the packaged and routinized communitas of club spaces are a priori remote from religiosity (for instance, see Chapters 5 and 8). But while large commercial raves and clubs may potentiate 'religious experiences', perhaps as they contextualize moments of 'extreme flow' (Malbon 1999: 141–3),[22] it nevertheless appears that smaller scale DIY parties are more likely conversion thresholds than refuelling depots – more likely liberatory (in the second sense) than clubs. Such events may be primal sites, like the original London acid house parties; unlicensed operations in disused industrial spaces, like the Blackburn warehouse parties (Hemment 1998); events facilitated by the early San Francisco Rave Community (Silcott 1999: ch. 2; Hill 1999); independent 'hardcore' events such as the original trance parties in Goa and proto electro-hippy 'drifter communities' (Cohen 1973: 97) at pre-crackdown Haad Rin on Koh Phangan, Thailand (Westerhausen 2002: ch. 9), Bahia Brazil, West Malaysia or Australian bush doofs in northeast New South Wales; intentional ritual gatherings like LA's Gathering of the Tribes; guided interactive rituals like those facilitated in New Mexico by the Circle of Tribes; or proto-zones within larger festivals, intentionally remote from the festal parent culture. In environments where a psy-trance sensibility seems to predominate, the consumption of LSD and 'teacher plants' (e.g. psilocybin, DMT and Salvia divinorum) is not uncommon. Possessing a pharmacologically 'progressive edge' (Reynolds 1998: 406), events like Exodus Cybertribal Arts Festival in northeast New South Wales – where chillout zones possess an ashramic ambience, and 'healing' areas, specialist 'herbal' stalls and panels on entheogens and zine libraries appear – are more likely 'psychedelic communities' (Tramacchi 2000), in which mystical states or primary religious experiences are not only enabled but perhaps more likely integrated. Many outdoor events are exalted as the 'primal point of contact' (Rawnsley, in Fritz 1999: 47), even way stations *en route* to 'the Eschaton'. They are contexts for the experience of trance, the loss of amnesia or *anamnesis*,[23] and for the experience of the sacred, or, perhaps more accurately, 'sacred madness' which, as D'Andrea claims (Chapter 12), possesses both rewards and dangers.

It appears that a higher proportion of the population of such events are older and more widely travelled than that of metropolitan clubs/raves and less preoccupied by a 'pleasure principled acquisitiveness' said to characterize the latter (Reynolds 1998: 425). Having transformed life into 'a work of the art of sensation gathering and sensation enhancement', there are many among their number whom Bauman would deem 'paragons and prophets' of the 'aristocracy of consumerism' (1998: 70). Yet what of the phenomenal quality of the 'peak experiences' in which Bauman is apparently uninterested? Participants at renegade parties like those mounted in the desert by Los Angeles' Moontribe through the 1990s or Melbourne's Green Ant are akin to pilgrims who have often sojourned from a great distance – gravitating toward communitas with fellow liminars, receptive to visions, metamorphoses and spiritual healing (Hutson 2000: 44).

Yet there is more to these events than the 'peak experience' or trance-state, as they sometimes require a high level of participation – the kind of personal sacrifice embodied in the rule of 'no spectators'. The *in situ* sacrifice – of self to the party – generates a sense of fulfilment and fraternity, of reward, unlikely to be achieved simply by turning up and dropping an E. As Pini (2001: ch. 5) conveys, ravers 'work' hard for the freedom to 'lose it' on the dance floor, but such a 'peak experience' requires a different order of sacrificial commitment. The widely held view from those who contribute to the planning, websites, logistics, décor, altars, performances, community safety, first aid, clean-up and so on of free parties, such as those described by Collin (1997: ch. 6), Rietveld (1998b) Tramacchi (2000) and St John (2001a), is that such participation confers an experience differentiated markedly from the 'consensus trance' of event-consumption predominant in the commercial party environment. Like Moontribe or Oracle Gatherings, such events are 'the work of the people'. There is perhaps a sense that the gifting of time, skills, resources, 'sacraments', venue/property, domain-hosting, etc. procures *mana*. Community forged through mutual self-sacrifice is also a striking feature of fund- and consciousness-raising events where, for instance, compassion for the environment (St John 2001c), for people living with AIDS, the oppressed or, more widely, 'planetary peace' and justice also confers redemption. Possessing an autonomous, immediate and 'instituant'[24] character, potentiating the sacralization of self and event-space through sacrifice, they facilitate the transformation of performer-inhabitants.

Yet, while we can locate variant salvation experiences within diverse venues and events, the reality is likely to be fuzzy and indeterminate – the boundaries obscure. Thus, in the fashion of the hyper-liminal party, a single event will occasion differential significance and outcomes for multiple participants, or even multiple effects and functions for an individual over an event's duration. Participants at an event possess different motivations.[25] The interactional complexity of events has been addressed by Malbon (1999) in his ethnography of London clubbing. For many habitués, at least initially, the club or party constitutes an escape route from the 'profane', a temporary release from work routines or underemployment, an opportunity for clubbers/ravers to 'resist' 'other aspects of their own lives' (Malbon 1999: 183). Yet 'holiday' or 'escapade' hardly exhausts the possibilities of such experiences, as they contextualize the realization of inner strength and effervescence. In such spaces, acts of 'playful vitality' enable freedom from old identities, while *at the same time* (or, more likely, over a period of years) cultivating alternative identities and identifications – catalysing new self and social fictions.

If ravers are like tourists, it is necessary to point out that, as with tourists, it is likely that age, region, socio-economic, ethnic and educational background serve to pattern a diversity of experience. It seems useful to characterize the raver experience on a possibility continuum whereby tourist experience similar to that identified by Erik Cohen (1992) may *modulate* over the event's duration. A dance party may thus provide a recreational interlude for rave-tourists whose experience approximates to Cohen's 'diversionary' or 'experiential' modes. Yet over the course of the event, which could last for several hours or several days, inhabitants might rupture the spectacular surfaces of a venue/space, to 'disrupt forever any pre-existing understanding of the organisation of nightlife pleasures', ensuring that 'nothing will be the same again' (Atkin and Lowe 1999: 155). Adopting 'experimental' or 'existential' modes, such foreigners may occupy the landscape (and go 'local'), nomads may settle (at least temporarily) and 'drifters' may feel like they belong. As events from indoor clubs to outdoor doofs contextualize the taking up of 'house' music and its various derivatives, initiates may discover 'a space in which to dwell...turning this house into a home' (Hemment 1996: 26). With occupants inhabiting and reinscribing space with an embodied collective significance, raves and post-raves are notorious reclaiming practices. Rushing on an heroic dose of familiarity, inhabitants join or reunite with 'family', recognizing their belonging, and identifying with place, in a fashion unparalleled in the lives of many young people.

Conclusion

An exploration of the rave imaginary provides useful insights on developments in post-traditional religiosity, expressive spirituality and global youth techno culture.

The ungoverned dance floor is a topos charged with *the possibility of becoming*. Partly inspired by Davis's *Techngnosis* (1998), this chapter has tracked the gnostic becoming manifest in the micro-narrative threads of ascensionism and re-enchantment. Within the prevailing circumstances of consumer-based identity production and the advent of new digital and body technologies, rave arrived as a super-sensory experience which, in its concatenation of meaning, offers insights on the possibility of postmodern religion and/or alternative spirituality. While the accelerating global dance party commonly stakes a claim to the utopic, accommodating inhabitants, narratives, zones and practices diverse and ramified, rave's space is no more utopian than *heterotopian*, no more solid commu-nitas than hyper-millennialist. Far from unifying the 'massive' under divine Truth, in the techno-carnival hybrid utopias are (re)configured from divined futures and putative pasts in the multitudinous present. As a *difference engine*, the post-rave party facilitates becoming, yet possesses little telos. While salvific modes are detected – they are modulated by the event-space and participant motiva-tion. Licensing escape from day-to-day experience or permitting the exploration of new pathways, revitalizing routinized cultural patterns or catalysing new self and social fictions, from metropolitan warehouse parties to international trance festivals, the hyper-liminal party contextualizes the contemporary youth riot of passage.

Notes

1 Much will come from an exploration of developments in 'rave-tourism' which facili-tate a 'neo-tribal' (Maffesoli 1996) or, more pertinently, *techno-tribal* (see St John 2003) 'massive', where the nodes in metropolitan, regional and global circuits represent many possible sites of identification and signs of difference for contemporary *techno-mads*.

2 www.raveistherapture.com (accessed 12 November 2001). Also see http://www.rave-theawakening.com/awakening/awakening.html.

3 www.neverworldmusic.com/ravers.html (accessed 10 June 2002).

4 As they did in Melbourne in 2002 at the 'Shangri-la Healing Oasis'.

5 From Tranc.ition 2001 Industry Directory, p. 15.

6 It should be noted that the efficacy of ingestion waned throughout the 1990s as the quality and reliability of E diminished for the majority of users.

7 http://www.rtts.com (accessed 12 September 2002).

8 http://www.oraclegatherings.com/intention.htm (accessed 8 November 2002).

9 For example, see Velayutham and Wise (2001), who discuss the sexualized exoticizing of Hinduism at 'Homosutra', the 1999 Sydney Gay and Lesbian Sleaze Ball.

10 McKenna from 'Re: Evolution', http://www.deoxy.org/t—re-evo.htm (accessed 3 November 2002).

11 http://www.crossroads.wild.net.au/lab.htm (accessed 17 November 2002).

12 http://www.technocosmicmass.org (accessed 7 May 2002).

13 http;//www.technocosmicmass.org (accessed 7 May 2002).

14 And otherwise described as inclusive 'non-differentiation' (Hutson 1999: 66), 'communal subjectivity' (Martin 1999: 94) or 'belongingness' (Pini 2001: 2).

15 Indeed Matsuri Productions is a prominent trance label.

16 But these 'poles' are almost chimeric, as one grasps the Afro-futurist 'conceptechnics' patterning, for instance, the European stylistic inspiration of seminal Black American

Detroit techno artists like Derek May – for whom 'Kraftwerk is the delta blues and Depeche Mode are Lead Belly' (Eshun 1998: 178).

17 Here, Pini is explicitly referring to female ravers but, without wishing to conflate the experiences of females and males within such contexts, the quote is no less applicable to males.

18 Thus dichotomies evoked by rave micro-narratives – progression/regression, transcendence/immanence, futurism/primitivism, posthuman/primal, future/past – seem unsustainable.

19 http://www.christianraves.com (accessed 13 October 2002).

20 http://wwwsacreddance.org (accessed 24 September 2002). Also see http://www.rave-theawakening.com/rave/rave.html.

21 http://www.raveistherapture.co (accessed 12 November 2001).

22 Or the maximal stimulation of the autonomous nervous system through integrated 'driving' mechanisms associated with alternative states of consciousness (see Takahashi, Chapter 7).

23 Which, according to Phillip K. Dick (from his *Valis*, as reported on Fusion Anomaly: http://fusionanomaly.net/anamnesis.html) is salvation-finding gnosis (accessed 1 August 2002).

24 Bastide, whose ideas are translated into English in this collection by Gauthier (Chapter 3).

25 See Saldanha (Chapter 14), who discusses this in relation to parties on a beach in the Third World – Goa.

Bibliography

Apollo (Henry Kielarowski) (2001) 'House music 101', available online at http://www.livingart.com/raving/articles/housemusic101.htm (accessed 16 September 2002).

Atkin, I. and M. Lowe (1999) 'Dances with shadows: dance clubs, mirrored balls and reflected pleasures', in R. Goodman (ed.) *Modern Organizations and Emerging Conundrums: Exploring the Postindustrial Subculture of the Third Millennium*, Lanham, MD: Lexington Books.

Bailey, E. (1997) *Implicit Religion in Contemporary Society*, Kampen, The Netherlands: Kok Pharos.

Bauman, Z. (1998) 'Postmodern religion?', in P. Heelas (ed.) *Religion, Modernity and Postmodernity*, Oxford: Blackwell.

Beck, J. and M. Rosenbaum. (1994) *Pursuit of Ecstasy: The MDMA Experience*, Albany, NY: State University of New York Press.

Bey, H. (1991) [1985] *TAZ: The Temporary Autonomous Zone – Ontological Anarchy and Poetic Terrorism*, New York: Autonomedia; available online at http://www.cia.com.au/vic/taz/index.html (accessed 13 October 2002).

—— (1995) 'Primitives and extropians', *Anarchy* 42, available online at http://www.t0.or.at/hakimbey/primitiv.htm (accessed 29 October 2002).

Bozeman, J. (1997) 'Technological millenarianism in the United States', in T. Robbins and S. Palmer (eds) *Millennium, Messiahs and Mayhem: Contemporary Apocalyptic Movements*, New York: Routledge.

Bradby, B. (1993) 'Sampling sexuality: gender, technology and the body in dance music', *Popular Music* 12(2): 155–76.

Brewster, B. and F. Broughton. (2000) *Last Night a DJ Saved My Life: The History of the Disc Jockey*, Cambridge: Grove Press.

Campbell, C. (1972) 'The cult, the cultic milieu and secularisation', in M. Hill (ed.) *A Sociological Yearbook of Religion in Britain 5*, London: SCM Press.

Chan, S. (1998) 'Music(ology) needs a context: re-interpreting Goa trance', *Perfect Beat* 3(4): 93–8.

Chatterton, P. and R. Hollands (2002) 'Theorising urban playscapes: producing, regulating and consuming youthful nightlife city spaces', *Urban Studies* 38(1): 95–116.

Cohen, E. (1973) 'Nomads from affluence: notes on the phenomenon of drifter-tourism', *International Journal of Comparative Sociology* 14(1–2): 89–103.

—— (1992) 'Pilgrimage and tourism: convergence and divergence', in A. Morinis (ed.) *Sacred Journeys: The Anthropology of Pilgrimage*, New York: Greenwood Press.

Cole, F. and M. Hannan (1997) 'Goa trance', *Perfect Beat* 3(3): 1–14.

Collin, M. (1997) *Altered State: The Story of Ecstasy Culture and Acid House*, London: Serpent's Tail.

Corsten, M. (1999) 'Ecstasy as "this worldly path to salvation": the techno youth scene as a proto-religious collective', in L. Tomasi (ed.) *Alternative Religions Among European Youth*, Aldershot: Ashgate.

Davis, E. (1998) *Techgnosis: Myth, Magic and Mysticism in the Age of Information*, New York: Three Rivers Press.

Dery, M. (1996) *Escape Velocity: Cyberculture at the End of the Century*, New York: Grove Press.

Eisner, B. (1994) [1989] *Ecstasy: The MDMA Story*, Berkeley, CA: Ronin.

ENRG, E. (2001) 'Psychic sonics: tribadelic dance trance-formation', in G. St John (ed.) *FreeNRG: Notes from the Edge of the Dance Floor*, Altona: Common Ground.

Eshun, K. (1998) *More Brilliant than the Sun: Adventures in Sonic Fiction*, London: Quartet.

Fatone, G. (2001) '"We thank the Technology Goddess for giving us the ability to rave": *gamelan*, techno-primitivism, and the San Francisco rave scene', *Echo* 3(1): http://www.humnet.ucla.edu/echo/volume3-issue1/fatone/fatone1.html (accessed 15 August 2002).

Fritz, J. (1999) *Rave Culture: An Insider's Overview*, Canada: Smallfry Press.

Gaillot, M. (1999) *Multiple Meaning: Techno – an Artistic and Political Laboratory of the Present*, Paris: Dis Voir.

Gilbert, J. and E. Pearson. (1999) *Discographies: Dance Music, Culture and the Politics of Sound*, London: Routledge

Green, D. (2001) 'Technoshamanism: cyber-sorcery and schizophrenia', paper presented at the 2001 Center for Studies on New Religions Conference, London; available online at http://www.cesnur.org/2001/london2001/green.htm (accessed 3 March 2002).

Handelman, D. (1990) *Models and Mirrors: Towards an Anthropology of Public Events*, Cambridge: Cambridge University Press.

Hannigan, J. (1998) *Fantasy City: Pleasure and Profit in the Postmodern Metropolis*, London: Routledge.

Heelas, P. (1996) *The New Age Movement: The Celebration of the Self and the Sacralization of Modernity*, Malden, MA: Blackwell.

—— (1998) 'Introduction: on differentiation and dedifferentiation', in P. Heelas (ed.) *Religion, Modernity and Postmodernity*, Oxford: Blackwell.

—— (2000) 'Expressive spirituality and humanistic expressivism: sources of significance beyond church and chapel', in S. Sutcliffe and M. Bowman (eds) *Beyond New Age: Exploring Alternative Spirituality*, Edinburgh: Edinburgh University Press.

Hemment, D. (1996) 'E is for ekstasis', *New Formations* 31: 23–38.

—— (1998) 'Dangerous dancing and disco riots: the northern warehouse parties', in G. McKay (ed.) *DiY Culture: Party and Protest in Nineties Britain*, London: Verso.

Hetherington, K. (2000) *New Age Travellers: Vanloads of Uproarious Humanity*, London: Cassell.

Hill, D. (1999) 'Mobile anarchy: the house movement, shamanism and community', in T. Lyttle (ed.) *Psychedelics Reimagined*, New York: Autonomedia.

Hobbs, D., S. Lister, P. Hadfield, S. Winlow and S. Hall. (2000) 'Receiving shadows: governance and liminality in the night-time economy', *British Journal of Sociology* 51(4): 701–17.

Hofmann, A. (1997) 'The message of the Eleusinian Mysteries for today's world', in R. Forte (ed.) *Entheogens and the Future of Religion*, San Francisco: Council of Spiritual Practices.

Hollands, R. (2002) 'Divisions in the dark: youth cultures, transitions and segmented consumption spaces in the night-time economy', *Journal of Youth Studies* 5(2): 153–71.

Hutnyk, J. (2000) *Critique of Exotica: Music, Politics and the Culture Industry*, London: Pluto Press.

Hutson, S. (1999) 'Technoshamanism: spiritual healing in the rave subculture', *Popular Music and Society* 23(3): 53–77.

—— (2000) 'The rave: spiritual healing in modern western subcultures', *Anthropological Quarterly* 73(1): 35–49.

Ivakhiv, A. (2001) *Claiming Sacred Ground: Pilgrims and Politics at Glastonbury and Sedona*, Bloomington, IL: Indiana University Press.

Jordan, T. (1995) 'Collective bodies: raving and the politics of Gilles Deleuze and Felix Guattari', *Body and Society* 1(1): 125–44.

Kozinets, R. (2002) 'Can consumers escape the market? Emancipatory illuminations from Burning Man', *Journal of Consumer Research* 29: 20–38.

Lasch, C. (1979) *The Culture of Narcissism*, New York: Norton.

McRobbie, A. (1994) *Postmodernism and Popular Culture*, London: Routledge.

Maffesoli, M. (1993) [1982] *The Shadow of Dionysus: A Contribution to the Sociology of the Orgy*, Albany, NY: State University of New York Press.

—— (1996) [1988] *The Time of the Tribes: The Decline of Individualism in Mass Society*, London: Sage.

Malbon, B. (1999) *Clubbing: Dancing, Ecstasy and Vitality*, London: Routledge.

Martin, D. (1999) 'Power play and party politics: the significance of raving', *Journal of Popular Culture* 31(4): 77–99.

Melechi, A. (1993) 'The ecstasy of disappearance', in S. Redhead (ed.) *Rave Off: Politics and Deviance in Contemporary Youth Culture*, Aldershot: Avebury.

Moore, D. (1995) 'Raves and the Bohemian search for self and community: a contribution to the anthropology of public events', *Anthropological Forum* 7(2): 193–214.

Niman, M. (1997) *People of the Rainbow: A Nomadic Utopia*, Knoxville, TN: University of Tennessee Press.

Phillips, J. (2002) 'The ultimate technology: BRAINS', in *Global Eyes Yearbook*, 2002 Tranc.ition Project, Melbourne.

Pike, S. (2001a) *Earthly Bodies, Magic Selves: Contemporary Pagans and the Search for Community*, Berkley, CA: University of California Press.

—— (2001b) 'Desert Goddesses and apocalyptic art: making sacred space at the Burning Man festival', in M. Mazur (ed.) *God in the Details: American Religion in Popular Culture*, London: Routledge.

Pini, M. (1997) 'Cyborgs, nomads and the raving feminine', in H. Thomas (ed.) *Dance in the City*, London: Macmillan.

—— (2001) *Club Cultures and Female Subjectivity: The Move from Home to House*, Basingstoke, Hampshire: Palgrave.

Possamai, A. (2002) 'Cultural consumption of history and popular culture in alternative spiritualities', *Journal of Consumer Culture* 2(2): 197–218.

Push and M. Silcott (2000) *The Book of E: All About Ecstasy*, Omnibus Press.

Ramy (1999) 'The meaning of a rave', *City Heat Magazine*, December, available online at http://www.livingart.com/raving/articles/article01.htm (accessed 22 September 2002).

Rietveld, H. (1993) 'Living the dream', in S. Redhead (ed.) *Rave Off: Politics and Deviance in Contemporary Youth Culture*, Aldershot: Avebury.

—— (1998a) *This is Our House: House Music; Cultural Spaces and Technologies*, Aldershot: Ashgate.

—— (1998b) 'Repetitive beats: free parties and the politics of contemporary DiY dance culture in Britain', in G. McKay (ed.) *DiY Culture: Party and Protest in Nineties Britain*, London: Verso.

Reynolds, S. (1997) 'Rave culture: living dream or living death?', in S. Redhead (ed.) *The Clubcultures Reader: Readings in Popular Cultural Studies*, Blackwell: Oxford

—— (1998) *Energy Flash: A Journey through Rave Music and Dance Culture*, London: Picador.

Ross, A. (1992) 'New Age technoculture', in L. Grossberg, C. Nelson and P. Treichler (eds) *Cultural Studies*, London: Routledge.

Rushkoff, D. (1994) *Cyberia: Life in the Trenches of Hyperspace*, London: Flamingo.

St John, G. (2001a) 'Doof! Australian post rave culture', in G. St John (ed.) *FreeNRG: Notes from the Edge of the Dance Floor*, Altona: Common Ground.

—— (2001b) 'Alternative cultural heterotopia and the liminoid body: beyond Turner at ConFest', *Australian Journal of Anthropology*, 12(1): 47–66.

—— (2001c) 'Techno terra-ism: feral systems and sound futures', in G. St John (ed.) *FreeNRG: Notes from the Edge of the Dance Floor*, Altona: Common Ground.

—— (2003) 'Post-rave technotribalism and the carnival of protest', in D. Muggleton and R. Weinzierl (eds) *The Post-Subcultures Reader*, London: Berg.

Saldanha, A. (1999) 'Goa trance in Goa: globalization, musical practice and the politics of place', in T. Mitchell and P. Doyle (eds) *Changing Sounds: New Directions and Configurations in Popular Music*, UTS: IASPM Conference Proceedings, Sydney.

—— (2002) 'Music tourism and factions of bodies in Goa', *Tourist Studies* 2(1): 43–62.

Sanders, J.Q. (2002) 'Keeping their faith alive: Christian raves give teens a place to soothe their hearts – and souls', *Philadelphia Inquirer*, 20 May; available at http://www.philly.com/mld/inquirer/3298878.htm.

Saunders, N. (1993) *E for Ecstasy*, London: Neal's Yard Press.

Saunders, N. and R. Doblin (1996) *Ecstasy: Dance, Trance & Transformation*, San Francisco: Quick American Archives.

Saunders, N., A. Saunders and M. Pauli. (2000) *In Search of the Ultimate High: Spiritual Experience through Psychoactives*, London: Rider.

Schechner, R. (1985) *Between Theatre and Anthropology*, Philadelphia: University of Pennsylvania Press.

Schütze, B. (2001) 'Carnivalesque mutations in the Bahian Carnival and rave culture', *Religiologiques* 24, fall: 155–63.

Shulgin, Alexander and Anne Shulgin (1991) *PIHKAL Phenethylamines I Have Known and Loved: A Chemical Love Story*, Berkeley, CA: Transform Press; partly available online at http://www.erowid.org/library/books—online/pihkal/pihkal.shtml.

Silcott, M. (1999) *Rave America: New School Dancescapes*, Quebec: ECW Press.

Sutcliffe, S. (1997) 'Seekers, networks and "New Age"', *Scottish Journal of Religious Studies* 15(2): 97–114.

—— (1998) 'Between Apocalypse and self-realisation: 'nature' as an index of New Age religiosity', in J. Pearson, R. Roberts and G. Samuel (eds) *Nature Religion Today: Paganism in the Modern World*, Edinburgh: Edinburgh University Press.

—— (2000) ' "Wandering Stars": seekers and gurus in the modern world', in S. Sutcliffe and M. Bowman (eds) *Beyond New Age: Exploring Alternative Spirituality*, Edinburgh: Edinburgh University Press.

Thornton, S. (1995) *Club Cultures: Music, Media and Subcultural Capital*, Cambridge: Polity Press.

Till, R. (2000) 'Clubbing: a new performance tradition', in T. Mitchell and P. Doyle (eds) *Changing Sounds: New Directions and Configurations in Popular Music*, IASPM Conference Proceedings, Sydney.

Tramacchi, D. (2000) 'Field tripping: psychedelic communitas and ritual in the Australian bush', *Journal of Contemporary Religion* 15(2): 201–13.

—— (2001) 'Chaos engines: doofs, psychedelics, and religious experience', in G. St. John (ed.) *FreeNRG: Notes from the Edge of the Dance Floor*, Altona: Common Ground Press.

Turner, V. (1969) *The Ritual Process: Structure and Anti-structure*, Chicago: Aldine.

—— (1973) 'The center out there: pilgrim's goal', *History of Religions* 12(1): 191–230.

—— (1974) *Dramas, Fields, and Metaphors: Symbolic Action in Human Society*, Ithaca, NY: Cornell University Press.

—— (1983) 'Carnival in Rio: Dionysian drama in an industrialising society', in F. Manning (ed.) *The Celebration of Society: Perspectives on Contemporary Cultural Performance*, Bowling Green, OH: Bowling Green University Press.

Twist, C. (ed.) (1999) *Guerillas of Harmony: Communiques from the Dance Underground*, San Francisco: Tribal Donut.

Velayutham, S. and A. Wise. (2001) 'Dancing with Ga(y)nesh: rethinking cultural appropriation in multicultural Australia', *Postcolonial Studies* 4(2): 143–60.

Weber, E. (1999) *Apocalypses: Prophecies, Cults and Millennial Beliefs through the Ages*, Cambridge, MA: Harvard University Press.

Weidner, J. (2000) 'Alchemical Kubrick. *2001: A Space Odyssey*, the great work – on film'; available online at http://www.rense.com/general7/alchemkubrick.htm (accessed 23 September 2002).

Westerhausen, K. (2002) *Beyond the Beach: An Ethnography of Modern Travellers in Asia* Bangkok: White Lotus.

2 Ephemeral spirit

Sacrificial cyborg and communal soul

Hillegonda C. Rietveld

The amplified dance music carries me into another plane of experience; its regular beat comforting me while a world of musical textures, rhythms and visual impressions whirls around me. I forget about how I arrived here, about my usual daily life, myself. My body seems to have shed its burdens of human existence, its limitations reduced: free at last, free at last. Time is now and always, fragments of seconds, breaking to a blur of party weekends, then smoothing out into a transcendental sense of forever. Bodies of fellow dancers brushing, strangers have gone, we are all friends, in it together; we are as one. Thinking in terms of differentiation eliminated, I am immersed. Stepping out of this sense of immersion, walking now around the periphery of the event, I notice the repetitive 4/4 beats of a house-music-related dance music that is pumped out of a rather oversized set of speakers, flanking a person wearing headphones, the DJ, playing recordings, mixing them seamlessly, taking control over the mood of the party. Meanwhile, lights and smoke are interfering with the visual field, making clear observations cumbersome. The dancing crowd of people looks like a unified mass, some people more individuated than others, swayed by musical manipulations, by visual fragmentation and enhanced by dance drugs.

The above descriptions could suit a range of post-disco and post-rave dance events, in a variety of geographical locations and adapted spaces. One could perceive them as contemporary rites of passage, rituals to mend and come to terms with identity gaps produced in a rapidly changing global urbanity, where one is part of a mass of a few hundred to a few thousand strangers, with a sprinkle of friends here and there, and where the abstract machine aesthetic of the music can somehow feel comforting. The participant, the dancer on the dance floor, can temporarily shed a sense of alienated self, instead submerging into a world of electronically produced powerful tactile-acoustic and fragmented visual impressions, held together by an incessant bass drum, which seems to beat in close proximity to the speed of one's heartbeat. Bataille, almost casually, once defined the spirit as 'subject–object' (1989: 56), the merging of self with the other. This involves the destruction of the object, to release its spirit in death, but in the case of rave-styled events almost the opposite occurs: subjectivity disappears, merges with the surroundings, with what otherwise would be conceived of as the 'other'. This other is either the object, such as presented in technological metaphors of techno, or other subjects, such as occur in a strong sense of community on the dancefloor. In this way, a contemporary sense of spirituality is achieved. Yet, despite the experience of the spiritual as universal, disembodied and transcendental, this is an illusion. The subject never exists in a vacuum; it is embodied. The subject's relationship with the other is never the same; it changes through time, discursively. As such, a notion of spirit is unstable, depending on historical and material contexts.

An overwhelming soundscape can act as a spiritual re-energizer, part and parcel of what Pratt, in the context of Gospel music, has called 'a larger strategy of survival' (1990: 49). For those who feel they have been dislocated in a political sense, made homeless in more ways than one, intense dance parties, such as raves, can provide a strong sense of community. At times, the cultural output of rave-styled events seems to take on a cultural logic, comparable to that of migrant and diasporic communities:

> The syncretic popular musics cultivated by such communities often exhibit...contradictions with particular clarity, combining pre-modern folk elements with the latest mainstream pop styles in a self-conscious and often deliberately ironic sort of eclecticism.
>
> (Manuel, cited in Rietveld 1998a: 260)

There seems to be a need for a deeper, pre-modern, meaning, which is often invented and constructed to suit the present circumstances. Such understanding of the pre-historical could be conceived of as, in fact, being post-historical, not unlike contemporary popular imagery found in science fiction fantasy. For example, in the context of an Australian setting for a trance-music-based rave, one of Cole and Hannan's interviewees remarked in 1995:

> Like the aborigines, aeons ago, that contemplated the planetsphere, whilst hitting their sticks, blowing thru a hollowed out pipe [i.e. a didjeridu]. These open-air, wilderness, tribelic, pagan-like parties (rituals) are along the line of primordial communion.
>
> (Cole and Hannan 1997: 5)

This longing for pre-modern roots can partially explain the adoption of a 'time-less' or seemingly transcendental shamanism in some of the more countercultural rave scenes. For example, Mark, from nomadic techno sound system Spiral Tribe, stated in the UK's rave days that 'you can call us techno-pagans, what ever', and that 'it is a shamanic thing' (Lowe and Shaw 1993: 168–9). Shamanism exists in a variety of forms around the world, and seems to include the forging of a close sense of community and, more frequently, reaching a form of spiritual peak-experience which the shaman produces through ritual (Rouget 1985; Taylor 1985). Such ritual can include an experience of death-rebirth, similar to unselfconsciously losing a sense of self on the dance floor, by breaking the boundaries of the self through exhaustion, repetitive beats and the use of dance drugs.

So, spirituality, like sexual joining, can be achieved ritually. However, the meaning of such experience is variable, depending on context. The encapsulation into a protocol of the formal aspects of spirituality (that sense of being part of something larger than one self) could be understood as a formation of religion. Made predictable, a formalized ritual can be used for political ends. The raver, in a spiritual moment of peak-experience, is vulnerable, as any person experiencing a religious ceremony or rite, during complete submission to a belief system. This vulnerability in a definable social group could work to enhance a sense of community, which is, for example, powerful when one belongs to a marginalized social class; hence the intensity of, say, gay dance gatherings. It can also serve other purposes. By solidifying the rave into a formal predictable ritual, comparable to a religion, it is easier to exploit this format for both commercial and countercultural ends. As such in intense cases, the nightclub could be regarded as a secular type of night-time church and the free open-air party as a post-historic tribal rite.

The ritual which produces this spiritual peak-experience at raves and post-rave events, and the specifically embodied contexts by which this is informed, will be the topic of this discussion. I am particularly interested in the machine aesthetic of techno and trance. I have often wondered why people bother to travel to beautifully quiet environments to unleash the pounding sounds of what seems like industrial work and war, and the sounds of urban bleeping office environments. Faraway beaches and deserts, which offer refuge to the global urbanite from ever-increasing surveillance, are ecologically disturbed by noise pollution, while the starry sky purrs on in its own pulses and rhythms. I will attempt to provide an understanding of what the merging of human and machine means, the spiritual rite of the post-industrial cyborg. I will do so by inquiring into techno as a spiritual man–machine interface, and by exploring its machine aesthetic. The discussion will suggest that the experience of the relationship with new technologies is, perhaps, different for men and women – a polemical point, no doubt. There seems to be a self-annihilating urge amongst contemporary men, an identity crisis, which requires an intense and, for some, often repeated rite of passage, an experience of self-destruction and redefinition as sacrificial cyborg. This may not be strategically beneficial for those who are currently engaged in defining their embodied selves and who could gain more from a sense of communal soul.

Post-industrial spirit

Although seemingly calming and maturing in the UK, at the time of writing (2002), (post-)rave dance events have erupted in the USA, Europe, Israel, South Africa, Southeast Asia, Australia, New Zealand, Japan, South America, India, China. Such geographical locations are, arguably, characterized as being in various stages of global urbanization and of (post)-industrial development. Admittedly, the notion of the post-industrial is problematic. It is based on the acceptance of an 'information revolution', which Robins and Webster aptly describe as a 'cocktail of scientific aspiration and commercial hype' (1999: 89) that obscures historical and material power relations in a neo-conservative fashion (Kumar 1995). Ignoring complex social and historical analysis, in popular culture technology appears to acquire immanent agency. Information communication technology (ICT), especially in its digital form, seems occult in its mystery, perfect for inspiring techno-paganism (Davis 1998: 183). The arrival of ICT seems like a divine deliverance from outer space, changing industrialized societies accordingly from manufacturing-industry to information-led economies. Yet the idea of the post-industrial era has inspired artists and policy-makers alike, since it is attractive in its apparent simplicity, making the hype a reality or, indeed, 'hyperreality' (Baudrillard 1987: 16). As a hegemonic myth, the post-industrial and its 'information revolution' identify a symbolic relationship between human and technology, especially between man and machine, which in turn is worked out in the cultural and subjective domain, such as in the dance rituals of rave-styled events.

Addressing spirituality in 'the information age', in *Techgnosis*, Davis proposes that the spirit could be regarded as 'a blast of the absolute' (1998: 6), pure information, subjectively comparable to digital data which, magically, seems to exist independent of matter. By contrast, Davis suggests, the soul is analogue, tied to the emotions and desires of the body as well as to mythologies. This separation of apparently non-physical entities offers an attractive construct in the context of a historical moment when analogue communication media are replaced by digital media. For example, in electronic music, as digital technologies were introduced into the production process, analogue technologies gained by contrast an aura of authenticity (Goodwin 1990), feeling 'warmer', fuller, more organic – in short, possessing a more soulful texture and sound. Davis's distinction between spirit and soul demonstrates a particular reworking of the problematic mind/body split of the European Enlightenment, removing the body one more step towards a post-human subjectivity; the digitized ghost now seems to operate in an analogue machine. This construct shows a shift of the spiritual into a domain of what Yurick calls 'electromagic' voodoo (1985: 24). The organic human brain is capable of operating in a complex ever-changing environment, yet the domain of the digital is invisible to the human eye, while its speed of processing information makes it impossible for the human mind to keep up with certain calculations. Only an interface can humanize such alienating digital processes.

It is important to recognize that the split between body and spirit is only an idea, one that makes little sense. Spirituality is an embodied experience, depending on the discursive context of the body, which depends on historical and material developments. The literary theorist Eagleton stated succinctly: 'Aesthetics is born as a discourse of the body' (1990: 13). Digital data have a human and social source – they are programmed. In addition, a spirit/matter duality does not quite explain how the embodied act of dancing to a musical aesthetic could indeed produce a spiritual experience. The aesthetic can be regarded as a type of empathy or subjective melting between self and other (Todorov 1984: 98). This could be comparable to orgasm, as well as to the peak-experience when dancing to a repetitive beat for a length of time at techno- and house-related dance parties, or to taking empathy-inducing drugs, such as Ecstasy.

For example, in her study of women at raves, Pini points out that 'raving' is 'commonly experienced as involving a dissolution of the division between self and other and between inner and outer' (2001: 160). The result of this melting of self and other, of subject and subject (community), or of human and thing (cyborg), of subject and object, produces a sense of encompassing intimacy with the spirit of the other. In the case of the spirit being 'subject–object', I suggest that the interface between technology and humans could be regarded as a spiritual tool.

Techno trance

As a musical genre with a machine aesthetic, techno operates as such an interface, demanding an active engagement with the idea of technology, especially with that of ICT. Toop suggests that techno 'seems to mirror the feeling of non-specific dread that many people now feel when they think about life, the world, the future; yet it also expresses a feeling of bliss' (Toop 1995: 89). As a musical genre, techno can be understood as both futuristic electronica and industrial nostalgia. It is abstract and foregrounds seemingly otherworldly machine noises rather than producing a simulated version of acoustic musical instruments. Its speeds, rhythms and structures can vary widely, from break and broken beat to chill out music. Most commonly, though, and of importance to the dance events discussed here, is when its syntagmatic structure is supplied by house music. As a post-disco party music, house features a repetitive 4/4 beat and a speed of 120 or more beats per minute, and is mostly produced with electronic instruments. House provides a ritual musical structure to a broad and inclusive 'church', can feature a range of textures, from electronic to organic, and may support a range of attitudes, from abstract to humanist, including techno's machine aesthetic (Rietveld 1998b). Fused with house, techno becomes a powerful physical and spiritual means of confirming a subjective relationship with technology.

The term 'techno' was initially inspired by Toffler, who in 1980 popularized the idea of an information-based post-industrial society in *The Third Wave*. Toffler suggested that the 'agents' of this new era, this new wave, were the 'Techno Rebels' (cited in Savage 1996: 315), people who would be able to take control over technology for their own purposes. As a genre, techno utilizes relatively accessible electronic music technologies, widening the use of ICT to a rebellious DIY underground resistance; music by the people for the people, in effect a type of electronic folk music (Rietveld 1998a). The term 'techno' and its vague futuristic implications struck a chord with producer Juan Atkins and his DJ-producer friends in early 1980s Detroit, as well as with the British music industry and press, who marketed their techno and the ideas around it to a wider world audience.

In 1980s Detroit, the car industry had vanished and businesses moved out to the suburbs, leaving this city to rethink its post-industrial future in terms of information technologies (Sicko 1999). Similar shifts in industrial and urban structures have occurred elsewhere. In New York, hip-hop spawned the electro genre (with the 'robot dance', globally popularized by Michael Jackson) during the early 1980s, which left its mark on early forms of techno. Also in the early 1980s, in one of Chicago's areas of deserted warehouse spaces, a black Latino gay club called the Warehouse lent its name to the musical selections of its resident DJ, Frankie Knuckles; this was music from 'the house' – in other words, house music. In the UK, sound-system parties utilized disused industrial storage and factory spaces. At the very end of that decade, similar events, much larger in scale attracting thousands, gained the tag of 'rave' in the UK; these were increasingly organized in the countryside, signifying an urban disappearance from intensifying surveillance by police and press, enabled by ICT and fuelled by moral panic (Collin 1997). Subsequently, one could find similar uses of empty warehouses elsewhere (San Francisco, Melbourne, Sydney, Bangkok, Lisbon, Berlin) and, increasingly during the 1990s, of non-urban spaces (Australian bush, Israeli desert or Japanese mountains for its urban 'refugees', and Thai islands, Peruvian mountains or Goan beaches for global urban tourists). At the same time, the UK's super-clubs developed during the mid-1990s as a result of the overwhelming success of this type of dance gathering. Since the middle of that decade, such clubs, like Ministry of Sound based in London, have attempted to gain a share of a potential global market.

Detroit techno was a combination of European and African-American futurisms; as Derrick May famously put it: 'It's like George Clinton and Kraftwerk are stuck in an elevator with only a sequencer to keep them company' (Barr 2000: vii). In Germany, back in the 1970s, Kraftwerk's 'Man–Machine' music had brought the electronic avant-garde, including its machine-aesthetic heritage, into the popular domain with tracks like 'Trans Europe Express' (1977). Meanwhile, in the same era USA funk music articulated changes in industry and in black civil rights politics; funk made sense of the identity crisis experienced by black male blue-collar workers as they lost jobs in the failing manufacturing industry in the 1970s economic downturn (Ward 1998). An intense sense of rootlessness found expression in 'the discontinuum of AfroDiasporic Futurism' (Eshun 1998: −003). In the case of George Clinton's Detroit-based spaced-out funk, Afro-centric imagery of Egypt's pyramid gods was combined with the idea that the black man came from outer space (Toop 1995). Hereby the Afro hair-do signified black pride, in a countercultural let-your-hair-grow manner, as well as the psychedelic antennae that reached out into the universe.

More convulsive psychedelic sentiments were tried out in excessively raw form in early to mid-1980s Chicago, again in a mostly African-American context. In competition with Frankie Knuckles' smooth gay-friendly sessions, DJ Ron Hardy was well known for his legendary drug-fuelled marathon DJ sessions, playing a mixture of edgy danceable electronic weirdness, including industrial punk funk from the USA and Europe. These sessions enabled, in 1987, the birth of acid house, a deconstructed post-human form of house music. The best example is Phuture's seminal track 'Acid Trax' (1987), with its unanchored incessant psychedelic or 'acid' squelchy bass sequence placed on top of a relentless 4/4 bass heavy beat. It was a simple concept, a wonderful example of how creative moments can occur when one ignores the manual and makes wetware mistakes (Rietveld 1998b). Without batteries, the Roland 303 (analogue) bass sequencer had lost its memory and pumped out random notes, which foregrounded the texture of its sound that could be manipulated with filters. The producers, Phuture, were amazed by the effect and, rather than dismissing it as 'improper', they recorded this sound to a house beat (Rietveld 1998b). Acid house inspired a generation of producers, including the techno creators of Detroit, the rave generation in the UK and, importantly, a range of trance tribes around the globe.

As a genre, trance can be described as an initially German abstracted marriage between techno and house music. Trance is favoured in the early 21st century at rave-styled events (often more 'psychedelic'), as well as by super-club DJs (favouring the 'epic' version). It exists in parallel fashion in a wide variety of geographical locations: Goa, Bangkok, Australia, Japan, Germany, the UK, South Africa, Israel, Greece; and in a diversity of spaces, from legislated clubs to squat and countryside parties. Alongside other forms of techno, during the late 1990s trance became a dominant genre at the Love Parade in Berlin. This is a yearly techno-driven political demonstration celebrating the reunification of Germany, attracting over a million young people in one day by the end of the 1990s. Another example can be found in the New Age realm: Earthdance is a yearly trance event, inspired by Tibetan Buddhist pacifism, taking place in 45 countries, from London to San Francisco to Melbourne, all venues linked by the internet, promoting world peace. Meanwhile, UK-based dominant dance music magazine *DJ* showed in its yearly poll of October 2002 that a significant number of non-English club DJs were applauded for their trance sets. Since it is extremely difficult for non-Anglo-American artists to break into the British music world, this shows the overwhelming effectiveness of trance across national borders. It could be seen as a global dominant for raves and post-rave events, even trickling into the corporate pop world, in stylistic terms.

Trance is extremely functional; it only makes sense within the specific ritual of DJ-led, rave-styled dance gatherings. In addition to a relentless industrial machine aesthetic (whether psychedelic or epic), the pulsating house beat and seamless disco mixing, it features a hypnotizing tonality. House's melodic content and groin-moving funk bass lines have been stripped and replaced by repetitive half-note shifts that leave the listener in a perpetual state of body-denying suspense while, occasionally, a randomized sequence weaves its psychedelic squelches through the mass of electronic sound. Skilfully manipulated by the DJ at a dance event, the tracks glide into each other, deleting individual differences between them. Breaks from the bass-drum pulse are programmed, as a rest from the physical exhaustion, where dancers can ritually predict a build-up of suspense, and where a succession of chords elevates the spirit and the arms, while a euphoric catharsis is produced (every time!) when the pulse of the 4/4 bass kick drum, the mechanical heart, returns, literally producing a 'kick', an adrenaline rush. The effect is comparable to a roller-coaster ride, where the car is pulled to its highest point, people bursting with suspense, higher, higher...and then let loose to the forces of gravity with thundering abandon.

Sacrificial cyborg

This experience, artificial and machine-like as it may be, can be perceived as transparently natural and tribal, somehow acutely pre-historic. The very dancing to house music at dedicated dance gatherings is ritualistic, in open-air events as well as in urban settings. This ritual context revolves, in the case of techno, around the merging, psychedelic, sexual, spiritual relationship with technology, especially ICT, in a post-industrial society. Bataille argues in *Theory of Religion* (1989) that humanity defines itself in separation from the non-human, from objects or things. He then proposes, inspired by the Aztec death cult of human sacrifice, that in death or in destruction of the object the thing/animal/body releases its spirit. Therefore, through sacrifice, the object-as-thing becomes intimate to the subject, the self, in a spiritual sense (Bataille 1989). An adaption of this idea, may be helpful to understand interface spirituality provided by techno on the dance floor. When we are conscious of the self, this is an imagined object of our observation. By suspending that particular object, the subject ceases to be. As the dancer 'gives up', as it is said, their body and soul to the rhythmical music, there is a temporary destruction of the imaginary self.

As self-consciousness disappears, the dancer enters into a spiritual world filled with impressions produced through the music and visuals. For example, trance (as a musical genre) can induce images spiralling psychedelically before our very eyes; techno can be like a forceful technological cyclone wrapping our beings; in the excesses of gabba (gabber house, an extreme type of techno), a masochistic serenity is produced when the pain of industrial pounding noise leads to comforting numbness; while deep house melts us communally into the dancing crowd. Roused by sensory over-stimulation, a dancer can be overcome by a state of trance, ranging from emotional/orgasmic ecstasy to, indeed, a type of spirit possession (Rouget 1985). Although trance seems to be purposefully made for such effect, this can be achieved by any of such genres.

This peak-experience is a trip into the void: time, space and sensory input fragmenting and collapsing, yet held together by the repetitive beat; suspended, the spiritual hedonist is rendered speechless and unable to articulate; being everything and nothing; part of the all; complete, yet empty. 'Zero is immense', notes Land, in the context of Bataille's ideas. 'The nihil of annihilation is the nothing from which creation brings forth the being' (Land 1992: 101). The techno DJ could, in this context, function as a type of shaman, taking the congregation on a journey of speed, in some cases with peaks and lulls, but mostly faster and faster into the void and to the other side of the night. It is only before and after the nothingness of the peak-experience that this unbearably ungraspable gap is filled by normalizing discourse, like domesticating a divine monster. In this case I would like to suggest that techno and its subgenres, such as trance, act out, or metaphorically articulate, the very ICT that affects and, for some, threatens to undermine everyday social identities. Dancers act out their becoming cyborg in their convulsive dance into the void, filling that void in turn with ways to connect and make sense of this experience. This can be a techno-pagan post-historic or a more refined spiritual feeling, abstract and indefinable, Zen-like.

In techno mutations of trance and gabba, the 4/4 beat of house and disco takes on a Teutonic 'motorik' (Reynolds 2000: 31), a metronome piston noise of industrial machines, reinstating a nostalgic masculinity of an imagined industrial modernity. This rigid machine beat was developed, according to Reynolds, by German bands like Neu! in the 1970s:

> Krautrock brought into focus an idea that had been latent in rock...that the rhythmic essence of rock – what made it different from jazz – was a kind of machine like compulsion.... There was a spiritual aspect to all this, sort of *Zen and the Art of Motorik Maintenance*: the idea that true joy isn't liberation from work, but exertion and fixation, a trance-like state of immersion in the process, regardless of outcome.
>
> (Reynolds 2000: 32–3)

It is in combination with this industrial rock aesthetic that techno has gained its global popularity. The 'protestant' North European work ethic, arguably underlying the first industrial revolution, is here translated into music and leisure. At dance events featuring trance, techno-house and rave-inspired dance gatherings, one sees this hard work taken to an extreme, in order to reach a peak-experience: the complex demanding logistics of a night out (requiring travel and sometimes complex information-retrieval skills), the pushing of the body beyond endurance in physical exercise, sleep deprivation and drug use. Malbon (1999) and especially Pini (2001) provide detailed descriptions of how their interviewees work hard to reach a drug-induced peak-experience and to maintain that experience.

Various dance scenes seem to display a 'macho' atmosphere around drug use, where it can be important to show off how much battering the (imagined once-warrior) body can endure. Dance drugs aid a dancing cyborg identity, as the chemicals enhance the ability of the nervous system to mesh with the technological sensibilities that techno offers. Dance drugs are body technologies, with a profound effect on the mind, on subjectivity. Yet, the body is disregarded in this process, just as '[t]he denial of the body...is but symptomatic of the lack of mind body integration within society at large' (McNiff, in Barrett 2002: 119). Like legal drugs in our post-industrial society, dance drugs work to abolish an awareness of the body, or, rather, to unmake an awareness of its limitations. Mind-altering drugs temporarily enhance required mental faculties, at the cost of the organism that supports them. Not only is the self tampered with subjectively; in some social environments (such as the post-industrial North of the UK) one can also see a tendency towards (an almost) physical self-annihilation.

As body technologies, dance drugs help the user to plug in, jack into or merge with a matrix of aural, tactile and visual whilst losing self-consciousness. The experience of the matrix is 'pre-historic' on an individual level, a vaguely remembered feeling that came before the conscious formation of the subject. Especially in enclosed environments, such as clubs, the warm, moist bodies of the crowd within a dark space or distorted visual field produce an environment akin to the womb, while the amplified pulse of the bass drum, inescapably entering and embracing the body in a tactile manner, acts like a mother's heartbeat. In the context of popular music, Middleton calls this pulse the 'primal metaphor' (1990: 288). This regularity, embracing heartbeat and 'motorik' at once, provides an androgynous 'pre-Oedipal' framework (Rietveld 1993), in which the dancer loses a sense of self, however temporarily, whilst feeling safe.

Such a repetitive musical structure synchronizes the crowd, affecting the body's own pulses, which can produce a profound experience of transcendental universality, where time seems suspended, a forever here and now (Bradley 2001). The continuous exercise, sometimes for hours on end, may stop an awareness of the limited body and self. This is combined with the ritualistic predictability of the DJ-led dance event. In the context of techno-paganism, Davis observes that 'ritual passes the intellect and stimulates…on a more subliminal level' (1998: 183). This is a powerful cocktail, slotting perfectly together in its effect on a subjectivity similar to the one found in Baudrillard's exploration of the disappearing dialectic of 'alternative strategy': 'The sublime has passed into the subliminal' (Baudrillard 1987: 54).

As the crowd moves in unison, the individual could gain an experience of being absorbed and becoming part of a larger timeless organism, of bodies, music, machine aesthetic, clearly tactile and acoustic but blurry in the visual field. As techno music and post-rave dance gatherings foreground their technological imagery as an abstraction, this metaphorical 'womb' has a machine-like quality, a matrix in terms of both womb and grid system, making the experience of self-annihilation and rebirth in the context of a machine aesthetic a deeply spiritual cyborgian suture. It is at the same time a sacrifice of the body as well as of a sense of the self. Hooked chemically and sensorially into the machine pulse of techno (Plant 1993), the post-industrial alienated individual sacrifices the self ritually to achieve a spiritual transition into a cyborg-like subjectivity. This is the peak-experience, one that does not always materialize, but one that is nevertheless profound and unspeakable when it occurs.

Man–machine

Although thousands of girls and women attend rave-related events (Pini 2001; Rajandran 2000), the 'man' in the techno-based man–machine relationship is quite male. A crisis in masculinity seems to have been produced due to a dread of the obsolete male body, no longer needed in heavy industries, while at the same time, arguably, a feminization of the labour force is occurring (Morley 1996; Springer 1996). Almost nostalgic for a futurist past, techno music channels this identity crisis. Men – black, white, Asian, straight, gay, teenage, middle-aged – energetically dance to a range of post-human techno versions on a mutated disco dance floor. This may seem a strange way to reconfirm one's masculinity. Unlike couple dancing, disco group dancing is historically associated with the feminine, with women and gays. House music, providing the dominant structure for techno, developed in the 1980s from the underground disco that structured highly sexualized gay scenes (Fikentscher 2000; Thomas 1995). However, drug use has physically 'loosened up' the heterosexual masculine body, while at male-dominated gatherings the homo-social gaze is deflected away from fellow dancers towards the DJ. The profoundness of this situation becomes clear when one realizes that the DJ is not particularly exciting to watch (someone wearing headphones, usually too absorbed with the equipment and music selection to look up) and who is sometimes even invisible (because of smoke and visual effects, or because the DJ is too far away). In techno, dancing can be regarded as a male bonding (Rajandran 2000), comparable to that of football matches (Verhagen 2001). In addition, it seems that the potentially threatening ICT is being fetishized (Springer 1996; Rietveld 1998b). The man–machine is a subject–object relationship, in which the machine plays a role in the game of (spiritual) seduction. Not only do dancers give themselves up to the machine metaphors of the music; there is also a self-absorbed masculine pleasure in taking control over this cyborg relationship, as DJs, producers and programmers. If 'subject–object' is spirit, it is also the experience of orgasm; this is what makes techno sexy to some.

Social and industrial relations are changing for women as well, as they too attempt to negotiate their relationship to the emerging 'paradigm' of ICT. Despite a male majority in the organization of techno events, there is an increasing involvement by women, as DJs and, sometimes, as producers. Since around 1997, up to 10 per cent of Top 100 DJs in the yearly UK-based *DJ* magazine poll have been female and the most successful ones play techno. Reactions from crowds are mixed, from male hecklers as well as supporters to friendly female admiration. However, there is a twist in the sexual politics of techno, exactly because the focus has moved from the people on the dance floor to the DJ. There have been reports of women on the dance floor who have displayed confusion when being led by a female DJ. Men, on the other hand, especially the dancers rather than the promoters, increasingly seem to welcome female DJs in the domain of techno. Huyssen (1986) has suggested, in context of the feminized robot in Fritz Lang's 1926 film *Metropolis*, that 'the vamp in the machine' normalizes the male experience of new technology. The potentially spiritual experience of cyborgian merging is thereby positioned in terms of a male-defined heterosexual sexuality. In the case of female techno DJs, the focus of male heterosexual energy on the female DJ powerfully deflects the idea of homo-eroticism in a homo-social environment, enabling both male bonding and a sexualized, as well as spiritual, man–machine bonding in a time of social transition.

The techno interface offers a precarious liberation to women, it seems, in the form either of androgyny or of a sexual metaphor for technology. A cyborg subject position is a 'body-without-organs' to borrow Deleuze and Guattari's concept in Potts (2001), who summarizes Irigaray's critique of this idea, in that it 'amounts to the annihilation of female embodiment before a female-defined corporeality even exists' (*ibid.*: 158). Although there is an undeniable presence of female techno fans, they are outnumbered by male fans. It seems as though many women in the dance scene care less about techno as a musical aesthetic than about the scene itself: the people, the androgynizing dance drugs, a variety of subcultural attitudes (less the hooligan culture of gabba, more the countercultural ideas of trance), the dancing (especially the intricate techno footwork called 'Melbourne Shuffle' in Australia, a speeded-up mix of Irish and jazz dance steps) and the socially produced fashions. In short, women seem to engage in the human relational experience outside the masculine self-annihilating ritual of devotion to the machine aesthetic.

Communal soul

Irigaray (2002) has suggested on the basis of comparative European sociolinguistic research with boys and girls that the definition of human self in relationship between subject and object, as Bataille proposed, is quite masculine. Instead, she found that girls define themselves more in relationship with other subjects, rather than with objects or things; instead of a masculine subject–object relationship, a feminine subject–subject relationship was noted. Similar findings are possible in contemporary dance culture. For example, it is striking that record-shop owners and promoters alike have noticed that, even in now, most women prefer more melodious and embodied forms of dance music. Such music sets up a relationship with the human world, rather than with the world of things. This includes soulful vocal club music and deep house music, which the techno fraternity often dismisses as 'handbag' music, referring to an accessory associated with the feminized realm.

Like soul music itself, the musical skills and attitudes of many African-American house singers and music-makers are rooted culturally in gospel music, where harmonies between the voices articulate an embracing community and where chord progressions 'lift up the spirit'. It is as if energy is channelled from the rhythmically moving lower part of the body into the cerebral, uniting all the seemingly disparate parts of body, mind, soul and spirit. In the case of old-school 1980s African-American and Latino house music, instead of directing one's devotion to Jesus, the gospel-inspired focus was to the community and to the sexual. This could mean that orgasm was occasionally bluntly celebrated, making the profane sacred in the process. This was a celebration of liberating the repressed, especially in the context of sexual politics. The sacred, according to Bataille, is 'a privileged moment of communal unity, a moment of the convulsive communication of what is ordinarily stifled' (1985: 242).

Although aimed at a gay crowd, the Chicago house scene also attracted heterosexuals, whereby it was 'hip to be gay' in order to gain access to the intense fun of the party (Rietveld 1998b: 21). Kevin Saunderson, part of the seminal (heterosexual) brotherhood of Detroit techno producers, observed the following about DJ Knuckles' early 1980s sessions at the Warehouse, where the sound system was allegedly fantastic:

I'm sixteen years old, don't know anything about gay people, so I'm sitting on the wall the whole night, you know, guarding my butt and everything, right. And anyway, after a while...you start to see the people having fun and getting into the music and these people [are] just so free. I mean, just animated, arms all over the place, jumping on top of speakers, dancing with this person, prancing over this side, on the wall, climbing the walls on top, above 'em.

(Bidder 2001: 18–19)

This quote illustrates the uneasy, yet curious, relationship between gay club culture and heterosexual masculinity. The dance style described was called 'jacking', a dance-floor variant of copulating movements. The term itself is a mechanistic metaphor, creeping into the early house imagination preparing for a discursive development towards techno. People jacked with each other to the music, with walls and with the speakers (Bidder 2001; Rietveld 1998b).

Deep house is tantalizingly tactile in its deep penetration and full embrace of the body through its loudly amplified low-frequency bass lines. The 4/4 'foot' of the bass drum, mostly an analogue sound, has a warm 'feel', while its African-American and Latino syncopations move the body in a variety of directions, in contrast to the unidirectional macho 'motorik' of trance. In the dark space of the dance floor, the dancer gives in to the musical soul of communal intimacy, a 'subject–subject' spirituality. There are some forms of techno which manage to achieve this as well, mostly African-American and mostly a crossover with deep house's bass lines and soulful analogue feel. In current deep house, deep in its emotional response, the sexual is often less explicit. While the 'motorik' accompanies a possession trance, with the machine as its imagined 'animal' (Rouget 1985), deep house's orgasmic ecstasy articulates a relationship with a communal soul. In both cases, however, such rituals strengthen vulnerable identities in times of change. Gay club cultures and African-American forms of dance music have pioneered in this, as subjectivities which have been under siege so long that powerful forms of dance music and partying have been produced to heal this sense of unease, this continuous need for a rite of passage.

Conclusion

Despite its transcendental and universal appearance, the spirit is produced in and by the material and historical context of the self's relationship to the 'other'; spirituality is thereby always embodied. In the case of raves, the favoured musical form is a marriage between techno (functioning as a man–machine spiritual interface) and house music (producing a powerful ritual framework). In the early 21st century, trance comes out on top in terms of global popularity, stripping house of its African-American and Latino syncopated rhythms and replacing these with a Germanic 'motorik' pulse. One could, perhaps, conclude that techno and trance are genres which help to make sense of a troublesome post-industrial relationship between human and ICT.

This relationship seems particularly significant in terms of a vulnerable sense of masculinity which is worked out at homo-social rave-styled events; by destroying a sense of self, the merging with technology becomes a cyborgian rite of passage which needs to be repeated for as long as the identity crisis prevails. More men than women seem to be actively engaged with techno, either on the dance floor or in the production process. Meanwhile, women at rave-related events seem to embrace androgyny as a perceived liberation from femininity, an experience that may be found in the abstract spirituality of techno's machine aesthetic. In this sense the experience of the spirit, which instead of Bataille's 'subject–object' would be more usefully regarded as the 'self–other', varies, according to subject position affecting the choice of spiritual interface. For example, those who are more occupied by defining their embodied self also embrace a more metaphorically embodied form of dance music. This shows an affirming spirituality which connects subjects with subjects instead of a sacrificial annihilation of the self to merge with the machine-as-object. Rather than losing the self in a (metaphorical) cyborgian merging with technology, we could, perhaps, find ourselves in an embrace towards a sense of communal soul.

Bibliography

Barr, T. (2000) *Techno: The Rough Guide*, London: Penguin.

Barrett, E. (2002) 'Knowing and feeling: new subjectivities and aesthetic experience', *International Journal of Critical Psychology* 5: 113–23.

Bataille, G. (1985) 'The sacred', in A. Stoekl (ed.) *Visions of Excess: Selected Writings, 1927–1939*, A. Stoekl with C. R. Lovitt and D. M. Leslie, Jr (trans.), Manchester: Manchester University Press.

—— (1989) *Theory of Religion*, R. Hurley (trans.), New York: Zone Books.

Baudrillard, J. (1987) *The Ecstasy of Communication*, New York: Semiotext(e).

Bidder, S. (2001) *Pump Up the Volume*, London: Channel 4 Books.

Bradley, B.S. (2001) 'An approach to synchronicity: from synchrony to synchronisation', *International Journal of Critical Psychology* 2: 119–41.

Cole, F. and M. Hannan (1997) 'Goa trance', *Perfect Beat* 3(3): 1–14.

Collin, M., with J. Godfrey (1997) *Altered State: The Story of Ecstasy Culture and Acid House*, London: Serpent's Tail.

Davis, E. (1998) *Techgnosis: Myth, Magic and Mysticism in the Age of Information*, London: Serpent's Tail.

Eagleton, T. (1990) *The Ideology of the Aesthetic*, Oxford: Basil Blackwell.

Eshun, K. (1998) *More Brilliant than the Sun: Adventures in Sonic Fiction*, London: Quartet.

Fikentscher, K. (2000) *'You Better Work!' Underground Dance Music in New York City*, Hanover, NH, and London: Wesleyan University Press.

Goodwin, A. (1990) 'Sample and hold; pop music in the digital age of reproduction', in Simon Frith and Andrew Goodwin (eds) *On Record; Rock, Pop and the Written Word*, London: Routledge.

Henderson, S. (1997) *Ecstasy: Case Unsolved*, London: Pandora.

Huyssen, A. (1986) 'The vamp and the machine', *After the Great Divide: Modernism, Mass Culture and Postmodernism*, Basingstoke and London: Macmillan Press.

Irigaray, Luce (2002) *The Way of Love*, in dialogue with Prof Judith Still (16 December), London: ICA.

Kumar, Krishan (1995) *From Post-Industrial to Post-Modern Society: New Theories of the Contemporary World*, London: Blackwell.

Land, N. (1992) *The Thirst of Annihilation: George Bataille and Virulent Nihilism*, London: Routledge.

Lowe, R. and W. Shaw (1993) *Travellers: Voices of the New Age Nomads*, London: Fourth Estate.

Malbon, B. (1999) *Clubbing: Dancing, Ecstasy and Vitality*, London: Routledge.

Middleton, R. (1990) *Studying Popular Music*, Milton Keynes: Open University Press.

Morley, D. (1996) 'Postmodernism: a rough guide', in J. Curran, D. Morley and V. Walkerdine (eds) *Cultural Studies and Communication*, London: Edward Arnold.

Pini, M. (2001) *Club Cultures and Female Subjectivity: The Move from Home to House*, Basingstoke: Palgrave.

Plant, S. (1993) 'Building the Hacienda', *Hybrid* 1: 3–11.

Potts, A. (2001) 'The body without orgasm: becoming erotic with Deleuze and Guattari', *International Journal of Critical Psychology* 3: 140–64.

Pratt, Ray (1990) *Rhythm and Resistance: Explorations in the Political Uses of Popular Music*, London: Praeger.

Rajandran, S. (2000) 'The female in rave culture: the adventures of Galactic Canary in Buenos Aires', a Richter Fellowship proposal, supervised by J. Tobin, University of California, Los Angeles.

Reynolds, S. (1998) *Energy Flash: A Journey through Rave Music and Dance Culture*, London: Macmillan.

—— (2000) 'Kosmik dance: krautrock and its legacy', in P. Shapiro (ed.) *Modulations: A History of Electronic Music, Throbbing Words on Sound*, New York: Distributed Art Publishers.

Rietveld, H. (1993) 'Living the dream', in S. Redhead (ed.) *Rave Off: Politics and Deviance in Contemporary Youth Culture*, Aldershot: Avebury/Ashgate.

—— (1998a) 'Repetitive beats: free parties and the politics of contemporary DiY dance culture in Britain', in G. McKay (ed.) *DiY Culture: Party and Protest in Nineties Britain*, London: Verso.

—— (1998b) *This Is Our House: House Music, Cultural Spaces and Technologies*, Aldershot: Ashgate.

Robins, K. and F. Webster (1999) *Time of the Technoculture: From the Information Society to the Virtual Life*, London: Routledge.

Rouget, G. (1985) *Music and Trance: A Theory of the Relations between Music and Possession*, Chicago: University of Chicago Press.

Savage, J. (1996) 'Machine soul: a history of techno', in J. Savage (ed.) *Time Travel. From the Sex Pistols to Nirvana: Pop, Media and Sexuality, 1977–96*, London: Chatto & Windus (first published in *Village Voice, Rock & Roll Quarterly*, Summer 1993).

Sicko, D. (1999) *Techno Rebels: The Renegades of Electronic Funk*, New York: Billboard.

Springer, C. (1996) *Electronic Eros: Bodies and Desire in the Postindustrial Age*, London: Athlone Press.

Taylor, R. (1985) *The Death and Resurrection Show*, London: Antony Blond.

Thomas, A. (1995) 'The house the kids built: the gay black imprint on American dance music', in C.K. Creekmur and A. Doty, *Out in Culture: Gay, Lesbian and Queer Essays on Popular Culture*, London: Cassell (first published in *Out/Look*, Summer 1989).

Thornton, S. (1996) *Club Cultures: Music, Media and Subcultural Capital*, Cambridge: Polity.

Todorov, T. (1984) *Mikhail Bakhtin: The Dialogical Principle*, Manchester: Manchester University Press.

Toop, D. (1995) *Ocean of Sound: Aether Talk, Ambient Sound and Imaginary Worlds*, London: Serpent's Tail.

Verhagen, S. (2001) 'To be or to wannabe: over gabbers, jeugdculturen en de media', Sociology Masters dissertation, Supervisor: F. van Wel, University of Utrecht.

Ward, B. (1998) *Just My Soul Responding: Rhythm and Blues, Black Consciousness and Race Relations*, London: UCL Press.

Yurick, S. (1985) *Behold Metatron, the Recording Angel*, New York: Semiotext(e).

Discography

Kraftwerk (1977) 'Trans Europe Express', Kling Klang, Germany.

Phuture (1987) 'Acid Trax', Trax Records, Chicago, US.

Part II

Dance, rapture and communion

3 Rapturous ruptures

The 'instituant' religious experience of rave

François Gauthier

My personal opinion is that savage religion is not so much something that is thought as something that is danced.

(R.R. Marett)[1]

What does the gathering of many thousands of youth on a regular basis foretell? Forcibly something.

(Emmanuel Galland 1997: 8)

Defining evanescence

This chapter will focus mainly on that which has fuelled the formidable diffusion of rave and continues to draw non-initiates by the thousands, even today, into the humidity and heat of all-night techno parties: namely, the nature and characteristics of the singular and intense moment of release of the techno trance. The hypothesis can seem uncanny or daring: that rave's ascension within Western youth subcultures is due to the *religious* nature of its experience. But it is also, as will be debated here, an insightful and fecund viewpoint for understanding the effervescence of rave in contemporary youth culture.

In order to address some questions raised by the intensity and otherness of the rave experience – questions which challenge the whole of contemporary social sciences and humanities – this discussion will call upon the works of two of the most original French thinkers of the 20th century: Roger Bastide (1898–1974) and Georges Bataille (1897–1962). If Bastide first enables us better to grasp the dynamics of rave culture as a whole, Bataille can help approach the more intimate dimensions of the state of rave. It is under the sign of consumption, abandon and transgression that we are here to penetrate the rapturous world of rave.

In regard to method, this discussion pursues a certain ideal-type of rave that can be defined as *instituant*.[2] I am bidding that it is by grasping the more vivid aspects of such a phenomenon that one can hope to understand what some have called the more 'degraded', 'commercial' or 'institutionalized' forms of rave. If the following analysis can be held to be widely applicable to emergent and clandestine rave scenes, the following must be stressed: first, that over a decade after the birth of raves in England, clandestine scenes still thrive in a number of cities;

second, that these vivid and transforming experiences can occur unexpectedly – for instance, at large commercial raves. In the course of my own research I have been astonished to hear young ravers holding little knowledge of rave history speak of their experiences in these large raves – the intensity of their experience, their commitment to the scene and the community forming around events – in virtually the same terms as those reported at the emergence of rave.

Religion: from disappearance to shifting

To tackle rave from a religious studies perspective, and thus grant it a full-fledged religious status, requires a few introductory comments. First of all, a distinction must be made between 'a' religion, from a theological, traditional, institutional-ized perspective, and 'religion' as a fundamental cultural phenomenon.[3] Opposing the social studies secularization theory and other modern views holding religion to be doomed to history's burial ground, the idea that religion and the religious experience do not end with the dwindling of traditional forms of instituted religion is becoming widespread.[4]

The French anthropologist Roger Bastide can be considered one of the most stimulating thinkers on the topic of contemporary religious phenomena, as he kept an eye on the cultural shifts in Western culture while concentrating the body of his work on Brazilian and African rituals. Late in his life, Bastide acknowl-edged that religion 'shifted' more than it disappeared or 'reappeared'. He pointed to urbanization- and secularization-induced phenomena such as star and hero cults, and their ecstatic rituals as contemporary modulations of an experience of the sacred and, therefore, manifestations of religiosity. That reli-gion transforms itself in less easily distinguished – or, as Edward Bailey (1997) would say, less *explicit* – cultural phenomena challenges classical definitions of religion. For Bastide, religion is not always 'in' what we are accustomed to call 'religions'. Religions, in fact, are often conservative contractions of the religious, or even institutions which aim to *defend against* the religious, and are thus merely moralistic or sentimental annexes of, for example, 'bourgeois class rule' (Bastide 1995). If this position is startling at first, closer analysis demonstrates that Bastide's ideas on religion, like those of Georges Bataille, are incisive toolkits enabling a comprehensive grasp of phenomena which would be elusive were we to limit religion to its traditional, institutionalized forms.

For Bastide, therefore, the 'death of God(s)' and the fall of traditional religious institutions (the *instituted*) by no means correlate to a disappearance of '*instituant*' experiences of the sacred. In other words, the crisis affecting various Christian churches, for example, does not signify a crisis of the *instituant* : the desire and need for experimentation with the dynamics of the sacred, as can be found, for instance, in transgressive behaviour or collective effervescence. It is the dialectical movement between these two polarities that I would like to introduce in order to shed some light on the dynamics of the rave phenomenon in contemporary society.[5]

As a first rule of thumb, we can state that the institution is always *instituted* by an *instituant*, and that the *instituant* is always a primary moment in the process of institutionalization.[6] Applying these categories to rituals, we can show how *instituant* and *instituted* are articulated. An instituted ritual, for example, can be the periodic re-enactment of a mythical foreground, aiming at maintaining a certain social order or structure. The ritual that seeks to be *instituant*, on the contrary, can be the source of major disorder, renewal and reorganization. Although these categories are set in opposition, they are not exclusive: an instituted ritual must possess a certain *instituancy*, or else its religiosity 'degrades' in a sense, becoming purely moral, its fervour dried up, unable to transcend the profane.[7] On the other end of the spectrum, the *instituant* must be wrapped in some amount of *domestication* and tied down by some sort of institutionalization to enable passage from the sacred back to the profane. In this articulation, when instituted forms no longer provide for the vividness of the *instituant* experience we witness the appearance of *savage* quests for *the vivid fervour of the instituant* that shun any regard for domestication.

Calling upon his extensive knowledge of Brazilian and African trance rituals, Bastide, in his essential article *Le Sacré sauvage* (1997: 209–29), shows how the contemporary rapport with the sacred differs from that in traditional and tribal religion. He argues that the traditional, 'organic' society is essentially geared towards restricting, controlling and channelling the dangerous but necessary *instituant* experience of the sacred, in a sense *domesticating* it. Far from being a hysterical free-for-all, the tribal trance ritual is tuned to a T, as religious (mythical reference) and social control (behaviour codes) transform the spontaneous, *instituant* trance into an institutionalized, domesticated one.

This general scenario, which also applies to larger social bodies, varies when two levels of social change occur. First, when the religious institution is weakened, its capacity to hold the experience of the sacred within its mythical frame proves largely handicapped. The *instituant* trance is then harder to transform and domesticate. Second, when community becomes eroded, this leads to feelings of solitude and helplessness. Synonymous with the erosion of instituted, conservative forms of religious experiences, these transformations induce an increased need for *instituant* experiences of the sacred – eventually through savage forms. Ferality and wildness are then expressed with increased intensity and periodicity in flourishing religious countercultures.[8] Often shying away from institutionalization, this quest for *instituancy* reveals a tragic disparity between a society's conservative superstructures and its more mobile social infrastructures.

Such would be the situation in much of the Western world today, where all institutions – religious, social and political – have their legitimacy affected by widespread disillusionment (Boisvert 1995, 1998). As any discourse or representation will be regarded as essentially relativistic, no authority will be accepted as a definite bearer of Truth. Rather, and given a new pragmatic reality that some have argued to be constitutive of a postmodern ethos (Boisvert 1995), truth and meaning must come from and be judged on the scale of *experience*. Consequently, far from wanting institutions to domesticate and control a dangerous and savage type of experience, contemporaries can actually *seek* these outside instituted forms.[9] This echoes Bastide, who states that any eventual solution to the 'problems' of a transitional society can only be found in a space 'beyond ideas': not from abstractions above (myths, ideologies, institutions, discourses and other representations) but from the 'immanence' of sociality and its correlate of affect, imagination and social 'heat' (Bastide 1997: 222).

The 'accursed share': Georges Bataille and the necessity of excess

Max Weber showed how Western culture was built on thoroughly rational foundations, an edifice in which nothing was to exceed the all-encompassing grip of Science, Progress and Reason. Here Bastide agrees with Bataille, for whom this enterprise is judged profoundly foolish since it ignores one of life's essential dimensions – that which is uneconomic, gratuitous, violent and expensive. To illustrate this, Bastide calls up the mythological image of Prometheus's Vulture, gnawing at his liver, a symbol of sapiens' inextinguishable *hubris*, or excessiveness (Bastide 1997: 163–82). Bataille, for his part, mobilized a whole theoretical system around what he calls the 'damned', 'blasted' or 'accursed share'[10] of humanity.

Bataille deems the principles of usefulness, propriety and productivity to be highly insufficient for understanding the foundations and workings of societies' economics. These principles, although necessary, only account for one share of human activity: that which is submitted to an end, inscribed within reason and projected into duration. Another share, the accursed one, is that of excess, expenditure, un-usefulness, waste, luxury, mourning, cults, games, aesthetics, war, debauchery, drunkenness, (sacrificial and erotic) consumption, that which cannot be 'accounted for' and must be spent (as lovers are) outside any productive end (Bataille 1949: 28).[11] It is exuberance and violence, an unproductive necessity, which limit the human realm through the accursed share and which, ultimately, open on to the possibility of a rapport with a radical *otherness*, the sacred: 'that prodigious effervescence of life that, for the sake of duration, the order of things hold in check, and that this holding changes into a breaking loose, that is, into violence' (Bataille 1989: 42).[12]

Modernity, through a fantasy of total control and domination over the arbitrary (and notwithstanding its project of liberation), made usefulness itself, work, into a sacred value. In so doing, modernity has negated the accursed share by trying to integrate it in a consumerist economy, substituting leisure and reason for religion and ritual. Tumultuous expenses and collective effervescence, therefore, were deemed characteristic of premodern, archaic, bygone, uncivilized and therefore lesser societies. Some anthropologists had consequently noted that proper religious celebrations, effervescences and festivities such as bacchanals, carnivals and orgies had virtually disappeared from the face of the (Western, and therefore civilized) earth (Duvignaud 1977; Caillois 1980). Rather, it seemed, luxury, expense and transgression had been emptied of their substance and anaesthetized, channelled into leisure activities or entertainment commodities.

The brazenness with which techno-rave fired up so many local subcultures could have been caused in part by a certain longing, otherwise unfulfilled, for expense and communion (Epstein 2001a). Incidentally, techno-rave could be defined as a hedonistic encounter of the technological and the archaic in which transient communities give voice to this accursed share. On a more general level, through excess and transgression raves participate in a cultural resurgence of the festive, providing new avenues for experiences of the sacred in an atomized society (Fontaine and Fontana 1996; Gaillot 1999, 2001).

Rave as festive ritual

I regard this radical experience of rave as a manifestation of the religious '*fête*',[13] or 'celebration'. The 'festive', a religious category different from that of ritual, is, for Georges Bataille specifically, a human fusion in which this accursed share is given expression. Fuelled by desire, an instinct, a call for destruction, exhilaration, dis-order, a motivation often understood as animalistic, the *fête*, in which the paradoxes of human and social life collide, is simultaneously harnessed and subordinated by a wisdom which enables the participants to *come back* from this confusional state with a feeling of replenishment, *as if* having received some kind of impetus from the 'outside' (Bataille 1989: 54).

Set in Bataille's economy, the festive amounts to the sacrificial consumption of order, usefulness and productivity. Its constitution and effectiveness are reliant on its ability to set up a contrast with the profane order. Through its instinct of preservation, the festive is necessarily ritual, as it must provide return from the uncertainty of the margin; but it also differs from ritual as it allows for an un-rivalled degree of spontaneity, play and creativity.

What also distinguishes the festive from the ritual is that the latter is disengaged from a telos: the celebration is not a re-enactment of an original myth, reporting meaning outside itself. Neither is it held to take after some sort of commemoration. The aim is in fact to escape time and duration and to elude all memory. If an occasion is given for celebrating, the celebration is only fully festive if what is celebrated is forgotten and recognized for what it really is – a pretext. The festive implicitly seeks forgetfulness, selflessness and oblivion. What this implies is that the prompted effervescence is sought after *for itself* and *in itself*. In other words, it is its own purpose and reason. By opening up to creativity, by staging an otherly, unlicensed temporary world, the festive need only contain *itself*. Disengaging from temporality, the festive bursts into an 'eternal' – or, to be more precise, 'indefinite' – present, and opens on to an *instituant* factuality.

This scenario is consistent with some of the characteristics of the rave-borne techno experience. Many interpreters, from within or on the edge of the rave scene, have likened rave to the festive (see Fontaine and Fontana 1996; Ben Saâdoune *et al.* 1997; Hampartzoumian 1999; Epstein 2001a; and Petiau 2001, for example), thus referring, more or less explicitly, to a symbolic mechanism making use of *transgression* (Bataille 1986, 1988, 1989). To understand how rave fits into this scheme and leads to abandon and rapture in the techno trance, the festive can be decomposed into three sacrificial stages: rupture (with the profane), consumption and communion in abandonment.[14]

Ruptures and transgressions: hastening otherness

If a fundamental characteristic of the festive is to set up contrast with the profane, the efficiency with which a rave can lead to an *instituant* religious experience depends to a great extent on how much it can depart from normal consciousness. As I will try to demonstrate, rave seeks this rupture by all means: temporal, spatial, corporeal and symbolic. These efficient ruptures can be first divided into two levels: cultural (collective, social) and intimate (individual-with-others).

Cultural ruptures

An analysis of the cultural (or socio-historical) – which may affect individual consciousnesses indirectly – provides us with an initial interpretative key to understanding rave's radical and original stance while setting it in the perspective of recent cultural history.

The first significant elements of rupture appear in techno music, rave's sonic stage and canvas. As musicologist Philip Tagg (1994) put it, techno could well represent the most significant shift in contemporary music since the advent of rock. He writes: 'perhaps techno-rave puts an end to nearly four-hundred years of the great European bourgeois individual in music' (*ibid.*: 219). As far as the individual in rave and techno music is concerned, it could be interpreted as supporting the thesis of a certain 'decline of individualism in Western societies'.[15] In regard to 'artistry', the stereotypical techno music producer and DJ eludes the instituted star-system of popular music by resorting to identity-blurring tactics, anonymity, white labels, parallel distribution systems and techno-tribe 'DJ-ing in the dark' – all strategies emphasizing that the dancing crowd of ravers (and not the DJs) are the stars.[16]

Could the simple fact of gathering be interpreted as transgression? In such an individualist and citizen-cum-consumer era, this could be so. Only the fact of gathering is obviously not the sole privilege of raves. What is particular here is that rave's gathering is set outside social institutions, namely stadiums, arenas, theatres and clubs, challenging established venues. Furthermore, as was noted in the case of Parisian raves (Epstein 2001b), while creative urban activities have always made good use of downtown centrality, raves use 'deterritorialization' (Deleuze and Guattari 1980) strategies by staging their 'Temporary Autonomous Zones' (Bey 1991) on the city's periphery: derelict post-industrial landscapes, abandoned army bases, fields, forests, etc.

As techno music makes use of sonic larceny and propriety rights baffling as *sine qua non* creation techniques (Reynolds 1999; Petiau 2001), raves blatantly (or else symbolically) hijack buildings and spaces at the expense of ownership. Clandestine warehouse parties are the best example of this transgression of propriety rights. Even in the case of licensed raves, what is determining is the purpose for which the ravers use the space, by contrast to the usual 'space-defines-use' formula. By redirecting such symbols of culture towards both a playful and feral use, rave catalyses its festive effervescence. The deliciously unreasonable absurdity of this ephemeral takeover of locations adds to rave's mythical construct and heightens the potential for subversive interpretation.

Another important and defining rupture in techno-rave is its rapport with technology. Until recently, technology was largely serving productive ends and the modern ideal of Progress. Techno culture thus marks a significant break from this handcuffed and stereotypical rapport with technology. In rave culture, technology is synonymous with *possibility*, and stands as a prerequisite for creation, gathering and effervescence.

The characteristics of early techno culture – subversion, a newfound freedom of expression through use of 'the technologies of pleasure' (Collin 1998) and recycling of the past and the symbolic, a new openness to ritual, a new imperative for togetherness outside instituted forms and discourses – contribute to a general ambiance of exploration, experimentation and new possibilities. Consequently, when techno-rave reached the urban crucibles of the West, feelings were ignited as though some kind of Kingdom had come. Of course, this idealism and glistening didn't last long, but the world, in a sense, *had* changed for youth, and post-rave culture carries this shift. The point is that the ruptures at work in techno-rave, on a cultural level, create a determining narrative, a first *disposition* that must be taken into account if we are to understand how the rave experience pushes itself on the individual consciousness.

Going elsewhere: intimate ruptures in the festive sphere

Incessantly, rave brews up mythologies of an 'elsewhere'. Representations are kept to a minimum in this subculture, blending the functional and pragmatic to the most effective and vivid expression of the symbolic. Party flyers (alongside posters and album covers) are virtually the only iconography in which this visual generation indulges. Flyer aesthetics exploit syncretism, covering a wide spectrum of cultural references in a given place at a given time. As Bernard Schütze puts it, writing about the Montreal scene:

> Their [the flyers'] particularity is that they announce nothing more than a colour, a date, an endpoint, an element, a quantity of memory, a connection, a state, a unit, a dimension. The title of the flyer is not even a word anymore, it is a technical abbreviation and a symbol, so we are really left with a bare minimum of linguistic substance.
>
> (Schütze 1997: 17)

We have been transported to the edge of language, where its multi-potentiality is fully exploited. Words here are only *forms* offered to symbolic enchantment. Umberto Eco's 'open work' is wide open here, overstretched, fully aesthetic. Interestingly, the universes depicted by rave and techno iconography are entirely insignificant without their ritual enactment. As Schütze writes, 'the flyer bears a sense/non-sense that is only fully revealed if one participates in the event of which they are the advent' (*ibid.*: 16). Here it is not the ritual that finds meaning through mythical re-enactment (as in the classical definition of ritual), but rather it is the mythological symbolism which acquires depth and significance through the ritual event. In other words, it is not the mythical framework that interprets the ritual gesture, but rather the experience that gives meaning to an imaginary mythological landscape.

What is common to this eclectic iconography is its portrayal and dream of an *elsewhere*: a nowhere that rave strives to realize in the margin of society. Simon Reynolds (1999: 248) appropriately noted that this 'no-where no-when elsewhere' corresponds to the epistemology of 'utopia', an ideal world outside reality, virtually unattainable and definitely unsustainable. This desire for a significant and meaningful elsewhere finds resonance in the explicit or symbolic references to Eastern, shamanic and primitive mysticisms which proliferate in various rave scenes.[17] These and other references work on the imaginary, on the idea – the *myth* – of rave as travel and ecstatic initiation. Raves do everything in their power to organize, stage, set up, provoke and condition a rupture. In this case, the popular expression 'going out' takes on a strong and full meaning: to extract oneself voluntarily and freely (in the double sense of liberty and gratuitousness) from regulated social life in order to experience 'something else' (Fontaine and Fontana 1996: 14).

If we were to concentrate mainly on the ritual aspect of rave, we could show how the threefold classical division of ritual is satisfied through segregation, marginalization and aggregation, which in the case of rave would translate as adventure, peak and plateau and, finally, comedown. The first stage of this sequence basically corresponds to the preparation for the event, which preludes rupture. Especially true of the implantation and emergence periods of rave (but still to a certain extent in today's post-rave culture, namely in the more underground currents), knowledge of a rave party requires energy and determination. It is essential to be 'in the know' – to know: where to access information and how to interpret it; where to buy tickets (if any); where to call for the event location (revealed hours before the actual party starts); how to get to the party; and where to get good drugs. In essence, then, and resembling other youth counter- or subcultures, rave thrives by feeding on a feeling of esotericism. For those who are already 'in the know', this builds identification and promotes commitment.[18] For the non-initiates, accessing this underground world provides both a thrill and an anxiety that can easily be measured through stories and accounts.

This esotericism sharpens the contrast with normal life. Consistent with what Maurice Boutin (1976) argued to be constitutive of the festive, a certain dose of exclusion is necessary for a rave to be a fully effective vehicle for sociality, effervescence and community. The over-mediated event, on the other hand, consequently less marginal, is already a few steps further towards institutionalization and reduces the festive to spectacle or leisure. The degradation of a certain sense of esotericism 'commonalizes' the experience and makes for a cheaper thrill – and thus jeopardizes the rupture from commonality.

Festive manifestations such as carnivals are well known for promoting disguises and occasioning particular attention to vestments and corporeal ornaments. Ravers massively confide in looking to make their attire special, more so than when clubbing (Ben Saâdoune *et al.* 1997). Substantial effort and/or money is often invested in an event-specific vestment, to which may be added corporeal markings (tattoos) and piercings. This constitutes a first strategy at deconstructing and reconstructing subjectivity, which involves here, as a first gesture, the outer self: the frontier that makes communication with others possible. It is a first visible sign of a desire for otherness, for reconfiguration, for abandonment of part of ordinary subjectivity. It is a first outward licence, an expression of the usually contained and forbidden, and the paradoxical show of both affront and vulnerability.[19]

Clandestine and emergent rave scenes have often been interpreted as 'initiatic journeys', partly because of the energy and craftiness required to make it to the party in the first place. Collin (1998), among others, has vividly portrayed such in the burgeoning London scene of the late 1980s. The story is well known: pirate radios and telephone info-lines with recorded messages giving out coded information, meeting places and car parks, caravans of cars and back alleys. Interestingly, knowingly or not, rave scenes emerged elsewhere using the same strategies. Furthermore, the info-line system and secrecy surrounding events are still the norm, although unnecessary from a strictly practical point of view. 'This is not like going to a club', rave seems to say. 'This isn't just going out, this is going *way out.*' Essentially, then, the greater the effort in preparing for and getting to an event, the greater commitment there is in being there with others and the more intensely the festive rupture will be felt – heightening its potentiality.

Creating a sense of rupture is to act simultaneously on the corporeal, the imaginary, the symbolic, the spatial and the temporal. There is a strong will in rave to camp outside the instituted club and leisure circuit, with their fixed venues and regulated timeframes. While other subcultures had already explored the excessive possibilities of the night (Silcott 1999), no other phenomenon had invested so massively in the all-night time slot. For this wasn't just an *evening* out clubbing, but a full-on *all-night until noon* (and sometimes beyond) extravaganza.

All of these considerations prepare ravers for the rave experience, instilling a sense of the extraordinary and gearing them towards an openness of both mind and body. The way from the door to the actual festive space enclosed by stacks of speakers often involves making it through various symbolic airlocks (such as the security, the ticket booth or the cloakroom) and tunnels, giving the impression of entering a secret world in which the heartbeat-like thumping of the bass drum shakes both air ducts and spines. Inside the rave, the experience can make for a brutal rupture. Everything in rave is oriented towards producing a confusional space where references are blurred through indistinctiveness or sensorial overkill. The first thing to notice in the typical hangar or warehouse rave, for example, is the absence of chairs, tables or any other objects which could define, structure and condition space. Apart from the chillout room lined with sofas and mattresses, where one can take part in orgiastic and organic sprawling, the space is what the raving bodies make of it. The rave environment stresses this disorganization of space and deters any attempt at resisting abandonment to the flow of bodies and sound. The vastness of the main rooms, the stroboscopic lighting, the colour hazes and smoke induce a confusional state, discouraging any attempt at seizing continuity or organizing information.

Techno music, stretched across high-frequency oscillations, waves, bleeps and low-end incessant thumping, also modulates consciousness in a specific fashion. Techno proves to be a truly efficient sculptor and architect of time, while space becomes thick or aerial in accordance. Through its insistent and repetitive beat structure, techno constantly reiterates a present, a new foundation, a Nietzschean eternal differential return, a new event of meaning – as though it were some sort of relentless immediacy machine. As Jean-Ernest Joos writes:

> Once the needle touches vinyl, there is no future – repetition has made it obsolete. The revolution of techno has been the creation of music that develops itself in its own interstices, the interstices of the present. The parasites of chronology, narrative, beginning, middle and end are all gone. Listening is pure, pure opening.
>
> (Joos 1997: 11–12)

Finally, drugs are another – truly radical – means of heightening rupture. Consciousness-altering and energy-liberating substances such as ecstasy, LSD and amphetamine (speed) are effective ways of catalysing and inducing a response to all other ruptures. To be truly effective in this economy, the drug must be accompanied by a context and a disposition enabling *ritual* consumption: the substance must therefore be acknowledged – and this can prove no small task – as a ritual *tool*, and not an end in itself.[20]

Drugs induce a significant rupture by affecting the apprehension of reality. Although they are not necessary for the rave experience to be *instituant*, a variety of alterants are used in the rave context as in various traditional festive contexts, exacerbating a feeling of otherness. If the festive is an 'inflation' of both the individual and social body (Caillois 1980), then subjective expansion through ritual drug use is an effective catalyst. As reverting to carnivalesque vestments had displayed a first *outer* disposition for a new subjectivity, drugs like ecstasy enable this exploration on an *inner* – Bataille would say 'intimate' – level.

Consumption

Rave's most important innovation is its break from the spectacle format of the rock show while blowing the club dance floor up to overwhelming proportions. In a way, the rock show is the result of an exacerbated individualism: the stage is the altar, where stands the deified figure of the band leader. Incidentally, the sociality of a rock show differs radically from that of a rave. The spectacle is a transfer of the self towards an incarnated Ideal, a live representation permitting an *ekstasis* of the self through identification. In rave, the uniform orientation towards the stage is short-circuited, freeing ravers from dogmatic spatial determinations while opening new possibilities for interaction. The result, were we to view a snapshot of the dance floor from above, would be something between a laboratory for Maffesoli's (1988) soft-core open-edge 'tribal' sociality and a portrayal of the Brownian particle dance: many interconnected and ever-shifting circles of oscillating individuals. This sociality facilitates contact and abandon, as no focus or adoration is sought from a stage.

In opposition to the more or less passive (but highly determined) *reception* involved in a spectacle, rave promotes *participation*. The investment required for rave differs significantly from that for leisure or spectacle, and even more so from the passive role of the consumer in the contemporary profane. Participation is creation and expression, and calls upon the whole of being. It is based on invest- ment and commitment (on a more or less short-term basis in this case but in a highly intense manner), as well as on all the gratuitous, puerile and excessive behaviours that make up rave's experience. Following Bataille, ravers enter a world of ruptures in which they consume in excess, and where they do not merely 'border' on the religious, but are deeply and wildly religious. Thus we could say that a profane 'logic of consumerism' is transcended into a fuller, more vivid 'logic of sacrificial consumption'.[21]

Through this consumption, rave recalls archaic and ecstatic manifestations of religion more than contemplative Christian piety. Of all the expensive and exces- sive behaviours in rave, dancing frenetically or in utter abandonment for hours on end is the most blatant and significant. In the rave context, with impressive stacks of speakers gushing out giga-levels of sound, techno comes into actual *being* (Boulé 2001), making it imperative to *dance*. Techno becomes a *presence* that cannot be ignored – more, it is a shock whose intensity is only matched by the body's urge to give in to it, an aggression made positive through the festive context (Métais 2001). Compared to rock and pop's 'sentimental' listening mode, techno music's 'sensitivity' bypasses verbal recognition and blurs subject/object division.

Dancing also modifies one's consciousness of space, time and body, and is readily judged to be therapeutic (Fontaine and Fontana 1996; Schott-Bilmann 2001). Benefits from dance can also be understood as resulting from its gratu- itousness, its essentially religious and erotic narrative, allowing for intimacy and contact with others outside usual social behavioural codes. This dance, various in styles, is an abstract, impulsive, desexualized body-in-motion that opens up to non-verbal communication. It is a dance in which gender and personality are transcended and the usual mode of negotiation and seduction yields to an orgiastic, confusional, indistinct openness, a state in which interconnectedness distils freedom. Added to the whole of rave's consumption, this becomes a means of opening subjectivity and prompting *encounter* in the festive interstice:

> The meaning of this profound freedom is given in destruction, whose essence is to consume *profitlessly* whatever might remain in the progression of useful works. Sacrifice destroys that which it consecrates.... This useless consumption is *what suits me*, once my concern for the morrow is removed. And if I thus consume immoderately, I reveal to my fellow beings that which

I am *intimately*: Consumption is the way in which *separate* beings communicate. Everything shows through, everything is open and infinite between those who consume intensely.

(Bataille 1988: 58–9; italics in original)

Abandonment

Through a confusional environment and a musical landscape which continually eludes a defined narrative, rave discourages any attempt at resisting its sensorial assault. The ruptures and excesses uncovered to date can incidentally be understood as prompting abandon. To achieve this effectively, though, raves must also provide for a minimum of security. This is ensured by rave's ritual structure and group solidarity. Ravers have abundantly reported mutual aid and cooperation within the parties: an anthropological constant arising when a group transgresses into the margin. Raves are known to function widely on the basis of small 'tribes' (Maffesoli 1988), each individual taking some responsibility for the others.

Correlatively to this safety net, many observers have resorted to psychedelic guru Timothy Leary's use of the terms 'set and setting' to illustrate how the ecstasy trip, for instance, will be influenced and secured (Collin 1998; Reynolds 1999; Push and Silcott 2000). Although simplistic, this expression refers to two polarities which interrelate in sculpting the subject's experience of an altered consciousness. These are:

1   The subject's disposition, motivations, desires, expectations, anguishes, past experiences, etc.
2   The environment and social narrative (meaning its web of symbolic references) in which the subject is directly involved with others.

In the cases discussed here, these different ritual fragments combine and complete each other to provide a frame in which to consume and let go.

Most ecstasy users know that the worst way to deal with this drug is to try to control it. This usually results in fear or insecurity and can lead to unpleasant experiences. 'E' (ecstasy), rave's most popular and prominent conscience-bender, requires it be *worked*. Supporting the participation thesis, ravers generally acknowledge that the ecstasy trip is not a passive thing: 'You have to dance to it, dance it until it's no longer an intruder, until it has become one with the flesh' (Joos 1997: 11). Everything boils down to the acceptance of an altered state, which the raver must resist resisting.[22]

The state of surrender to body, crowd and sound that is typical of rave has widely been called a 'trance', although the expression is seldom given any definition or granted further analysis. A trance, understood in the wide anthropological sense, is simply an altered state of consciousness, a significantly differed rapport with the world, with the self and with others. In this respect, it is not thoroughly uncommon. The question arises then as to the specific nature of the rave-borne trance. This will be the focus of the remainder of this chapter.

In our culture, where trance states are often understood as sharing an acute proximity with folly, the only accepted state of trance is hypnosis. Rather than collective, the hypnotic trance is defined as being necessarily individual (Fontaine and Fontana 1996: 23). Considering that other cultures recognize many different states of consciousness (Suissa 1997), the lack of subtlety here is disarming. Nonetheless, Joos translates this into the techno sphere:

> As such, the rave state is precisely one of hypnosis. Hypnosis occurs when, after one stares at a point until it becomes invisible, one's attention is decentralised. And that is exactly what happens at raves: all visual, auditory and tactile sensation is only peripheral, diffuse, like an immense and unfocused opening.
>
> (Joos 1997: 12)

The religious *fête* involves some sort of trance, a transgression of the self in a wider ensemble, an *ekstasis* (Duvignaud 1977). In normal life, individuality is understood as difference, and this difference, in turn, translates into divergence. In the midst of the festive consumption, this difference becomes a foundation for convergence: the presence of the self affirmed by the presence of others. It is, in other words, participating in an inflated social body and, both intimately and ultimately, the recognition of the need for others (Boutin 1976).

This reveals that lying deep beneath the impulse to consume is the call for abandon. Letting go in the festive arena of rave further recalls the parallel drawn with *sacrifice*. For Bataille, sacrifice, widely held by scholars to be 'the religious rite *par excellence*', is defined as violence – meaning *dis*-order: rupture and excess – consuming an offering.[23] The most important gesture in sacrifice is the gift of the ritual offering (abandon), which fire or blade seals as definite and irretrievable (Mauss 1968; Bataille 1988, 1989). Through its destruction, its own consumption in the sacrificial scheme, the offering is irrevocably torn away from any *use*, any determined productive end or value.

In a sacrificial scheme, abandon in the festive ritual of rave could be understood as holding subjectivity as an offering (and we can stress the radical vulnerability that this entails). Holding the self as an offering in a consumed moment of surrender, were we to pursue this logic, recalls in turn mysticism: another high-intensity area of religious experience. Sacrifice, when the violated offering becomes the self and is no longer symbolized by an outer object, opens on to the ultimate sacrifice, that of subjectivity, in utter renunciation and abandon of will. Here sacrifice bridges into mysticism, of which it can be argued to hold the seed (Gauthier 2001a). We can now fall back on the problem of defining the techno-induced trance. In other words: where in the array of these differently orientated logics of consumption – outward or inward – does the rave experience lie?

All analysts seem to have noted the intensity and particular nature of the rave experience, variously referred to as being 'beyond words', 'iridescent', 'oceanic', 'empty', 'pure presence', 'a pure space of non-thinking', 'intense, more abundant life', and even 'mystical', 'comparable to a mystic's trance' or 'peak of human experience' (Collin 1998). What this reveals is that, essentially, for the protagonists normality is clearly transgressed and transcended. Furthermore, the fact that 're-entry' from this state is known to be 'notoriously difficult' (*ibid.*: 38) indicates that this experience is a savage, hardly domesticated quest for the *instituant*.

In essence, then, the rave experience amounts to *losing oneself*, preferably in bliss. Can we conclude that it is an experience of the sacred? First, it is important to reconfigure the debate on the sacred. If we want to be able to understand fully what is at stake here we must draw away from theorists such as Mircea Eliade and Rudolf Otto, for the sacred is not an essence, and even less a 'thing' – even indefinable – that could by itself 'erupt' into the profane.[24] We must also put the axe to conceptions of religion and the sacred riven with obligations to such phantoms as divinities, gods, the supernatural or any unattainable transcendence – conceptions that are still, in many respects, hostages to Christian theology.[25] Rather, the sacred is a fundamental anthropological category, since any social or cultural order has an exteriority, an otherness. Therefore, all societies, all cultures involve the sacred, which can be experienced – to varying degrees – by individuals as a structuring and/or dangerous force.

The *instituant* rave experience, because of its intensity, otherness and singularity, then, is clearly one of the sacred. Yet there is no God here, nor 'spirits'. This is not a possession trance, unless perhaps possession by 'nothing'. But ravers do not feel 'something' (or indeed 'nothing') is overcoming them. On the contrary, it seems this overwhelming feeling originates from within, only they cannot say *how* or *where*. To agree with Duvignaud (1977), the festive trance is one of destructuration, not possession. Through this ontological disorientation, the rave experience generates more pleasure than one can handle, and it is this overflow that ravers feel the need to share with others. By contrast with other ecstasies, such as those brought by seduction, the source and direction of this pleasure (*jouissance*) remains unknown and consequently difficult to deal with (Joos 2001).

Compared with monastic mysticism, where trance and ecstasy are generally obtained through silence, isolation and immobility (all these being excesses, but of a 'negative', *hypo* nature), the techno trance is possible only because of the ephemeral social effervescence in which it takes place and the 'positive', *hyper* nature of its excesses. Yet it is not a collective trance (this could be the case in a homogenous society where the trance would be inserted into a common defined mythical frame), but rather an individual trance enabled by the presence of others. Sensitivity blushes to the surface of the skin and subjectivity opens indefinitely, as rubbing with the collective whole. Abandon is measured in openness, bringing meaning to being-together:

> The extreme moment of static pleasure...'the rift', when you are absolutely dispossessed of any goal, any expectation, any centre, is also the moment of greatest sociality, because at that moment the opening of the surface [of both skin and subjectivity] is as wide as possible. And it's precisely at that

moment that you seek eye contact and recognition from the other in order not to be alone with your pleasure, and to say that because your bodies are one, you can open up indefinitely.

(Joos 1997: 12)

In mysticism, desire for the sacred is stretched as a teleology, even though it is the sacrifice of this very desire that leads to the ultimate levels of bliss. Here, inserted in the festive context of rave, the ecstatic state arrives, in a sense, 'out of the blue': out of the confusional scape of a rupture turned rapture. The experience is therefore unhinged from a defined and institutionalized – and therefore explicit – religious system that could explicate its meaning. By contrast to a mystical experience, the techno trance is sought *in itself* and *for itself*, detached from any defined meaning, aim or purpose. This parallels Roger Bastide's savage trance, applied to contemporary youth movements. He writes that today's savage, *instituant*-seeking trance, unlike that administered by religious *institutions*, is 'dysfunctional', as it does not seek any result. Pushed to its furthest limit, this quest can even become suicide. This trance is the desire for pure *instituancy*, pure experimentation with an otherness that remains confused and diffuse – a purely gratuitous act, or a simple gesture of revolt. It is not release, compensation or catharsis in violence and delirium, as psychiatrists would have it, for the trance would then be functional again, and would lose its revolutionary edge. But it is, paradoxically, both an *insurgence against limits* and a *recognition of the anthropological necessity of limits* (Bataille 1986) on two levels: on the social level by transgressing the forbidden; and on the individual level by 'raising from its depths the anarchic herd of censored desires' (Bastide 1997: 225), which are consumed in the non-desire of the techno trance. The savage, as a quest for purest *instituancy*, is above all decomposition, destructuring, the essence and aim of a counterculture that, paradoxically, desires not – a priori – to be instituted in a new *definable*, and therefore possibly recuperated and commodified, culture.[26]

A mystical experience is not reducible to intensity. If it does share some sort of kinship with the rave rift, folly or other experiences that occur at the limits of human experience and language, mysticism, as a limit-case of the religious, requires insertion in a way of life and a whole system of beliefs and meaning. Mysticism and the rave rift nevertheless share abandon in an indefinite present – except in rave this spending in immediateness is made possible by the presence of others. Bataille (1986) held that the individual body could not be kept indefinitely to the 'minuscule fold' of private life: it must be opened, shared and delivered, made collective. Participating in the social body's need for the festive and the individual body's need for orgiastic sharing, rave's body-in-motion satisfies itself, thwarting the rules of the profane. The techno trance, therefore, is not mystical, although it perhaps contains the *possibility* of some kind of mysticism, if the potential for transformation is seized. The individual, then, as if partly domesticating this *instituancy*, becomes his or her own pontiff.

If this scenario holds interesting potential for promoting personal responsibility, it is also tragic since it falls short of making it into a large-scale collective cosmology. If this experience is understood as festive in nature and thereby immediate and ephemeral, the rave experience can still become a manner of being-in-the-world by providing a differential point of view from which to construct meaning and identity. If it is interpreted as highly spiritual or explicitly religious *by the individual* (and possibly his or her surroundings), then, the rave experience and its rift-like peak might approximate 'savage mysticism', to keep with Bastide's terminology. On the other hand, the particularly fulfilling and fleeting nature of this trance-with-others can become an easy escape route in which communion and openness dissolve into autism – meaning essentially shunning the depths of its own religiosity.

Conclusion

In the *instituant* rave experience, rupture and excess lead to abandon. And in abandon's consumption, in this rapture brought by the heat of rupture, communion is found: the dissolution of the individual in sharing, the union of the separate. On the anthropological level, we find the recognition of the need for others in an altered environment as a structuring limit of human experience. On the sociological level, this 'rift', the state of rave, is a paroxysmal state, both collective and individual, that answers how sociality is effected through *'reliance'* (Ménard 1991). Deriving from the Latin 'to bind', *'religare'*, the etymology of *reliance* pinpoints an essential function of religion, and demonstrates how sociology bridges into – and could even be said to stem from – *religiology*.[27] Far from dying out, religion can be found thriving in contemporary quests for meaning and ritual, although in a more *instituant* and fragmented manner (and thus shunning dogmas, credos and institutions). Hence the importance of challenging our traditional understanding of religion (and its science) in order to better – and more fully – apprehend the effervescence of contemporary youth phenomena such as rave.

Notes

1 *The Threshold of Religion*, p. xxxi; quoted in Kerr (1991: 249).
2 A draft of this ideal-type as well as further outlooks highlighting the religiosity of rave can be found in Gauthier and Ménard (2001). The ideal-type was drawn from personal observation and from printed material on rave, most of which can be found cited in the bibliography.
3 For a more thorough discussion on the odds and ends of this distinction as a basis for a comprehensive understanding of religion today, see Ménard (1999).
4 Even Peter Berger (1999) is acknowledging today the mistake social sciences and humanities made by ruling out the religious component from cultural and political analysis. Berger's understanding of the religious, meanwhile, remains more restricted than the views presented here.
5 As far as I know, there has yet to be any translation of Roger Bastide's text *Le Sacré sauvage* (Bastide 1997: 209–29); nor do I know of any use made of his categories *'institué'/'instituant'* and *'sauvage'/'domestique'*. The difficult task of introducing this terminology in English therefore falls upon my shoulders and I hope that the liberty and responsibility this involves will be greeted with some leniency.

6 While 'instituted' religion is easily translated from the French '*institué*', the case of *instituant* religion is somewhat problematic. '*Instituant*', in French, is the present participle of the verb '*instituer*' (to institute), and could therefore warrant the use of the English equivalent 'instituting'. However, the present participle in French is more restricted in its use, rarer, almost specialized, compared to its relatively common use in English (Morton 1979: 42). Therefore, calling on a certain tradition of translating concepts verbatim while aiming to maintain the specific meaning and depth of Bastide's theory, I will plead for the introduction of the term '*instituant*'.

7 It is the aim of the Christian mass, for example, to help relive the *instituant* experience of Christ. When the mass no longer purports *instituancy* and is unable to renew itself, the ritual dies out and new ones emerge. The Protestant Reformation, for this matter, is an excellent example of the instituted ritual of mass renewing with the *instituant* fervour that drives the Christian faith.

8 Bastide gives the Brazilian *macumba*, a highly syncretistic and feral version of African religion, as an example of this (1997: 209–29).

9 The profusion of anything and everything 'extreme' (either lived or mediated) is an example of this. The French anthropologist David Le Breton has written substantially on this phenomenon (see Le Breton 2000).

10 As Robert Hurley translates (Bataille 1989), from the French 'part maudite'. This is not the place to discuss such things at length, and so I will stick to Hurley's English terminology for the remainder of this contribution. Personally, though, I think 'damned' or even 'blasted' has a somewhat punkish and provocative feel that could better serve Bataille's radical ideas than the priestly 'accursed'.

11 The original version of *La Part maudite* (Bataille 1949) was prefaced by *La Notion de dépense*, which is close to essential for understanding the latter and which is unfortunately absent in Hurley's translation.

12 Bataille understands violence as being essentially a rupture or transgression of an order.

13 Hurley (Bataille 1989: 52) translates the French '*fête*' as 'festival'. While 'festive' (or even 'celebration') refers to some extent to the semantics of Bataille's '*fête*', 'festival' is, I find, too mellow and too highly determined to express thoroughly what is meant here: images of summer festivals, for example, can spring to mind, hinting more towards light-hearted entertainment than sacrificial consumption and orgiastic behaviour. I will therefore retain '*fête*' or the more versatile 'festive'.

14 This scheme, which I have explored briefly elsewhere (Gauthier 2001a), has also been noted by Petiau (1999).

15 'Postmodernity' is still synonymous with an individualistic culture (Lipovetsky 1983: 2002), only more inclined towards what Maffesoli (1998) calls an affective tribal behaviour.

16 The institutionalization and normalization of raves have struck a serious blow to this ideal, but more clandestine scenes still hold this to be a fundamental characteristic of their events.

17 As is abundantly illustrated in Collin (1998) and Reynolds (1999), for example, in the case of the UK. See Gauthier (2001a) for a hypothesis as to the reasons for the resort to so many of these often highly religious symbolisms.

18 It is important to note, as further support to a religious studies reading of rave, that commitment is one of the defining axioms of Edward Bailey's (1997) 'implicit religion'.

19 Consider the pride and/or shame that is felt when passing 'normal' people on the street on the way to the party, for example.

20 For the sake of this discussion, we can recognize the delicate nature of the question of drugs and keep to the best-case scenario (which is not so rare an instance) in which drug intake supports rave's total experience. For further discussion on the question of

drugs and ritual intake, see Gauthier (2001a). (See also Peterson 1996; Saunders and Doblin 1996; Fontaine and Fontana 1996; Collin 1998; Reynolds 1999; Fallu 2001).

21 The French language opposes the verb '*consumer*' (to burn: excessive consumption in the sense of Bataille) to '*consommer*' (to ingest: consumerist consumption), making this articulation somewhat clearer. See Gauthier (2001a) for more on this 'consumption logic' as opposed to a consumerist conservative order.

22 Following the scheme given by Fontaine and Fontana (1996), the first phase of consciousness altering is fear, felt during the temporary (but, especially in the case of ecstasy, extremely intense) transition between states. This is where letting go is most difficult but also most important. The second phase involves maintaining the rupture and restructuring this new consciousness. A third phase could be added, this being the (sometimes very difficult) comedown from the altered state. Ecstasy and other drugs thus enable individual de-conditioning, making it possible to see and feel the world otherly.

23 It can be noted that, following this definition, it need not be specified to *what* (supernatural being or suchlike) the offering is vowed, in the same way that the definition of religion can spare reference to the otherworldly. The space here is obviously not suited for a detailed argumentation of this point, but the reader can refer to Bataille (1988, 1989) and Gauthier (2001b).

24 Which is exactly what Eliade (1992) defines as a *hierophany*, central to his archetypal theory on the sacred.

25 On the unnecessary status of these 'phantoms' in a comprehensive and functional theory of religion, see Ménard (1999).

26 This whole paragraph refers to Bastide (1997: 225).

27 'Religiology' ('*religiologie*') is a constituent term of the heuristic pledge of the Université du Québec à Montréal's Religious Studies Department (Sciences des religions): as was argued in this chapter, that, despite secularization theories, the experience of religion does not die out but rather moves to other manifestations in culture. Refer to Ménard (2001). And as the intellectual itineraries of such prominent thinkers as Durkheim, Mauss, Lévi-Strauss and Turner, to name but a few, would suggest, there can be no... sociology nor anthropology without a profound questioning of the religious.

Bibliography

Bailey, Edward I. (1997) *Implicit Religion in Contemporary Society*, Kampen, the Netherlands: Kok Pharos.

Bastide, Roger (1995) 'Anthropologie religieuse', *Encyclopaedia Universalis*, vol. 2, Paris: Éditions Encyclopaedia Universalis.

—— (1997) [1975] *Le Sacré sauvage et autres essais*, Paris: Stock.

Bataille, Georges (1949) *La Part maudite*, prefaced by *La Notion de dépense*, Paris: Minuit.

—— (1986) [1962] *Erotism: Death and Sensuality*, Mary Dalwood (trans.), San Francisco: City Lights.

—— (1988) *The Accursed Share*, vol. 1, Robert Hurley (trans.), New York: Zone.

—— (1989) *Theory of Religion*, Robert Hurley (trans.), New York: Zone.

Ben Saâdoune, Nora, Caroline Hayeur and Emmanuel Galland (eds) (1997) *Rituel festif/ Festive Ritual*, Montreal: Macano.

Berger, Peter (ed.) (1999) *Desecularization of the World: Resurgent Religion and World Politics*, Grand Rapids, MI: W.B. Eerdmans Publishers.

Bey, Hakim (1991) *T.A.Z.: The Temporary Autonomous Zone, Ontological Anarchy, Poetic Terrorism*, Brooklyn, NY: Autonomedia.

Boisvert, Yves (1995) *Le Post-modernisme*, Montreal: Boréal.

—— (1998) *L'Analyse post-moderniste: une nouvelle grille d'analyse socio-politique*, Montreal: Harmattan.

Boulé, Éric (2001) 'L'Ouvrage sonore', in Gauthier and Ménard (eds) *Religiologiques* 24, '*Technoritualités. Religiosité rave*', fall: 81–96.

Boutin, Maurice (1976) 'Fête et événement', in Maurice Boutin, Éric Volant and Jean-Claude Petit (eds) *L'Homme en mouvement: le sport. Le jeu. La fête*, Montreal: Fides.

Caillois, Roger (1980) [1950] *Man and the Sacred*, Meyer Barash (trans.), Westport, CT: Greenwood Press.

Collin, Matthew (1998) *Altered State: The Story of Ecstasy Culture and Acid House*, updated 2nd edition, London: Serpent's Tail.

Deleuze, Gilles and Félix Guattari (1980) *Mille Plateaux*, Paris: Minuit.

Duvignaud, Jean (1977) *Le Don du rien: essai d'anthropologie de la fête*, Paris: Stock.

Eco, Umberto (1989) *The Open Work*, Cambridge, MA: Harvard University Press.

Eliade, Mircea (1992) *Mystic Stories: The Sacred and the Profane*, Ana Cartianu (trans.), Boulder, CO: East European Monographs, in cooperation with Editura Minerva, Bucharest; New York: distributed by Columbia University Press.

Epstein, Renaud (2001a) 'Les Équipements de la nuit techno à l'épreuve de la critique techno', *Annales des ponts et chaussées* 99, July–September: 1–10.

—— (2001b) 'Les Raves ou la mise à l'épreuve underground de la centralité parisienne', *Mouvements*, January–February; available online at http://www.acadie-reflex.org/JeuCadre1.html (accessed 8 January 2003).

Fallu, Jean-Sébastien (2001) 'Drogue et techno: une approche alternative', in Gauthier and Ménard (eds) *Religiologiques* 24, '*Technoritualités: Religiosité rave*', fall: 115–24.

Fontaine, Astrid and Caroline Fontana (1996) *Raver*, Paris: Anthropos.

Gaillot, Michel (1999) *Multiple Meaning: Techno, an Artistic and Political Laboratory of the Present*, Warren Niesluchowski (trans.), Paris: Dis Voir.

—— (2001) 'Les Raves, "part maudite" des sociétés contemporaines', in Anne Petiau (ed.), *Sociétés* 72, '*Pulsation techno, pulsation sociale*', Paris and Brussels: De Boeck.

Galland, Emmanuel (1997) 'Réveillez-vous!/Wake up!', in Nora Ben Saâdoune, Caroline Hayeur and Emmanuel Galland (eds) *Rituel festif/Festive Ritual*, Montreal: Macano.

Gauthier, François (2001a) 'Consumation. la religiosité des raves', in François Gauthier and Guy Ménard (eds) *Religiologiques* 24, '*Technoritualités. Religiosité rave*', fall: 175–97.

—— (2001b) 'La Finitude consumée: le sacrifice dans l'Inde ancienne', in *Religiologiques* 23, spring: 247–76.

Gauthier, François and Guy Ménard (eds) (2001) *Religiologiques* 24, '*Technoritualités: religiosité rave*', fall; available online at http://www.unites.uqam.ca/Religiologiques (accessed 8 January 2003).

Hampartzoumian, Stéphane (ed.) (1999) *Sociétés* 65, '*Effervescence techno*', Paris and Brussels: De Boeck.

Kerr, Philip (1991) *La Théologie après Wittgenstein*, Paris: Cerf.

Joos, Jean-Ernest (1997) 'Ouvertures: à la surface de la peau/Opening on the surface', in Nora Ben Saâdoune, Caroline Hayeur and Emmanuel Galland (eds) *Rituel festif/Festive Ritual*, Montreal: Macano.

—— (2001) 'Transformations de la subjectivité dans la culture techno', in François Gauthier and Guy Ménard (eds) *Religiologiques* 24, '*Technoritualités: religiosité rave*', fall: 107–14.

Le Breton, David (2000) [1991] *Passions du risque*, Paris: Métailié.

Lipovetsky, Gilles (1983) *L'Ère du vide: essais sur l'individualisme contemporain*, Paris: Gallimard.

—— (2002) *Métamorphoses de la culture libérale: éthique, medias, enterprise*, Montreal: Liber.

Maffesoli, Michel (1985) *L'Ombre de Dionysos: contribution à une sociologie de l'orgie*, Paris: Méridiens-Klinsieck.

Maffesoli, Michel (1988) *Le Temps des tribus*, Paris: Méridiens-Klinsieck.

Mauss, Marcel (1968) *Oeuvres 1. Les fonctions sociales du sacré*, Paris: Minuit.

Ménard, Guy (ed.) (1991) *Religiologiques* 3, '*Jeux et traverses. Rencontre avec Michel Maffesoli*'; available online at http://www.unites.uqam.ca/religiologiques (accessed 8 January 2003).

—— (1999) *Petit Traité de la vraie religion*, Montréal: Liber.

—— (2001) 'Les dÉplacements du sacré et du religieux', in Guy Ménard and Jean-Marc Larouche (eds) *L'Étude de la religion au Québec. Bilan et prospective*, Sainte-Foy, Québec: Presses de l'Université Laval and Canadian Corporation for Studies in Religion.

Métais, Aline (2001) 'Les Émotions "core": commotion du présent et experience du Soi', in Anne Petiau (ed.) *Sociétés* 72, '*Pulsation techno, pulsation sociale*', Paris and Brussels: De Boeck.

Morton, Jacqueline (1979) *English Grammar for Students of French*, Ann Arbour, MI: Olivia and Hill Press.

Peterson, Robert (1996) '*Ecstasy': synthèse documentaire et pistes de prevention*, Saint-Charles-Borromée, Québec: Direction de la santé publique de Lanaudière.

Petiau, Anne (1999) 'Rupture, consumation et communion: trois temps pour comprendre la rave', in Stéphane Hampartzoumian (ed.) *Sociétés* 65, '*Effervescence techno*', Paris and Brussels: De Boeck.

—— (ed.) (2001) *Sociétés* 72, '*Pulsation techno, pulsation sociale*', Paris and Brussels: De Boeck.

Push and M. Silcott (2000) *The Book of E: All About Ecstasy*, London: Omnibus Press.

Reynolds, Simon (1999) *Generation Ecstasy: Into the World of Techno and Rave Culture*, New York: Routledge.

Saunders, Nicholas and Rick Doblin (1996) *Ecstasy: Dance, Trance and Transformation*, San Francisco: Quick American Archives.

Schott-Bilmann, France (2001) *Le Besoin de danser*, Paris: Odile Jacob.

Schütze, Bernard (1997) 'Flyer power', in Nora Ben Saâdoune, Caroline Hayeur and Emmanuel Galland (eds) *Rituel festif/Festive Ritual*, Montreal: Macano.

—— (2001) 'Carnivalesque mutations in the Bahian Carnival and rave culture', in François Gauthier and Guy Ménard (eds) *Religiologiques* 24, '*Technoritualités: Religiosité rave*', fall: 155–63.

Silcott, Mireille (1999) *Rave America: New School Dancescapes*, Toronto: ECW Press.

Suissa, Amnon J. (1997) 'Toxicomanies et rituels', in Denis Jeffrey, Guy Ménard and Jacques Pierre (eds) *Religiologiques* 16, *Rituels sauvages*, fall: 77–90; available online at http://www.unites.uqam.ca/religiologiques/no16/16index.html (accessed 8 January 2003).

Tagg, Philip (1994) 'From refrain to rave: the decline of figure and the rise of ground', *Popular Music* 13(2): 209–22.

4 'Connectedness' and the rave experience

Rave as new religious movement?

Tim Olaveson

Is rave simply about the dissipation of utopian energies into the void, or does the idealism it catalyzes spill over into and transform ordinary life?

(Reynolds 1999: 10)

As William Pickering published his second edition of *Durkheim on Religion*, he remarked upon the increased interest in the work of Émile Durkheim (Pickering 1994: 2). The observation remains accurate today, partly through growth in the popularity of the social anthropologist Victor Turner, prominent in a tradition of scholars adapting Durkheim's project. Regular contributors to journals like *Durkheimian Studies* and scholars publishing through the British Centre for Durkheimian Studies have launched reinterpretations of Durkheim's thought on various subjects,[1] and Turner's work has been recast, reformulated and extended by scholars of the sociology/anthropology of religion, ritual and other social phenomena, including pilgrimage, performance, education and tourism.[2] For my own part, in another work (Olaveson 2001) I demonstrate the equivalence of Durkheim's *collective effervescence* and Turner's *communitas*, indicating that similar models of cultural creativity and revitalization underlay the work of both scholars, resembling more recent attempts to map new religious movements.

In recent years, the concepts of effervescence and communitas have been employed in efforts to understand and map a range of youth social practices falling under the rubric rave or post-rave (Hutson 1999, 2000; Malbon 1999; St John 2001a; Tramacchi 2000). Scholars have begun to conceptualize raving as a transformational and spiritual practice, raising the possibility of viewing rave as a new religious movement (Tramacchi 2001) or, as Corsten suggests, 'a symbolic and proto-religious practice of a modern urban youth scene' (1999: 91).

Addressing various criticisms, this chapter illustrates how collective efferves-cence/communitas (often viewed as separate entities) is useful for investigating the most often reported experience in rave literature around the world – *connect-edness*. The evidence I use consists primarily of a review of the existing literature on rave cultures, along with the results of the initial eight months of an ongoing ethnographic study of the central Canadian rave scene. I then delineate how the model of cultural revitalization latent in the work of Durkheim and Turner has been adapted by scholars of religious movements. Finally, I suggest that rave cultures do in fact exhibit many features of *new religious movements* and, while that phrase may lack precision here, the dance culture phenomenon of the past 15 years demonstrates sociocultural revitalization on a massive scale.

Raves as contemporary techniques of syncretic ritualizing

A recent collaborative ethnography of the rave scene in central Canada in which the author participated (Takahashi and Olaveson 2003) demonstrated that, contrary to the majority of academic analyses of rave culture, *raving is a highly meaningful and spiritual practice for many ravers* (see also Fritz 1999; Reynolds 1999; Silcott 1999 for popular sources on rave as spirituality). By contrast to medical health research largely focusing on harm reduction and the demographics of drug use at raves,[3] and cultural studies and postmodern analyses tending to examine rave's politics and gender dynamics or critique its 'meaningless glittering surfaces' (Melechi 1993; Pini 1997; Rietveld 1993), other researchers have arrived at conclusions congruent with our findings – that dance events are meaningful and transformative. These studies tend to be based on direct ethnographic evidence, including discussions with ravers themselves. Both Scott Hutson and Ben Malbon, two of the few researchers who have seriously solicited ravers' views and performed fieldwork at rave events, discuss the shortcomings of some postmodern analyses of the rave (and, for Malbon, the clubbing) experience:

> Though I find this 'rave-as-empty-joy-of-disappearance' thesis both plausible and informative, it is incomplete because it ignores the poignant and meaningful spiritual experiences that ravers say they get from raves.
>
> (Hutson 1999: 54)

> Far from being a mindless form of crass hedonism, as some commentators suggest, clubbing is for many both a source of extraordinary pleasure and a vital context for the development of personal and social identities.
>
> (Malbon 1999: 5, see also 127)

Recent studies also tend to view the rave as a new rite of passage for Euro-American youth (Corsten 1999) or as an example of formal ritual (Becker and Woebs 1999; Gauthier and Ménard 2002; Tramacchi 2000). While raves unquestionably contain ritual elements, I am disinclined to apply the term 'ritual' to all raves and rave-derived events, due to the usual variation of the elements comprising them. Rather, my approach approximates that proposed by Ronald Grimes in categorizing such phenomena. Grimes (1995) proposes conceptualizing practices experimenting with ritual techniques as instances of *nascent* or *syncretic ritualizing* rather than formal rituals. The advantage of framing raves in this way is that it captures their nascence, their self-conscious creativity and their definitive place on the (often stigmatized) margins of society – elements highlighted as characteristic of ritualizing phenomena (see Grimes 1990: 10).

This approach facilitates a theoretical engagement with the fluidity and creativity of raves and their socioculturally revitalizing effects.

The experience of connectedness at raves

The catalyst for such revitalization appears to be the phenomenological experience most consistently reported by ravers of an intense sensation of interpersonal and sometimes universal connection between participants, often described as 'connectedness', 'unity' or 'love'. Both popular and academic sources on rave and rave-derived cultures have discussed this at length.[4] In the ritualized setting of a rave, participants often experience profound feelings of communality, equality and basic humanity, as Fritz so poignantly notes:

> Although ravers don't feel the need to give their superhuman power a name or personality, when a rave 'goes off', everyone has a shared experience of connectedness and hundreds or even thousands of people can feel like one being with a shared purpose and direction.
>
> (Fritz 1999: 179)

My own fieldwork on the rave experience in central Canada validated such statements, which pervade written descriptions and personal accounts of the rave experience. Not only did I witness and experience connectedness myself, but quantitative analyses conducted in the collaborative study confirmed its existence. A content analysis was performed on 84 ravers' personal accounts of the rave experience, as posted on rave websites by participants from Canada, the United States, the United Kingdom, Germany, France and Australia. We also analysed 121 completed surveys at more than 20 rave events in the cities of Toronto, Ottawa, Montreal and Quebec. Of the seven central themes of the rave experience emerging from the data, connectedness was most frequently reported.[5]

Other ethnographers of rave cultures have also written about the connectedness or unity experience, recognizing its affinity with Victor Turner's 'communitas'. For example, in research on raving as a spiritual/healing practice, Scott Hutson (1999, 2000) argues that the sense of unity and connection ravers claim to achieve resembles Turner's communitas, and facilitates healing at raves. On the post-rave 'doof' party movement, Tramacchi states that Turner's 'analysis of counter-cultures is highly applicable to the contemporary developments of rave and *doof*...which use rituals of alterity, ecstasy and community' (Tramacchi 2000: 210; see also Tramacchi 2001).

Without regarding rave as a single culture/subculture, as Hutson does, other commentators make similar claims. Writing about the Australian biannual alternative lifestyle event ConFest, a component of which is the rave-derived *Tek Know* 'village', St John applies Turner's communitas, yet finds it lacking in respect of its homogeneity and non-corporeality (a critique he revisited with regard to rave in Chapter 1 of this volume). As St John notes, some authors have highlighted the problematical essentialism underlying Turner's *limen*, of which communitas is a modality. Especially in its application to pilgrimage phenomena, communitas has become a reified and all-encompassing 'primal unity' that fails to account for the underlying and backstage diversities, tensions and multiplicity of competing voices in such phenomena. St John also notes that, despite a late theoretical interest, Turner was not an anthropologist of the body, and 'the communions he had in mind tended to be clinically social, not somatic' (St John 2001a: 60).

Ben Malbon's *Clubbing: Dancing, Ecstasy and Vitality* (1999), thus far the longest academic publication seriously to treat the embodied experiential dimension of clubbing or raving, also draws on the concept of communitas, along with Maffesoli's (1996) concept of 'unicity'. While Malbon's book is a turning point in ethnographies/geographies of dance-based cultures, he neither understands nor adequately analyses Turner's ideas, rejecting the heuristic value of communitas according to the unsubstantiated assumptions of other dance ethnographers rather than addressing Turner's work directly. On the other hand, St John's critique of the essential and disembodied communitas is a useful corrective, highlighting the need to heed the complexity and carnality of contemporary ritualized social movements and gatherings, such as rave and dance events. Acknowledging this critique, in the next section I further probe the early formulations made by Hutson and Tramacchi.

Connectedness and the rave experience as collective effervescence/communitas

Émile Durkheim's concept of 'collective effervescence' was given its fullest treatment in his last and greatest work, *The Elementary Forms of Religious Life* (Durkheim 1995). While it has recently experienced something of a revival in the social sciences in the works of such theorists as Michel Maffesoli, Chris Shilling, Philip Mellor and other 'neo-Durkheimians' who discuss the resurgence of sacred, communal social gatherings and collectives, it had originally received little attention – a circumstance likely due to the fact that Durkheim had never given it precise definition, often using it interchangeably with such terms as 'moral density', 'concentration', 'heat', 'sentiments', 'emotion' and 'delirium' (Jones 1986; Nielsen 1999; Ramp 1998). Nevertheless, it is important to note that Durkheim did not intend the term to be epiphenomenal. As I discuss below, he thought collective effervescence was a feature of certain types of social assemblies, especially religious rituals. Possessing several characteristics, it is: inherently communal and collective; energetic, electric, or ecstatic; an essentially non-rational affective state or experience; ephemeral or temporary in nature; and a possible source of great cultural creativity.

Victor Turner's widely cited concept of 'communitas' is central to his theories of ritual and social creativity. Like Durkheim, Turner often had difficulty precisely defining communitas, but cautioned that it was not a mere epiphenomenon, but an ontological reality: 'Just because the communitas concept is elusive, hard to pin down, it is not unimportant' (V. Turner 1969: 29; see also 1974: 231). Turner described it variously as: an unstructured or rudimentarily structured community of equal individuals (1967: 99ff.; 1969: 96; 1982: 47); an essential and generic human bond (1969: 97; 1985: 233); a set of egalitarian, direct, non-rational bonds between concrete and historical individuals (1969: 131, 177; 1974: 47); and a deep, inherently emotional experience or state (1969: 136ff.; 1974: 46, 201, 205, 274). Also paralleling Durkheim's collective effervescence, Turner thought that communitas emerges in ritual and characterizes certain social gatherings. He distinguished three different types of communitas: spontaneous or existential communitas, which is characteristic of events such as counterculture 'happenings', rock concerts and pilgrimage phenomena; normative communitas, in which spontaneous communitas is translated into a set of moral and behavioural codes and doctrines in order to normalize and regulate social behaviour along the lines of the original experience; and ideological communitas, in which the ethos or ethic of the communitas experience is translated into an ideology or blueprint, such as in utopian societies or cults, or the 'hippie' communes of the American counterculture (V. Turner 1969: 132; 1973: 191–230; 1974: 169; 1979: 45–8; see also B.C. Alexander 1991).

The ontological experience of connectedness ravers so often report as central to raving is the experience of existential collective effervescence/communitas, and possesses five distinct characteristics.

Electricity, exaltation, enthusiasm

Both the scant treatment and lack of clarity attending to sociological discussions of effervescent rituals are partly due their ethereal nature. Durkheim described such rituals as events infused by electricity, ecstasy and enthusiasm:

> [Effervescence]…quickly launches [ritual participants] to an extraordinary height of exaltation. Every emotion expressed resonates without interference in consciousnesses that are wide open to external impressions, each one echoing the others. The initial impulse is thereby amplified each time it is echoed, like an avalanche that grows as it goes along. And since passions so heated and so free from all control cannot help but spill over, from every side there are nothing but wild movements, shouts, downright howls, and deafening noises of all kinds that further intensify the state they are expressing.
>
> (Durkheim 1995: 217–18)

Turner echoed Durkheim's descriptions, and wrote that such rituals produce 'direct, immediate, and total confrontations of human identities' and 'for the hippies – as indeed for many millenarian and "enthusiastic" movements – the ecstasy of spontaneous communitas is seen as *the* end of human endeavour' (V. Turner 1969: 132, 138–9). As St John (2001a) notes, these and other descriptions of communitas bear a decidedly clinical ring to them, despite the fact that, as I have pointed out elsewhere (Olaveson 2001), both scholars were writing about – and Turner was actually observing – embodied and extraordinary physical feats and mental states during ritual performances. Yet, despite their clinicality, these passages betray a resemblance to contemporary descriptions of the effervescent and ritualized atmosphere of raves and clubs, such as the following: raving is 'frenzied behaviour, extreme enthusiasm, psychedelic delirium…instantaneous, high-impact, sensation-oriented' (Reynolds 1999: 77).

The 'electricity' referred to by Durkheim is also captured in a phrase associated with the rave experience: *the vibe*. Ravers describe 'the vibe' as a kind of energy or pulse which cannot be expressed or understood in words, but as that which can only be physically experienced. As an amplified feeling or emotional state, the rave 'vibe' mirrors the 'exaltation' and 'enthusiasm' described by Durkheim:

> It's the feeling that makes 500 people cry when a certain tune is played. It's the feeling that you can trust everyone around you, that everyone is sharing in one experience that somehow touches them deep in their soul and that you all understand each other.
>
> (Orion, in McCall 2001: 59)

Ravers are cognizant of the fact that, in addition to the music, it is the people and the sense of community and connectedness at raves that create and sustain 'the vibe'. Further evoking Durkheim's effervescence, 'vitality' is another term used to describe the energy, electricity and ecstasy of the dance experience. In the concluding paragraph of *Clubbing*, Malbon describes vitality (which he derives from the work of Durkheim, Maffesoli, LeBon and Csikszentmihalyi[6]) as the experience, and *raison d' être*, of clubbing:

> Playful vitality is…partly a celebration of the energy and euphoria that can be generated through being together, playing together and experiencing 'others' together. Yet playful vitality is also partly an escape attempt, a temporary relief from other facets and identifications of an individual clubber's own life – their work, their past, their future, their worries. Playful vitality is found within a temporary world of the clubber's own construction in which the everyday is disrupted, the mundane is forgotten and the ecstatic becomes possible.
>
> (Malbon 1999: 164)

Embodied, non-rational, emotional

A hallmark of the rave experience, and another quality of collective effervescence/communitas, is its quintessentially non-rational, embodied and affectual nature.[7] Simon Reynolds remarks that, at 'massive volume, knowledge [of rave's meaning] is visceral, something your body understands as it's seduced and ensnared by the paradoxes of the music' (1999: 349). Ravers often indicate that they don't attend raves to listen to music, but rather to *feel* the music that 'communicates directly with the body' (Poschardt 1998: 414). Sense-enhancing drugs such as MDMA further intensify the process, creating effects 'so that sounds seem to caress the listener's skin' (Reynolds 1999: 84).

As rave's transgressive medium of embodied expression, the significance of dance (and especially new forms of dance) was early recognized by scholars of rave culture. As McRobbie noted, while dance 'is where girls were always found in subcultures…[n]ow in rave it becomes the motivating force for the entire subculture' (1994: 169). Pini (1997) also highlighted rave culture's creation of new socio-sexual spaces, in which women are free to explore new forms of identity and pleasure through dance. Yet dance is not only a prime agent in the rave's remoulding or dissolution of gendered spaces; it catalyses the experience of connectedness. In *This is Not a Rave* (2001), Toronto raver Tara McCall repeatedly highlights connectedness or 'connection' as the essence of the rave experience, and specifically, *connection through dance*:

> This is what lies at the foundation of rave: everyone in tune with the same rhythm. Once you feel this connection you bare part of your soul by dancing your dance. Once you get inside the music it's like a heartbeat in a womb. It validates your existence with a constant reminder that you are quite literally connected to all that encompasses you.
>
> (McCall 2001: 18)

Malbon too emphasizes the centrality of dance to club (rave) cultures, and of attending to 'embodied information' (1999: 27) in studying them. Like McCall, he also directly links dance to the production of the 'unity experience' of clubbing.

Along with being intractably embodied, the experience of unity in rave is also an intensely emotional one. Fuelled at least partially by ecstasy, raves are sites of intense outpourings of emotion, especially empathy and compassion. Popular sources on rave culture are filled with countless testimonials by ravers of the experience of deep and powerful emotional states during events: '…deep feelings of unlimited compassion and love for everyone' (Fritz 1999: 43; see also Silcott 1999; Reynolds 1999; McCall 2001; Malbon 1999).

As many have noted, the experience of unity with the crowd while raving or clubbing, paralleling other religious experiences, is intense and ineffable. Discussions with informants reinforced this:

MC (24-YEAR-OLD RAVER FROM TORONTO):
> If I could have a wish, and it would be coming from my experience with raves, I would give everybody what I have been able to experience. One night. And they could take that information and do whatever they want with it. But, I can't believe that it's possible to live life and, not, wow, not have experienced that. Like, I feel fortunate. Really, I feel, like, especially, we really didn't know what we were involved in in '92 [in the Toronto jungle scene], we didn't realize. And now I feel lucky,

> I feel lucky enough to have tasted it even. Because, Tim, like, there are moments, I mean, the world *stops*.

TIM: Is it the most intense experience you've ever had in your life?

MC: Oh my gosh. I can't believe I'm going to say this. Yes. I knew right away but I had to think about it just to make sure, because I kind of didn't believe it.

Survey respondents also described raving as a deeply spiritual and emotional experience:

> [Raving] makes me feel like being in tune with the eternal cosmic pulsation. For me it is a kind of spiritual experience to be in a rave.
>
> (survey respondent, male, 20–24 years old; quoted in
> Takahashi and Olaveson 2003)

Communal and collective

One of the central characteristics of collective effervescence/communitas is its communal and collective nature,[8] paralleling the 'unity' and 'love' experienced at countless rave and post-rave dance events, even without the aid of 'empathogenic' drugs like ecstasy. Former New York rave promoter Dennis the Menace discusses such an intense communal and spiritual experience at a Storm Rave in 1993:

> At the end of the party, we were winding down, the sun was out, everyone was feeling pure and alive, in that communal unity feeling. Then someone in the middle of the floor started holding hands and putting their hands up in a circle. Kids were jumping from the back to put their hands up to touch the centerpoint where all the hands interlocked. People had tears in their eyes. We were just looking at each other, so happy, so open to everything.... Group energy, where one person triggers the next person who triggers the next person. ... You could just feel it vibrating between everyone. You can't put that in a pill. There's kids I know that were totally straight, who never did drugs, and who were there dancing as hard as anyone 'cos they could feed off that energy.
>
> (Dennis the Menace, in Reynolds 1999: 149)[9]

Based upon his own experiences at Australian psy-trance 'doofs', Tramacchi also emphasizes the communal nature of the connectedness experience:

> This collective consciousness is especially pronounced at parties where MDMA is a conspicuous element. During the plateau of MDMA effects, interpersonal differences appear to evaporate producing a condition of almost total identification of self with other. Within the psychedelic dance rapture, participants may lose or suspend subjective experience of

themselves and merge into a kind of collective body, a place where desire and production meet in a state of flow.

(Tramacchi 2001: 174; see also 181)

Tramacchi's description of the 'melding of selves' during the connectedness experience recalls the same language used by Turner to describe the communitas attending the Ndembu rites of passage he observed in Zambia (then Northern Rhodesia), as well as the hippie happenings of the 1960s. Such an experience, he wrote, is an exchange between 'total and concrete persons, between "I" and "Thou". This relationship is always a "happening", something that arises in instant mutuality, when each person fully experiences the being of the other' (V. Turner 1969: 136).

Transgressive, levelling and humanizing

As 'settings of intensely emotional assembly, association and, by implication, breakdown of established social barriers and structures' (Nielsen 1999: 208), effervescent rituals evince 'a compulsion to dissolve limits, differentiation and particularity.... Effervescent assemblies are in this light ambiguously dangerous arenas' (Ramp 1998: 144). Collective effervescence thus presents 'a transgressive possibility fuelled by a de-differentiating impulse in moments of heightened emotional intensity' (*ibid.*: 146). It implies dissolution of regular social and normative structures, and is sometimes seen as a danger to these structures. This closely matches Turner's well-known discussions of communitas as dialectically opposed to social structure. While social structure keeps people apart, defines their differences and constrains their actions (V. Turner 1974: 47), communitas is a liberating, equalizing, humanizing and transgressive force and experience, a necessary counterbalance to the dehumanizing effects of social structure. It therefore represents an inherent threat to social and political structures.

The rave experience has also been universally recognized as a transgressive, levelling and humanizing experience. Although rave has become a middle-class phenomenon in North America, early acid house parties and raves teemed with and were in fact imported as a concept from Ibiza by working class British youth such as Danny and Jenni Rampling, the creators of the legendary club Shoom (Collin 1997: 47ff., 168; see also Critcher 2000; Reynolds 1999: 59). Furthermore, as Reynolds notes, house music and its ethos were 'born of a double exclusion': the gay African-American club and party circuit of Chicago (Reynolds 1999: 24). Therefore, for its progenitors and for many today, rave is perceived to be inclusive, a place where race, class and gender lines are dissolved, where people can just be themselves and be accepted (see Reynolds 1999; Silcott 1999; Fritz 1999), although theories of homogeneous and universal inclusion within rave and dance cultures must be moderated with analysis of the politics of particular dance spaces. For example, Thornton (1995) points out that 1990s English club scenes did (and undoubtedly still do) possess tacit norms around notions of subcultural style and 'coolness' (and would-be patrons were sometimes denied access for violating them).

At the time of writing, in the central Canadian rave scene such exclusionary practices as highlighted by Thornton appear to be largely absent, at least in the trance, jungle/drum 'n' bass and Goa communities. In fact, many informants in Toronto, Montreal, Quebec and Ottawa reported preferring rave events to clubs for this reason. Although these divergent rave musical styles and event genres have emerged, and often cater to particular socio-economic groups and ethnic communities within metropolitan centres, many central Canadian raves still do attract diverse ethnicities, classes and social groups, especially in the city of Toronto. When I asked participants in Canadian metropolitan centres how they would characterize the social atmosphere at raves, the typical answer I received was that 'rave is totally open to anyone'. Fritz's informants, many of whom were from Canada's west coast, expressed the same thing:

> The value of rave culture is an acceptance of everyone and everything. If you're black you can come to my party, if you're gay you can come to my party, if you're a beautiful woman you can come to my party. Everyone can come and be themselves and be welcome and be free.
> (Logan, a.k.a. 'Beats Off', in Fritz 1999: 268)

Raves are also renowned for their extremely low levels of violence. During the height of rave in late 1980s Britain, rival football gangs could even be found embracing each other at events while under the influence of ecstasy: they 'were so loved-up on E they spent the night hugging each other rather than fighting' (Reynolds 1999: 64; see also Silcott 1999: 34). In addition to violence, sexual difference and sexual tension are also markedly reduced at raves. Women report being attracted to the rave scene because they feel safer there, and because they are less likely to be propositioned by men (McRobbie 1994; Pini 1997; see also Critcher 2000 on this). Female informants in the cities of Toronto, Montreal, Quebec and Ottawa repeatedly stated that they greatly preferred raves to night-clubs, as the sexual atmosphere at raves is much less aggressive. Some informants did report being propositioned by men, but this was the exception rather than the rule.

Despite their heavy commercialization, mainstream Canadian raves in the trance, jungle/drum 'n' bass and Goa genres do appear to create a social space where difference, status and inequalities are temporarily suspended. As sites of dissolution of the social and political distinctions through which states regulate their citizens, such events therefore also possess an inherent danger for governing bodies. This is undoubtedly one of the reasons why authorities in North America have begun to adopt similar regulatory measures to those imposed upon ravers by the English government in the early 1990s at the height of that country's 'moral panic' about rave culture (Thornton 1994).

The rave experience as temporary and utopian

Although popularly perceived otherwise, Émile Durkheim actually ascribed both a re-creative (culturally conservative) and a creative (culturally revitalizing) function to ritual. That which he called '*effervescence créatrice*' (creative effervescence) is a phenomenon that can spontaneously produce new moral codes, as well as ideal conceptions of society (Pickering 1984: 387). Nielsen (1999: 208) reiterates that new collective representations (cultural symbols) may, and usually do, result from collective effervescences (see also Allen 1998: 150; Mellor 1998; Shilling and Mellor 1998: 203). Also, due to its volatile, destabilizing and even sacred nature, collective effervescence can only be temporary in its existence; it is a fundamentally transitory state (Durkheim 1995: 228). It is thus akin to spontaneous communitas, 'the spontaneity and immediacy [of which] – as opposed to the jural-political character of structure – can seldom be maintained for very long' (V. Turner 1969: 132). In fact, liminality, the state in which communitas can emerge, can be both creative and destructive (V. Turner 1979: 44). Communitas is equated with movement and change (V. Turner 1974: 285), and with transient humility or modelessness (V. Turner 1969: 97). Regarded as a timeless condition, the eternal now, a moment in and out of time (V. Turner 1974: 238; 1979: 41), communitas-like experiences depicted by members of religious, millenarian or revivalist groups often portray an Edenic, paradisiacal or utopian state (V. Turner 1974: 231, 237).

Much has been written about the similarly temporary nature of raves – chronologically, spatially and socially. For example, rave music, characterized by hyper-extended, repetitively rhythmed tracks and sets, creates a sense of timelessness echoing the eternal present of collective effervescence/communitas:

> Timbre-saturated, repetitive but tilted always toward the *next now*, techno is an immediacy machine, stretching time into a continuous present – which is where the drug-technology interface comes into play. Not just because techno works well with substances like MDMA, marijuana, LSD, speed, etc., all of which amplify the sensory intensity of the present moment, but because the music itself *drugs* the listener, looping consciousness then derailing it, stranding it in a nowhere/nowhen, where there is only sensation, '*where now lasts longer.*'
>
> (Reynolds 1999: 55)

Raves are timeless places, removed social spaces where utopias are both imagined and lived: 'With its dazzling psychotropic lights, its sonic pulses, rave culture is arguably a form of *collective autism*. The rave is utopia in its original etymological sense: a nowhere/nowhen wonderland' (*ibid.*: 248). The temporary and socially unstructured character of the rave has been likened to anarcho-mystic writer and philosopher Hakim Bey's concept of the 'temporary autonomous zone' (TAZ) (Collin 1997: 5; Gibson 1999: 22–3; Luckman 2001; Reynolds 1999: 169; St John 2001a; Tramacchi 2001). The TAZ, like the rave, is quintessentially liminal or marginal. It occupies the 'cracks and vacancies' left by the state, including abandoned industrial complexes – the detritus of Euro-American post-industrial society. As manifestations of the TAZ, raves are utopian social formations temporarily convened in Turner's cracks, crevices and interstices of social structure – in the margins of society.

Moreover, the attribution of utopian urges and visions to rave cultures and the rave experience is not a casual one. As Reynolds and others note, rave scenes 'in their early days buzz with creativity and we're-gonna-change-the-world idealism' (Reynolds 1999: 90; see also Fritz 1999; Silcott 1999). In *Rave Culture*, Fritz states that rave events are now being used as tools for political change:

> It could be said that rave culture is essentially a revolutionary political move-ment in that it represents the will of a significant portion of society to organize and gather for the purposes of creating a new community model and that these activities are carried out despite fervent opposition from governing bodies....A rave makes the political statement that we are all equal, and that no matter how different we may think we are, on a more tribal level, we all have the same basic needs as human beings. In this light, rave culture offers a firm foundation on which to build a new political order which may, in the not so distant future, lead the way to a more humanistic and personal system of government.
>
> (Fritz 1999: 216–17)

One of the findings from our study of the central Canadian rave scene was that the urge for sociopolitical change and the drive toward utopian social models, as described by Fritz and others, is closely linked with personal transfor-mation at rave events. For example, several informants made a causal connection between epiphanic experiences at rave events and new perspectives on wider social issues and their own culture. One 22-year-old Montreal raver's description of his awakening was typical:

> The first time you rave, you go in blind. You come out and you can see....Everything's fucked up. Nothing's right. Why is the news always bad? Rave is just a generation of kids who don't know what the future is. We're waiting for the Earth to explode.
>
> (personal interview, 30 March 2002)

While the pessimism expressed in this passage has been critiqued by many as encapsulating commercialized rave culture's failure to effect real political change, utopian and oppositional urges have had more success in some post-rave move-ments and collectives, and dance parties are being harnessed for political ends in various locations around the globe (for example, see Marlin-Curiel 2001).

Connectedness, sociocultural revitalization and new religious movements

As I discussed above, Émile Durkheim and Victor Turner both viewed ritual and the extraordinary, ecstatic experiences common to religious rituals as real and important sociocultural phenomena. For them, such experiences as connectedness, in its ecstatic, non-rational, embodied, humanizing and utopian dimensions, are fundamental to sociocultural revitalization. In fact, they saw all societies operating according to dialectics of structured, norm-governed states and ecstatic, effervescent experiences of connectedness. There is no question that they would not be surprised to witness the rave phenomenon were they alive today; nor would they wonder, as so many politicians, anxious parents and even social scientists currently do, why the rave experience so strongly attracts contemporary youth.

Durkheim and Turner were not the only writers to think about ritual, the connectedness experience and sociocultural revitalization. Anthony Wallace (1956, 1966), a psychological anthropologist who specialized in North American native cultures, formally developed the concept of the revitalization movement. Like the former theorists, Wallace saw religions and entire cultures following patterns of alternating states of religious and cultural intensity and innovation, and routinization and stagnation. He viewed revitalization movements as conscious and deliberate efforts to construct a more satisfying culture, and saw such objects of social scientific study as cargo cults, messianic movements, new religious sects and revolutions as examples (Wallace 1956: 265).

Wallace argued that revitalization movements occur when a culture or religion no longer adequately meets the needs of its members, a phenomenon that could manifest itself as increased individual stress, decay or decrease in the efficacy of religious symbols and rituals, and a general cultural malaise such as that which Durkheim lamented was affecting France while he was writing *The Elementary Forms*. Without such revitalizing rituals, he wrote, a society is apt to disintegrate as a system (Wallace 1966: 160). Revitalization occurs with the formulation of a new, utopian or idealized vision of society (often embodied in a charismatic leader and fresh ecstatic experience), its dissemination and ritualization, and then its routinization into a formal code of behaviour. Once this code begins to lose its efficacy for the group, a new code will appear in a rash of ecstatic practices, and the process will begin again. Wallace thought that all societies follow this cycle.

Wallace's ideas on revitalization movements were coloured and limited by his historical functionalism. However, the revitalization movement as a concept has received renewed interest lately, for example in the analysis of new religious movements such as Soka Gakkai and Shambhala (Dawson and Eldershaw 1998; Eldershaw and Dawson 1995; Shupe 1991), and within broader theoretical projects (Laughlin *et al.* 1990). Wallace's ideas, along with those of Durkheim and Turner, have also found their way into new religious movement (NRM) theory. For example, Eileen Barker states that one of the reasons why NRMs are significant is 'that they may occasionally function as a barometer of what at least some members of a society feel they need but is not being supplied by other means' (Barker 1999: 26). In other words, they show us the 'gaps' in cultures. This same point has been made by a number of other scholars of NRMs. George Chryssides, among others, notes that people who join NRMs are usually those who are 'disaffected' or 'alienated' from the generally accepted norms of their society (Chryssides 1999: 5). Similarly, Rodney Stark and William Bainbridge's theory of NRMs and religion in general is based upon the premise that as religions and cultures begin to secularize and stagnate (a perennial, evolutionary process), individuals seek out or form sects and cults in the search for more vivid and consistent 'supernatural compensators' (Bainbridge 1997; Stark and Bainbridge 1985, 1987). And finally, in his explanation for the current explosion of NRMs, Lorne Dawson encapsulates Wallace's and Durkheim's sense of a 'general cultural malaise' and decline in meaningfulness as a precursor to the irruption of revitalization movements:

> In the private sphere everything is seemingly now a matter of choice. There are no set and secure behaviours with regard to courtship, marriage, childrearing, sexuality, gender relations, consumption, vocation and spirituality. Consequently, many individuals are left yearning for more guidance. In the public sphere, all are compelled to conform. Guidance is manifest, but in ways which belie the meaningfulness of participation. Institutions are guided increasingly by a strictly formal rationality geared to the satisfaction of the functional requirements of social systems, with little or no regard for the desires, needs, or even character of the individual members of these institutions. In the face of this social dissonance, the proliferating NRMs provide a more holistic sense of self; a sense of self that transcends the constellation of limited instrumental roles recognized by modern mass society and anchored in a greater sense of moral community and purpose.
>
> (Dawson 1998: 582; see also Robbins 1988)

Thus, from the writings of Durkheim at the turn of the last century right up to current scholarship on NRMs, there has been a persisting recognition that religious and cultural innovation and revitalization constitute a perpetual and dialectical process in which intense, embodied, communal, ritualized experience plays a key role.

Rave as NRM?

Many would argue that Dawson's description of both public and private life in Euro-American societies hits the mark. Modern consumer cultures are routinely critiqued for their alienating impact, their absence of meaning and superficiality. It has also been argued that extreme levels of individual stress and adverse health result from these features, and are an effect of the relativization or outright deterioration of particular sociocultural contexts due to the process of globalization (Dawson 1998: 587). The advance and proliferation of technology and communications media contribute to these effects, facilitating the processes of globalization and the destabilization of both individual subjects and communities (Baudrillard 1983; Giddens 1991; Lash and Urry 1994; Mellor and Shilling 1997; Strinati 1995). Acid House and rave cultures themselves have been regarded as prime examples of this process. In an oft-cited passage in which he draws on the work of Jean Baudrillard, Antonio Melechi likens the rave to a giant void, a touristic ritual of individual and cultural disappearance: mediated, simulated, hyperreal (Melechi 1993: 32).

As scholars of NRMs have recognized, modern consumer cultures are therefore ideal hosts for the formation of sects, cults and other NRMs. This is why we are currently witnessing cultural and religious diversity and experimentation perhaps unprecedented in human history, manifested in such developments as the New Age movement, alternative lifestyle movements, and mass importation of and experimentation with other religious traditions. What these experimental cultural exercises have in common is an attempt to make sense of life, an attempt to formulate efficacious cultures, an attempt at a re-sacralization or re-enchantment of the world (Maffesoli 1996: xiv; Mellor and Shilling 1997). While, in a sense, Melechi is right in describing rave as symptomatic of the void of consumer cultures, what he fails to recognize is that it is simultaneously an adaptational strategy, conscious or otherwise, to the meaninglessness of existence within them. Ravers, doofers and trance-dancers have reappropriated from the appropriators, have re-harnessed the products of consumer capitalism in the drive to recreate community and meaningful modes of existence. Dance cultures are examples *par excellence* of the sociocultural revitalization and innovation stirring within consumer cultures.

Corsten (1999) and Tramacchi (2001) have recognized this, suggesting that 'youth techno scenes' and 'doofs' should be included in the category of NRMs. They may be right. To varying degrees, rave and dance cultures contain several features common to NRMs: cultural and social dissatisfaction and disaffection by potential members; occurrence within host cultures with decaying and declining religious symbols, rites and institutions; occurrence within host cultures of religious and social pluralism and accelerated intercultural communications and technology; religious iconography appropriated syncretically from other traditions; hallucinatory, ecstatic or altered consciousness experiences transpiring in embodied, visceral and emotional states; radical personality transformation as a result of such ecstatic experiences; the creation of 'surrogate' family and community units and support mechanisms; the formation of ideal or utopian social visions and programmes; charismatic leadership and the development of cultic formations in the form of the DJ and his/her followers; and opposition and resistance from existing authorities, social institutions and power structures (the technique of 'deviant' labelling; the fear, similar to other NRMs, that the practice of raving 'breaks up families'; and regulatory measures introduced in many states and metropolitan centres around the world) and the concomitant adaptation of ritual performances (licensed raves, more 'underground' raves).[10]

On the other hand, certain features of rave cultures seem to defy the label 'NRM'. For example, while 'rave' as a practice is now universally recognized and has certainly transformed Euro-American popular culture, most rave 'communities' possess little to no formal social structures and are perhaps more accurately characterized as collectives or 'neo-tribes' (Bennett 1999; Gibson 1999; Maffesoli 1996). Applying the term 'cult' (in the sociological sense of the term) to rave cultures is thus a bit of a stretch. In relation to this, while revelatory and ecstatic experience, such as pervades rave practices, is certainly instrumental in the formation of NRMs, Chryssides and others note that an 'NRM's *teachings* are the fuel by which the religion is driven, and without which it would fail' (Chryssides 1999: 4; emphasis mine). There appears to be no central body of revelations, teachings or beliefs common to rave culture, but rather the emergence of translocal, idealized narratives of the gnostic wisdom inherent in 'tribal rituals', 'drumming' and psychoactive substances (Gibson 1999; Hutson 1999; Takahashi and Olaveson 2003; and see St John Chapter 1 in this volume). Raving as a practice tends to de-emphasize verbal and linguistic communication, although individual communities have certainly developed their own foci and symbolic codes. In addition, the likelihood of dance culture, or even dance *cultures*, congregating around a single charismatic leader with a unique message, is low.[11] Taking this point further, it could be argued that in the contemporary context the creation of NRMs with 'closed' and tightly controlled belief systems and doctrines is becoming ever more difficult with the advent of global communications and the Internet. With regard to rave, this may be quite impossible due to the geographically diverse nature of rave communities and events, as well as to today's accessible technologies used to make, share and reshape the 'movement's' principle symbolic medium – electronic music; the idea of one prophet with one message seems an unlikely prospect, as compared with a diaspora of techno-disciples mixing their own gospels and revelling in their own private ecstasies.

Conclusion

Scholars of rave, post-rave and other dance cultures have recently suggested that these movements may be viewed as NRMs. My own research on the central Canadian rave scene supports these conclusions to a limited extent. While it may not be entirely accurate to call rave culture(s) NRMs, there is clearly something important happening at both individual and societal levels. In particular, one of the central features of the rave experience – the experience of connectedness – is often interpreted by ravers as a religious experience. Further, the experience of connectedness is a key element in ritual performances and religious and sociocultural revitalization as these have been modelled by Émile Durkheim, Victor Turner and other prominent scholars of religion. When viewed in this light, the development and primary characteristics of rave cultures should not surprise us. Rave is just the latest example in the process of sociocultural revitalization that underlies the development of all religions and the health and regeneration of cultures throughout human history.

Notes

1 Including religion (Allen *et al.* 1998; McCarthy 1982; Nielsen 1999; Pickering 1984; Thompson 1993; Wallwork 1985), ritual (Carlton-Ford 1993; Smith and Alexander 1996), postmodernity (J.C. Alexander 1988; Featherstone 1991; Mestrovic 1992; Shilling and Mellor 1998), morality (Miller 1996; S.P. Turner 1993), collective effervescence (Allen 1998; Carlton-Ford 1993; Mellor 1998; Ono 1996; Ramp 1998; Shilling and Mellor 1998; Smith and Alexander 1996; Tiryakian 1995), collective representations (Pickering 2000), (non-)rationality and embodiment (Mellor and Shilling 1997; Ono 1996; Shilling 1993) and various other topics.
2 See B.C. Alexander 1991; Ashley 1990; Bell 1989; Cohen 1985; Deflem 1991; Gay 1983; Grimes 1976; Grimes 1985; Handelman 1993; MacLaren 1985; Moore 1983; Oring 1993; Pechilis 1992; Salamone 1988; Schechner 1977; St John 2001a; Walker Bynum 1995; D. Weber 1995.
3 See Adlaf and Smart 1997; Brown *et al.* 1995; Forsyth 1996; Forsyth *et al.* 1997; Lenton *et al.* 1997; Measham *et al.* 1998; Pedersen and Skrondal 1999; Power *et al.* 1996; Shewan *et al.* 2000; Topp *et al.* 1999.
4 See Collin 1997; Fritz 1999; Lenton and Davidson 1999; Malbon 1999; McCall 2001; Reynolds 1999; Silcott 1999; T. Weber 1999.
5 For detailed results of these analyses, see Takahashi and Olaveson (2003).
6 Whose concept of *flow* Turner likened to communitas (V. Turner 1979: 46, 55ff.).
7 See Carlton-Ford 1993; Durkheim 1995: 212; Mellor 1998; Mellor and Shilling 1997; Nielsen 1999: 156, 207; Nisbet 1965: 74; 1966; Ono 1996: 80; Ramp 1998; Shilling and Mellor 1998: 197; V. Turner 1969: 136ff.; 1974: 46, 201, 205, 274.
8 See Gane 1983a, 1983b; 1988: 156, 159; Nielsen 1999: 207; V. Turner 1967: 99ff; 1969: 96; 1982: 47. Durkheim was sometimes criticized for placing at the heart of his notion of effervescent assembly a type of crowd psychology or hysteria (Douglas 1966: 20; Evans-Pritchard 1965: 68; Goldenweiser 1915, 1917), but, as Pickering (1984: 395–417) explains, this was not his intended meaning. Turner has been similarly erroneously critiqued.
9 Dennis the Menace's description of 'straight' ravers experiencing the same states of collective effervescence/communitas as those using ecstasy accords with my findings from research in the central Canadian rave scene. On some occasions, both myself and some of my informants experienced what can most accurately be described as the experience of communitas while raving, without the use of ecstasy or any other psychoactive substances. See also Takahashi (Chapter 7) on this phenomenon.
10 For a good example of this dynamic in the Canadian context, see Hier (2002).
11 Although, of course, the DJ can be viewed as a type of charismatic leader or 'techno-shaman' controlling his/her 'congregation' (see Hutson 1999; Takahashi and Olaveson 2003).

Bibliography

Adlaf, E. and R. Smart. (1997) 'Party subculture or dens of doom? An epidemiological study of rave attendance and drug use patterns among adolescent students', *Journal of Psychoactive Drugs* 29(2): 193–8.
Alexander, B.C. (1991) 'Correcting misinterpretations of Turner's theory: an African-American pentecostal illustration', *Journal for the Scientific Study of Religion* 30(1): 26–44.
Alexander, J.C. (1988) *Durkheimian Sociology: Cultural Studies*, Cambridge: Cambridge University Press.
Allen, N.J. (1998) 'Effervescence and the origins of human society', in N.J. Allen, W.S.F. Pickering and W.W. Miller (eds) *On Durkheim's Elementary Forms of Religious Life*, London: Routledge.

Allen, N.J., W.S.F. Pickering and W.W. Miller (eds) (1998) *On Durkheim's Elementary Forms of Religious Life*, London: Routledge.

Ashley, K.M. (ed.) (1990) *Victor Turner and the Construction of Cultural Criticism: Between Literature and Anthropology*, Bloomington, IN: Indiana University Press.

Bainbridge, W. (1997) *The Sociology of Religious Movements*, New York: Routledge.

Barker, E. (1999) 'New religious movements: their incidence and significance', in B. Wilson and J. Cresswell (eds) *New Religious Movements: Challenge and Response*, London: Routledge.

Baudrillard, J. (1983) *Simulations*, New York: Semiotext(e).

Becker, T. and R. Woebs (1999) 'Back to the future: hearing, rituality and techno', *World of Music* 41(1): 59–71.

Bell, C. (1989) 'Ritual, change, and changing rituals', *Worship* 63: 31–41.

Bennett, A. (1999) 'Subcultures or neo-tribes? Rethinking the relationship between youth, style and musical taste', *Sociology* 33(3): 599–617.

Brown, E.R.S., D.R. Jarvie and D. Simpson (1995) 'Use of drugs at raves', *Scottish Medical Journal* 40(6): 168–71.

Carlton-Ford, S.L. (1993) *The Effects of Ritual and Charisma: The Creation of Collective Effervescence and the Support of Psychic Strength*, New York: Garland Publishing, Inc.

Chryssides, G. (1999) *Exploring New Religions*, London: Cassell.

Cohen, E. (1985) 'Tourism as play', *Religion* 15: 291–304.

Collin, M. (1997) *Altered State: The Story of Ecstasy Culture and Acid House*, London: Serpent's Tail.

Corsten, M. (1999) 'Ecstasy as "this worldly path to salvation": the techno youth scene as a proto-religious collective', in L. Tomasi (ed.) *Alternative Religions Among European Youth*, Aldershot: Ashgate.

Critcher, C. (2000) ' "Still raving": social reaction to ecstasy', *Leisure Studies* 19(3): 145–62.

Dawson, L. (1998) 'The cultural significance of new religious movements and globalization: a theoretical prolegomenon', *Journal for the Scientific Study of Religion* 37(4): 580–95.

Dawson, L. and L. Eldershaw (1998) 'Shambala warriorship: investigating the adaptations of imported new religious movements', in B. Ouellet and R. Bergeron (eds) *Les Sociétés devant le nouveau pluralisme religieux*, Montreal: Fides.

Deflem, M. (1991) 'Ritual, anti-structure, and religion: a discussion of Victor Turner's processual symbolic analysis', *Journal for the Scientific Study of Religion* 30(1): 1–25.

Douglas, M. (1966) *Purity and Danger: An Analysis of Concepts of Pollution and Taboo*, London: Routledge & Kegan Paul.

Durkheim, E. (1914) 'Contribution to discussion: "Une Nouvelle Position du problème moral" ', *Bulletin de la Société française de philosophie* XIV: 26–9, 34–6.

—— (1995) *The Elementary Forms of Religious Life*, New York: Free Press; originally published in French in 1912 as *Les Formes élémentaires de la vie religieuse*.

Eldershaw, L. and L. Dawson (1995) 'Refugees in the dharma: the Buddhist church of Halifax as a revitalization movement', *North American Religion* 4: 1–45.

Evans-Pritchard, E. (1965) *Theories of Primitive Religion*, Oxford: Clarendon Press.

Featherstone, M. (1991) *Consumer Culture and Postmodernism*, London: Sage.

Forsyth, A. (1996) 'Places and patterns of drug use in the Scottish dance scene', *Addiction* 91(4): 511–21.

Forsyth, A., M. Barnard and N. McKeganey (1997) 'Musical preference as an indicator of adolescent drug use', *Addiction* 92(10): 317–25.

Fritz, J. (1999) *Rave Culture: An Insider's Overview*, Canada: Small Fry Press.

Gane, M. (1983a) 'Durkheim: the sacred language', *Economy and Society* 12(1): 1–47.

Gane, M. (1983b) 'Durkheim: woman as outsider', *Economy and Society* 12(2): 227–70.

—— (1988) *On Durkheim's Rules of Sociological Method*, London: Routledge.

Gauthier, F. and G. Ménard (2002) *Religioloqiques 'Technoritualites: religiosite rave'* 24.

Gay, V.P. (1983) 'Ritual and self-esteem in Victor Turner and Heinz Kohut', *Zygon* 18(3): 271–82.

Gibson, C. (1999) 'Subversive sites: rave culture, spatial politics and the Internet in Sydney, Australia', *Area* 31(1): 19–33.

Giddens, A. (1991) *Modernity and Self-Identity*, Cambridge: Polity Press.

Goldenweiser, A. A. (1915) '[Review] *Les Formes élémentaires de la vie religieuse*', *American Anthropologist* 17: 719–35.

—— (1917) 'Religion and society: a critique of Emile Durkheim's theory of the origin and nature of religion', *Journal of Philosophy, Psychology and Scientific Methods* 14: 113–24.

Grimes, R. (1976) 'Ritual studies: a comparative review of Theodor Gaster and Victor Turner', *Religious Studies Review* 2(4): 13–25.

—— (1985) 'Victor Turner's social drama and T.S. Eliot's ritual drama', *Anthropologica* 27(1–2): 79–99.

—— (1990) *Ritual Criticism: Case Studies in its Practice, Essays on its Theory*, Columbia: University of South Carolina Press.

—— (1995) *Beginnings in Ritual Studies*, Washington: University Press of America.

Handelman, D. (1993) 'Is Victor Turner receiving his intellectual due?' *Journal of Ritual Studies* 7: 117–24.

Hier, S.P. (2002) 'Raves, risks and the ecstasy panic: a case study in the subversive nature of moral regulation', *Canadian Journal of Sociology* 27(1): 33–57.

Hutson, S. (1999) 'Technoshamanism: spiritual healing in the rave subculture', *Popular Music and Society* fall: 53–77.

—— (2000) 'The rave: spiritual healing in modern western subcultures', *Anthropological Quarterly* 73(1): 35–49.

Jones, R.A. (1986) *Emile Durkheim: An Introduction to Four Major Works*, Beverly Hills, CA: Sage.

Lash, S. and J. Urry (1994) *Economies of Signs and Space*, London: Sage.

Laughlin, C.D., J. McManus and E.G. d'Aquili (1990) *Brain, Symbol, and Experience: Toward a Neurophenomenology of Consciousness*, New York: Columbia University Press.

Lenton, S. and P. Davidson (1999) 'Raves, drugs, dealing and driving: qualitative data from a West Australian sample', *Drug & Alcohol Review* 18(2): 153–61.

Lenton, S., A. Boys and K. Norcross (1997) 'Raves, drugs and experience: drug use by a sample of people who attend raves in Western Australia', *Addiction* 92(10): 327–37.

Luckman, S. (2001) 'Practice random acts: reclaiming the streets of Australia', in G. St John (ed.) *FreeNRG: Notes from the Edge of the Dance Floor*, Altona: Common Ground Press.

McCall, T. (2001) *This is Not a Rave: In the Shadow of a Subculture*, Toronto: Insomniac Press.

McCarthy, G.D. (1982) 'The elementary form of the religious life', *Scottish Journal of Religious Studies* 3(2): 87–106.

MacLaren, P.L. (1985) 'Classroom symbols and the ritual dimension of schooling', *Anthropologica* 27(1–2): 161–89.

McRobbie, A. (1994) 'Shut up and dance: youth culture and changing modes of femininity', in A. McRobbie (ed.) *Postmodernism and Popular Culture*, London: Routledge.

Maffesoli, M. (1996) *The Time of the Tribes: The Decline of Individualism in Mass Society*, London: Sage.

Malbon, B. (1999) *Clubbing: Dancing, Ecstasy and Vitality*, London: Routledge.

Marlin-Curiel, S. (2001) 'Rave new world: trance-mission, trance-nationalism, and trance-scendence in the "New" South Africa', *TDR – The Drama Review – A Journal of Performance Studies* 45(3): 149–68.

Measham, F., H. Parker and J. Aldridge (1998) 'The teenage transition: from adolescent recreational drug use to the young adult dance culture in Britain in the mid-1990s', *Journal of Drug Issues* 28(1): 9–32.

Melechi, A. (1993) 'The ecstasy of disappearance', in S. Redhead (ed.) *Rave Off: Politics and Deviance in Contemporary Youth Culture*, Aldershot: Avebury.

Mellor, P.A. (1998) 'Sacred contagion and social vitality: collective effervescence in *Les Formes élémentaires de la vie religieuse*', *Durkheimian Studies* 4: 87–114.

Mellor, P.A. and C. Shilling (1997) *Re-forming the Body: Religion, Community, and Modernity*, London: Sage.

Mestrovic, S.G. (1992) *Durkheim and Postmodern Culture*, New York: Aldine de Gruyter.

Miller, W.W. (1996) *Durkheim, Morals and Modernity*, London: UCL Press.

Moore, R. (1983) 'Contemporary psychotherapy as ritual process: an initial reconnaissance', *Zygon* 18(3): 283–94.

Nielsen, D.A. (1999) *Three Faces of God: Society, Religion, and the Categories of Totality in the Philosophy of Emile Durkheim*, Albany, NY: State University of New York Press.

Nisbet, R.A. (1965) *Emile Durkheim*, Englewood Cliffs, NJ: Prentice-Hall, Inc.

—— (1966) *The Sociological Tradition*, New York: Basic Books.

Olaveson, T. (2001) 'Collective effervescence and communitas: processual models of ritual and society in Emile Durkheim and Victor Turner', *Dialectical Anthropology* 26(2): 89–124.

Ono, M. (1996) 'Collective effervescence and symbolism', *Durkheim Studies/Etudes Durkheimiennes* 2: 79–98.

Oring, E. (1993) 'Victor Turner, Sigmund Freud, and the return of the repressed', *Ethos* 21(3): 273–94.

Pechilis, K. (1992) 'To pilgrimage it', *Journal of Ritual Studies* 6(2): 59–91.

Pedersen, W. and A. Skrondal (1999) 'Ecstasy and new patterns of drug use: a normal population study', *Addiction* 94(11): 695–706.

Pickering, W.S.F. (1984) *Durkheim's Sociology of Religion: Themes and Theories*, London: Routledge & Kegan Paul.

—— (1994) 'Introduction', in W.S.F. Pickering (ed.) *Durkheim on Religion*, Atlanta: Scholars Press.

—— (ed.) (2000) *Durkheim and Representations*, London: Routledge.

Pini, M. (1997) 'Women and the early British rave scene', in A. McRobbie (ed.) *Back to Reality? Social Experience and Cultural Studies*, Manchester: Manchester University Press.

Poschardt, U. (1998) *DJ Culture*, Hamburg: Rogner & Bernhard GmbH & Co.

Power, R., T. Power and N. Gibson (1996) 'Attitudes and experience of drug use amongst a group of London teenagers', *Drugs: Education, Prevention and Policy* 31(1): 71–80.

Ramp, W. (1998) 'Effervescence, differentiation and representation in *The Elementary Forms*', in N.J. Allen, W.S.F. Pickering and W.W. Miller (eds) *On Durkheim's Elementary Forms of Religious Life*, London: Routledge.

Reynolds, S. (1999) *Generation Ecstasy: Into the World of Techno and Rave Culture*, New York: Routledge.

Rietveld, H. (1993) 'Living the dream', in S. Redhead (ed.) *Rave Off: Politics and Deviance in Contemporary Youth Culture*, Aldershot: Avebury.

Robbins, T. (1988) *Cults, Converts, and Charisma*, Newbury Park, CA: Sage.

St John, G. (2001a) 'Alternative cultural heterotopia and the liminoid body: beyond Turner at ConFest', *The Australian Journal of Anthropology* 12(1): 47–66.

—— (2001b) 'Doof! Australian post-rave culture', in G. St John (ed.) *FreeNRG: Notes from the Edge of the Dance Floor*, Altona: Common Ground Publishing.

Salamone, F.A. (1988) 'The ritual of jazz performance', *Play and Culture* 1(2): 85–104.

Schechner, R. (1977) *Essays on Performance Theory: 1970–1976*, New York: Drama Book Specialists.

Shewan, D., P. Dalgarno and G. Reith (2000) 'Perceived risk and risk reduction among ecstasy users: the role of drug, set, and setting', *The Internation Journal of Drug Policy* 10: 431–53.

Shilling, C. (1993) *The Body and Social Theory*, London: Sage.

Shilling, C. and P.A. Mellor (1998) 'Durkheim, morality and modernity: collective effervescence, homo duplex and the sources of moral action', *British Journal of Sociology* 49(2): 193–209.

Shupe, A. (1991) 'Globalization versus religious nativism: Japan's Soka Gakkai in the world arena', in R. Roberson and W.R. Garrett (eds) *Religion and Global Order*, New York: Paragon House.

Silcott, M. (1999) *Rave America: New School Dancescapes*, Toronto: ECW Press.

Smith, P. and J.C. Alexander (1996) 'Durkheim's religious revival', *American Journal of Sociology* 102(2): 585–92.

Stark, R. and W. Bainbridge (1985) *The Future of Religion*, Berkeley, CA: University of California Press.

—— (1987) *A Theory of Religion*, New York: Peter Lang.

Strinati, D. (1995) *An Introduction to Theories of Popular Culture*, London: Routledge.

Takahashi, M. and T. Olaveson (2003) 'Music, dance and raving bodies: raving as spirituality in the central Canadian rave scene', *Journal of Ritual Studies* 17(2): 72–96.

Thompson, K. (1993) 'Durkheim, ideology and the sacred', *Social Compass* 40(3): 451–61.

Thornton, S. (1994) 'Moral panic, the media and British rave culture', in A. Ross and T. Rose (eds) *Microphone Fiends: Youth Music and Youth Culture*, New York: Routledge.

—— (1995) *Club Cultures: Music, Media and Subcultural Capital*, Cambridge: Polity Press.

Tiryakian, E. (1995) 'Collective effervescence, social change and charisma: Durkheim, Weber and 1989', *International Sociology* 10(3): 269–81.

Topp, L., J. Hando, P. Dillon, A. Roche and N. Solowiji (1999) 'Ecstasy use in Australia: patterns of use and associated harm', *Drug & Alcohol Dependence* 55(1–2): 105–15.

Tramacchi, D. (2000) 'Field tripping: psychedelic *communitas* and ritual in the Australian bush', *Journal of Contemporary Religion* 15(2): 201–13.

—— (2001) 'Chaos Engines: doofs, psychedelics, and religious experience', in G. St John (ed.) *FreeNRG: Notes from the Edge of the Dance Floor*, Altona: Common Ground Press.

Turner, S.P. (ed.) (1993) *Emile Durkheim: Sociologist and Moralist*, London: Routledge.

Turner, V. (1967) *The Forest of Symbols: Aspects of Ndembu Ritual*, Ithaca, NY: Cornell University Press.

—— (1969) *The Ritual Process: Structure and Anti-structure*, Ithaca, NY: Cornell University Press.

—— (1973) 'The center out there: pilgrim's goal', *History of Religions* 12(3): 191–230.

—— (1974) *Dramas, Fields, and Metaphors: Symbolic Action in Human Society*, Ithaca, NY: Cornell University Press.

—— (1979) *Process, Performance and Pilgrimage*, New Delhi: Concept Publishing.

—— (1982) *From Ritual to Theatre: The Human Seriousness of Play*, New York: Performing Arts Journal.

Turner, V. (1985) *On the Edge of the Bush: Anthropology as Experience*, Tucson, AZ: University of Arizona Press.

Walker Bynum, C. (1995) 'Women's stories, women's symbols: a critique of Victor Turner's theory of liminality', in R. Grimes (ed.) *Readings in Ritual Studies*, Upper Saddle River, NJ: Prentice-Hall.

Wallace, A.F.C. (1956) 'Revitalization movements', *American Anthropologist* 58: 264–81.

—— (1966) *Religion: An Anthropological View*, New York: Random House.

Wallwork, E. (1985) 'Durkheim's early sociology of religion', *Sociological Analysis* 46: 201–18.

Weber, D. (1995) 'From limen to border: a meditation on the legacy of Victor Turner for American cultural studies', *American Quarterly* 47(3): 525–36.

Weber, T. (1999) 'Raving in Toronto: peace, love, unity, and respect in transition', *Journal of Youth Studies* 2(3): 317–36.

5 The flesh of raving

Merleau-Ponty and the 'experience' of ecstasy[1]

James Landau

The ecstasy of raving is problematic.[2] Often characterized in the same manner as its more 'traditional' cousins – as ineffable, numinous and overwhelming – it is said to have changed lives, and it is for many the draw, and perhaps even the *raison d'être*, of raving itself. Yet no real consensus exists about its shape, manner or form – its constitution, its 'essence', remains remarkably disputed. Caught within a web of contentious and proliferating discourses – medical, political, academic and subcultural – the ecstasy of raving is multiply situated and inordinately multi-layered, a veritable palimpsest of meaning. Making matters worse, ecstasy's hermeneutic ambiguity further complicates the picture: for, governed by immediacy and engagement, ecstasy obviates the analytic authority of detached observers even as its ineffability opens up an epistemological gap between the actual 'experience' and its subsequent embodiment in discourse.

Beneath this interpretive minefield, though, lies a deeper, more fundamental concern, namely ecstasy's transgressive relationship to binary thought. For in dissolving the mind's organizational dualisms, including, most profoundly, that of the self/Other dichotomy, ecstatic raving is an 'experience' discursively dominated by recurring motifs of unity, holism and interconnectedness. In the crucible of the rave, barriers are said to disintegrate as once disparate entities overlap and intermingle. Ravers become not only 'one with the music' (Stiens 1997: 2), but also one with the crowd, losing 'subjective belief in their self [as they] merge into a collective body' (Jordan 1995: 5). As Douglas Rushkoff has noted, 'there is a magic moment that can happen at a rave – at 2 or 3 in the morning, when everyone is dancing, [during which] you experience a feeling of collective organism' (Eisenberg 1997: D5), of being a part of what another raver describes as a 'big, coordinated animal that just moves' (Pini 1997: 120). Melting into the crowd, the raver participates in an ecstatic collectivity, a unity that challenges the ontological certainties of Western thought by destabilizing such foundational oppositions as self/Other and mind/body.

That said, ecstatic practitioners often conceptualize this collectivity in terms of antinomian spiritualities known for both their frequent disavowal of mainstream religion[3] and their emphatic deployment of non-traditional concepts. As one rave-proselyte notes, the electronic music and dance scene has long flirted with the idea of spiritual connections. Names of events such as 'Spiritual Signals', record companies such as 'Conscious Records', and spiritual imagery like buddhas and mandalas [abound].... And let's face it, many of us have had deeper religious experiences at a full moon rave or a good night at [a club] than we ever had in church.

(Gris 2000)

Coded here as a 'deeper religious experience' than church, and thus evocative of mystical intensities, raves revolve around what Simon Reynolds describes as the 'gnosis of drug-knowledge', around 'a truth that cannot be mediated or explained in words' (1999: 245), a profound secret that another practitioner describes as:

Ecstasy. Not a drug, a feeling. Overpowering, almost overwhelming joy. Better than life. It is life, the love of living.... A religious experience; God has come down from the heavens to give YOU a hug. Heaven is here, now and forever. The awakening of the Gaian mind. Ethereal energy joining each of the beautiful party people, forming a greater collective consciousness.

(Parsons 1996)

Explicitly referencing 'God' and 'religious experience', this account is exemplary in that it also ties together New Age threads (of the 'Gaian mind') with themes of collectivity and interconnectedness to produce novel religious forms. Indeed, as is made evident by such terms as 'vibes', 'group minds' and 'ethereal energies', ravers freely appropriate religious concepts in their attempt to fashion personal spiritualities that adequately address their peak experiences.

Intrigued and wholeheartedly respectful of these emergent religious forms, I am nevertheless in agreement with Marghanita Laski, who argues 'that the attachment of religious "overbeliefs" to experiences of aesthetic or ecstatic intensity is gratuitous rather than essential' (Tramacchi 2001: 175). While not necessarily agreeing with her perspective that ecstasy results from an eruption of the sacred into the profane, I do concur with Laski that ecstasy, as an overwhelming ineffability, does not require conceptualization for its existence – that it just is.

Significantly, though, I also disagree with Laski's noble sentiment that 'ecstasy is more important than ideology' (*ibid.*: 175). Viewing ecstatic overbeliefs as nothing more than culturally situated narratives traded within a social economy, I cannot help but recognize their political positioning and potency. For whether assimilationist or countercultural, ecstatic overbeliefs have very real social and cultural repercussions, including, most frequently, demonization and illegalization. Moreover, with its 'truth' predominately constituted by medical and political agendas, ecstasy is often reduced – both in mainstream *and* underground formulations – to the neurological activity of MDMA and its chemical analogues, a reduction that continues to discount those individuals who have attained ecstasy *without* chemical intervention.[4]

In opposition to this unyielding empiricism, the religious overbeliefs of ravers describe the *experience* of ecstasy as a 'transcendent' or 'spiritual' moment occurring within the ritual context of the rave, which is itself often conceived as a contemporary religious practice possessed of numerous historical and crosscultural correlates (see Chapter 6). Similarly, an anonymous contributor to the Hyperreal web archives has contended that rave's religious influences include 'Taoism (Tai Chi), Sufism, Hinduism (Yoga), Buddhism (Meditation), Cabalism (the tree of life), Shamanism (navigating consciousness), [as well as the] Mysticism of all religions and tribes of aboriginal people' (see Anonymous n.d.). Unfortunately overshadowed by the media's prolific drug scare, this noteworthy *bricolage* has gone largely unnoticed by both mainstream and academic communities – its religious neomorphisms, when acknowledged, often being mocked, ridiculed or dismissed in much the same manner as those of the New Age movement.

With this in mind, it is the purpose of this chapter to produce a theory of ecstatic raving that avoids spiritual formulations even as it maintains a high degree of respect for them. Drawing on first-person accounts that are frequently laced with religious motifs, I will be constructing an ecstatic 'overbelief' grounded in contemporary philosophical and psychoanalytic theory. Myself a one-time practitioner of these 'techniques of ecstasy', of these 'technologies of pleasure', I am writing this piece out of a desire to understand my own 'experiences' *without* resorting to the disembodied articulations frequent to religious rhetoric, which tends to emphasize spirit and mind over body and perception. Wary of the mind/body hierarchy inherent in conceptions of ecstasy where the self transcends its immanent reality in order to commune with an incorporeal godhead, supernatural reality, or spiritual energy, I will be beginning from the premise that ecstatic raving is first and foremost an embodied activity. Especially interested in what one raver describes as the 'profound sense of connectedness with people' (Alissa 1995) that raving confers, I will be developing an approach that conceives of ecstatic raving, when fully achieved, as a momentary glimpse of ideological autonomy.

It is my ultimate hope to show that the phenomenology of Maurice Merleau-Ponty can especially clarify and make sense of ecstasy's effects, including its disruption of binary thought, exactly because his philosophy – as epitomized in his 'ontology of the flesh' – is *already* a non-dualistic framework. Emphasizing the lived body, this framework actively undermines the series of mind/body lateral associations (e.g. masculine/feminine, active/passive and reason/emotion) that have had far-reaching and often detrimental consequences for not only Western thought but also individuals of non-dominant race, gender and sexuality.

Resolving binary oppositions through a 'thesis of reversibility' that emphasizes interconnectedness and ambiguity via a subtending logic of difference-within-identity, Merleau-Ponty contends that the perceived world not only pre-dates consciousness, but is also its foundation – a foundation, I argue, to which we 'return' during ecstatic raving.

The 'experience' of ecstasy: subjectivity and the flight from language

Perhaps indicative of our culture's unfortunate marginalization of transgressive and emergent religious forms, it is not uncommon for the more exuberant claims and testimonials of ravers to be repeatedly dismissed as nothing more than the ramblings of honeymooners not yet tolerant to MDMA. Mired in the rhetoric of drug use, experiential accounts of ecstasy, like other drug-related phenomena, are continually stripped of epistemological value. All too often, these emotionally invested accounts are disregarded wholesale, their claims ignored as perverse, irrational and irrelevant.

Yet these experiential accounts are all we have. Indicative of the available fictions about ecstasy circulating within our culture, they reveal not only the term's dependency on religious and psychedelic themes, but also important information about the ideological placement of the authors themselves. Since 'experience is not outside social, political, historical and cultural forces, and in this sense, cannot provide an outside position from which to establish a place for judgment' (Grosz 1999: 148), experiential accounts must be understood as overdetermined narratives of ideology that can be read in terms of a subject's 'making sense' of the world *through* their particular cultural background. Experiential accounts of ecstasy that make use of appropriated religious concepts must accordingly be recognized as more than just attempts to illustrate, defend and legitimize ecstatic raving to others; they must be seen as the very *construction*, in a sense, of ecstasy's 'reality' through language usually reserved for traditional religiosity.

It must not be forgotten, though, that this 'reality' is ever and always a 'fiction', a 'text' that comes about within a matrix of internal and external discourses inseparable from language, and thus, by extension, ideology, identity and culture.[5] Born within the symbolic order, experience operates within – *and is read through* – a field of culturally situated narratives that can be deployed for political purposes – which is exactly what Maria Pini, for example, does in her groundbreaking feminist analyses of rave.

Conceiving of subjectivity, rightfully, as a series of fictions, Pini contends that in rave 'lies the potential for re-figurations of the here and now, the possibilities for creating alternative fictions or narratives of being, and the opportunities for the development of new (albeit temporary, incomplete and constituted partly in fantasy) "identities" ' (Pini 2001: 3). While Pini's project boasts an admirable aim, namely a revolution in feminine subjectivity, it is perhaps an irony that her inter-pretive framework is exactly what prevents her from fully recognizing ecstasy for what it is. For, overly concerned with opposing any conception of the raver 'as a non-sexed, non-raced, and otherwise non-specific generality' (*ibid.*: 46), Pini fails, because of her interpretive model's implicit fear of an 'apolitical' rave, to truly listen to the claims of 'freedom' made by her interviewees, subsequently fore-closing any possibility of finding an alternative conceptual model that could explain this apolitics without sacrificing sexual specificity – a model, it is my argument, that can be found in Merleau-Ponty's ontology of the flesh.

Before we can examine this ontology, though, we must follow the lead of Pini's apt invocation of Angela McRobbie's 'call to lived experience' (McRobbie 1997: 170): we must attend to the actual experiences of ecstasy, 'experiences' that must be interrogated through the lens of subjectivity. Toward that end, ecstasy must be understood beyond the empiricist's context of neurobiology; it must also be theorized in terms of the subject's relationship to itself, its body and the world. As Pini notes, in concordance with most theorists of rave,

> one can see a radical reframing of the body within rave and, as a conse-
> quence, the emergence of experiences which many claim are entirely new to
> them [such that] participants often refer to rave as constituting a different
> 'world' [within which] the 'self' is no longer an individual, boundaried
> one…[Here,] subjectivity is restated in terms which do not reproduce tradi-
> tional distinctions between mind and body, self and other.
>
> (Pini 1997: 118)

Interestingly, while Pini both correlates the 'emergence of new experiences' to a refiguring of subjectivity *and* explicitly references ecstasy's strange relationship to binary thought, she at the same time fails to mention, even implicitly, another significant characteristic of ecstasy: its ineffability.

Strangely absent from Pini's work, the widely documented ineffability of ecstatic raving echoes one of the major attributes of classic mystical experiences. As one rave apologist argues,

> the experiential nature of such spiritual moments transcends any beliefs
> that we might have…coming into the experience, i.e. what we believe the
> reasons/explanations for what is happening are completely irrelevant. All
> that matters is that we can have these amazing, *undefinable*, shareable experi-
> ences – [ultimately,] they are real/valid/meaningful and the beliefs we
> construct to help us understand them are secondary and not even important
> compared to the experience itself.
>
> (Fogel 1994; italics mine)

Echoing Laski, Lee Fogel highlights here the 'undefinability' of the ecstatic moment which, for him, supersedes its intellectual positioning: the experiences are 'real' and 'valid', while the beliefs constructed to explain them are 'secondary' in comparison.

This ineffability, though, does not require a mystical explanation: it is my contention that the format of raves inherently yields indescribable 'experiences'. Taking the phrase 'It's so loud I can't even hear myself think' to its logical extreme, the rave event's volume leaves little space for thought. Overwhelmed by the bass, 'language', Hillegonda Rietveld argues, is 'unable to catch the event; participants…do not seem to be able to describe their experience as anything else than "it was wild, absolutely wild", "unbelievable", "there wasn't anything like it", or "great"' (Rietveld 1993: 63). With the visual field fracturing beneath the incisions of lasers, participants are transported to a perceptual realm of inconstancy, a place where words are swallowed whole by the darkness and the fog. Add to this the peculiar 'meaninglessness' of electronic music, which Reynolds attributes to the emphasis on percussion and timbre, 'the two elements of music that are the hardest to remember...[i.e.] ineffable, untranscribable elements' (Reynolds 1999: 054), and you have an 'experience' that does not lend itself to memory or communication. A space where meaning fails, where representation collapses, the rave-assemblage deconstructs language through the deployment of its materiality.

Yet Pini takes issue with this. Stemming directly from her political desire to reaffirm and protect the category of 'woman' against poststructuralist formulations of ecstasy that emphasize an 'undoing of the constructed self within rave' (Pini 2001: 46), Pini opposes analyses that see rave as mass 'disappearance' or postmodern meaninglessness. Emphatically, she declares that,

> although it is true that ravers may well experience a sense of 'losing' themselves within an event, this does not mean that identity has been 'escaped' from. Body-subjects within rave may well experience a merging into a larger 'body' (such as the 'body' of the dancing crowd) but as far as raving women go, this does not mean that femininity is ever fully 'escaped' from.
>
> (Pini 2001: 46–7)

Denying the classical conception of ecstasy as a 'transcendental' movement beyond the ego and its identities, Pini deploys a textualized approach wherein 'the lived practices of rave cannot be separated from the 'texts' or 'fictions' which make up its meanings' (Pini 1997: 113). Pini's model, accordingly, necessitates an immediate and *contemporaneous* constitution of every ecstatic moment as meaningful, enlanguaged experience – her ecstatics are forever the prisoners of ideology, forever the prisoners of their inscribed skins. Arising from her wish to safeguard rave's ability to restructure cultural narratives of sexuality, Pini refuses to accept raving as a mute, afictional activity – as an ineffable. Instead, it must 'speak' (Pini 2001: 157), it must be active in its production of 'otherwheres'; it must exist dialogically in relation to oppressive structures.

Because of this, Pini cannot part with subjectivity. She needs it to remain not only the nexus of fictions, but also the seat of activity and agency. Pini therefore conceives of ecstasy as *re*subjectification, not *de*subjectification. Understanding the subject as the result of subjectification into the Symbolic (and inherently political) order of language, Pini feels that all claims of desubjectification abnegate the political efficacy of rave. For if ecstasy is 'nothing more' than a desubjectification, a movement beyond language into a realm of ineffability, then the dancing body that was once a self becomes nothing more than an apolitical anonymity, a state of affairs Pini adamantly denies, arguing that it is 'naïve and problematic' to deny that 'identity classifications do not continue to have very real effects' (*ibid.*: 49).

Concurring with Pini that hierarchical and thus oppressive identity categories are at work within rave, I nevertheless feel that her arguments suffer from an inadequate separation of the ecstatic moment from the cultures of clubbing and raving within which it is embedded. Finding it more useful to examine raving as a continuum of experiential zones bracketed at one end by 'everyday life' and at the other end by 'ecstasy', I contend that between these poles of cultural subjectification and acultural desubjectification can be found a gradient of 'experiences' whose trajectory involves a gradual unfixing and eventual dissolution of normative identity and its concomitant ideologies. A night of raving can accordingly be read as the experiential progression from normal everyday life into, first, the oppositional subculture of the rave, club or doof itself, second, the backdrop-liminality of the rave-as-carnival and, finally, the embodied intensities of ecstasy itself.

A state 'beyond' language, ecstasy opens up a breech, an epistemological gap, between itself and its subsequent discursive products. Because of this, all testimonials and other experiential accounts must be seen as *retroactive* renderings, as attempts *after the fact* (perhaps mere seconds after the fact) to make sense of, to conceptualize, what is inherently ineffable: a desubjectified cognitive state that can best be understood as a corporeal style of being, i.e. a non-reflective awareness autonomous in its 'freedom' from ideology, language and culture. An 'experience' only *after* the fact, ecstasy is opposed to rationality and higher-order thought. Ultimately, it is indeed the 'transcendence' of the thematic, Cartesian *cogito*, albeit in a manner distinct from the idealistic formulations of traditional religion.

The only metaphysical 'void,' accordingly, into which the ecstatic escapes is the 'emptiness' of direct and unmediated perception. For while there's still neurological activity, cognition of *some* form, it's *not* that of the subject – the 'I' heavy with preoccupied self-reflection – but rather that of the unbound body, suddenly weightless in its joyous exploration of itself and the world.

The Body-without-Organs: ecstasy and its pleasures

As it is discussed here, ecstasy is like a mathematical limit: it is an idealization of an event not always reached. For not everyone at a party achieves pure ecstasy. Perhaps they only experience a playful liminality, or maybe just an intense physical pleasure. An escape from the trap of ecstasy/sobriety, the experiential gradient allows us to understand raving from a functionalist standpoint, i.e. in terms of efficiency – a standpoint well addressed by the analyses of Tim Jordan and Simon Reynolds.

Jordan, in employing the conceptual creativity of Gilles Deleuze and Felix Guattari, explains that 'raving's production, or what is desired by ravers through constituting a rave-event, is an ongoing inducement into a desubjectified state of something like rapture' (Jordan 1995: 129). Seeing ecstasy as that which ravers desire, as the 'purpose' of assembling such disparate material elements as music, bodies, drugs and lights – not to mention temporality and spatiality – Jordan frames the rave within the context of the BwO, or the Body-without-Organs. Composed of all 'the potentials in the human nervous system for pleasure and sensation without purpose: the sterile bliss of perverse sexuality, drug experiences, play, dancing and so forth' (Reynolds 1999: 246), the BwO, Grosz elaborates,

> is the body in abundance of its (biological, psychical, and signifying) organization and organs...[It is an] attempt to denaturalize human bodies and to place them in direct relations with the flows of particles of other bodies or things...[and it] refers indistinguishably to human, animal, textual, sociocultural, and physical bodies.
>
> (Grosz 1994: 168)

'Beyond' the organizations and stratifications of subjectivity and culture, the BwO, operative at multiple levels, 'refers indistinguishably' to both individual and communal bodies such that Jordan can contend that

> the BwO of raving is the undifferentiated state that supports the connections that the rave-machine makes between its different elements. This undifferentiated state is a collective delirium produced by thousands of people jointly making the connections of drugs to dance, music to dance, dance to drugs, drugs to time, time to music and so on, thereby gradually constructing the state of raving and so the BwO of raving. The delirium is non-subjective and smooth, as all the connections and functions of the [rave-]machine give way to simple intensities of feeling.
>
> (Jordan 1995: 130)

Attempting to collapse the stratifications of subjectivity, ravers are trying to reconstruct themselves as Bodies-without-Organs, as 'smooth', fiction-less spaces across which intensities and pleasures may flow unhindered:

> as we negotiated the stairs down to the dancefloor, we began to slide into the contours of the rhythm, becoming immersed in it, the bass curling around the spine which felt like it had been loosened of its inhibiting rigidity, like it had slipped the bounds of all that was holding it – us – back, and could just flow, loose, warm, *alive*.... And in a second we were amongst the throng, synched right into the matrix of bodies and sound.
>
> (Collin 1997: 3)

With his body free of 'inhibiting rigidities', Matthew Collin evokes here the autonomy and collectivity inspired by Jordan's analysis. Similarly, another raver, speaking specifically about the chemical component of the assemblage, explains that ecstasy 'heightens all five senses to the point that the music becomes hypnotic and the sense of touch becomes so pleasurable that a crowd is comforting. It's sensory overload... It's totally sensual. Touching becomes so intense' (McPhee 2000). Frequently catalysing synaesthesia with the help of MDMA, the rave-assemblage embodies a relationship where the greater the sensory intensities – whether tactile, aural or visual – the greater the degree of desubjectification.

'Measuring' these intensities through a 'physics' of efficiency, Deleuze and Guattari's functionalist approach subsequently asks not 'what does it mean?' but 'how does it work?' Sidestepping the neurodeterministic reduction of ecstasy to MDMA, this approach asks by what means, and to what degree, a particular assemblage of music, bodies, chemicals and lights induces desubjectification amongst its participants.

It is worth noting, however, that subjectivity in this model is nothing more than a surface effect. Emphasizing the tangible body over the untenable mind, Deleuze and Guattari envision the subject as nothing more than a series of cultural stratifications that transform a BwO into a codified body. Fitting well into postmodern agendas of superficiality, ephemerality and hyperreality, this model arises from a series of contemporary philosophies that see the body 'as a purely surface phenomenon, a complex, multifaceted surface...whose incision or inscription produces the (illusion or effects) of depth and interiority' (Grosz 1994: 116). In this view, individuality, consciousness and subjectivity, while experientially 'real', are nothing more than fictive illusions, dimensionless holograms on the surface of the body.

Significantly, while I feel much can be gained from philosophies such as this – and while I also feel that the Deleuzo–Guattarian approach, with its intensities, connections and flows, speaks gracefully to the *jouissant* pleasures of ecstasy – I am hesitant to invest *wholly* in such an approach and would rather, for the purposes of this chapter, explore what traditional philosophies of depth, such as psychoanalysis and phenomenology, can reveal about the ecstatic 'experience'.

The disappearing ego: ecstasy and psychoanalysis

Examining the rave as a ritual of disappearance in which no meaning could be found other than pure escape, Rietveld (1993: 54) approaches ecstatic subjectivity from a psychoanalytic viewpoint that presumes the body's interior to be private, depthful and libidinally cathected. Drawing on Freudian thought, she argues that E makes the user return to a pre-Oedipal stage in which libidinous pleasure is not centred in the genitals – a stage in which sexuality is polymorphous as sensuality engages the entire body (*ibid.*: 54). Crucially, while she could have easily posited these sensations in terms of a Deleuzo–Guattarian BwO, she instead conceived of ecstasy as a developmental retrogression, as an infantilization within the context of adulthood.

In this model, ecstasy 'rewinds' the individual backward into a pre-Oedipal period of inchoate sensations that play across the body free of patterning, grouping and organization. This process occurs through a dissolution of the ego, which in Freudian terms is something akin to a 'psychical map of the body's libidinal intensities...,a kind of bodily tracing, a cartography of the erotogenic intensities of the body, an *internalized* image' (Grosz 1994: 33) that provides unity and a sense of bodily cohesion. With their body's libidinal impulses emancipated, ecstatics are awash with the pleasures inherent to sensation.

Yet, for Rietveld, pleasure does not complete the analysis: ineffability must be addressed. Moving from Freud to his successor Lacan, she adds that ecstasy marks the ' "return" to a stage in psychological development which is before the acquisition of language, thereby undoing the self that is constituted in and by language.... A break is caused with the established order at a basic level, however temporary' (Rietveld 1993: 65). Emphasizing its alinguistic character, Rietveld's argument implicitly correlates ecstasy to the Lacanian Real, a period of undifferentiated sensations chronologically prior to the development of the ego. To simplify grossly: children in this model are initially unaware of their physical distinctiveness and are thus 'at one with the universe'. This phase ends only when they successfully identify and internalize their mirror-image, thus birthing the category of 'self' or 'I' in opposition to the 'other' of everything else.

Serving as the border between the chaos of the immanent interior and the provisional stability of the transcendent exterior, this *body image*, according to Lacan, is the primordial seed from which all language and identity emerge, inasmuch as the categories of 'self' and 'other' act as the foundational model from which all other linguistic oppositions evolve. Consequently, language and the self are so intertwined that, in the psychoanalytic view, ecstasy's transgressive relationship to binary thought stems from the rave-assemblage propelling its participants into the Real, a cognitive space 'beyond' the ego and its organizational structures. Indeed, facilitated by the metronomic mandala of electronic music, whose repetitive beats reinscribe temporality as the dancing ecstatic 'trances out' (Reynolds 1999: 203), the music–drug–dancing interface 'sings to a very visceral, ancient part of us deep down inside. It draws us out, perhaps from the "reptilian" brain, past our egos, and beckons us to dance with abandon, to surrender ourselves to the beat' (Casey 1993), a beat beyond language and subjectivity.

The Lacanian approach, though, useful as it is, must be understood within the context of its manifold difficulties. For, apart from Lacan's rampant phallocentrism and mis/appropriation of women, his linguistic turn, the basis for so much of postmodern and contemporary thought, draws around human subjectivity an impenetrable linguistic immanence that forever taunts us with an unobtainable Real, an impossible, transcendent and unavoidably lost reality. What's more, Lacan's approach cannot fully explicate intersubjectivity (Fielding 1999: 186). Enmeshed in the Symbolic Order, and subsequently unable to bridge the epistemological and ontological gap between itself and the other, the Lacanian mind cannot escape itself.

Merleau-Ponty and the corporeal schema

A critical dilemma for Western philosophy, the problem of intersubjectivity and its shadow, solipsism, can be summated as follows: since 'I cannot witness your *cogito*, I cannot know that you exist as a thinking thing. Consequently, if one defines human beings as *res cogitans*, the only human being I can be certain is a human being is myself' (Dillon 1997: 112). A frequent philosophical enterprise, explorations of intersubjectivity have failed, according to M.C. Dillon, because of their inability to resolve the immanence/transcendence divide (*ibid.*: 114–29). Inevitably rooting themselves in the neo-Cartesianisms of empiricism or intellec-tualism, no Western philosopher has truly escaped solipsism because they have all emphasized the mind, the *cogito* – with the exception, Dillon contends, of Merleau-Ponty.

Resonating with the work of Lacan, Merleau-Ponty's vision of psychogenesis depends as well on a mirror-stage through which the disordered perceptions of the infant's body are unified into a coherent whole. In concordance with Lacan that the period before the ego is a time of 'indistinction of perspectives, [in] which the mine–alien or self–other distinction is absent' (*ibid.*: 119), Merleau-Ponty specifically understood this period, which he called syncretic sociability, as a 'first phase, which we call pre-communication, in which there is not one individual over against another but rather an anonymous collectivity, an undif-ferentiated group life' (Merleau-Ponty 1964: 119). Agreeing as well that the thematic structures of consciousness arise out of this cognitive bedrock, Merleau-Ponty *does* depart from Lacan in that he emphasizes perception over language:

> to recognize his image in the mirror is for [the baby] to learn that *there can be a viewpoint taken on him*.... By means of the image in the mirror he becomes capable of being a spectator of himself. Through the acquisition of the specular image the child notices that he is visible, for himself and for others.... The mirror image makes possible a contemplation of self.
>
> (Merleau-Ponty 1964: 136)

Whereas Lacan emphasizes the specular image as a deceptive alienation that governs the child's entire psychic development, Merleau-Ponty posits it in terms of visibility and the child's emergent conceptualizations of space.

For Merleau-Ponty, though, the body image, otherwise known as the corpo-real schema, is more than just the barrier between the interior and exterior. It is the very ground of intersubjectivity. For since 'we have no idea of a mind that would not be *doubled* with a body, that would not be established on this ground' (Merleau-Ponty 1968: 259), the corporeal schema itself, the body image, is repre-sentative of *what it means* to be a human being, thus resituating the search for other minds as a search for other bodies.

Encrusted with libidinal and cultural inscriptions, with fictions of identity and power, the corporeal schema, according to Merleau-Ponty, determines the extent of the individual's 'I-can', i.e. the range of their movements and actions as psychically and socially proscribed. Fluid and malleable, open to the incorpora-tion of instruments, clothing and prostheses, the body image in its plasticity is conformative to the world, enabling us to develop a practical relationship to objects and situations.[6] Synaesthestic, it allows the possibility of voluntary action inasmuch as it 'unifies and coordinates postural, tactile, kinaesthetic, and visual sensations so that these are experienced as the sensations of a subject coordinated into a single space' (Grosz 1994: 83).

What is crucial here is that the body possesses inherent corporeal knowledges, awarenesses of its own kinaesthetic abilities and conformative relationships to the world that *subtend* self-reflective consciousness. It is ultimately these subconscious knowledges that are thematized to produce the corporeal schema, the interface between the mind and body.

Therefore, if the self is delineated from the world by the corporeal schema, if the subject is indeed dependent on its body image for existence, then the dissolution of the self during ecstasy would require a concomitant transformation in the corporeal schema, which would seriously affect not only the raver's sense of self and body, but also their mobility. For in removing the psychosocial limitations on movement and posture imposed by culture, ecstasy allows ravers to attain the oft-proclaimed state of 'flow' (Csikszentmihalyi 1990), in which liquid movements undulate across a body open to a much wider field of possibilities, of 'I-cans'. Central to the ecstatic 'experience', dancing is reframed here as the release from routine movement. Cinnamon Twist iterates that:

> this kind of dance...is FREEING MOTION. Not just moving to the beat but letting the beat help you throw off all the restricted robotic movements that have been imprinted in your heart, your eyes, your ears, your arms, your ass, your dreams, by all the tricks, traumas, and seductions of society...dancing with the world, but dancing off the consensus-trance.
>
> (Twist 1992)

Significantly, the corporeal schema possesses one other bodily knowledge worth mentioning before finally turning to the ontology of flesh: that of perception's reflexivity. Stemming from the body's simultaneous immanence and transcendence, perception can only occur because the body exists in the world: 'pure consciousness cannot *touch* anything. The body can touch things, but it can touch things only to the extent that it is touched *by* things' (Dillon 1997: 155). A necessarily reflexive act, perception occurs in what Merleau-Ponty originally called the tacit *cogito*, which is opposed to the thematic, or Cartesian, *cogito*. 'The tacit *cogito* is silent: it sees the world and does not thematize its seeing. The [Cartesian] *cogito* speaks: it thematizes its relations with things and posits itself in the statement, "I think" ' (*ibid.*: 108).

Reflecting Merleau-Ponty's wish to return to 'prediscursive experience, experience before the overlay of reflection, the imposition of a meta-experiential organization, [and] its codification by reason, language or knowledge' (Grosz 1999: 151), the tacit *cogito* is pure perception, an anonymous perceptual field antecedent to the thematic ego, the cognitive structure that inculcates the subject into an experiential matrix of language, culture and identity. Accordingly, if ecstatic raving is indeed an unravelling of the thematic, Cartesian *cogito*, then in phenomenological terms it can be read as a return to the tacit *cogito*, a prediscursive awareness 'unaware of itself in its fascination with the world' (Dillon 1997: 105). As Catherine explains:

> When I dance at a rave I feel very...close to, if not at, this non-thinking state. I hardly notice the passage of time and I am free of the tensions and worries of daily life.... I notice the things around me in a closer way: the lights, the people, the all-encompassing vibration of the bass, even the feel of the grainy dirt on my palms when I sit down on the floor for a rest.
>
> (Catherine 1998)

Perception: the hidden depth of flesh

An elaboration of the concept of the tacit *cogito*, the ontology of the flesh was developed in opposition to traditional ontologies that presuppose 'a bifurcation of being into disjunct and mutually exclusive spheres of immanence (the sphere of consciousness, subjectivity...) and transcendence (the sphere of things, objectivity...)' (Dillon 1997: 154). Hovering ambiguously between dualism and monism, flesh is a phenomenological ontology that holds that all dichotomies are actually subtended by an encompassing unity that makes difference not only possible, but also necessarily interdependent. A fabric of 'divergence and non-coincidence' (Grosz 1994: 100), the flesh interweaves subjects and objects, bodies and their world, into an unfolding and dynamic unity permeated with difference and alterity. All things, whether the 'visibles' of bodies and objects or the 'invisibles' of subjectivity and thought, interweave and intersect within a flesh that presents itself to us as the world's perceptible surface.

Unifying perception and existence through its thesis of reversibility, the ontology of flesh states simply that nothing, no one, can perceive without first being perceptible:

> the flesh of the world perceives itself through our flesh which is one with it. Just as the worldly thing must touch my body for my body to touch it, so, in general, must my perception of the world be correlated with my own perceptibility.
>
> (Dillon 1997: 105)

Hinged on the critical and self-evident realization that perception requires distance – that there must be a gap between the perceiver and the perceived – the thesis of reversibility requires an inherent alterity within the flesh: subjects and objects must be distinct, separate; they cannot coincide. At the same time, though, for them to 'perceive' one another they must also exist within the same flesh, the same world.

It is ultimately this distance, or *chiasm*, that allows us to recognize Merleau-Ponty's approach as a philosophy of depth: for while one might be likely to examine the ontology of flesh as a philosophy of exteriority, of surface phenomena, perception requires a distance through the *depth* of flesh's 'invisible' underside. Not a pure play of superficial phenomena, the flesh has depth: folding over itself to create 'hollows' and 'enclosures', the flesh creates 'invisibles' such as the mind, thought and language, fleshy interiorities that are irrevocably embodied.

Difference-within-identity: the gnosis of ecstatic flesh

> Rave...allows us to access a space (within ourselves) completely outside the realm of subjective vs. objective. I think that space represents a state of being rather than thinking.... Suppose for a moment that I stopped 'thinking', that I just 'AM'.... I would just perceive...which leads to an awareness of being 'one' with everything.
>
> (Tanya 1994)

Speaking to 'the motif of communality [that] has been one of the more recurrent elements in discourses about psychedelic parties' (Tramacchi 2001: 174), Tanya expresses above an 'experience' of 'being one with everything' that is often echoed by other practitioners. Eric Stiens, for example, recounts the tale of one participant who testified that 'for one night, I was one with the universe, I was one with my neighbor, and I was one with the music' (Stiens 1997: 2). Frequently catalysed by the empathetic qualities of MDMA, this transpersonal blending of the self with the other has been one of the primary areas of inquiry throughout this chapter. Often linked to feelings of being 'connected to everyone around me, like we are one organism in synch with the music' (Fogel 1994), this sense of unity and interconnectedness has led to the invocation by many of a 'super-organism' composed of the crowd's ecstatic bodies. Flying in the face of modernity's rigid individualism, this sense of unity resonates, I feel, with one of the major goals of religion – namely the production of solidarity and community – thus partially explaining the discourse of ecstatic raving's frequent deployment of religious rhetoric.

For example, incorporated into the full-moon rave rituals of the Moontribe, this transgressive unity occurs, according to Ralph Perring, when 'by by-passing the conscious mind and plugging into a deeper level of the psyche, the short-sighted understanding of ourselves as separate individuals is ruthlessly blown apart to make way for *a higher consciousness*' (Perring 1997), a 'consciousness' intrinsic to the Moontribe's sense of spiritual interconnectedness.

For some, though, this 'consciousness' is never quite complete. For running perpendicularly to the rhetoric of unity that permeates ecstatic discourses is a contrary thread of continued identity. Ravers, even as their egos melt, even as their bodies dissolve into a larger 'organism', still speak of something *apart*, of some undefinable 'thing' distinct from the crowd. Ask them if they completely disappear into this unity while ecstatic, and they will often vacillate, equivocally answering both 'yes' and 'no' as they search for the terminology to describe, to produce, their 'experience'.

While this alternation between unity and identity could be explained simply in terms of functionality, as a matter of the particular rave-assemblage's efficiency or the individual's psychological disposition, these answers shy away from confronting the matter head on. Therefore, having already elaborated various models of desubjectification that situate the raver's apprehension of unity as the result of an unreflective perceptual awareness free of oppositional thought, and therefore of any *thematized* concept of 'difference', the task remains to explain this continued sense of separation and identity. Cognizant of Pini's shortcomings, we must recognize as well that neither the Deleuzo–Guattarian BwO nor the Lacanian Real, with their smooth, undifferentiated terrains, can adequately address this tension. And neither, in truth, can a model based solely on Merleau-Ponty's tacit *cogito*. If, though, we conceptualize the reversibility of the flesh as an innate *bodily knowledge*, as an aspect of what it *means* (in a non-thematic, subconscious way) to be a living organism, then we can begin to apprehend how the ontology of flesh can adequately address this tension within the heart of the ecstatic 'experience'.

For, no different than 'knowing' what it 'means' to blink an eye or to have weight, the body 'knows' in a pre-reflective manner that it is one entity, just as it 'knows' it is *also* a part of the world. Without being told, and in a non-linguistic manner, the body understands the thesis of reversibility and the difference-within-identity of flesh because *it itself is of the flesh*. Similarly, the body understands the 'distance' inherent to perception. Indeed, it is this *gap* that ultimately serves as the template for binary thought. For rooted in the inherent distances of perception, the self/Other dichotomy is the thematization of this bodily knowledge such that, during ecstasy, when all themes and conceptual models have disappeared, only the body's subconscious, non-linguistic 'knowledges' remain. Destabilizing and eventually dissolving the boundaries between such fundamental oppositions as self/Other, mind/body and here/there, ecstasy frees the body from its thematic veil so that it can become aware again, at a 'deeper' level, of identity and difference.

Accordingly, we can now resolve the ambiguous yes/no response from above. For if the ecstatic raver is indeed an anonymous body of textless flesh, one that has shed its identity, ideology and language, one that has either divested or radically altered its culturally inscribed body image, then the thematic boundaries that normally delineate our edges are destabilized and perhaps even dissolved. Dancing amidst a crowd of ecstatic bodies, the raver is consumed not only by an immediate 'experience' of the phenomenal world, but also by his or her body's subconscious knowledges of unity and alterity (not to mention genderless sexual specificity) – knowledges that are quite different from those of self-reflective thought. Lost in the reflexivity and natural transgressivity of the flesh, in its indeterminacy and interwovenness, the raver is a mute witness to the blurring of once clear demarcations between himself and the crowd, between herself and the rave. For, as Merleau-Ponty asks, 'where are we to put the limit between the body and the world, since the world is flesh?' (1968: 138).

Conclusion

In this chapter I have attempted to explore ecstasy and the rhetoric of unity that surrounds it through a variety of theoretical approaches. Most of these have understood ecstasy as desubjectification, an understanding with which I agree. My own situating of ecstatic raving within a phenomenological framework ultimately arises out of a desire to *ground* it in perception, sensation and the body, all of which, while eagerly praised by practitioners, are frequently ignored in these same practitioner's neo-mystical articulations.

At the same time, I am fully cognizant that the problem inherent in adopting a phenomenological approach to ecstasy is its dependence on first-person accounts, which are ultimately linguistic artifices incapable of grasping what they are attempting to describe – ecstasy being antithetical, after all, to language. As I mentioned earlier, though, first-person accounts are all we have to work with. This epistemological gap, accordingly, must be acknowledged as not only inevitable but also central to the ecstatic 'experience'.

Finally, my situating of ecstasy within the ontology of the flesh must be recognized as only an introductory manoeuvre. In truth, much more can and should be said about this approach, including a further investigation of ecstasy's relationship to the 'sensory overload' of the rave-assemblage, as well as an exploration of emotion that might draw on, for example, the work of Susan Cataldi (1993). Similarly, I only briefly employed dance within this chapter, itself a topic that would benefit greatly from Merleau-Ponty's conceptions of flesh since dance is already understood by some as a means of non-dualistically restructuring subjectivity. Further investigations into the 'flesh of raving' might also explore gender, dis/ability and temporality, all of which could greatly benefit from being 'fleshed out'.

Notes

1   While many people have contributed to the development of this work and its ideas, I would like to especially acknowledge the academic guidance of Mary Klages and Sam Crill, as well as the intellectual and moral support of Devery Holt, Caryn Margolis, Dave Dolezal and Hope Albrecht.

2   For the purposes of this chapter, I am using the term 'rave' to describe a wide array of psychedelic and ecstatic dance events that more properly might be described as 'post-rave' gatherings. I have chosen to retain this terminology, despite being slightly 'out of date', in order to accommodate the term 'raving', which I feel still possesses a distinct and communicable meaning. 'The ecstasy of raving', as a phrase, can therefore be translated as 'the ecstasy of clubbing' etc. The reader may insert whatever terminology they like, as long as it is recognized that I am referring to the ecstatic state engendered by all-night dancing to the beat of predominately electronically engineered music.

3   See 'Christianity and Raving', available online at:
www.hyperreal.org/raves/spirit/culture/Xtianity—And—Raving.html
(accessed 1 November 2002).

4   Gore notes that 'it is not...the fact of taking Ecstasy which ensures the happy outcome in raving. Rather it is the *repetition* of the same formula on each occasion, the *ritualisation*' (1997: 53).

5   Which is not to deny wholesale the possibility of ecstatic raving being a mystical event, an eruption of the divine into the mundane; it is only to adopt a sceptical approach that recognizes that such claims are difficult to corroborate or legitimize.
6   For further information, see Grosz (1999) for her study of Freud and his notion of the body ego, as well as Schilder, whose work on the corporeal schema was foundational for Merleau-Ponty.

Bibliography

Alissa (1995) 'What do we get out of raves?', March, available online at www.hyperreal.org/raves/spirit/testimonials/What—We—Get—From—Raves.html (accessed 1 November 2002).

Anonymous (n.d.) 'Goa trance and mystical traditions', available online at www.hyperreal.org/raves/spirit/technoshamanism/Goa—Trance.html (accessed 1 November 2002).

Casey, S. (1993) 'Techno and raving', July, available online at : www.hyperreal.org/raves/spirit/technoshamanism/Techno—and—Raving.html (accessed 1 November 2002).

Cataldi, S. (1993) *Emotion, Depth, and Flesh, a Study of Sensitive Space: Reflections on Merleau-Ponty's Philosophy of Embodiment*, Albany, NY: SUNY Press.

Catherine (1998) 'Rave as meditation', available online at: www.csp.org/nicholas/A63.html (accessed 1 November 2002).

Collin, M. (1997) *Altered State: The Story of Ecstasy Culture and Acid House*, Britain: Serpent's Tail.

Csikszentmihalyi, M. (1990) *Flow: The Psychology of Optimal Experience*, New York: Harper-Perenniel.

Dillon, M.C. (1997) *Merleau-Ponty's Ontology*, 2nd edition, Evanston, IL: Northwestern University Press.

Eisenberg, R. (1997) 'It's all the rave. Interview with Douglas Rushkoff', *SF Examiner*, 22 June 22.

Fatone, G. (2000) 'We thank the technology goddess for giving us the ability to rave: gamelan, techno-primitivism, and the San Francisco rave scene', available online at www.humnet.ucla.edu/echo/volume3-issue1/table-of-contents/table-of-contents.html (accessed 1 November 2002).

Fielding, H. (1999) 'Envisioning the other: Lacan and Merleau-Ponty on intersubjectivity', in Dorothea Olkowski and James Morley (eds) *Merleau-Ponty, Interiority and Exteriority, Psychic Life and the World*, Albany, NY: SUNY Press.

Fogel, L. (1994) 'Christianity and raving', March, available online at: www.hyperreal.org/raves/spirit/culture/Xtianity—And—Raving.html (accessed 1 November 2002).

Gore, G. (1997) 'The beat goes on: trance, dance and tribalism in rave culture', in Helen Thomas (ed.) *Dance in the City*, New York: St Martin's Press.

Gris, S. (2000) 'Is electronic music and dance culture spiritual?', available online at www.sflnc.org/index/readthis/news/food—for—thought/6.html (accessed 1 November 2002).

Grosz, E. (1994) *Volatile Bodies: Toward a Corporeal Feminism*, Indianapolis: Indiana University Press.

—— (1999) 'Merleau-Ponty and Irigaray in the flesh', in Dorothea Olkowski and James Morley (eds) *Merleau-Ponty, Interiority and Exteriority, Psychic Life and the World*, Albany, NY: SUNY Press.

Herzogenrath. B. (2000) 'Stop making sense: fuck 'em and their law (it's only I and O but I like it', available online at www.iath.virginia.edu/pmc/text-only/issue.100/10.2 herzogenrath.txt (accessed 1 November 2002).

Jordan, T. (1995) 'Collective bodies: raving and the politics of Gilles Deleuze and Felix Guattari', *Body and Society* 1(1): 125–44.

Lacan, J. (1977) 'The mirror stage as formative of the function of the I as revealed in psychoanalytic experience', *Ecrits*, Alan Sheridan (trans.), New York: Norton.

McPhee, M. (2000) ' "Hug drug" intoxicating Denverites', *Denver Post*, 27 February.

McRobbie, A. (1997) 'The E's and the anti-E's: new questions for feminism and cultural studies', in M. Fergusson and P. Golding (eds) *Cultural Studies*, London: Sage.

Malbon, B. (1999) *Clubbing: Dancing, Ecstasy and Vitality*, New York: Routledge.

Melechi, A. (1993) 'The ecstasy of disappearance', in Steve Redhead (ed.) *Rave Off: Politics and Deviance in Contemporary Youth Culture*, Aldershot: Avebury.

Merleau-Ponty, M. (1964) *The Primacy of Perception*, ed. James Edie, Evanston, IL: Northwestern University Press.

—— (1968) *The Visible and the Invisible*, ed. Claude Lefort, Alphonso Lingis (trans.), Evanston, IL: Northwestern University Press.

—— (1981) *Phenomenology of Merleau-Ponty*, Athens: Ohio University Press.

Parsons, J. (1996) 'The vibe tribe', May, available online at:
www.hyperreal.org/raves/spirit/vision/The—Vibe—Tribe.html
(accessed 1 November 2002).

Perring, R. (1997) 'Moontribe voodoo', available online at:
www.csp.org/nicholas/A28.html (accessed 1 November 2002).

Pini, M. (1997) 'Cyborgs, nomads and the raving feminine', in Helen Thomas (ed.) *Dance and the City*, New York: St Martin's Press.

—— (2001) *Club Cultures and Female Subjectivity*, New York: Palgrave.

Reynolds, S. (1999) *Generation Ecstasy: Into the World of Techno and Rave Culture*, New York: Routledge.

Rietveld, H. (1993) 'Living the dream', in Steve Redhead (ed.) *Rave Off: Politics and Deviance in Contemporary Youth Culture*, Aldershot: Avebury.

Stiens, E. (1997) *On Peace, Love, Dancing and Drugs: A Sociological Analysis of Rave Culture*, available online at:
www.phantasmagoria.f2s.com/writings/raveindex.html (accessed 1 November 2002).

Tanya (1994) 'Christianity and raving', available online at:
www.hyperreal.org/raves/spirit/culture/Xtianity—And—Raving.html
(accessed 1 November 2002).

Tramacchi, D. (2001) 'Chaos engines: doofs, psychedelics and religious experience', in G. St John (ed.) *FreeNRG: Notes from the Edge of the Dance Floor*, Altona: Common Ground.

Turner, V. (1969) *The Ritual Process*, Chicago: Aldine.

Twist, Cinnamon (1992) 'The imaginal rave', July, available online at:
www.hyperreal.org/raves/spirit/vision/Imaginal—Rave.html (accessed 1 November 2002).

Weiss, G. (1999) 'Body image discourse: a corporeal dialogue between Merleau-Ponty and Schilder', in Dorothea Olkowski and James Morley (eds) *Merleau-Ponty, Interiority and Exteriority, Psychic Life and the World*, Albany, NY: SUNY Press.

6 Entheogenic dance ecstasis: cross-cultural contexts[1]

Des Tramacchi

Participation in psychedelic dance parties can produce experiences with apparent similarities to those accessed in various ecstatic and shamanic religious traditions, especially those that utilize *entheogens*.[2] This chapter discusses some of the structural nuclei of group-oriented entheogenic rituals, and explores broad parallels that exist between community-focused entheogenic dance rituals in three separate cultures. These shared structural elements are also core features of the nocturnal terpsichorean excursions of the outdoor psychedelic dance cultures that flourish in northern New South Wales and Southeast Queensland, Australia. It is my hope that this brief cross-cultural tour of the use of entheogens in conjunction with collective dance is broad enough in scope but nonetheless rich enough in detail to provide useful perspectives on the function and meaning of the Western psychedelic dance rituals known as 'bush-parties' or *doofs*.[3]

Entheogenic rituals

The ceremonial use of entheogens as catalysts for achieving states of communal ecstasis has a wide geographical spread. A broad survey of the world's entheogenic practices reveals that the majority of the more frequently used entheogenic sacraments contain substances that are pharmacological equivalents of the Western category of 'psychedelics' (Ott 1996; Schultes and Hofmann 1980). Entheogens are used in a number of different ritual contexts, including healing, divination, ensorcelment, *rites de passage*, and rituals of public celebration and social affirmation. It is these socially affirming, collective rituals, as reconstructed from ethnography, that are the focus of this chapter.

The principal ethnographic sources to be analysed are Stacy B. Schaefer's description of the ritual uses and meanings of peyote among the Mexican Huichol, focusing on the annual 'peyote pilgrimage' (Schaefer 1996), supplemented with the observations of Barbara Myerhoff's (1974) description of the Huichol pilgrimage; G. Reichel-Dolmatoff's account of *yajé* (*ayahuasca*) sessions among the Barasana of Colombia (Reichel-Dolmatoff 1975); and James W. Fernandez's monograph on the ritual use of *eboka* by members of the Bwiti cult among the Fang and Metsogo of Gabon, West Africa (Fernandez 1982). In selecting examples of rituals, I have been influenced by two factors. First, size restrictions prohibit an exhaustive treatment. Second, because I wish to present the rituals in some detail, I have chosen accounts that are representative and thorough. Together, the accounts range across three continents and three very different societies, and they are representative of the wide range of cultural approaches to the sacred generally and to entheogens in particular. Also, to simplify the analysis I have chosen accounts where the entheogen is ingested by the same route – orally – rather than as an ointment, enema, snuff, smoke, vapour or injection. I have selected just three examples of rituals, which I believe are exemplars of community-oriented entheogenic ritual as a class.

Peyote and Huichol community

The *Wixárika* or Huichol are an indigenous Mexican people, who live in several independent, self-governing districts or *comunidades indígenas* with economies based on sedentary slash-and-burn agriculture supplemented by gathering and hunting (Schaefer and Furst 1996). The animistic or panentheistic Huichol religious worldview maintains that all things in the environment are sensate and animate. The Huichol pantheon bustles with beings generically referred to by the obscure term '*Kakauyaríte*' – conceptualized as personae or faculties of nature, and addressed in kinship terms – who are revered and invoked for aid (*ibid.*).

In Huichol religion ecstatic states are greatly valued; consequently, peyote is greatly esteemed. The Huichol ingest the visionary *hikuri* or peyote cactus (*Lophophora williamsii*) as a religious sacrament and as a 'unifying force in ideology and society' (Schaefer 1996: 140–1) . Peyote contains upwards of 57 alkaloids, alkaloidal amines and amino acids (Anderson 1996). The most psychoactive of these substances is the alkaloid mescaline (*ibid.*), one of the classic psychedelics (Peyton and Shulgin 1994). The Huichol employ *hikuri* in a wide range of religious and ethnomedicinal contexts. Two of the major public rituals involving the ingestion of peyote are the peyote pilgrimage and the *Hikuri Neixa*, or 'Peyote dance'. Here I will focus primarily on the rituals associated with the pilgrimage. Every year a group of Huichol undertakes the lengthy pilgrimage to Wirikúta, a high desert where peyote grows abundantly (Lamaistre 1996). The Huichol peyote pilgrimage is interpreted by the pilgrims or *hikuritámete* as a spiritual return to the mythic *fons et origo* (Myerhoff 1974). In the preparatory phases of the pilgrimage, participants – beautifully clothed in the highly ornate and colourful traditional dress so pleasing to their deities (Valadez and Valadez 1992) – express their solidarity and openness to one another through the public confession of sexual misconduct, after which

> the shaman ties knots in a special string, with each knot representing a pilgrim and the uniting of the souls of all participants. They are thus …symbolically tied together for the entire pilgrimage, as well as afterwards, up to and including the completion of Hikuri Neixa, months later, when in one of the concluding rituals the knots are untied.
>
> (Schaefer 1996: 163)

Group solidarity is paramount. As one Huichol shaman put it: 'all must be of one heart, there must be complete unity among us' (Myerhoff 1974: 135). The journey to Wirikúta is lengthy – about 200 miles – and the pilgrims consume very little food (Schultes and Hofmann 1992). Barbara Myerhoff (1974) argues that confession, fasting and making pilgrimage are all techniques for reducing, concealing or escaping functions associated with mortality, and that this assists the pilgrims to gradually shed their human identities. On arrival in Wirikúta the travellers ritually wash and pray. The shaman or *mara'akáme* who leads the expedition begins to sing as part of a ritual in which the pilgrims, now fully identified with divinities, make the transition back into the origin-world through a magical portal (*ibid.*).[4] For people on their first pilgrimage there is a complex rite of passage, replete with ritual blindfolding and the reciting of stories associated with Wirikúta and peyote.

Eventually peyote – which is closely associated mythologically with both deer and maize – is found. The *mara'akáme* shoots an arrow into the first 'deer' (Schaefer 1996). The Huichol present offerings to this first peyote. Later, large baskets of peyote are gathered, some to be consumed in Wirikúta, others to be stored or traded. Preparation and ingestion of peyote occur in a strictly ceremonial context. The Huichol gather on the crest of a hill in Wirikúta:

> Everyone sat on the rocks crowning the summit, positioning themselves so as to face east.... The shaman purified everyone with his feather wand and sacred water and touched the peyote to their cheeks, throat and wrists. The white tufts on the peyote were removed and placed as offerings. Then the peyotéros peeled the tough skin at the base of the cactus and consumed small amounts of the first peyote of the pilgrimage.
>
> (Schaefer 1996: 149)

The Huichol pilgrims next return to their encampment:

> the sacred fire was kindled and that night the shaman, with the help of his assistants, sang. Throughout the night all the pilgrims circled the area five times. Five is the sacred number for the Huichols and all the members consumed peyote five times during the night. At the first rays of dawn, they painted designs on the faces of their ritual companions, *compañeros* in Spanish, with the ground-up yellow root of a desert shrub known as *uxa*.... They also exchanged peyote they had selected especially, each giving some to all the others and receiving some in turn from everyone else.
>
> (Schaefer 1996: 149–50)

The two most important ceremonial roles in the Huichol peyote pilgrimage are those of the *Saulizika* (the primary mara'akáme), who presides over ceremony, and the *Nauxa*, or 'Keeper of the Peyote' (*ibid.*). The person acting in the ceremonial capacity *Nauxa* is charged with the responsibility of ensuring that other participants are able to travel along the 'road' of the *Saulizika*'s song. The

Nauxa blesses the peyote with a plumed wand, or *muviéri*, and then distributes the peyote to the pilgrims seated about the fire:

> Everyone eats his or her peyote and the mara'akáme begins the chanting that will continue through the entire night. While the mara'akáme carries the souls of the pilgrims along the journey of his song, Nauxa makes certain that the pilgrims are in the physical and mental states that facilitate their out-of-body travel along this path. Five times during the night, when the pilgrims circle the fire after a cycle is completed in the mara'akáme's song, Nauxa places the same amount of peyote as originally consumed in front of each pilgrim.
>
> (Schaefer 1996: 152)

During the course of the night the peyote visions unfold. Initially these visions tend to consist of brilliantly coloured fast-moving geometric forms (*ibid.*). After a few hours the visions start to take the forms of more complex scenarios (*ibid.*; Valadez and Valadez 1992):

> Upon completing this ritual, and having spent the night consuming peyote at regular intervals, the pilgrims had reached the state in which they were journeying inwards, caught up in their own visions, their own communications with the divine Huichol entities.
>
> (Schaefer 1996: 149–50)

Peyote visions are a culmination of a long process of de-differentiating the profane, flawed, time-conditioned self from the sacred, perfect, timeless Huichol divinities (Myerhoff 1974). The process of coming home to Wirikúta and dwelling there for a short time is a temporary repossession of 'innocence, godhood, and prehuman bliss' (*ibid.*: 244). The visions are engrossing and intensely personal, there is little verbal communication during the visions and attention is largely directed inwards (*ibid.*). Nonetheless, this is also a deeply shared undertaking:

> In Wirikuta, the *hikuritámete* are in a state of intense communion with each other, where the social self is shed and men stand beside each other as totalities, in spontaneous, joyous vulnerability, without the protection or requirements of social structure. This state of fusion of the individual with the group is antithetical to everyday life. Indeed, it is anathema to the allocation of roles and resources, the division of labor, the organizational, restrained, rational considerations which are the inevitable accompaniments of providing the daily dole of bread. This concern cannot be suspended for long.
>
> (Myerhoff 1974: 246)

Indeed, Victor Turner (1974) suggests that the climax of the Huichol pilgrimage is a kind of cosmic anti-structure and communitas:

In Wirikúta, according to Huichol mythology, divisions dissolve between sexes and ages, leaders and led, men and animals, plants and animals, men and demigods...three complexes of symbols, deer, maize, and peyote, become functionally interdependent, and, for the Huichols, even seem to fuse, at Wirikuta. The deer designates the Huichols' past as nomadic hunters, the maize their present as sedentary cultivators, and the peyote the incommunicable 'idioverse' of each individual.

(Turner 1974: 9)

The pilgrims' sojourn in *Wirikúta* is exceedingly brief. Having joyously 'come home' as divinities and having collected sufficient peyote for their community's annual needs, the *hikuritámete* are ready to return to their previous mortal, structural condition. For while the experience of Wirikúta is the compass of Huichol spiritual life, it is also replete with the spiritual dangers associated with the *mysterium tremendum*:

The special task of the Huichol mara'akame is to guide his people out of Wirikúta quickly and firmly, disregarding their desire to linger. His guardianship in escorting them back to reality, in persuading them to relinquish the longing for Paradise, is as important as leading them there in the first place.

(Myerhoff 1974: 248)

Yajé *and Barasana community*

The Barasana are one of several small Tukanoan subgroups who live in a section of the Vaupés[5] drained by the Pirá-paraná river (Hugh-Jones 1979). Their economy is based on subsistence agriculture supplemented by gathering, hunting and fishing (*ibid.*). Barasana live in large communal malocas or longhouses situated near running water and spaced in such a way that it often takes an hour or more to travel between them. The larger of these houses also function as ceremonial centres or *basaria wi* (dance-houses) (*ibid.*; Reichel-Dolmatoff 1975). The Barasana hold many communal ceremonies and dances. Barasana ethnographer Stephen Hugh-Jones reports that the relatively prestigious house in which he worked for 20 months held 12 communal rituals during that time, including seven 'Fruit House' rituals (in which fruit is ceremonially brought into the house to the accompaniment of the sound of *He* instruments), one '*He* House' ritual (the major initiatory rite), three social dances, and one ritual exchange of food (Hugh-Jones 1979). The Barasana frequently make use of the vision-inducing potion *yajé* in their ceremonies.[6] The entheogenic properties of *yajé* are the result of a unique and sophisticated pharmacological synergy (Ott 1996). The basic ingredient is nearly always the stems of the vine *Banisteriopsis caapi*. Depending on the region, leaves of other plants, especially *oco-yagé* (*Diplopterys cabrerana*) and *chacruna* (*Psychotria viridis*), are added to intensify the enchanting properties of the drink (Schultes and Raffauf 1992). These latter plants are rich in the N,N-dimethyltryptamine or DMT –

another of the archetypal psychedelics (Peyton and Shulgin 1994). Substances (beta-carbolines) found in *Banisteriopsis caapi* have distinct psychoactive properties, but also facilitate the more spectacular visionary action of DMT (McKenna and Towers 1984).

Reichel-Dolmatoff (1975) provides an outstanding ethnographic description of his attendance at a social dance and *yajé* session among the Barasana Indians of the Pirá-paraná.[7] Unlike the Huichol peyote pilgrimage, the *yajé* session described by Reichel-Dolmatoff was not part of a predetermined ritual cycle, but rather something that came together in a more spontaneous and informal way, requiring only a few days notice to prepare and send invitations to neighbouring communities. The session itself, however, unfolded in a highly formalized way:

> It was becoming dark now and we entered the maloca. Just inside the door the men had arranged two rows of little wooden stools, and now they began to open the large boxes containing the feathercrowns, the rattles, and the painted loincloths. Bëhpó, the oldest of the men present and the headman of the visiting party, opened a box lying before him on the floor, lifted up a large feather headdress with both hands, and put it slowly on his head. It was 6:20 P.M. He now took another feathercrown and handed it to his neighbor; then another and another. More boxes were brought, and all the men adorned themselves.... It was about an hour before all the men were properly dressed.
>
> (Reichel-Dolmatoff 1975: 159–60)

After the men had adorned themselves, they sat in a semicircular formation facing the interior of the maloca:

> There were twelve men, who were now talking and laughing. It was dark now and one of them lit the *turí*, the large resin-covered torch standing near the center of the room, and it began to shed intense red light over the scene.
>
> (Reichel-Dolmatoff 1975: 160)

The men next tied rattles made from strings of tinkling seeds around their ankles. Bëhpó shook his stick-rattle in a highly stylized series of gestures. There was a general playing of flutes, whistles, and turtle-shell instruments. *Cashirí*, a kind of beer, was ritually served. Bëhpó then lifted an ornate ceramic horn which produced a long-drawn sound like a foghorn. The men now rose for the dance:

> The deafening sound of the rattles filled the room as the men took up their positions once more, facing the interior of the house, stamping the floor – once, twice, three times – 'Hö!' they exclaimed. 'Hö-hö!' Then they advanced and turned, singing and marking their steps with the hollow thud of the stamping tubes. The line advanced into the open space of the center. Turning around in a circle, each man with one hand on the shoulder of the one before him, they appeared again in the light, dancing slowly, round after round. The

voices rose and fell, the thumping approached and receded, over and over, from light to darkness and back again into the red glow of the torch.

(Reichel-Dolmatoff 1975: 163)

Shortly after 8 o'clock the painted ceramic vessel used to prepare and hold *yajé* was brought out and stirred with a rattling sound. The men returned to their seats. The *yajé* was distributed in small gourd cups and imbibed with much grimacing and spitting. *Cashirí* beer was again served. Having drunk the *yajé* the participants became more relaxed and boisterous. The women now joined the men in a slow solemn dance. At about 9.30 the men took another round of *yajé*. By 10 o'clock most of the men were having visions, talking to one another about them in drowsy voices. As the men began to enter deeply into the *yajé* trance their dancing became more animated and they became more synchronous in their movements:

> The general rhythm of the dance had become more and more coordinated as time went on. After the men had drunk three or four cups of yajé the steps, turns, and gestures had reached a precision that made the group appear to be one single organism moving in a highly controlled and precise way. The same was true for the songs; there was never a false note or an eccentric movement; song and dance had become completely fused. Moreover, the entire scene was far from being a frenetic orgy; it was extremely formalised and solemn.

(Reichel-Dolmatoff 1975: 163)

Some of the men exchanged entheogenic *vihó* snuff. Participants avoided 'facing others and looking into their eyes' (Reichel-Dolmatoff 1975: 163). The quality of sociality oscillated mostly between private introspection and impersonal interaction as undifferentiated members of a group. The cycles of dancing and resting continued throughout the night and *yajé* was taken at regular intervals:

> At 2:10 A.M. the men took another round of yajé, and at 3:20 the eighth and last one. They were dancing now in almost complete darkness. Then they rested, and occasionally there were long monotonous recitals. The music never stopped completely, and the croaking noise of the turtle shell continued hour after hour. Dawn was coming. Bëhpó slowly took the feathercrown from his head and handed it to Muhipu, saying 'má' take! in a loud voice. The other men followed his example. It was exactly 6:20 A.M.; the ceremony had lasted twelve hours to the minute. Muhipu handed the different ornaments to Biá, who carefully packed them away in their boxes. The men left the maloca and gathered in the chilly air in front of the house, yawning and stretching their limbs. There was but little conversation. The men look tired but content. After a while some of them put up their hammocks and went to sleep.

(Reichel-Dolmatoff 1975: 167)

The Barasana *yajé* ritual described by Reichel-Dolmatoff has a number of similarities to Huichol peyote ritualism. Ritual adornment, a ceremonial fire, chanting, music, dancing through the long night, and the synchrony and coordination of participants are elements common to both ceremonies. These elements also occur in the following account from tropical West Africa.

Eboka *and Bwiti community*

Bwiti is a new religious movement found among the Fang and Metsogo peoples of Gabon in equatorial West Africa. This ecstatic, syncretic cult, influenced by the Bieri ancestral cult and Christian evangelism, has been characterized as a reformative movement and as a dynamic form of resistance and response to colonialism (Fernandez 1982). The polymorphous Bwiti religion is spread throughout Fang territory, but chapels are relatively autonomous, and there is little organization beyond that found at the level of individual villages (Fernandez 1972). The religion deals with the maintenance of satisfactory relationships with the dead, and also seeks to make available to its members experiential knowledge of the transition from the realm of the living to that of the dead. This experiential knowledge is arrived at primarily through the initiation rite in which the novice becomes a Banzie,[8] or member. Bwiti incorporates a number of psychoactive plants, the most esteemed of which is *eboka* (prepared from the roots of the shrub *Tabernanthe iboga*). *Eboka*, or *eboga*, contains many alkaloids, including an unusual psychedelic drug, ibogaine (Pope 1969). *Eboka* is used in two distinct ways. First, the powdered roots are taken in enormous, visionary doses to symbolically 'break open the head' in order for one to become experientially aware of the presence of the Ancestors during intensive, once-in-a-lifetime initiation rites. Subsequently, smaller quantities of *eboka* are taken by Banzie as ceremonial stimulants during periodic all-night rituals, accompanied by song, dance, and 'the insistent rhythms of the cult harp (*ngombi*) and the soft beat of the bamboo staves (*obaka*)' (Fernandez 1972: 240).

> The lighter regular dosage of two to five teaspoons does not produce hallucinations, though adepts of Bwiti claim that once a man has 'met eboga' and been taken by 'him' to the 'other side', any subsequent amount will raise in his mind many of his former experiences. The regular dosage...is taken primarily to enable the adepts to engage in the arduous all-night ceremonies without fatigue. Members often say that eboga taken in this way also lightens their bodies so that they can float through their ritual dances. It enables them to mingle more effectively with the ancestors at the roof of the chapel. They do not report visions under the influence of such amounts, only modest change in body perception and some dissociation.
>
> (Fernandez 1982: 475)

Fernandez provides an account of a Metsogo Bwiti *engosie* – an all-night celebration 'along the path of birth and death' – which was preceded in the mid-afternoon by a preliminary shared meal. *Eboga* was also eaten in the afternoon, a séance was performed, and a spirit curse was 'lifted' from an afflicted man through an elaborate ritual. The Bwiti *engosie* proper commenced around 9 o'clock in the evening, with a series of long shuffling entrance dances that commenced out in the forest and were designed to attract lingering spirits into the chapel. These were followed by songs arranged according to cosmological themes and dances 'of superb quality and highly coordinated' (*ibid.*: 437).

The choreographic highlights of the evening were the 'amazements' or *akyunge*. *Akyunge*, sometimes translated as 'miracles', refer to things done with 'such surpassing skill and subtlety as to amaze and be beyond ordinary understanding and imitation' (*ibid.*: 436).[9] The *akyunge* consisted of highly competent performances of illusions, for example the appearance of levitating torches and even the 'miraculous' appearance of the local French District Administrator (skilfully impersonated by Bwiti members). These dramatic performances are designed to 'confound the ordinary categories of experience.... Things are confused, lose their categories – Metsogo "miracles" make things "amazingly ambiguous"' (*ibid.*: 468). Soon after midnight, the energies of the *engosie* are channelled into an experience of satisfaction and communitas. After a brief circumambulation of the surrounding forests,

> the membership, following the *nima na kombo*,[10] enter the chapel and, just before the central pillar, begin to weave a tighter and tighter circle until they are compressed, virtually, into one being around the *nima na kombo*. Raising their candles above their heads (ideally they should be able to make one flame out of all candles) they intone *bi antô nlem mvôre* (now we become one heart).
>
> (Fernandez 1982: 454)

One-heartedness is usually followed by a short, highly figurative sermon. The following five hours are dedicated to the recital of songs drawn from 'the Path of the Harp' – a collection of 115 songs relating cosmological events, commencing with creation *ex nihilo*. Banzie one-heartedness is again enacted at first light:

> this time it does not occur within the chapel but rather before the ancestors' welcoming hut (*ôtunga*). And the members, instead of raising the candles in their right hands raise and bring together the yarn umbilical cords in their left hands.... They are reaffirming the 'umbilical linkage' that binds them to the departing ancestors. 'Oneheartedness' may otherwise be celebrated by men and women in separate groups in the midst of nearby streams. But midnight and first light are the two occasions for this celebration in the process of the engosie. It is a climactic celebration in the engosie.
>
> (Fernandez 1982: 454)

As the process of the *engosie* moves towards its conclusion it becomes apparent that the membership has achieved an accentuation of aesthetic sensitivity, a renewed appreciation of life and the satisfaction of communitas:

What seemed to me the most beautiful music is performed in the early morning hours, after the spirits of men and ancestors have mingled in the cult chapel and after the membership has achieved a state of 'one-heartedness' – *nlem mvore*. . . . Dawn is faintly evident over the equatorial forest wall to the east. The first cock has crowed. All cult activities must be concluded before the sun rises, for Bwiti is a night cult, a cult of the female principle of the universe, Nyingwan Mebege, the Sister of God, who is the moon. There is deep satisfaction in the membership born of the fact that they have danced all night, achieved 'one-heartedness', and can look forward to the fellowship of the communal meal, which comes immediately after the cultic activities. It is an afterglow brought to them by *eboka* as well, for the drug is not usually associated with undesirable aftereffects.

(Fernandez 1972: 240–1)

Ceremonial constants

The entheogenic rituals discussed above share a number of structural elements. These can be organized under the rubrics preparation, ritual space and time, music and dance, pharmacological aspects and social relations. In this section I will discuss the similarities in each of these areas, as well as discussing how these same elements are also intrinsic to the dance-ecstasy of Western psychedelic parties. Such a 'side-by-side' comparison will accentuate the continuities between these rituals.[11]

Preparation

All three rituals involve preliminary ritual modifications of the self. Fasting, special diets, sexual abstinence or libido-regulating practices, prayer, confession and the fulfilment of ritual or social obligations may be required for the participants to attain a ritually 'pure' condition. Such preparations are a common feature of ritual contact with the sacred and are not peculiar to entheogenic ritualism, although they may take on new physiological and psychological significance within the entheogenic context. Fasting can impact on the extent and rate of absorption of psychoactive substances, and minimize potentially unpleasant food/drug interactions. The physical strain induced by hunger may also lower the psychological threshold for visions, as might sexual abstinence. The practice of fasting prior to 'tripping' or 'e-ing' appears to be widespread among psychedelic drug users, and is based on sound pharmacological principles: drugs are absorbed more efficiently by the body when the stomach is empty and the possibility of nausea is reduced. Besides pharmacological considerations, fasting is also in and of itself a powerful technique for altering consciousness – serving to radically disrupt both cultural and physiological habits.

The transformation of appearance through elaborate and beautiful ceremonial costume or cosmetic modifications also occurs in all three rituals. Practices such as beautification, fulfilling or releasing obligations, confession and prayer exert a strong influence on 'set' – the mood and expectation factors that can impact on an individual's experience of entheogenic ritual. Many dance-party participants pay a great deal of attention to their appearance, and some don highly elaborate and beautiful costumes. Examples that I have observed at doofs include a Halloween witch costume; a rainbow-coloured, plumed headdress and a long white robe; Chaplinesque garb; bizarre, electronic, bleeping glove puppets; leonine prosthetic tails; and other childlike, colourful and interesting costumes composed of furry, shiny, luminescent or metallic-looking materials. For those who make use of psychoactive substances at dance parties, ritual preparations may commence some time before the actual dance party with a pilgrimage to procure taboo sacraments such as LSD or MDMA through informal and esoteric systems of exchange.

Ritual space and time

Ritual space is established in all three rituals. In the case of the Huichol, all of Wirikúta is sacred space, the point of cosmic origin. The campfire provides a further sacred centre within this space, while the orbits of circling candles outline a sacred perimeter (Schaefer 1996). The Barasana ritual takes place in any of several large malocas. These communal houses are also modelled on the form of the sacred cosmos (Hugh-Jones 1979; Reichel-Dolmatoff 1971, 1975). The space is prepared for ritual by clearing the central area for dancing and by lighting special resin torches which emit intense red light (Reichel-Dolmatoff 1975; Schultes and Raffauf 1992). The Bwiti rituals take place in and around chapels replete with esoteric meanings. The centre of the chapel is a pillar which serves as *axis mundi*, conceptualized as linking the living and the dead, above and below, in an enduring relationship (Fernandez 1982). The chapel also has a female and a male side, the setting up of polarities being an important preliminary to their synthesis – the Bwiti 'one-heartedness'. The Bwiti chapel also represents an androgynous cruciform human figure (*ibid.*).

A further similarity between these rituals is their overnight duration and nocturnal setting. While the Huichol pilgrimage is lengthy, the actual time spent in the intense, visionary world of Wirikúta is relatively brief. The climax of the pilgrimage is a night-long ritual of music, circumambulation and meditation. The Barasana *yajé* session lasts a single night, as does the Metsogo Bwiti ritual described by Fernandez. There is perhaps an endeavour here to preserve the integrity of routine patterns by temporally locating the majority of the ritual in the depths of night, beyond the regular realm of waking consciousness. In each instance the rituals transport the participants through the undifferentiated amorphousness of night to emerge eventually into the pristine splendour of a new day. Here, the cosmic order of day and night are given human meaning through ritual. The emphasis on ritual expression through space at doofs is quite distinctive and pervasive. Doof organizers aim to imbue the events with an atmosphere of sacrality and may perform ceremonial and magickal activities to consecrate their selected site. The remote places in which these outdoor psychedelic parties are held become transformed into vast countercultural cathedrals, in which various icons are arranged to create a sacred landscape in which humans are 'naturalized' and 'nature' is humanized.[12] There is a precision also to the temporal trajectory of dance parties. The rituals generally last for the duration of one full night, and occasionally a few consecutive nights. DJs play different kinds of music at different stages of the night and these stages may well correspond to different phases and moods associated with the process of 'tripping'.

Music and dance

Another common feature of these rituals is their employment of music – especially sustained percussive sound and sonorous chanting. The Huichol *mara'akáme* is a 'singing shaman' whose chanting transports souls along a 'journey'. The Huichol pilgrims circle the ceremonial fire in precisely determined patterns to the accompaniment of the *mara'akáme*'s song. The voices of Barasana participants in a *yajé* ceremony rise and fall to the croaking of a turtle-shell instrument and to the thumping of dancing feet and stamping tubes, song and dance becoming 'fused'. The Barasana dance becomes precise and highly coordinated. Similarly, the Bwiti ceremonial dances are 'of superb quality and highly coordinated' (Fernandez 1982: 437). Over many hours the music of the various Bwiti instruments reaches a plateau of aesthetic sensitivity which echoes the attainment of deep solidarity and psychic interrelatedness.

A great many styles of electronic dance music are associated with psychedelic parties, including techno, trance, hard house, jungle, trip-hop, electro-funk, speed bass and ambient. High volume is an essential element in all these musical genres. Loudspeakers are a source of such esoteric qualities as 'vibes', 'power' and 'ambience'; they are not simply the utilitarian medium of transmission, but an intrinsic instrument for sound production (Bull 1997). Ideally, the DJs direct the collective trance with insight and dexterity, pleasuring listeners by stretching out and sustaining enjoyable sonic moments, drawing from a well-honed palette of pleasurable frequencies, tones and rhythms, but also moving the listener into more challenging and rewarding sound environments. Because DJs select and present as well as create music, they have been described as 'curators' of 'galleries of sound' (Rietveld 1993). DJs also function as guides to an unfamiliar and powerfully charged synaesthetic realm and in this sense have been described as 'electronic shamans' (Bull 1997).

Psychedelic dance music is imbued with certain para-religious qualities. The soundscapes of psychedelic dance music are frequently juxtaposed with surreal mantra-like 'samples' that reinforce decategorization and anti-structure. Sometimes a 'techno anthem' may contain explicit instances of prayer, as for example the track 'Halleluja' (Sash! 2000), which incorporates ecstatic gospel music sounds and themes including exuberant choruses of 'Hallelujah, Lord!' and 'I wanna thank you!' The content of the prayers in 'Halleluja' is, however, strongly oriented towards ebullient MDMA and dance-associated forms of consciousness, and thanks are given (perhaps ironically) for such seldom appreciated facets of life as mobile phones, shopping malls, perfect skin, faster food, pay TV, remote control, 'quality time', the Internet and global warming. The musical effluvium of gratitude continues:[13]

> Thankyou, for plastic surgery, thankyou, for safer sex.
> Thankyou for the World Cup finals, thankyou, for radar control.
> And thankyou for a brilliant future, in a peaceful world.
>
> (Sash! 2000)

Quite apart from the frequently religious or quasi-religious ideation of psychedelic dance music, the very form and structure of the music promote and support trance states. The repetitive, hypnotic, rapid beat of techno (generally 110–30 beats per minute) may induce a classic auditory driving scenario (Neher 1962). Percussion and tintinnabulation are frequently used to accent ritual 'transformations', possibly because these sonic bursts 'overload' the autonomic nervous system via the limbic system (which controls the hypothalamus), resulting in an inhibition of 'rational thought' and an increase in suggestibility (Needham 1967). Percussive sounds may also augment synaesthesia and the depersonalizing effects of entheogens (Johnston 1977), effects that may be further compounded by 'photic' driving from the kaleidoscopic lighting and animations present at many parties. It has been speculated that repetitious stimuli can induce a 'collective tuning-in' relationship among participants in ritual:

> the various ecstasy states, which can be produced…after exposure to rhythmic auditory, visual, or tactile stimuli, produce a feeling of union with other members participating in that ritual. In fact, the oneness of all participants is the theme running through the myth of most human ritual…. This state may vary in intensity, but it always has the effect of unifying the social group.
>
> (d'Aquili and Laughlin 1975: 38)

Prolonged, vigorous dancing can be sufficient in itself to induce mood-altering biochemical changes and altered states of consciousness. An important feature of psychedelic dance music is its great duration, and partygoers may find themselves dancing for extended periods of time in a state of blissful depersonalization (Bull 1997). Over time, the movements of bodies become aligned to the same rhythms, lighting patterns and economies of social circulation, so that the participants may develop a sense of merging in unison. This effect may be assisted by the use of LSD and MDMA, if we are to grant them the 'ego-dissolving' and 'heart-opening' properties frequently attributed to them. Like the Barasana *yajé* rituals, the doof is 'far from being a frenetic orgy'; the movements of dancers become an expression of unity. Participants may end up dancing synchronously, facing the same direction or feeling as if linked into a single, connected system. The doof ritual gains in intensity through the night, reaching a plateau of liminality and excitement after midnight, which continues through the early morning hours and gradually winds down after sunrise. The music generally becomes lighter and more melodic in the morning light; people recognize friends they had not known were present. Many people continue to dance; others wander about exploring the environment. Many don sunglasses[14] or seek out caffeinated beverages.

> the mornings are an incredible time at these parties, very different to the night, like the night's a more intense dance thing and then the morning, it's suddenly more like 'here's the community together, still playing around'.
>
> ('K', from tape-recorded interview)

Pharmacological aspects

The substances or combinations of substances used in dance rituals share a number of key pharmacological similarities. The major similarities are that they each produce a sense of dissociation or depersonalization, they all have a net stimulating effect, and they are all capable of producing visions or a sense of contact with transpersonal realities. Peyote produces wakefulness, depersonalization and visions. The entheogenic effects of peyote are largely referrable to its principal active constituent mescaline, although small amounts of related alkaloids are also present (Anderson 1996). Drinking *yajé* can also produce depersonalization and visions. *Yajé* visions are partly attributable to its DMT content. *Yajé* by itself is not an effective stimulant; indeed, it tends to produce an irresistible torpor. However, when *yajé* is used for ceremonial dances it is often taken in conjunction with large quantities of Amazonian coca (*Erythroxylum coca* var. *ipadu*), which helps to counter the *yajé* lassitude so that participants may easily remain awake through the night (Ott 1996). The effects of *eboka* are somewhat more difficult to classify. The most studied alkaloid of *eboka*, ibogaine, is a tryptamine derivative chemically related to DMT, psilocybin and LSD (Shulgin and Shulgin 1997). In large doses it produces visions and a 'depersonalizing' effect comparable to those produced by mescaline or DMT; however, it is generally taken at lower doses that function as a strong stimulant to increase 'ritual output' (Fernandez 1972).

The use of psychedelics at doofs has been widespread, though not at all universal. By far the most common material taken at doofs seems to be LSD, colloquially known as 'acid' or 'trips'. LSD is one of the classic psychedelics, with strong vision-inducing properties comparable to those of peyote or *yajé* (Peyton and Shulgin 1994), although it generally causes less nausea than either and is longer acting. LSD has some resemblance to *eboka* in that it has pronounced stimulating properties and its ingestion can give rise to dissociated states of consciousness. MDMA (Ecstasy) has also been very popular within Australia. The combination of MDMA and LSD is referred to by some doofers as 'candy-flipping' – a practice also associated with mainstream raves (Saunders and Doblin 1996) – and is widely esteemed. Interestingly, underground psychedelic psychotherapists have also recommended pre-dosing with MDMA to enhance subsequent LSD experiences (Stolaroff 1994, 1997).

Social relations

The structural continuities found in these rituals are not arbitrary; rather, they are present in all the cited instances because they are effective in inducing ecstasy at the collective level. These ecstatic elements appear to orient the participants in the various rituals toward a similar *functional* goal – renewed and intensified group identification at an immediate level. This is precisely the condition that Victor Turner (1969) referred to as communitas. Paradoxically, the collective entheogenic ceremonies also accentuate awareness of the individual self – Schaefer speaks of the 'quest for the self', and Fernandez remarks on 'greater possibilities of the self' accessed by Banzie – but these excursions into selfhood occur in parallel to a reciprocal atonement (in the more archaic sense of that word) with the matrix of the communal self. While visions also constitute a powerful form of experiential transcendence for the individual, it is as affirmative and shared signs of community that entheogenic ecstasies are primarily valued. Throughout the accounts we repeatedly find references to related ideas of one-heartedness, moving as one, or being as one, membership, and the 'uniting of the souls' based on shared, ecstatic experience of the numinous, and especially in the sublime *mysterium fascinans* facets of the numinous. The motif of communality has been one of the more recurrent elements in discourses about raving (Hill 1999; Jordan 1995; Nolan 1998) and there exists a general consensus about the centrality of experiential transcendence – sometimes conceptualized as 'dance-delirium' or the 'implosion' or 'disappearance' of subjectivity among ravers (Hopkins 1996; Lyttle and Montagne 1992):

> The overall impression is of losing oneself or transforming oneself through shared, multifaceted sensation.... Here again rave rituals may be a sign of the times, representing fascination not with forces but with metamorphosis.... Metamorphosis occurs as the self is destabilised, disembodied and 'dispersed across social space'.
>
> (Hopkins 1996: 15)

Occasionally parties are described in terms of the Great Mother, Gaia, or womb, with the bass rhythm of the music being compared to the foetal heartbeat. When a party is likened to the womb there is also the implication of a shared sibling status between ravers, which raises a symbolic 'incest taboo', thus attenuating sexual tensions and replacing them with familiarity and friendliness. Images of infants and young children were a recurrent motif of early rave promotional fliers (Akland-Snow *et al.* 1996). These figures may signify the pre-sexual, hedonistic and polymorphic perverse nature of psychedelic sociality. Sam Keen has suggested that 'LSD, DMT, and mescaline' may give rise to a 'Dionysian consciousness...based upon a body ego of the polymorphously perverse body', in which the self is transformed into a focused awareness of sensations (1969: 182). Collective consciousness may be especially enhanced at parties where MDMA is a conspicuous element. During the plateau of MDMA effects interpersonal differences appear to evaporate, producing a condition of almost total identification of self with other. Participants in public MDMA *agapae* may form 'puppy-piles' – protracted and unconditional collective embraces.

Dynamics of play and creativity are a prominent catalyst of social relations at both doofs and raves. Activities from which people can derive acute pleasure via a sensory modality are popular. In the mornings people may stroll about viewing the environment, art and one another, listening to the music or blowing bubbles. In the liminal arena of doofs, world elements are appropriated and juxtaposed in carnivalesque ways which serve to disrupt categories – not unlike the 'amazements' of Metsogo Bwiti. The 'amazements' of doofs include people in 'freaky' costumes, skilful acrobatic displays and fire-twirling,[15] kaleidoscopic lightshows and elaborately constructed soundscapes and art spaces.

Conclusion

Psychedelic parties, like their non-Western counterparts, incorporate multiple trance techniques. Both rave and doof rituals can be seen as different but analogous kinds of 'social machines' which draw power from various Dionysian 'engines', including an ecstatic dance-delirium (Jordan 1995), ritual costume, substance-induced 'ergotrophic stimulation' (Fischer 1971) and rhythm-induced 'tuning in' (d'Aquili and Laughlin 1975). Psychedelic dance parties share many elements with other entheogenic dance rituals. These similarities are not superficial; rather they are functionally analogous; in all these instances social energy generated through ecstatic dance is harnessed and directed by ritual virtuosos in accord with the collective desires of the group to enhance the possibility of producing a definite product: spontaneous communitas.

Notes

1 This chapter draws in part on an honours thesis I wrote under the supervision of Associate Professor Richard Hutch of the Department of Studies in Religion, University of Queensland, whose ongoing advice and interest I gratefully acknowledge.

2 Jonathon Ott has recommended the term '*entheogen*' to supplant the pejorative term *hallucinogen* and the ethnocentric neologism *psychedelic* when discussing shamanistic substances, and provided the following definition:

> Entheogen[ic] was proposed as a name for a subclass of psychotropic or psychoactive plants (and, by extension, their active principles and derivatives 'both natural and artificial'), as a broad term to describe the cultural context of use, not specific chemistry or pharmacology; as an efficient substitute for cumbersome terms like shamanic inebriant, visionary drug, plant-sacrament, and plant-teacher.
>
> (Ott 1996: 205)

3 A doof is essentially an event – usually held in a remote outdoor setting rather than in a metropolitan nightclub – where people assemble in an anarchic formation to celebrate psychedelic community and culture, as expressed through characteristic psychedelic arts and music, and where people are free to explore consciousness (often

via dance, psychedelic drugs) in a safe, supportive and stimulating environment. Those attending doofs frequently report a sense of connectedness, community and sacrality. One field consultant described it as 'an almost tribal, spiritual thing for some of the people there' (Tramacchi 2000: 203). For a comprehensive discussion of doofs within the constellation of Australian post-rave cultures, see St John (2001).

4 Barbara Myerhoff (1974: 249) suggested that the desire for a return to a paradisiacal *'illud tempus'* via a magical portal may have a psychological relationship to Carl Jung's notion of 'uroboric incest' – the desire to return to the safety of the womb.

5 The Vaupés is the largest of a number of states or *comisarías* in the Colombian Amazon. The Vaupés is home to a culturally diverse Indian population, comprising speakers of many different languages and dialects. One of the major language groups of this region is known as Tukanoan (Schultes and Raffauf 1992).

6 The use of *yajé* – also known as *ayahuasca, dápa, mihi, kahi, natéma, caapi* and *pindé* – is widespread in the western parts of the Amazon Basin, including parts of Brazil, Colombia and Peru (Luna and Amaringo 1991; Schultes and Hofmann 1980, 1992) . *Yajé* is often taken in conjunction with tobacco, *ipadú* (*Erythroxylum coca* var. *ipadú*), and *chicha* (a mildly alcoholic beverage made from the fermented starchy tubers of *Manihot esculenta*) during all-night collective rituals, as well as for magical and healing purposes (Schultes and Raffauf 1992).

7 Reichel-Dolmatoff's ethnographic account not only includes the structures and processes of a *yajé* session, but is of the utmost interest to the phenomenologist of consciousness as it also furnishes a rare and almost microscopically detailed account of the visions and impressions that the author experienced during the acute phases of *yajé* inebriation.

8 The members of Bwiti are known as 'Banzie', which means 'those of the chapel', but which has also come to be associated with the French term *'ange'* or 'angels' (Fernandez 1982). Participants in Bwiti are also called *ndzi-eboka* or 'eaters of Iboga' (Schultes and Hofmann 1992).

9 *Akyunge* are also the means by which supernaturals are thought to intervene in human affairs, and Bwiti 'amazes' its members by enabling them to 'surpass themselves and come to an understanding of the extraordinary, the unseen, the "death side" of things' (Fernandez 1982: 436). The substance *eboga* is itself 'miraculous': 'It amazes by opening up both the initiate (once in a lifetime by massive doses) and all the Banzie (regularly by smaller doses) to greater possibilities of the self' (*ibid.*: 492).

10 *Nima na kombo* is the title for the leader of a Bwiti chapel (*ibid.*).

11 Elsewhere (Tramacchi 2001) I have discussed discontinuities between the symbolic expression of Western psychedelic dance parties and non-Western entheogenic dance rituals. Essentially, the theme of 'sacrifice' is extremely significant in the mythology of the majority of entheogenic sacraments, but greatly downplayed in the Western psychedelic context.

12 St John (1997) notes that within the discourses of Australian 'edge-culture' nature as Earth/Gaia assumes an increasingly sacred ambience, perhaps reflecting a postcolonial quest for organic meaning and spiritual connectedness to place (Tacey 1995).

13 One is reminded of Zaehner's (1972: 95) bemusement at accounts of LSD-induced 'psychedelic love' experiences such as 'Love. Love. Love. Love. Big yellow chrysanthemums and the sun and pancakes and Disneyland and Vermont and cinnamon and Alexander the Great' etc., etc.

14 The donning of sunglasses in the morning following a rave or doof is quite ubiquitous. Glasses protect both the dilated pupils and the sometimes fragile psyches of 'returning' trippers. La Barre mentions that young Plains Indian men also 'affect colored glasses' to protect their eyes in the mornings following peyote meetings (1975: 20).

15 In 186 BC the Roman Senate moved decisively against the orgiastic, nocturnal rites of Bacchanalia held 'in the groves of Stimula' and elsewhere. The Senate was primarily

alarmed at the large, ungoverned crowds associated with the worship of Bacchus. Fire twirling was one of the elements in these excessive, ecstatic celebrations of the god of inebriation and madness which led to its condemnation. The cult, according to Livy (1976), seduced women into running about with blazing torches while sporting untidy hair, a sight not unfamiliar to doof participants.

Bibliography

Ackland-Snow, N., N. Brett and S. Williams (1996) *Fly: The Art of the Club Flyer*, London: Thames & Hudson.

Adamson, S. and R. Metzner (1988) 'The nature of the MDMA experience and its role in healing, psychotherapy, and spiritual practice', *ReVision: The Journal of Consciousness and Change* 10(4): 59–72.

Anderson, Edward F. (1996) *Peyote: The Divine Cactus*, 2nd edition, Tuscon, AZ: University of Arizona Press.

Bull, Rick (1997) 'The aesthetics of acid', available online at: http://www.cia.com.au/peril/youth/rickacid.htm (accessed 20 March 1998).

Bye, R.A. Jr (1979) 'Hallucinogenic plants of the Tarahumara', *Journal of Ethnopharmacology* 1: 23–48.

d'Aquili, E.G., and Laughlin, C., Jr (1975) 'The biopsychological determinants of religious ritual behavior', *Zygon* 10(1): 32–58.

Dobkin De Rios, Marlene (1992) *Amazon Healer: The Life and Times of an Urban Shaman*, Dorset: Prism Press.

Eisner, Bruce (1994) *Ecstasy: The MDMA Story*, Berkeley, CA: Ronin Publishing Inc.

Fernandez, James W. (1972) 'Tabernanthe iboga: narcotic ecstasis and the work of the ancestors', in P.T. Furst (ed.) *Flesh of the Gods: The Ritual Use of Hallucinogens*, London: George Allen & Unwin.

—— (1982) *Bwiti: An Ethnography of the Religious Imagination in Africa*, Princeton, NJ: Princeton University Press.

Fischer, Roland (1971) 'A cartography of the ecstatic and meditative states', *Science* 174: 897–904.

Grof, Stanislav (1976) *Realms of the Human Unconscious: Observations from LSD Research*, New York: E.P. Dutton & Co., Inc.

Hill, Desmond (1999) 'Mobile anarchy: the house movement, shamanism and community', in T. Lyttle (ed.) *Psychedelics ReImagined*, New York: Autonomedia.

Hopkins, Susan (1996) 'Synthetic ecstasy: the youth culture of techno music', *Youth Studies Australia* 15(2): 12–17.

Hugh-Jones, Stephen (1979) *The Palm and the Pleiades: Initiation and Cosmology in Northwest Amazonia*, Cambridge: Cambridge University Press.

Johnston, Thomas (1977) 'Auditory driving, hallucinogens, and music–color synesthesia in Tsonga ritual', in A.A. Balkema (ed.) *Drugs, Rituals and Altered States of Consciousness*, Rotterdam: A.A. Balkema.

Jordan, Tim (1995) 'Collective bodies: raving and the politics of Gilles Deleuze and Felix Guattari', *Body and Society* 1(1): 125–44.

Keen, Sam (1969) *Apology for Wonder*, New York: Harper & Row.

La Barre, Weston (1975) *The Peyote Cult*, 4th (enlarged) edition, Hampton, CT: Archon Books.

Lamaistre, Denis (1996) 'The hunt in the Huichol trinity', in S.B. Schaefer and P.E. Furs (eds) *People of the Peyote: Huichol Indian History, Religion, and Survival*, Albuquerque, NM: University of New Mexico Press.

Landriscina, Franco (1995) 'MDMA and states of consciousness', *Eleusis* 2: 3–9.

Livy (1976) *Rome and the Mediterranean: Books XXXI–XLV of the History of Rome from its Foundation*, Henry Bettenson (trans.), Harmondsworth: Penguin.

Luna, Luis Eduardo and Pablo Amaringo (1991) *Ayahuasca Visions: The Religious Iconography of a Peruvian Shaman*, Berkeley, CA: North Atlantic Books.

Lyttle, Thomas and Michael Montagne (1992) 'Drugs, music and ideology: a social pharmacological interpretation of the acid house movement', *International Journal of the Addictions* 27(10): 1,159–77.

McKenna, Dennis J. and G.H.N. Towers (1984) 'Biochemistry and pharmacology of tryptamines and beta-carbolines: a minireview', *Journal of Psychoactive Drugs* 16(4): 347–58.

Myerhoff, Barbara G. (1974) *Peyote Hunt: The Sacred Journey of the Huichol Indians*, Ithaca, NY: Cornell University Press.

Needham, Rodney (1967) 'Percussion and transition', *Man* 2: 606–14.

Neher, Andrew (1962) 'The physiological explanation of unusual behaviour in ceremonies involving drums', *Human Biology* 34(2): 151–60.

Nolan, Rhonda (1998) 'Transcendence, communality and resistance in rave culture: an observation of youth at a Townsville rave', *Northern Radius* 5(1): 7–8.

Ott, Jonathon (1978) 'Recreational use of hallucinogenic mushrooms in the United States', in B.H. Rumack and E. Salzman (eds) *Mushroom Poisoning: Diagnosis and Treatment*, West Palm Beach, FL: CRC Press.

—— (1996) *Pharmacotheon: Entheogenic Drugs, Their Plant Sources and History*, 2nd densified edition, Kennewick, WA: Natural Products Co.

Peyton, Jacob, III, and Alexander T. Shulgin (1994) 'Structure–activity relationship of the classic hallucinogens and their analogs', available online at: http://itsa.ucsf.edu/ddrc/SARHallucin.html (accessed 19 August 2000).

Pope, Harrison G., Jr (1969) '*Tabernanthe iboga*: an African narcotic plant of social importance, *Economic Botany* 23(2): 174–84.

Reichel-Dolmatoff, G. (1971) *Amazonian Cosmos: The Sexual and Religious Symbolism of the Tukano Indians*, Chicago: University of Chicago Press.

—— (1975) *The Shaman and the Jaguar: A Study of Narcotic Drugs among the Indians of Colombia*, Philadelphia: Temple University Press.

Rietveld, Hillegonda (1993) 'Living the dream', in S. Redhead (ed.) *Rave Off: Politics and Deviance in Contemporary Youth Culture*, Avebury: Aldershot,

St John, G. (1997) 'Going feral: authentica on the edge of Australian culture', *Australian Journal of Anthropology* 8: 167–89.

—— (2001) 'Doof! Australian post-rave culture', in G. St John (ed.) *FreeNRG: Notes from the Edge of the Dance Floor*, Altona: Common Ground.

Saunders, Nicholas and Rick Doblin (1996) *Ecstasy: Dance, Trance and Transformation*, Oakland, CA: Quick American Archives.

Schaefer, S.B. (1996) 'The crossing of the souls: peyote, perception, and meaning among the Huichol Indians', in S.B. Schaefer and P.E. Furst (eds) *People of the Peyote: Huichol Indian History, Religion, and Survival*, Albuquerque, NM: University of New Mexico Press.

Schaefer, S.B. and P. Furst (eds) (1996) *People of the Peyote: Huichol Indian History, Religion, and Survival*, Albuquerque, NM: University of New Mexico Press.

Schleiffer, H. (1973) *Sacred Narcotic Plants of the New World Indians: An Anthology of Texts from the Sixteenth Century to Date*, New York: Hafner Press.

Schultes, R.E. and A. Hofmann (1980) *The Botany and Chemistry of the Hallucinogens*, revised and enlarged 2nd edition, Springfield, IL: C.C. Thomas.

—— (1992) *Plants of the Gods: Their Sacred, Healing and Hallucinogenic Powers*, Rochester, VT: Healing Arts Press.

Schultes, R.E. and R.F. Raffauf (1992) *Vine of the Soul: Medicine Men, Their Plants and Rituals in the Colombian Amazon*, Oracle, AZ: Synergistic Press Inc.

Shulgin, Alexander and Ann Shulgin (1997) *TIHKAL: The Continuation*, Berkeley, CA: Transform Press.

Stewart, Omar C. (1987) *Peyote Religion: A History*, Norman, OK: University of Oklahoma.

Stolaroff, Myron J. (1994) *Thanatos to Eros: 35 Years of Psychedelic Exploration*, Berlin: Verlag für Wissenschaft und Bildung.

—— (1997) *The Secret Chief: Conversations with a Pioneer of the Underground Psychedelic Therapy Movement*, Charlotte, NC: Multidisciplinary Association for Psychedelic Studies (MAPS).

Tacey, David J. (1995) *Edge of the Sacred: Transformation in Australia*, Blackburn, Victoria: HarperCollins Publishers.

Tramacchi, Des (2000) 'Field tripping: psychedelic communitas and ritual in the Australian bush', *Journal of Contemporary Religion* 15: 201–13.

—— (2001) 'Chaos engines: doofs, psychedelics and religious experience', in G. St John (ed.) *FreeNRG: Notes from the Edge of the Dance Floor*, Altona: Common Ground.

Turner, Victor (1969) *The Ritual Process: Structure and Anti-structure*, New York: Aldine Publishing Company.

—— (1974) 'Foreword', in B.G. Myerhoff (ed.) *Peyote Hunt: The Sacred Journey of the Huichol Indians*, Ithaca, NY: Cornell University Press.

Valadez, M. and S. Valadez (1992) *Huichol Indian Sacred Rituals*, Oakland, CA: Amber Lotus.

van Gennep, Arnold (1909) *The Rites of Passage*, Monika B. Vizedom and Gabrielle L. Caffee (trans.), London: Routledge & Kegan Paul.

Zaehner, R.C. (1972) *Drugs, Mysticism and Make-believe*, London: Collins.

Discography

Sash! (2000) 'Halleluja', *Trilenium*, Edel Records.

7 The 'natural high'

Altered states, flashbacks and neural tuning at raves[1]

Melanie Takahashi

Since its emergence in the late 1980s, the subculture referred to as 'rave' has become a significant global youth phenomenon. The electronic and rhythmically repetitive nature of the music, the long hours of dancing, the semi-legal secret location and the ingestion of psychoactive substances are what distinguish raves from other youth parties. When combined, these features are designed to promote feelings of connectedness, spirituality and the state of ecstasy among participants. Though members of this subculture can be identified through their choice of music, jewellery and clothing, recent media attention has made the raver's selection of drug the most salient indication of subcultural belonging. In Canada, this relationship is particularly apparent in the recent initiatives that have taken place to restrict rave events.[2] Bylaws that now limit legal raves to establishments meeting the outlined specifications for ventilation, emergency exits and running water are designed to safeguard ravers from the harmful effects of MDMA (3,4-methylenedioxymethamphetamine) and other popular designer drugs.[3] Similar harm-reduction strategies have appeared worldwide, resulting in a continuously evolving scene where the defining boundaries between raves and nightclubs have begun to blur.

While the notion of 'locale' no longer adequately distinguishes raves from other dance events, the subculture's most prevalent drug, MDMA, also referred to by ravers as 'E', 'XTC' and 'ecstasy', has become a demarcating feature of the subculture, at least in the Canadian rave scene. The centrality of MDMA to the rave scene is apparent in the number of publications which have incorporated 'ecstasy' into their titles, including *Clubbing: Dancing, Ecstasy and Vitality* (Malbon 1999), *Generation Ecstasy* (Reynolds 1999) and *Ecstasy: Dance, Trance and Transformation* by (Saunders 1996a). The underlying presence of MDMA and its influence on the subculture are also evident at many levels. A number of accessories which have become symbolic of raving are connected to the physiological effects of ecstasy: glow-sticks enhance the visual, and Vicks Vapo Rub the tactile effects of MDMA, while suckers and baby soothers (dummies) alleviate the drug's side-effects of bruxism and jaw tension. Additionally, bottled water and the designated 'chillout' areas at events reduce overheating and dehydration, effects which can have fatal consequences on ecstasy users (see Kalant 2001; Malberg and Seiden 1998). Accessories such as infant hair barrettes, 'kiddie' backpacks, teddy bears and friendship bracelets have been correlated with MDMA's ability to stimulate an innocence reminiscent of childhood; it was the drug's ability to bring out one's 'inner child' that gave it the nickname 'Adam' in the late 1970s, when psychologists realized its potential in therapy sessions (Reynolds 1999: 82). Even PLUR (peace, love, unity and respect), the acronym that has been referred to as the principal philosophy of raving (Fritz 1999: 203), an ideology that is intended to reflect the love and connectedness of the rave community, can be traced to the empathogenic[4] effects of MDMA.

To date, the majority of publications on substance use at raves focus on the escalating presence of drugs at events and the associated health risks, the range and quantification of illicit substance use, polydrug use and strategies for harm reduction. The subjects employed in these studies generally exhibit overrepresentation by habitual drug users, with the varying categories of rave participants overlooked. Further, these studies fail to delineate the motivations, experiences and attitudes of regular drug users, as well as those of occasional consumers and abstainers. Consequently, a wide range of data has been missed. While MDMA's connection to the rave culture is undeniable, it should also be noted that a reactionary trend to the emphasis on drugs has begun to take place as an increasing number of participants choose to abstain or to reduce or limit their consumption of illicit drugs. Fieldwork in the central Canadian rave scene has suggested that ravers' attitudes toward drugs do appear to contradict their otherwise focal position as portrayed in the literature. Analysis of participants' views concerning drugs suggests that an underlying code of 'acceptable' behaviour with respect to drug use has not only influenced participants' choice of drug, but also fostered the development of an underreported class of rave participants – those who limit their consumption of drugs and those who discontinue use altogether.

Drawing on recent studies of the flashback phenomenon, in addition to Gellhorn and Kiely's work (1972) on autonomic nervous system tuning, I suggest that exposure to a psychoactive substance at a rave can produce neural tuning such that a similar state can later be reached 'naturally' while in the rave environment. Further, some participants are in fact aware of this, and it is the effect of this process which motivates this underreported pattern of drug use.[5]

'Dance drugs' and raves

The appearance and increasing popularity of designer drug use among youth populations has been reported in many countries around the world, and Canada is no exception. Reported ecstasy-related deaths (see Kalant 2001; NIDA 2000), records of designer drug-associated emergency room visits (see NIDA 2000), police reports on drug seizures (*ibid.*), in addition to a small body of published literature (CAMH 2000; Adlaf and Smart 1997; Weir 2000), suggest that synthetic drug use is clearly on the rise in Canada. MDMA-related deaths have been the most prominent measuring stick used to gauge the influence and popularity of raves and dance drugs among Canadian youth; however, quantitative reliability is often confounded by the fact that 'ecstasy' pills may be combined or even replaced with other substances. Polydrug use, a common pattern of behaviour among ravers (see Adlaf and Smart 1997; Boys *et al.* 1997; Forsyth 1996; Pedersen and Skrondal 1999; Topp *et al.* 1999) presents another factor contributing to the inability to operationalize the content and dosage of substances ingested and the specific cause of drug-related deaths. These circumstances also fail to elucidate general patterns of use since the majority of serious cases demonstrate blood levels 40 times higher than the average recreational dose (Kalant 2001: 924). Overheating and dehydration are additional factors that complicate the epidemiological data. Post-mortem analyses of ecstasy-attributed deaths suggest that many cases are the result of hyperthermia rather than the direct toxicity from MDMA (Measham *et al.* 1998: 25). Much of the literature in the Canadian context has also relied on data obtained from samples directed toward the secondary-school population (see Adlaf and Smart 1997). These patterns of use cannot be generalized to the rave population as a whole, however, since most rave attendees fall into the post-secondary age bracket. For example, our survey results revealed 62 per cent of ravers to be over the age of 20 (Takahashi and Olaveson 2003).

Our study also found that psychoactive substance use was prevalent among those sampled: 81 per cent reported regular drug use at raves, 6 per cent reported occasional use and 13 per cent indicated that they abstain (*ibid.*). While a variety of substances were reported, ecstasy was the most frequently reported substance, at 67 per cent, followed by cannabis and crystal methamphetamine (*ibid.*). Ecstasy, LSD (Lysergic acid diethlamide) and the amphetamines appear to have the most consistent international presence. A number of other studies illustrate that regional variation exists in the patterns of drug use at raves. For example, Power *et al.* (1996) cite MDMA, LSD and amphetamine sulphate as the drugs of choice among a group of London youths examined. Amphetamine and MDMA use are also cited as the drugs of choice by Forsyth (1996) in the Scottish dance scene. Forsyth lists nitrates or 'poppers' with amphetamines and ecstasy as the most prevalent drugs among London youths, whereas 'poppers' seem to have a very minor presence in the Canadian rave scene to date. In our own study, references to a homemade concoction referred to as 'peach' were reported only by survey respondents sampled in Quebec.[6]

Weir (2000) and Weber (1999) note that alcohol use at Canadian raves is low, attributing this to the fact that, while it loosens inhibitions, it can also generate aggression amongst participants. For this reason, the general view among ravers is that alcohol has no place in the scene. Our survey data also confirmed this. According to one 22-year-old male, 'having alcohol there changes everything, I've seen a lot more people get sick and lose control from drinking – at raves there's a lot less incidents of people getting sick or hurt'. Females also attributed the 'non-sexual' atmosphere at raves to the absence of alcohol and felt this to be a positive feature of the rave environment.

Attitudes toward drugs: a 'moral' code of conduct?

Centrality of the music, dance and people

The position of the rave community toward drugs tends to be an ambivalent and paradoxical one. Psychoactive substance use is undeniably widespread among the rave population; survey results suggested that the majority of individuals who attend raves use drugs in this context or have done so in the past. At the same time, however, respondents emphasized that the rave experience and culture is fundamentally about the music, the people, the dancing and PLUR, rather than the drugs. Those who attend raves for the sole purpose of buying and ingesting psychoactive substances were perceived by some as 'phoney' ravers who frequent events for the wrong reasons (see also Lenton and Davidson 1999; Weber 1999). As one 18-year-old male states:

> I don't use drugs, I don't believe they are necessary. I think they make your night fake. Sadly it's necessary for some people, but to each his own. I just don't like people who don't have a clue about music, just use the venue for drugs.
>
> (18-year-old male)

Individuals who rave 'clean' were even admired for demonstrating a greater commitment to the music and the culture. According to one 18-year-old female informant:

> Even though I usually dose at raves, I really respect people who can rave without drugs because these people are really devoted to the music, I mean they can get high just from the music and the dancing and that's pretty cool.
>
> (18-year-old female)

Some ravers were aware of the shift in mental state that can result from prolonged dancing. As one 24-year-old male stated:

> I can have the same response whether taking the drug or not. In fact even better, there are times when I will go and dance for 15 hours straight and feel like I'm brought to a state of consciousness on par if not greater than those who had popped 15 pills.
>
> (24-year-old male)

The sentiment that these naturally induced altered states embody the core principles of the culture is illustrated in the following raver's statement: 'But there is the respect, the liberation, the space to simultaneously be an individual and part of a group. This natural high, not the chemical sort, is the true allure of a rave' (Park 2001). These attitudes are consonant with the finding that only 8 per cent of the subjects we surveyed mentioned drug use as the primary reason for attending raves, compared with the 92 per cent who referred to either the people, the music or dancing as the main attractants (Takahashi and Olaveson 2003). This finding is supported cross-culturally as two-thirds of Australian ravers surveyed by Lenton and Davidson deemed the music, lighting and dancing to be the primary appeal of raves (1999: 154). Similarly, van der Wijngaart *et al.* concluded that in The Netherlands psychoactive substances are only part of the larger rave context, with music and dancing having the dominant appeal (1999: 701).

The philosophy of the rave subculture – peace, love, unity and respect – is then thought to take precedence over drugs, with some ravers attributing what they refer to as the degradation of the scene and its *vibe*[7] to the increased availability and consumption of drugs at raves (see also McCall 2001; Lenton and Davidson 1999; Reynolds 1998; Weber 1999). While some informants were troubled over the decreasing quality of psychoactive substances and the introduction of novel street drugs such as 'special K' (ketamine) and GHB (Gamma-hydroxybutyrate) into the scene, others expressed concern over the effects of drugs on young participants (see also Lenton and Davidson 1999; Weber 1999). Some felt that young, inexperienced ravers are more susceptible to the dangers of polydrug use and overdose. As one raver observes: 'I see more and more irresponsible kids e-tarded out on the floor. You know it when you see it. Blatant drug use is starting to get out of hand' (cited in McCall 2001: 121). For this reason, recent bylaws and safety regulations were welcomed by some as a positive step towards harm reduction. In reference to the presence of security and law enforcement at raves, one 22-year-old male stated: 'I'm all for it and I appreciate it, it's reassuring to know that there's people there to help you.' In Canada, the rave community has also taken measures to address these safety concerns, as harm-reduction organizations such as OATS (Ottawans Actively Teaching Safety) and TRIP (Toronto Rave Information Project) are managed by volunteer ravers, and the presence of these groups at raves is viewed as positive and non-threatening by most rave-goers. The appearance of 'Smart Bars' at raves offering fruit and natural energy-boosting drinks for sale further provide participants with natural alternatives for staying awake, compensating for some of the negative side-effects of dehydration and drug use.[8]

Motivations for taking drugs: transformation as an intended outcome

An individual's motive and subsequent synthesis of the drug experience into his or her life were additional themes of concern voiced by subjects. It was suggested that adolescents will often lack the maturity to integrate their drug encounters for spiritual and psychological growth and in this way fail to respect, emulate and contribute to the PLUR edict. Underlying these sentiments is the suggestion of a code of acceptable conduct; there is a difference between individuals who attend raves to 'get high' and those who choose to integrate a psychoactive experience with personal development and transformation, the latter being consistent with the philosophy of raving. Many emphasized that obtaining a level of maturity and self-awareness is key before entering the rave environment, particularly when ingesting a psychoactive:

> Well you have to know yourself. You have to know exactly who you are when you go into a rave. The drugs, they can open up like ideas and possibilities in your head that you never knew you could possibly have. And for some people who have a hidden dark side like everybody does, it can be very traumatic if you're not ready for it. If you have some mental instability, weaknesses, it's not the right time.
>
> (24-year-old male)

> Not everybody can be a raver. Ecstasy will heighten who you are and that's probably why some people snap, 'cause there are things that they try to hide or are not aware of themselves, and they'll be shown. There's going to be a big light projected on it so that's why it's not for everybody. You have to have a certain maturity.
>
> (23-year-old male)

It was also noted that this kind of maturity is lacking among adolescents, and for this reason young ravers should refrain from drug use:

> I don't like seeing 15-year-old kids at raves, I just don't. You have to have a reality base before you escape it. I believe that you need to know who you are, you need to have ground rules in your head before you take any drug. You need to have a footing of knowledge and I had no clue what the hell I was when I was 15…I don't think you should be taking ecstasy when you're 15.
>
> (23-year-old male)

The following individual attributes his transition from taking drugs to 'get high' to taking drugs for personal growth as a combination of maturation and involvement in the rave scene:

> When we were young, we got high much less productively. I didn't grow really out of it. I had wonderful stories to talk about, weird stuff I saw in the sky, but I never really grew from my experiences with drugs. You learn something but you don't necessarily grow, and now I realize you do always like to keep something after a rave if you did it properly…. When you leave a rave you have to be more than you were when you came in.
>
> (22-year-old male)

This kind of division in terms of intended outcome of a drug experience was noted by Beck and Rosenbaum (1994), who discovered that MDMA users tend to be either spiritually/therapeutically focused in their pursuits or recreationally oriented. Among the recreational users, the benefits of MDMA rest solely within the experience itself, whereas the therapeutically oriented individual feels that positive experiences and insights gained from MDMA could and should be incorporated into everyday life (*ibid.*: 83). Ecstasy's ability to foster spirituality, personal development and life change has been documented at length (Cohen 1998; Eisner 1994; Metzner and Adamson 2001; Saunders 1996a, 1996b; Watson and Beck 1991) and has been reported by ravers:

> Thanks, I think, to ecstasy, I was able to *feel* each person's situation, in all of its pain and implications.... I have a new, real awareness of the global situation. I am graduating this semester and am now considering doing aid work in a Third World country for a while.[9]

> Still I've grown a lot from E....The emotional vision, becoming wiser, becoming more aware of yourself is far more important than what E takes from you. You take from drugs and they take from you too. I always say that I took more out of drugs than drugs took out of me.
>
> (24-year-old male)

Ecstasy is significantly the most widely used drug at raves and the ingestion of MDMA for its characteristic transformational and empathogenic properties is consistent with the finding that spirituality and personal transformation are central themes associated with the rave experience (Takahashi and Olaveson 2003). A content analysis on 84 personal rave accounts revealed that 42 per cent of accounts characterized the rave experience as religious or spiritual, and well over one-third of the accounts sampled made reference to a life change or personal growth as a direct result of rave attendance (*ibid.*). Another theme revealed by these accounts was the desire to create a better world through the application of PLUR (*ibid.*). Correspondingly, there is an expectation placed upon ravers to apply the knowledge gained from the rave experience outside the rave context to make a difference in the lives of others. This theme is evident in the following statement made by an anonymous raver who implores others to think about their motives for taking MDMA, encouraging users to promote the insights gained from ecstasy outside the rave environment:

> To all you E-heads out there, please, please, take the time to consider what you are doing to yourself, how it affects you and why you do it. E should be held as a sacred thing, not just something to do when you're bored. Get into the music, or something else, invite your passions to entrance you. Express what you've felt on E in the 'real world'. Make a difference in people's lives.[10]

Similarly:

> Raves have indeed changed my life, and lucky as I am I have many wonderful friends with whom to share those changes! As I see it there

wouldn't be any point to have been raving and living the whole rave experience without being able to extend those feelings and changes with my friends outside of raves.

(22-year-old male)

A hierarchy of drugs: 'good' versus 'bad' drugs

A hierarchy of drugs and substance users is a further indication of an underlying standard of conduct in operation. Many ravers emphasized the point that the ingestion of MDMA and other related substances is reserved for the rave environment, and it is this pattern of use which distinguishes ravers from drug addicts. The reference to ecstasy as a 'holy sacrament' reinforces the view that the rave experience is a ritual process wherein MDMA use is appropriate only in that ritual or sacred space (see Saunders 1996a: 112; Malbon 1999: 119–20). In reference to MDMA, one 21-year-old male informant stated: 'For me the experience is sacred and special, by not doing it all the time it stays that way.' Many informants stressed that the rave experience is a process that includes more than the event alone; prescribed pre- and post-rave behaviours are well thought out and ritualized (see Saunders 1996a: 112–13; Malbon 1999: 170–9).

Thus, ecstasy, cannabis and LSD, substances known to elicit a change in perspective, are deemed by some ravers to be more 'acceptable' than the 'feel-good' drugs such as heroin and cocaine.[11] Heroin and intravenous drug use is often considered socially unacceptable and taboo in the rave community (Power *et al.* 1996; Topp *et al.* 1999). According to one 21-year-old male, 'heroine and cocaine are for stupid people with too much money'. Nitrous oxide was also viewed negatively by some subjects: 'Some people will inhale nitrous oxide but that's just pure stupidity' (20-year-old female). The ability to transform is a key component of the rave scene's most popular rave drug, ecstasy. It is this unique property of the drug which may provide insight into the discontinued and infrequent drug user. The observation that the extraordinary nature of one's first experience on MDMA can never be recaptured, making subsequent encounters less satisfying, was a consistently reported theme among subjects. The opinion that 'ecstasy can teach you things, force you to see things differently, but there's a limit and once you've reached it, you're better off letting it go and preserve your neurons' (20-year-old female) was a common sentiment. The decision to limit or discontinue ecstasy use also has a physiological basis; frequent and excessive use of the drug will gradually deplete serotonin levels in the brain, meaning that the empathogenic and 'ecstatic' qualities of the drug will eventually cease, leaving only the amphetamine-like properties (Reynolds 1999: 86). While some ravers attempt to preserve MDMA's core properties by resorting to polydrug use, many others opt to limit MDMA consumption, and some elect to discontinue drug use altogether. I encountered a number of individuals in the latter two groups throughout the course of my research – individuals who were specific in pointing out that the transformations resulting from past psychoactive substance encounters provided them with the ability to attend raves and attain similar experiences naturally. As I will now discuss, there are biological and psychological explanations for this commonly reported phenomenon.

Ritual, flashbacks and neural tuning

Neural tuning refers to a 'permanent change in the central nervous system (CNS), resulting from repeated experience of a particular condition of the nervous system which makes the individual more susceptible to re-establishment of that same condition' (Castillo 1995: 25). Neural tuning occurs when the balance of the sympathetic (ergotropic) and parasympathetic (trophotropic) activity of the autonomic nervous system (ANS) shifts as a result of continued stimulation of one system resulting in an activation response in the other (see Gellhorn 1969; Gellhorn and Kiely 1972). Under normal conditions these systems are antagonistic to each other, meaning that stimulation of the one will inhibit activation of the other. However, maximal stimulation of either system can produce a kind of spillover effect, resulting in the simultaneous discharge of both systems. Maximal stimulation of the ergotropic and trophotropic systems is associated with 'the most intense forms of mystical experience and may lie at the heart of compelling spiritual experiences, meditative states, near death experiences and other types of human experiential phenomena' (Newberg and d'Aquili 2000: 256). Many of the elements present in ritual (i.e. repetitive auditory and visual stimuli, dancing and the ingestion of psychoactives) lead to the simultaneous discharge of the ANS subsystem, which can be expressed as profound alterations in consciousness and even a reorganization of personality (Laughlin *et al.* 1992: 146). Mechanisms such as these are commonly referred to as drivers (*ibid.*: 146), and there now exists extensive literature on the psychobiological effects of driving mechanisms, drawn from cross-cultural research (see d'Aquili and Laughlin 1975; 1996; Gellhorn and Kiely 1972; Lex 1975; Mandell 1980; Neher 1961, 1962; Turner 1983; Winkelman 1986, 1997, 2000). Although neural tuning can occur after initial exposure to one or more of these driving mechanisms, learning plays an essential role as rituals are usually repeated throughout the life-cycle, fostering the development of new neural network patterns and the reinforcement of existing structures (re-tuning). Research on the mind states referred to as *trance* and *ceremonial possession* indicates that personal beliefs and expectations, setting and, most importantly, past experience are essential to trance induction (see Ervin *et al.* 1988; Rouget 1985; Ward 1984).

I argue that what has been commonly referred to as the *flashback phenomenon* can be grounded within the framework of neural tuning. Recent publications on psychedelic drug flashbacks have departed from the classical biochemical and pathological explanation to suggest that the spontaneous re-experience of sensations originally associated with a previous drug encounter are the product of learning, environmental context and personal expectation. Ecstasy, in addition to other synthetic drugs associated with the rave scene, has been reported to induce flashbacks among its users (see Batzer *et al.* 1999; Leikin *et al.* 1989; Lerner *et al.* 2000; Matefy *et al.* 1978; Metzner and Adamson 2001; Seymour and Smith

1998). I contend that psychoactive ingestion (specifically MDMA), in tandem with additional driving mechanisms present in the rave context, may produce simultaneous discharge of the sympathetic and parasympathetic nervous system and subsequent neural tuning. Continued participation in the rave environment and repeated exposure to the rave event's driving mechanisms, such as dancing and repetitive auditory and visual stimuli, strengthen and develop previously tuned structures such that participants through time become adept at re-attaining these states naturally. Previous experiences can therefore be elicited with the presence of a limited subset of the original driving mechanisms, including, in some cases, only one. The reported change in perspective and the indication that after a period of raving one can eventually attend events and 'tap into' a previously drug-induced state naturally are consistent with what has been reported cross-culturally among societies where ritual and the experience of multiple realities are integrated in the culture's cosmology.

MDMA and neural tuning at raves

The altered states of consciousness fundamental to raving are not only regularly sought out by participants, but DJs are quite proficient at actively stimulating these experiences among the dancers. The ability to drive participants to the state of 'ecstasy' is part of the DJ's craft. It is inscribed in their technique and is a measurement of their skill. DJs are ultimately responsible for the group's consciousness and experience at a rave as 'they create the state of mind and the buzz for everybody in the room...they can crash it or they can take it up as they choose' (25-year-old male). It is for this reason that some have referred to the DJ as a 'techno-shaman' (see Hutson 1999; ENRG 2001). Techno music has been correlated with an increase in heart rate and systolic blood pressure, alterations in levels of neurotransmitters, peptides and hormonal reactions, in addition to changes in emotional state (Gerra *et al.* 1998). As well as the auditory constant of techno music, participant use of drums and whistles and the photic stimulation of lasers and strobe lights have the potential to activate alpha and theta brain waves characteristic of trance and visionary states (Neher 1961). Conditions of extreme physical exertion such as prolonged dancing activate the body's endogenous opiate system, wherein endorphins are secreted from the pituitary gland, resulting in an increase in delta and theta waves (Winkelman 1997: 400) and the symptom of euphoria and analgesia. Prolonged dancing leading to fatigue, hyperventilation and oxygen and blood sugar depletion may synergistically produce hypoglycaemia and a hallucinatory experience (Winkelman 2000: 148). Overheating from such extensive motor activity, in addition to exposure to the high temperatures generally present at raves, are further triggers which activate the release of endogenous opiates (*ibid.*: 151). The tendency for ravers to fast or limit food intake before, during and after an event, as was observed during fieldwork, is yet another trigger of alteration in consciousness.[12] Winkelman notes that fasting not only makes individuals more susceptible to trance states (1986: 179), but hypoglycaemia, a consequence of fasting, can intensify auditory driving produced from repetitive rhythmic stimuli (*ibid.*: 178). Further, sleep deprivation has been noted to invoke brain activity typical of trance states (*ibid.*: 176).[13]

Despite the presence of these natural driving mechanisms at raves, MDMA continues to have a dominant role in the subculture, and this may be due to the fact that the altered experience being sought out can be achieved with little effort. While over 90 per cent of the world's cultures recognize and seek out altered states of consciousness (ASCs) (Bourguignon 1973), Euro-American society has tended to discount ASCs in favour of 'rational' thought as represented by the waking phase of consciousness. The failure to explore these states of consciousness in our culture has led to what Laughlin *et al.* (1992) label *monophasic* consciousness. Individuals socialized in a monophasic culture are not trained to attend to or develop their own personal phenomenology. For the monophasic individual, psychoactive experimentation provides an easy and immediate access to an ASC, and these substances have the ability to tune and retune the autonomic nervous system with little effort (Laughlin *et al.* 1992). According to Seymour and Smith, 'when one takes a psychedelic drug, that conditioning breaks down and one is aware of a whole new range of sensory material' (1998: 241). This kind of new awareness was described by one informant as 'a key that opens you up to new ways of seeing things; it doesn't expand your mind but rather places you in a higher position from which you can see the world' (23-year-old male). Some ravers who have taken psychoactives describe being 'on the same wavelength' with other psychoactive users (see also Malbon 1999: 132), and this kind of mutual understanding implies a level of shared neural tuning among users. Statements such as 'when I meet someone who has raved, we don't even need to say a word to each other, we just know how the other feels' (22-year-old male), in addition to the frequently reported feeling of 'connectedness' at rave events, are indicative of the shared experience of neural tuning. Not only did ravers refer to other members of the subculture as 'family,' but the opinion that one is better understood by another raver as opposed to a family member or friend who doesn't rave was frequently expressed:

> I have a childhood friend who doesn't take drugs, doesn't drink alcohol, doesn't rave. I know him very well but he doesn't know me very well. He knows me in a way, but there's a whole aspect of emotions and experience that he has no idea I have.
>
> (24-year-old male)

Consistent with the aforementioned code of conduct, personal growth and transformation are expected outcomes of the drug experience among ravers. This expectation not only prescribes the context of drug ingestion for the rave setting, but also favours the selection of substances which enable the individual to obtain new knowledge or awareness from the experience. Research on trance states suggests that learning and past experience are fundamental to ASC induction, and this process is also alluded to by rave participants. Many informants were aware of the fact that the music and dancing alone are enough to produce an ASC; however, they also emphasized that one must learn to attend to these natural driving mechanisms and MDMA can accelerate and facilitate this process. As I mentioned earlier, a number of informants pointed out that after a period of taking psychoactives, drugs were no longer required to achieve an altered state. This sentiment is expressed in the following 25-year-old male's statement:

> Once you're done experimenting, you've done this for two years of your life, once you've done that, you don't have to search for that, you can go to events sober and still have just as much fun as you did when you were messed up five years ago, it's not necessary to find that state of consciousness through drugs.
>
> (25-year-old male)

Neural tuning is not only implied in these statements; some participants are very precise about how MDMA and other psychoactive substances operate in their systems. In referring to his own personal experience with ecstasy, Simon Reynolds suggests that an appreciation for and bodily reaction to the music can only be attained through an initial encounter with MDMA:

> Could you even listen to this music 'on the natural', enjoy it in an unaltered state? Well, I did and do, all the time. But whether I'd *feel it* if my nervous system hadn't been reprogrammed by MDMA is another matter. Perhaps you just need to do it once, to become sens-E-tized, and the music will induce memory rushes and body flashbacks.
>
> (Reynolds 1999: 139)

To an outsider, techno music can sound repetitive, monotonous and incomprehensible as it defies the characteristics of conventional music. Rave music is comprised of rhythm and sound; it is anonymous, continuous, cyclical, and in this way it challenges the listener to develop new listening skills (Fritz 1999: 76). According to Fritz, rave music demands a certain concentration and focus so the 'listener becomes closer to being a part of the musical process rather than a passive audience' (*ibid.*: 6). Characterized as a three-dimensional sound specifically designed to penetrate the body (*ibid.*: 76), according to many participants MDMA facilitates the ability to grasp the music such that musical receptivity transcends the auditory to include all the senses. The natural outcome of this embodied musical awareness is expressed through dancing, and MDMA's role in this kind of learning sheds light on the consistent finding that music and dancing outweigh drugs as the dominant appeal of raves. Although the relationship between techno music and ecstasy is noted by Reynolds to be one that has evolved into a 'self-conscious science of intensifying MDMA's sensations' (1999: 85), it would seem that the reverse is also true: MDMA functions to intensify sensations already evoked by the music. The embodied experience of musical perception, and MDMA's facilitation in acquiring this knowledge, is evident in the following respondents' statements:

> Like you can listen to a techno song and get shivers down your spine, but if you've never taken ecstasy, you'll never get those shivers. You don't know that it's possible, it opens like a certain kind of love that you won't have before.
>
> (22-year-old male)

> My first indication that I was rushing was the beat of the bass from the techno began to fill my brain and I was unable to sit still any longer on the couch. I reached the middle of the dance floor and let the music take me to heights I never dreamed imaginable. I lost all self consciousness, and felt in tune with the music, as though the bass was a life force and I was connected to it. My movements became fluid and I was able to dance along with it in utter freedom and abandon.[14]

Flashbacks at raves: neural tuning

The term 'flashback' most often refers to a spontaneous re-experience of images, physical sensations or emotional states associated with a previous drug encounter (McGee 1984: 273). Although the etiology of flashbacks has long been a focus of debate, I argue that the association between the flashback phenomenon and a psychoactive substance is our culture's way of explaining and categorizing the process of driving mechanisms and neural tuning. Generally it is the individual who experiences psychological disturbances with flashbacks who seeks out medical attention (Seymour and Smith 1998: 247), and this has introduced a sampling bias which has supported the tendency to regard flashbacks as pathological. Analysis of flashback occurrences among a random sample of psychedelic users, however, suggests that most individuals characterize flashbacks as positive and non-threatening in nature (see Batzer *et al.* 1999; McGee 1984; Matefy 1980; Matefy *et al.* 1978; Schick and Smith 1970; Wesson 1976).

Examination of the triggers known to elicit flashbacks shows them to parallel a number of agents present at raves. Environmental stimuli which resemble the context in which the original experience occurred may trigger a flashback (see Matefy 1980; McGee 1984; Heaton 1975), and this has led some to view flashbacks as learned phenomena. Stimuli associated with specific experiences operate as memory cues which can trigger the re-experience of emotionally salient encounters that may or may not be associated with a particular drug. According to McGee, 'the more similar the contextual stimuli are to those conditions prevailing at the time of the original storage of memories, the more likely the probability of their retrieval' (1984: 277).

While the location of rave events varies, there are a number of 'contextual stimuli' that are consistently present at raves. The techno music, crowds of dancers, glow-sticks, projections of psychedelic imagery and elaborate lighting systems can be expected at every event. These environmental factors are also conducive to this phenomenon since flashbacks are more likely to occur in conditions known to induce ASCs, such as stress, fatigue or reduced sensory input (Heaton 1975: 157). Whether the association is connected to a past drug encounter or previous exposure to a natural occurring ASC, the sensorial components of raves seem to trigger memory recall. Many informants noted immediate shifts in physical sensations and/or mind state upon entering the rave environment:

> Fourteen thousand people jumping up and down and all you could hear was the banging of the floor, it was absolutely incredible. You walk in and all you see was this sea of people and all they had was two glow-sticks each, so 28,000 glowing objects jumping up and down, and just bang, that's all you could hear. You couldn't even hear the music 'cause the banging on the floor was so loud. Absolutely incredible, I'm shivering just talking to you about it, but yeah it was phenomenal, it was an incredible feeling to walk in and just see this mass of people going nuts. I literally have goose bumps just talking about it.
>
> (24-year-old male)

> Sometimes when I walk into a rave and smell the familiar scent of incense, the sight of the glow-sticks, and feel the overpowering beat of trance, I get this light-headed sensation and sense of weightlessness in my body that reminds me of the first experience I had on E. It's awesome.
>
> (21-year-old female)

Similar sensations have also been reported by ravers when exposed to only one of the variables present at raves, such as listening to techno music at home:

> It was 3.00 in the morning and this DJ played this song called 'Air Tight' and it's an incredible track, unbelievable song and the mode of response just listening to it at home, it still elicits the same response that it did that night when I was listening to it, and I have that experience every single time.
>
> (24-year-old male)

Personal expectation is also correlated with flashback experiences (see Matefy *et al.* 1978; Heaton 1975), suggesting that flashbacks are often sought out by drug users. According to one DJ, people attend raves with the expectation of reaching a transcendent experience. It is this anticipated physical and emotional ordeal that distinguishes a rave from a nightclub:

> When you're going to a rave, you're going there particularly to experience a certain type of event. That's what you're going there for. You're going there to get this particular emotion, this particular sensation in this particular environment that you're looking for. You're going there to get it.
>
> (25-year-old male)

Heaton (1975) found that by attending to relevant stimuli and blocking out external inputs subjects were more likely to become aware of a broad range of psychedelic sensations. Some informants attributed their ability to recreate MDMA-like experiences by focusing on the music and bodily sensations while dancing:

> I believe that there's a very strong conditioned response when you take music and the pleasure that Ecstasy gives you, so I think that the mind can very easily extend that feeling of pleasure if you just focus on the music. I think lots of people don't take advantage of this, 'cause there is a way to extend the experience without drugs.
>
> (32-year-old male)

Ravers also talked about the ability to completely 'let go' while dancing and refer to this process as 'trance-dancing'. Although participants dance in groups, socialization on the dance floor is rare, as ravers will often refer to 'being alone among a crowd'. Some ravers described experiences involving the dissolution or disappearance of the ego through the process of dance. As one 32-year-old male recounts, 'like I'm dancing, feeling empty, I cut all input from my senses and not physically, but I'll close my eyes sometimes and once all the perceptions are gone, it's like being dead, like I don't exist anymore'. This also supports the notion that ravers are likely more proficient in inducing flashbacks, since flashbackers have illustrated greater adeptness than non-flashbackers at being able to lose themselves or 'relinquish personal control for the sake of a peak experience, and altering of consciousness' (Matefy 1980: 552).

Finally, there is an association between flashbacks triggered by marijuana, particularly in conjunction with LSD (see McGee 1984; Wesson 1976). This may shed some light on its widespread use in the Canadian rave scene; the underlying effects of state-dependent learning[15] may encourage users to quit the class of synthetic drugs, favouring marijuana for its potential to induce MDMA flashbacks.

Conclusion

The majority of individuals who attend raves use psychoactive substances, and clearly the range and availability of synthetic drugs is on the rise in Canada. However, in the process of ascertaining the range and quantification of illicit substance use at events a growing category of rave participants has been ignored by academics. Examination of ravers' attitudes toward drugs has suggested that most ravers use these substances as tools to enhance the extraordinary bodily and emotional aspects of raving, which they believe to be primarily a product of the music, the dancing and the crowd rather than the drug itself. Underlying these attitudes is the existence of a code of acceptable behaviour wherein psychoactive ingestion is associated with an intended outcome of learning, personal growth and transformation. This expectation not only dictates that the context for ingestion should be limited to the rave locale, but has also influenced the drug of choice to be MDMA, a substance noted for its therapeutic and spiritual potential. In many cases this kind of learning, which I have argued is 'neural tuning', has imparted to individuals the ability to reach a 'natural high' while in the rave environment. Although neural tuning can occur through repeated exposure to the natural driving mechanisms present at raves, psychoactive experimentation among individuals from a monophasic culture enables neural tuning that is immediate, and relatively effortless, among those who would otherwise be unacquainted with the potentials of natural ASC induction.

The flashback phenomenon is evidence of this process of immediate tuning. Examination of the triggers known to elicit flashbacks has illustrated that these triggers are all present at raves and many participants have learned to manipulate these mechanisms to re-create natural highs that mirror past drug experiences. As this learning takes place, a growing number of participants have argued that the same sense of community, abandonment and transcendence can be attained from the music and dancing alone, and that these are the primary reasons for attending events.

Although many ravers long for the 'good old days' when raves were not contaminated by novel street drugs and blatant drug abuse, this research suggests that the original philosophy and perhaps vision of the rave movement are being kept alive by a small but potentially growing number of individuals who are clearly committed to the music, the dancing and the vibe.

Notes

1 I would like to thank Charles Laughlin, Gwyneth Parry, George Takahashi and Tim Olaveson for helpful feedback on earlier drafts of this chapter. I also acknowledge Ian Prattis and Marie-Françoise Guédon for their continued support in this research. Finally, I am grateful to those members of the rave community who were kind enough to share their time and experiences with me.

2 The death of a 21-year-old male at a Toronto rave prompted Ontario's Chief Coroner to order an inquest into the MDMA-related death. Pressure from the media and politicians motivated city councillors to consider having raves banned. Protest from the rave community halted prohibition, and instead 19 recommendations were made to increase participant safety at rave events. These recommendations formed the basis of a city bylaw requiring promoters to obtain permits and follow specified guidelines to hold legal raves. Other cities in Canada, such as Ottawa, Vancouver and Calgary, have created similar bylaws in an effort to regulate rave events.

3 Originally the term 'designer drug' referred to legal substances that were designed to mirror the effects of illicit substances (Saunders 1996a: 10). Today, however, the terms 'synthetic' and 'designer drugs' are used synonymously to refer to illicit drugs that are created to evoke a specific effect. MDMA, MDA and LSD are examples of designer drugs. This term is also used for drugs that are considered 'new', or old drugs such as LSD which have acquired a renewed popularity (Saunders 1996a: 10). Designer drugs are also referred to as club or dance drugs, reflecting the popularity of designer drugs in the club and rave scenes.

4 The term 'empathogenic' refers to the unique qualities of MDMA and its related class of drugs. Such characteristics include a heightened sense of interpersonal communication, emotionality and sensory perception (see Tramacchi 2000: 211; Metzner and Adamson 2001: 182).

5 My examination of neural tuning in the rave context is informed by a collaborative anthropological study of rave culture conducted over an eight-month period (Takahashi and Olaveson 2003), in addition to ongoing fieldwork. In the collaborative project, a total of 121 surveys were distributed to ravers through the target and snow-ball sampling method. In this chapter the terms 'we' and 'our' in relation to survey results refer to both authors. Material was also obtained from personal accounts of ravers posted on Internet list-servs and rave websites. Semi-structured interviews of rave participants were the primary source of data for this study. Finally, participant observation was conducted at 21 events in the metropolitan centres of southern and eastern Ontario and Quebec. Recognizing the blurring of boundaries between clubs and raves, I attended both types of venues as both are identified with rave culture, although ravers themselves still feel that there remains a distinction. Observations at raves and after-hours clubs generally took place during the peak hours of these events (12.00–5.00a.m.), although I did remain to the end at eight events and this resulted in up to 12 hours of observation per event.

6 Some informants indicated that 'peach' is a mixture of MDMA and various other drugs, such as LSD or heroine.

7 Ravers recognize the vibe as a kind of energy, pulse or feeling that can only be experienced physically. Reynolds describes the vibe as 'a meaningful and *feeling*-full mood that materially embodies a certain kind of worldview and life stance' (1999: 372). The DJ, the music and the people attending the event are identified by ravers as factors which contribute to the quality of the vibe.

8 In addition to preventing dehydration, these energy drinks contain the amino acids that are believed to be the key products used by the body to produce neurotransmitters such as serotonin (Seymour and Smith 1998:241). It should also be noted that many of these 'smart' drinks are associated with enhancing a drug's effect.

9 http://www.hypereal.org/raves/spirit/testimonials/Harmony-SanFrancisco.html (accessed 8 August 2001).

10 http://www.ecstasy.org/experiences/trip82.html (accessed 8 August 2001).

11 It should be noted that, although common themes and features of the rave scene are visible, it is not a homogenous subculture. The fragmentation of a unified genre of rave music and an accompanied style of raving to multiple genres – i.e. jungle, gabba, trance, Goa, hardcore and breakbeat, to name a few – has been witnessed worldwide. Thus not all ravers prescribe to PLUR and not all ravers are interested in personal growth and transformation. Individuals who are interested in the spiritual aspects of raving are more likely to listen to trance music and attend Goa trance events (Fritz 1999: 190). Our survey research indicated that individuals who have had religious experiences at raves are much more likely to listen to trance music. The association between music preference and drug choice has also been noted by Weber (1999) and Reynolds (1999). Weber observed that in the greater Toronto area crystal methamphetamine is associated with jungle and techno and cannabis with hip-hop (1999: 327). Similarly, Pedersen and Skrondal (1999) found ecstasy use to be highest among house/techno rave-goers.

12 Most informants felt that the full effects of a psychoactive are more likely to be experienced on an empty stomach. The vomiting that can accompany the initial onset of MDMA was another reason for limiting food intake. Aside from beverages to prevent dehydration, food is generally avoided both during and after rave events since substances such as ecstasy and methamphetamine act as appetite suppressants.

13 That is, high-voltage slow-wave EEG, synchronous activity and parasympathetic dominance (see Winkelman 1986, 1997, 2000).

14 http://www.ecstasy.org/experiences/trip58.html (accessed 8 August 2001).

15 This term refers to the effect that what is learned under the influence of a drug-induced state is best recalled in that state.

Bibliography

Adlaf, E. and R. Smart (1997) 'Party subculture or dens of doom? An epidemiological study of rave attendance and drug use patterns among adolescent students', *Journal of Psychoactive Drugs* 29(2): 193–8.

Batzer, W., T. Ditzler and C. Brown (1999) 'LSD use and flashbacks in alcoholic patients', *Journal of Addictive Diseases* 18(2): 57–63.

Beck, J. and M. Rosenbaum (1994) *Pursuit of Ecstasy: The MDMA Experience*, Albany, NY: State University of New York Press.

Bourguignon, E. (1973) *Religion, Altered States of Consciousness and Social Change*, Columbus, OH: Ohio State University Press.

Boys, A., S. Lenton and K. Norcross (1997) 'Polydrug use at raves by a Western Australian sample', *Drug and Alcohol Review* 16: 227–34.

Castillo, R.J. (1995) 'Culture, trance, and the mind-brain', *Anthropology of Consciousness* 6(1): 17–32.

Centre for Addiction and Mental Health (2000) 'Rave attendance among Ontario students, 1995–1999', *CAMH Population Studies eBulletin*, June (1), Toronto, Ontario: CAMH.

Cohen, R.S. (1998) *The Love Drug: Marching to the Beat of Ecstasy*, Binghampton: Haworth Medical Press.

d'Aquili, E.G. and C.D. Laughlin (1975) 'The biopsychological determinants of religious ritual behavior', *Zygon* 10(1): 32–59.

—— (1996) 'The neurobiology of myth and ritual', in R. Grimes (ed.) *Readings in Ritual Studies*, Englewood Cliffs, NJ: Prentice-Hall Inc.

Eisner, B. (1994) *Ecstasy: The MDMA Story*, Berkeley, CA: Ronin Publishing Inc.

ENRG, E. (2001) 'Psychic sonics: tribadelic dance trance-formation (an interview with Ray Castle)', in G. St John (ed.) *Free NRG: Notes from the Edge of the Dance Floor*, Altona: Common Ground Publishing.

Ervin, F.R., R.M. Palmour, B.E.P. Murphy, R. Prince and R.S. Simons (1988) 'The psychobiology of trance II: physiological and endocrine correlates', *Transcultural Psychiatric Research Review* 25: 267–84.

Forsyth, A. (1996) 'Places and patterns of drug use in the Scottish dance scene', *Addiction* 91(4): 511–21.

Fritz, J. (1999) *Rave Culture: An Insider's Overview*, Canada: Smallfry Press.

Gellhorn, E. (1969) 'Further studies on the physiology and pathophysiology of the tuning of the central nervous system', *Psychosomatics* 10: 94–104.

Gellhorn, E. and W.F. Kiely (1972) 'Mystical states of consciousness: neurophysiological and clinical aspects', *Journal of Nervous and Mental Disease* 154: 399–405.

Gerra, G., A. Zaimovic, D. Franchini, M. Palladino, G. Giucastro, N. Reali, D. Maestri, R. Caccavari, R. Delsignore and F. Brambilla (1998) 'Neuroendocrine responses of healthy volunteers to "techno-music": relationships with personality traits and emotional state', *International Journal of Psychophysiology* 28: 99–111.

Heaton, R.K. (1975) 'Subject expectancy and environmental factors as determinants of psychedelic flashback experiences', *Journal of Nervous and Mental Disease* 161(3): 157–66.

Hutson, S. (1999) 'Technoshamanism: spiritual healing in the rave subculture', *Popular Music and Society*, fall: 53–77.

Kalant, H. (2001) 'The pharmacology and toxicology of "Ecstasy" (MDMA) and related drugs', *Canadian Medical Association Journal* 165(7): 917–28.

Laughlin, C.D., J. McManus and E.G. d'Aquili (1992) *Brain, Symbol & Experience: Toward a Neurophenomenology of Human Consciousness*, New York: Columbia University Press.

Leikin, J., A.J. Krantz, M. Zell-Kanter, R.L. Barkin and D.O. Hryhorczuk (1989) 'Clinical features and management of intoxication due to hallucinogenic drugs', *Medical Toxicology and Adverse Drug Experience* 4(5): 324–35.

Lerner, A.G., M. Gelkopf, I. Oyffe, B. Finkel, S. Katz, M. Sigal and A. Weizman (2000) 'LSD-induced hallucinogen persisting perception disorder treatment with clonidinean open pilot study', *International Clinical Psychopharmacology* 15: 35–7.

Lenton, S. and P. Davidson (1999) 'Raves, drugs, dealing and driving: qualitative data from a West Australian sample', *Addiction* 92(10): 1,327–37.

Lex, B.W. (1975) 'Physiological aspects of ritual trance', *Journal of Altered States of Consciousness* 2(2): 109–21.

McCall, T. (2001) *This Is Not a Rave: In the Shadow of a Subculture*, Toronto: Insomniac Press.

McGee, R. (1984) 'Flashbacks and memory phenomena', *Journal of Nervous and Mental Disease* 172(5): 273–8.

Malberg, J.E. and L.S. Seiden (1998) 'Small changes in ambient temperature, cause large changes in 3,4-methylenedioxymethamphetamine (MDMA)-induced, serotonin neurotoxicity and core body temperature in the rat', *Journal of Neuroscience* 18: 5,086–94.

Malbon, B. (1999) *Clubbing: Dancing, Ecstasy and Vitality*, London: Routledge Press.

Mandell, A. (1980) 'Toward a psychobiology of transcendence: god in the brain', in D. Davidson and R. Davidson (eds) *The Psychobiology of Consciousness*, New York: Plenum.

Matefy, R.E. (1980) 'Role-play theory of psychedelic drug flashbacks', *Journal of Consulting and Clinical Psychology* 48(4): 551–3.

Matefy, R.E., C. Hayes and J. Hirsch (1978) 'Psychedelic drug flashbacks: subjective reports and biographical data', *Addictive Behavior* 3: 165–78.

Measham, F., H. Parker and J. Aldridge (1998) 'The teenage transition: from adolescent recreational drug use to the young adult dance culture in Britain in the mid-1990s', *Journal of Drug Issues* 28(1): 9–32.

Metzner, R. and S. Adamson (2001) 'Using MDMA in healing, psychotherapy and spiritual practise', in J. Holland (ed.) *Ecstasy: The Complete Guide*, Rochester: Park Street Press.

Neher, A. (1961) 'Auditory driving observed with scalp electrodes in normal subjects', *Electroencephalography and Clinical Neurophysiology* 13: 449–51.

—— (1962) 'A physiological explanation of unusual behavior in ceremonies involving drums', *Human Biology* 34: 151–60.

Newberg, A.B. and E.G. d'Aquili (2000) 'The neuropsychology of religious and spiritual experience', in J. Andresen and K.C. Forman (eds) *Cognitive Models and Spiritual Maps*, Thorverton: Imprint Academic.

NIDA (2000) *An Overview of Drug Use in Toronto*, National Institute on Drug Abuse, available online at:
http://www.ccsa.ca/ccendu/Reports/NIDAfinalpaper.doc (accessed 19 June 2001).

Park, E. (2001) 'Floss talk: riding the raves', *Asian Week Archives*, available online at http://www.asianweek.com (accessed 19 June 2001).

Pedersen, W. and A. Skrondal (1999) 'Ecstasy and new patterns of drug use: a normal population study', *Addiction* 94(11): 1,695–706.

Power, R., T. Power and N. Gibson (1996) 'Attitudes and experience of drug use amongst a group of London teenagers', *Drugs: Education, Prevention and Policy* 3(1): 71–80.

Reynolds, S. (1998) 'Rave culture: living dream or living death?', in S. Redhead (ed.) *The Clubcultures Reader: Readings in Popular Cultural Studies*, Malden: Blackwell Publishers.

—— (1999) *Generation Ecstasy: Into the World of Techno and Rave Culture*, New York: Routledge.

Rouget, G. (1985) *Music and Trance: A Theory of the Relations between Music and Possession*, Chicago: University of Chicago Press.

Saunders, N. (1996a) *Ecstasy: Dance, Trance and Transformation*, Oakland, CA: Quick American Archives.

—— (1996b) 'High church: can drugs bring you spiritual enlightenment?', *The Face* 98: 106–12.

Schick, J.F.E. and D.E. Smith (1970) 'Analysis of the LSD flashback', *Journal of Psychedelic Drugs* 3(1): 13–19.

Seymour, R.B. and D.E. Smith (1998) 'Psychological and psychiatric consequences of hallucinogens', in R.E. Tarter, R.T. Ammerman and P.J. Ott (eds) *Handbook of Substance Abuse: Neurobehavioral Pharmacology*, New York: Plenum Press.

Takahashi, M. and T. Olaveson (2003) 'Music, dance and raving bodies: raving as spirituality in the Central Canadian rave scene', *Journal of Ritual Studies* 17(2): 72–96.

Topp, L., J. Hando, P. Dillon, A. Roche and N. Solowij (1999) 'Ecstasy use in Australia: patterns of use and associated harm', *Drug and Alcohol Dependence* 55: 105–15.

Tramacchi, D. (2000) 'Field tripping: psychedelic *communitas* and ritual in the Australian bush', *Journal of Contemporary Religion* 55(2): 201–13.

Turner, V.W. (1983) 'Body, brain and culture', *Zygon* 18(3): 221–45.

van de Wijngaart, G.F., R.V. Braam, D.E. de Bruin, M. Fris, N.J.M. Maalste and H. Verbraeck (1999) 'Ecstasy use at large-scale dance events in The Netherlands', *Journal of Drug Issues* 29(3): 679–702.

Ward, C. (1984) 'Thaipusam in Malaysia: a psycho-anthropological analysis of ritual trance, ceremonial possession and self-mortification practices', *Ethos* 12(4): 307–34.

Watson, L. and J. Beck (1991) 'New Age seekers: MDMA use as an adjunct to spiritual pursuit', *Journal of Psychoactive Drugs* 23(3): 261–70.

Weber, T.R. (1999) 'Raving in Toronto: peace, love, unity and respect in transition', *Journal of Youth Studies* 2(3): 317–36.

Weir, E. (2000) 'Raves: a review of the culture, the drugs and the prevention of harm', *CMAJ* 162(13): 1,843–49.

Wesson, D.R. (1976) 'An analysis of psychedelic drug flashbacks', *American Journal of Drug and Alcohol Abuse* 3(3): 425–38.

Winkelman, M. (1986) 'Trance states: a theoretical model and cross-cultural analysis', *Ethos* 14: 174–203.

—— (1997) 'Altered states of consciousness and religious behavior', in S.E. Glazer (ed.) *The Anthropology of Religion*, Westport, CT: Greenwood Press.

—— (2000) *Shamanism: The Neural Ecology of Consciousness and Healing*, Westport, CT: Bergin & Garvey.

Part III

Music

The techniques of sound and ecstasy

8 Selecting ritual

DJs, dancers and liminality in underground dance music

Morgan Gerard

This chapter seeks to explore a contemporary performance arena where the liminal space the anthropologist Victor Turner believed once belonged to tribal ritual can be located – namely, that of underground dance music and its performance at raves and clubs. Following the processual model initially established by Arnold van Gennep (1960) and later refined by Turner, I argue that ritual transformation in rave and club events is made possible by both the spatialization and performance of music and the ways in which participants negotiate liminality throughout the course of events. Drawing from a brief ethnographic case study of Toronto's Turbo Niteclub, and by focusing on the interstitial moments of music and dance, I investigate how liminally located interactions between performers and audiences generate potentially transformative experiences.

In his quest to locate contemporary manifestations of liminal performance, Victor Turner wrote about 'retribalization as an attempt to restore the original matrix of ritual' (1984: 25). Vague as to what constitutes 'retribalization', Turner seemed to be subtly mandating his readers to seek out those communities, organizations or 'tribes' in their own immediate geographies whose activities or events were somehow distinguished from the more ritually impoverished mainstream of Western society. Through investigating and, more importantly, participating in events which embody the multidimensionality of tribal ritual – speech, music, dance, art and so on – Turner suggested that the transformative experiences of our agrarian forebears could be rejoined and recovered by post-industrial citizens long separated from such creative activities by the division of labour and other changes in society. It is a suggestion he made throughout his writing, first appearing in *The Ritual Process* (1969), where he briefly mentioned the liminality of Halloween, attempts made by hippies to recreate certain ritual conditions under which spontaneous communitas might be conjured, and the ritual-ness of participating in groups as diverse as black youth street gangs, the Ku Klux Klan and Hell's Angels. In *Dramas, Fields and Metaphors* (1974), he grants three pages of (somewhat condescending) discussion to rock music scenes and how they might figure in his understanding of tribal communitas and ritual. In *Process, Performance and Pilgrimage* (1979a), he extended his acknowledgments of Western liminal practices to include the activities and initiation rites of religious or quasi-religious organizations such as churches, sects, clubs, fraternities,

Masonic orders and secret societies. And by the publication of *From Ritual To Theatre* his scope of interest had widened so far as to include 'theatre, ballet, opera, film, the novel, printed poetry, the art exhibition, classical music, rock music, carnivals, processions, folk drama, major sports events and dozens more' (V Turner 1982: 85, 86).

Notwithstanding his perpetual distinction between the liminal and liminoid,[1] Victor Turner believed that such activities and groups have discovered 'the cultural debris of some forgotten liminal ritual' (1979a: 58) and somehow managed to excavate a connection to a numinosity thought lost to large-scale, complex societies. Following his introduction to Richard Schechner in 1977 and a subsequent two-week workshop in experimental theatre, Turner discovered something of that elusive liminal energy and a sort of 'retribalization' among a spontaneous communitas of anthropology and drama students while 're-enacting' a series of Ndembu rituals. Perhaps encountering his own transformative threshold where, like the essence of liminality itself, he was betwixt and between the anthropologist's analytic endeavour to understand ritual and the dramatist's performative experience of ritualizing, Turner's accounts (1979b) of the workshop are suggestive of those anti-structural moments he characterizes as particular to ritual. Much of his final writing, some of it collected and edited after his death by his wife, Edith, took this to heart in declaring that '[t]he theatre and other performance arenas have taken over the liminal space that belonged to ritual' (E. Turner 1986: 10).

Writing ritual-ness

The idea that performances of underground dance music are a contemporary manifestation of some ancient form of ritual is well established among participants of so-called rave and club cultures. From 'techno-shamanism', through 'neo-tribalism' to 'trance dancing', the language of ravers and clubbers is replete with references to a subculturally excavated sense of primitive numinosity. In the introduction to *This Is Not a Rave*, an insider's guide to Toronto's rave scene replete with first-person accounts, author Tara McCall expresses her own spiritual experience of the events:

> Something magical happens to me during those twilight hours on Sunday morning. It is on the Sabbath that I always find my god. I am as nomadic as the others wandering from warehouse to warehouse to have my soul awakened. The music thunders through my flesh, the notes swim within my veins. DJs spin their scriptures with eloquence, zest and assurance. The bass rattles my lungs and beats in unison with my heart. If I close my eyes I can watch my flesh melt away and my soul rise between the spaces of sound.
>
> (McCall 2001: n.p.)

McCall's testimonial is but one example of how both ravers and clubbers often invoke, acknowledge and even promote the potentially transcendent experiences that occur while participating in underground dance music events. Among scholars, many of whom count themselves as either longstanding or temporary participants in rave or club culture, there also seems to be an almost intuitive understanding and appreciation of the events as somehow transformative, transcendent and quasi-religious. For example, Rietveld refers to early house music events in Chicago as 'a night-time church' (1998: 129), Gore characterizes 'the DJ as [a] high priest whose instrument is not the drum but the turntable' (1997: 61), and Hutson suggests that a DJ 'guides the ravers on an ecstatic journey to paradise – a presocial state of nondifferentiation and communitas' (1999: 54). Such references have become central to the academic canon of rave and club cultures and reveal a set of a priori assumptions concerning underground dance music's ritual-ness. Given the theoretical prevalence of Birmingham's Centre for Contemporary Cultural Studies (CCCS) in the literature on underground dance music, this is no surprise. It is, however, something of an obstacle to understanding the processes through which rave or club events as socially interactive rituals unfold. Following Hall and Jefferson's (1976) study of British youth and the suggestion that virtually any collection of young bodies gathered under the banner of a subculture was engaged in rituals of resistance, Birmingham-inspired sociology and cultural studies have fallen short of addressing the structures and experiences of such rituals. This is largely because analyses informed by CCCS theory and method are marked by a disturbing lack of ethnographic material on the interactiveness of subcultural sites or events and the mediating role played by music and dance in many of those events – a disturbing trend considering the prevalence of music scenes in CCCS-inspired literature over the past 25 years. Instead, music and dance are considered not as lived experiences but as static texts or signs to be read for some decodable political significance or as socially disembodied reference points used to illustrate current theories on deviance, class consciousness, commodity consumption and stylistic resistance to the mainstream (Hall and Jefferson 1976; Hebdige 1979).

Sarah Thornton's *Club Cultures* (1996) is one such example of this approach. In her neo-Marxist analysis of British ravers and clubbers, Thornton makes a number of allusions to underground dance music spaces as ritual, suggesting that clubbing is 'a rite of passage' for British youth and that raves involve a 'ritualistic passage' for their participants (*ibid.*: 57). Yet her discussion does not attend to any sense of movement or participation through such passages. In a discussion of what might otherwise be deemed, following Turner, 'social drama', Thornton investigates how specific and supposed conflicts (authentic/phoney, classless/classed, underground/mainstream) are played out through particular symbols (clothes, VIP rooms, record collections) of 'subcultural capital'. In identifying 'subcultural ideologies' (*ibid.*: 6) shared by hierarchically ranked groups of participants, Thornton's analysis also seems relevant to the idea that rituals can be performances of contested power relations, directed towards the group and outsiders (see Harrison 1991). But in avoiding the central role played by music and dance as performed events and concentrating on how conflict is played out through the successful consumption and signification of subcultural signs, Thornton misses the most active illustrations of how her all-important insider/outsider dichotomy is resolved or transformed.

This inattention to dramaturgical features is also characteristic of the post-structuralist approaches to rave and club cultures (Redhead 1993; Pini 1997; Rietveld 1998; Stanley 1997; Martin 1999) which, when invoking the ritual-ness of underground dance music without accounting for the central role of music and dance, construct idealized versions of raves and clubs rather than actual instances of situated, performed events. The result is that references to raves and clubs as ritual events or to DJs as ritual specialists remain primarily metaphorical, anecdotal and often culled from what might be called the 'who feels it knows it' approach of privileging informant testimonials. Readers interested in the co-construction of events by multiple participants are given little or no analysis of the specific performative contexts from which to understand how a house music event is like a church, how a DJ can be likened to a shaman and how communitas is built from the dance floor.

Not even a recent initiate in rave or club culture would expect that what was lost can now be found simply by magically dressing up a venue, hoping a DJ will perform as he might have previously, or expecting a crowd of dancers instantly to commune. If an event is like a church, a DJ like a shaman and a dance floor like communitas, it is because they are actively transformed as such through ongoing interactions between performers and participants as they experience music and dance. How DJs and dancers engage in this potential for transformative experiences has only recently emerged as a topic for serious consideration by scholars. Until Fikentscher's (2000) ethnomusicological study of interactivity at New York City clubs, most authors simply provided clues as to the 'direct and reciprocal relationship between the DJ and his audience' (Langlois 1992: 236). While the dance music press, insider accounts and testimonials from DJs and dancers suggested a fertile ground for investigation, scholars tended to avoid the dialectical possibilities inherent in performance analyses or phenomenologically inspired investigations by simply treating such interactions as somehow ineffable. With the publication of *You Better Work!* (2000), however, Fikentscher provided the first academic framework for understanding how a successful event is co-constructed *vis-à-vis* DJ–dancer interactions. I have taken up this general theme elsewhere in reference to the interactional work conducted by MCs in tandem with DJs and dancers at Toronto drum 'n' bass events (Gerard and Sidnell 2000). Both studies point to the temporalization and spatialization of events combined with structured performance techniques and social context as central features of what most participants consider to be essential ritualized events in their lives. Here, music and dance are the 'molecules of ritual' (V. Turner 1969: 14), the combined and recombined aesthetic symbols or forms responsible for 'the structuring of structure' in all such events (Kapferer 1986: 202). Such structuring and the process by which the aforementioned phenomena might occur can be further elaborated by considering van Gennep's three phases of ritual as they are applied to music (primarily) and dance (secondarily).

To investigate this process in the context of rave and club events, and with the intention of contributing a more descriptive analysis of the 'rave as ritual' hypothesis, I discuss an event at Turbo Niteclub on Friday, 20 October 2001, in Toronto, Canada. By investigating the spatialization of music, DJ–dancer inter-actions and DJing as a ritually structured narrative, I illustrate how liminality is a constantly revisited theme and, indeed, the root paradigm of rave and club cultures.

The spatialization of music

In his cross-cultural review of rites of passage, van Gennep maintained that transformation occurs during the successful movement between demarcated phases of separation (pre-liminal), transition (liminal) and incorporation (post-liminal). By suggesting that a 'rite of spatial passage has become a rite of spiritual passage' (1960: 22), van Gennep locates transformative stages in space. If raving or clubbing can be likened to ritual there must be some indication to participants that a separation from profane or secular space and time has occurred. Van Gennep characterized this phase as 'passing through the door' (*ibid.*: 20). Thus, the obvious starting point for the study of the ritual process in underground dance music events would be outside the venue itself where people are awaiting entry.

Turbo Niteclub is located in the centre of what is known as Toronto's entertainment district, a 2-kilometre stretch of clubs, restaurants, offices and resi-dential lofts in which traffic is directed one way west along Richmond Street and one way east along Adelaide Street. The club portion of Turbo's building is divided into two floors; during the night in question, local promotion company Lifeforce schedules drum 'n' bass in the basement, and house, tech-house and techno on the main floor. The entrance door of the club faces south on Adelaide Street and is accessible by one of two line-ups: those entering the door from its west side are either ticket holders or waiting to pay cash at the admission door just inside the entrance; those entering the door from its east side hope to do so because their names are on the guest list. It's 10.30 p.m. and, arriving earlier than usual to take notes on DJ Tim Patrick's set upstairs, I wait in the guest-list line and hear Patrick's first record through the doors. Generally, two security personnel stand by the door conducting patrons to their respective line, while at the front of the guest-list line a Lifeforce employee checks names on a clipboard and, if confirmed, gives tickets to those listed by the promoters, club owners or featured DJs.

While Thornton has suggested we look at the line-ups and door policies of raves and clubs in order to understand how qualifiers based on age, race, gender and sexuality allow for a culling of potential participants from the crowd inside (a process she connects to the inclusive/exclusive nature of such events), Turbo has no such policy except with regard to age.[2] Even with an open-door policy, the highly structured organization of participants as they prepare to enter the club generates a great deal of anxiety: underage patrons worry they will be checked for identification and, if they have fake ID, wonder if it will get them through the door; those hiding drugs dread losing their party favours; ticket holders and those hoping to pay inside, if arriving during peak hours (1.00–3.00 a.m.), are concerned the club might be at capacity and they will have to wait until enough people leave before they are permitted entry; and, if they arrive before the official 1.00 a.m. cut-off, being asked to join the ticket line can be particularly humiliating for those who believe their insider status should exclude them from paying. The waiting and uncertainty posed by entering Turbo and the mandatory body search for items deemed 'ritual pollutants'[3] seem to correspond somewhat to the pattern of separation rites as van Gennep understands them. But Turner has argued that separation 'is more than just a matter of entering a temple – there must be in addition a rite which changes the quality of time *also*, or constructs a cultural realm which is defined as "out of time"' (V. Turner 1982: 24). That rite, I suggest, is music. Arriving at Turbo by foot or by car, the anticipation generated by a thumping bass reverberating through the club is particularly dramatic. As each familiar record and mix is played by the DJ inside the club, those waiting outside become excited and expectant. Neither in the club nor the public realm, time spent in line is suspended time where patrons dutifully await music's power to restructure their temporal sense of 'being-in-the-world' (Rouget 1980: 122).

It then follows that the interior of Turbo could be characterized as the transitional space. For van Gennep, this is a 'neutral zone' between worlds, standing outside of culture (1960: 18); for Victor Turner it is 'a no-man's-land betwixt-and-between the structural past and the structural future' (1990: 11). In the context of underground dance music events, the liminal territory in question is that which Fikentscher (2000) calls the 'counterpublic sphere'; Stanley (1997), Martin (1999) and St John (Chapter 1) refer to as 'heterotopia' (Foucault 1986); and Gibson and Pagan (1997) and May (2000) designate the 'temporary autonomous zone' (Bey 1991). All of these characterizations suggest a realm of the subjunctive (V. Turner 1982) and the intersubjective (Pini 1997), an arena where participants might construct alternate identities and, perhaps, apply experiences of the liminal to their post-liminal lives. At Turbo, immersion in the liminal is reflected in the club's design.

Having passed the guest list, cleared security and presented my ticket through a glass booth, I am immediately directed inside by another security guard. Entering the club down a flight of stairs (which leads to the drum 'n' bass room in the basement), I then go upstairs, where Tim Patrick is playing a set of minimal house and tech-house to a sparsely populated room. At 10.45 p.m. this is no surprise; club events in Toronto rarely attract large crowds until 1.00 a.m. Although a number of people are mingling at bars, standing around the edges of the dance floor and sitting in the small area serving as a VIP room, nobody is dancing.

At Turbo, whether drum 'n' bass downstairs or house, tech-house and techno upstairs, for those 'watching' the dance floor from the vantage point of the VIP room or from the downstairs foyer or the bar, music is omnipresent and its palpable presence mediates all forms of social activity inside the club. But if dance is generally considered the central activity of such events, how do we account for non-dancing patrons in the context of raves and clubs as ritual? Previous scholarly works on underground dance music point us towards understanding dance's figurative role in relation to altered states of consciousness (Thornton 1996: 60), building communitas (Fikentscher 2000: 60), and going 'mad' or 'losing it' (Pini 2001). Like Turner's 'fertile nothingness' of liminality, where participants find themselves 'striving after new forms and structures' (V. Turner 1990: 12), such accounts indicate that participants construct their own free, gestative cultural space, one that can be likened to spontaneous communitas. Removed from the dictates of discreet, polite Torontonian culture and given an opportunity to engage in ecstatic dance, participants discover those moments 'when compatible people...obtain a flash of lucid mutual understanding on the existential level, when they feel that all problems, not just their problems, could be resolved; whether emotional or cognitive, if only the group which is felt (in the first person) as "essentially us" could sustain its inter-subjective illumination' (V. Turner 1979a: 45). Yet throughout the course of the event it was observed that many occupants of the VIP room (as well as some of those drifting around the edges of the club) never once strayed on to the dance floor. Are such individuals peripheral to the ritual proceedings and, if so, who are they and what, if any, is their role?

On this particular night, as is the case for most other events at the club, the occupants of Turbo's VIP room were mostly DJs, club and rave promoters, niche media pundits and other industry insiders and their guests – in short, a demographic typical of most VIP rooms in contemporary club culture. While Thornton's analysis indicates that such figures are in possession of the most subcultural capital – markers of greater insider status which, she argues, betray the so-called egalitarian ethos of underground dance music events – I prefer to characterize their presence and role as indications of 'normative' communitas. Occupying a position removed from the dance floor, these 'insider' patrons (and a number of 'regular' clubbers allowed into the VIP room on this occasion) have a unique vantage point from which to observe and assess key aspects of the ritual proceedings: the conduct of the DJ; how occupants of the dance floor are attending to the music played, the DJ and each other; and the reactions of their industry colleagues. Put simply, they are able to monitor events in such a way as to make alternative judgements on the etiquette and efficacy of the performance.

While it is common for promoters, DJs, media and club owners to locate their participatory origins as former neophytes by regularly intoning such claims as 'I'll always be a raver' or 'I'll always be a club kid', there is little doubt from the dance floor or from other VIPs that they stand out from the spontaneous and are staunchly rooted in the realm of the normative. As professionals, performers, entrepreneurs, etc., they are rarely caught in the throes of ecstatic dance. Instead, they are recognized for organizing, maintaining and promoting the 'utopian blueprint' (V. Turner 1977: 46) of the dance floor through activities which serve to contextualize events within a wider social and historical framework. Here, gossiping and networking serve to reinforce the social bonds of the community as one which exists both inside and outside dance (the activity) and clubs (the location); critically evaluating the event at hand affords promoters and DJs the opportunity to plan for and produce 'better' events in the future; attending events provides journalists and photographers with potentially valuable content for publication (which, in turn, serves reflectively to contextualize past performances); and informal business dealings enable entrepreneurs to perpetuate the ritual project as one which, if it is to continue, must confront the realities of event organization, commerce and the concerns of local law enforcement. As brokers of what is variously labelled 'the scene', 'the culture' and/or 'the community', one might even suggest that, following Victor Turner's (1979a) characteristics of normative communitas, VIPs acts as representatives (to the outside world) of a new social structure. This is particularly the case if one considers how promoters, DJs, club owners and media collaborate in contextualizing and disseminating the reformative paradigm(s) of raving and clubbing to the everyday world.[4]

The central paradigm rave and club cultures offer to the everyday world is liminality itself. Occurring record by record and interaction by interaction, liminality is presented and promoted as a transformational experience realized through music and dance. In order to illustrate this phenomenon it is necessary to consider underground dance music both as an event which occurs through the programming and mixing of vinyl records[5] by DJs for a dance floor, and as a variety of recorded music genres available on both vinyl records and CD. Both contexts reveal that liminality is the central aesthetic feature of underground dance music.

Techniques of liminality

As a recorded medium, underground dance music has been subject to a number of postmodernist investigations which marginally inform a discussion of liminality. Following Hebdige's (1987) analysis of the intersemiotic nature of sampling and pastiche in rap music, other scholars have pursued similar investigations into how techniques of composition locate underground dance music betwixt and between high and low culture, real and hyperreal music, black and white identity, and masculine and feminine subjectivity (Bradby 1993; Tagg 1994; Noys 1995; Thornton 1996; Rietveld 1998; Hutson 1999). For participants engaged in performances, however, there are less theoretical, more relevant features which directly evoke liminality. Because most dance music records are produced by DJs primarily for their consumption by other DJs, reading underground dance music as a static text defeats the purpose of the music which, ultimately, is to structure performances through vinyl records. That is, house, techno and drum 'n' bass records work as tools DJs employ in the programming and mixing of sets. If one were to speak of emotion and meaning in house music, liminal features in underground dance music provide the most relevant starting point for understanding how DJs collaborate with participants to construct successful events.

During Tim Patrick's performance at Turbo, I observed four techniques of liminality as they occurred in both the records in his programme and the techniques he used to play them: filtering and looping, EQing and mixing. As the first DJ of the evening, Patrick's set began at 10.30 p.m. to an empty club. Twenty minutes later, there were 30 people mingling at bars and four people on the dance floor, only one of whom was dancing. By midnight there were 35 people on the dance floor and approximately another 120 in the room. At this point, Patrick played what I identify as the first record of the evening exhibiting liminal characteristics: the combination of the filter and the loop.[6] Both the filter and the loop, when heard individually or in tandem, like liminality in general, are not meant to produce immediate satisfaction (Broadhurst 1999). Rather, they are tension-, excitement- and expectation-inducing effects intended to draw participants more fully into dance. Building from an ascending pattern, this particular filtered loop occupied 32 bars of the record in question. Its effect on the crowd was mixed: a number of the dancers recognized the effect as one which would likely precede a return to the thumping 4/4 pattern of the kick drum and thus began throwing their hands in the air energetically; others were unsure of the potential outcome and slowed their dancing in order to survey other participants, while approximately 10 people previously standing by the western bar abandoned their drinks for the dance floor. In each case, use of the filtered loop not only produced expectation and excitement but afforded participants an opportunity quickly to reflect on the state of the dance floor and their position *vis-à-vis* dance. With the dance floor half empty, by playing a record with a filtered loop Patrick addressed and transmitted to the crowd the possibilities of what *might* be if participants would more fully attend the dance space.

The third liminal technique I wish to address is EQing.[7] Throughout the course of his (and virtually every underground dance music DJ's set) Patrick was constantly manipulating the bass, mid and treble frequencies of the records, either as a means of mixing from record to record (i.e. dropping the bass out of the playing record to replace it with the bass of the next) or as an effect during the course of a single record. In cases where EQing is used during the body of a single record it is done to affect the sense of time transmitted through music. From the familiar 4/4 pulse of the kick drum, which in house, tech-house and techno makes up much of the performance's rhythmic narrative, Patrick temporarily suspended the dancers by dropping the bass out of the mix. Throughout the course of my field research I have observed two very distinct patterns in the way dancers react to this effect. The first involves club-culture neophytes; from the very beginning of the set there were a group of four college-age women dancing together while facing each other in a circle. In Toronto, dancing together in a circle usually indicates novice status.[8] When Patrick dropped the bass out of this first record, as if losing their footing or their timing all four women paused, looked at each other in slight confusion, stopped dancing completely and faced the DJ booth in unison as if looking for further instruction. The second pattern observed involves club-culture initiands; approximately one metre to the left of the group of four was a single woman of a similar age dancing alone. While her Snug[9] clothes indicated a certain insider status, her reaction to the EQing demonstrated a practised engagement with liminality. Although there was a slight pause in her dancing as Patrick dropped the bass out of the mix, this woman maintained the flow of her movement and, likely counting the record's time signature, increased the pace of her dancing at the exact point the bass was reintroduced into the mix.

Both reactions point to different levels of ritual experience. As such, dropping the bass out of a record demonstrates to dancers that they must obey the DJ not only by dancing but also by dancing together. Dropping the bass out of a record essentially functions as a levelling device – by interrupting the flow of time as measured through the kick drum the DJ is able to assess and re-synchronize the dance floor. As Turner has noted, such actions on the part of those conducting rituals are essential in creating the prerequisite 'uniform condition' (V. Turner 1969: 95) of spontaneous communitas. Within the span of twenty minutes, with four records played and two additional cases of similar EQing, the effects of this 'grinding down' of neophytes was observed: the group of four women continually surveyed the more experienced dancer to their left and, becoming more familiar with both the effects of EQing and the single woman's corresponding reaction to the technique, no longer hesitated as noticeably and, progressively, reacted in a similar fashion.

Mixes are the fourth, and most important, liminal technique.[10] In all performances of underground dance music, every mix is a period of ambiguity for both the DJ and the dancers. Generally favouring the longer, more drawn-out mix in which he overlays two records simultaneously through EQing for a minute or longer, Tim Patrick is considered to be one of Toronto's best technical DJs and rarely 'trainwrecks' a mix.[11] However, there is always the possibility of error or a skipping record, which will reflect poorly on his supervisory, 'shamanic' role in the proceedings. Although Fikentscher has noted that the programming of records is one mark of a 'good' DJ, mixing is equally important as both a technical skill and an art. A DJ's reputation and career are, in part, based on mixing skill, and between every record played mistakes can be costly for both performer and participants. For dancers, mixes are liminal in that they can sometimes be uncertain periods between the rhythmic structures of records. During this period, the 'total involvement' characteristic of Victor Turner's (1979a: 55) notion of flow can be broken by a poor mix. In such cases, the flash of spontaneous communitas is potentially threatened; dancers are often drawn out of their ecstatic state; they return to an increased awareness of both setting and self, and sometimes abandon the dance floor. A successful mix, however, allows for a continuous flow between mental, musical and physical states. It is generally in this transitional period that DJs (when their mix is recognized as not only technically successful but also innovative and/or daring) and dancers (when enthusiasm, energy, drugs and alcohol seem to best motivate a packed dance floor) find themselves caught up in those moments of spontaneous communitas that ravers and clubbers refer to as a 'peak'. In his popular pseudo-ethnography of New York City clubs, Miezitis describes this experience as:

1 Cream, Montreal 1999

Source: © Caroline Hayeur – Agence Stock Photo

2 Free party at Summit of America organized by activists against ZLEA (Zone de libre échange des Amériques), Quebec city, April 2001

Source: © Caroline Hayeur – Agence Stock Photo

3 Trance – Festive Ritual, Portrait of the Rave scene in
  Montreal, 1996–7

Source: © Caroline Hayeur – Agence Stock Photo

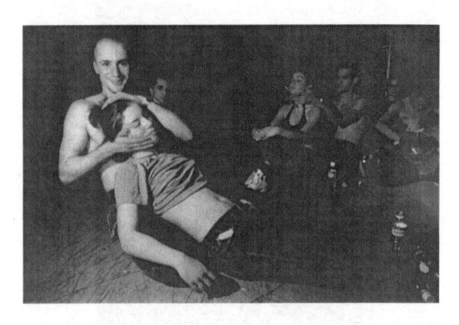

4 Massage – Festive Ritual, Portrait of the Rave Scene in Montreal, 1996–7

Source: © Caroline Hayeur – Agence Stock Photo

5 Beach Party at Half Moon Bay, Black Rock, Victoria, Australia, 21 February 1999

Source: © Saskia Fotofolk

6 Beach Party at Half Moon Bay, Black Rock, Victoria, Australia, 28 February 1999

Source: © Saskia Fotofolk

7 Exodus Cybertribal Festival 2003, Bald Rock Bush Retreat, New South Wales, Australia

Source: © Saskia Fotofolk

8 Shed 14, Melbourne, 5 September 1998
Source: © Saskia Fotofolk

9 Outback Eclipse Festival, Lyndhurst, South Australia, 3–6 December 2002
Source: © Saskia Fotofolk

10 Outback Eclipse Festival, Lyndhurst, South Australia, 3–6 December 2002

Source: © Saskia Fotofolk

11 Earthdance (Free Tibet Party), Melbourne, 2 October 1999

Source: © Saskia Fotofolk

12 Earthdream2000 Dance Floor, Alberrie Creek, South Australia
Source: © Saskia Fotofolk

13 Adam Beyer at Awakenings, NDSM Warehouse, Amsterdam, New Year's Eve 2002–3
Source: © Alexander Browne

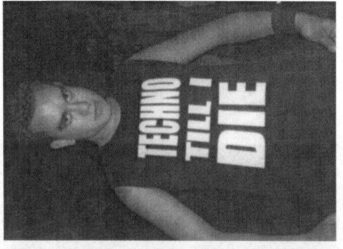

14 Planet Rose, Nijmegen, Netherlands, November 2002

Source: © Alexander Browne

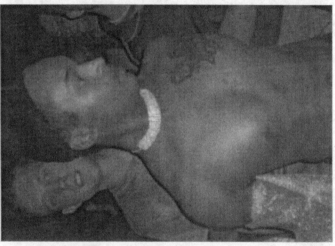

15 Awakenings, NDSM Warehouse, Amsterdam, New Year's Eve 2002–3

Source: © Alexander Browne

16 Awakenings, NDSM Warehouse, Amsterdam, New Year's Eve 2002–3

Source: © Alexander Browne

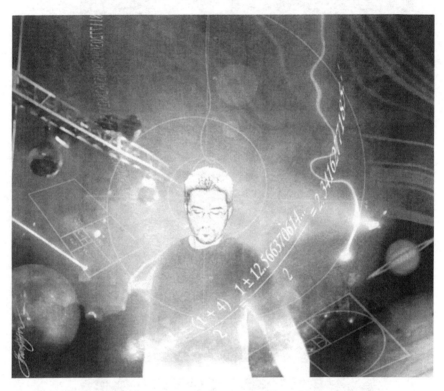

17 Finding Fibonacci, 2002

Source: © Steve Wishman

18 Rainbow Serpent Festival,
    Victoria, Australia, 2003

Source: © Martin Reddy

19 Outback Eclipse Festival, South Australia, December 2003

Source: © Martin Reddy

20 Hacienda by Todd Fath

Source: From the cover of Hillegonda C. Rietveld's *This Is Our House*

21 Drop Bass Network's Jesus Raves, 29 June 2002, Racine, Wisconsin

Source: Drop Bass Network

22 Drop Bass Network's Second Coming, 31 December 2000, Madison, Wisconsin

Source: Drop Bass Network

a peak of excitement and energy when the music is most stimulating, when the crowd is the largest and the most loosened up, most energetic, and when the lights and theatrics resemble a grand stage finale. The peak is like a sexual climax when everything and everyone flows together, a moment when time seems erased.

(Miezitis, in Fikentscher 2000: 41)

Variously signified by dancers throwing their hands in the air, blowing whistles, shouting or, in the case of drum 'n' bass, calling for a 'rewind',[12] peak moments unite the dance floor often through the release of tension built up during the mix and the fulfilment of expectations delivered by an almost prescient programming on behalf of the DJ. Whether such moments are triggered by the introduction of new rhythms, feints or breaks in rhythmic structure, an acceleration of tempo (Rouget 1980), or simply by mixing from one 'hot' record to another, the result is often a trance-like euphoria that, ultimately, defines a DJ's set and the dancers' experience as 'successful'. Much of that success rests on the DJ recognizing that every set is a narrative with ritualistic consequences received and reflected in dance. With the traditional Western predilection for a beginning, middle and end (Grimes 2000: 107), that narrative is often likened (by DJs and dancers using metaphors that are clearly spatial) to a journey. As a joint endeavour, the DJ or, as Fikentscher calls him or her, the 'soundscape architect' (2000: 8), skilfully draws from a blueprint of performance techniques to resituate the dance floor as a place transported (ideally) from 'here' to 'there', a task more complex than simply beginning and ending a set with a series of interspersed peak moments. Rather, as van Gennep has noted in cases 'where the transition possesses an autonomy of its own as a secondary system inserted within a ceremonial whole' (1960: 185), the passage process in a DJ's set is primarily encoded in every mix between records.

Often taken from published accounts of historical, religious or cultural events, van Gennep's understanding of the transitional process is based largely on observable phenomena. While music announces those spatial boundaries – particularly on the dance floor, where to 'dance is to inscribe music in space' (Rouget 1980: 121) – identifying the stages as they unfold in a DJ's performance relies on an intricate observation of mixing techniques and an ear trained in the complexities of the specific musical forms. Given these, it is possible to isolate stages in a mix corresponding to van Gennep's tripartite model. First, separation is essentially that point where the DJ indicates structural and temporal change through a type of narrative foreshadowing. By EQing the bass out of the forthcoming record, brief vocal, instrumental and secondary rhythmic segments (such as a high-hat or snare) of the forthcoming record can be inserted into the mix so as not to clash with the 4/4 rhythm of the main record. While this does not interrupt the temporal or structural flow of the main record, it does hint at the next movement. Second, transition is the ambiguous phase during which, for those trained in underground dance music's performance idiom, it is apparent that two tracks are being played simultaneously. Depending on the DJ, this phase can last between one and five minutes, usually involving a delicate manipulation of the EQ in which the 4/4 pulse of one or both records is removed from the mix in order to synchronize 'the structural past and the structural future' (V. Turner 1990: 11) of two rhythmically distinct records into a seamless mix. Finally, incorporation is that point at which the DJ fully completes the transition to the proceeding track, leaving behind all traces of the former record and returning listeners/dancers to the more familiar simplicity of one record. This can be achieved by progressively EQing all three channels from one record out of the mix: immediately, by punching a kill switch; gradually, by lowering the main volume control of the channel in question; or quickly, by moving the cross-fader completely to the desired channel.

Dancing passages

As noted in the case of EQing as a liminal technique, mixing as a passage process is received in a variety of ways depending largely on a dancer's knowledge of underground dance music's performance aesthetics. While neophytes make their first ritual passage through events somewhat tentatively, the initiated are more sure-footed. Throughout many of Patrick's mixes, the excitement and expectation of the separation phase often went relatively or completely unnoticed by less experienced participants, while more experienced dancers displayed their cognizance of impending changes through gestural shifts such as sweeping or stabbing hand movements in sync with the impending record's secondary rhythmic structure or a monitoring glance to the DJ booth. Recognizing this initial threshold in the mix, such reactions illustrate the extent to which experienced dancers are fully embedded in the ritual process and how less experienced dancers are yet to develop the same level of ritual skill and/or knowledge. For example, it was observed that less experienced dancers often hesitated and surveyed others for cues throughout each phase. In the case of more experienced dancers, many of whom seemed either to know or to predict forthcoming changes, there were no awkward pauses and their understanding of, and participation in, the structure and timing of mixes was displayed through the blowing of whistles, throwing hands in the air and glances of affirmation between friends.

This final phase of the mix presents opportunities for dancers to distinguish themselves from non-dancers as actively managing their membership or sense of belonging in a collaborative community at the nucleus of the ritual proceedings. For dancers, successful movement through the mix completes the passage process in a way not accessible to those off the dance floor. One might even suggest that the more mixes one dances through, the more fully incorporated one becomes in the new community. Furthermore, over the course of a DJ's set, and after each cycle is successfully repeated (particularly in cases when peaks occur), participants might undergo an accelerated transcendence where the combination of music, dance and, sometimes, drugs results in a heightened awareness of what informants often refer to as the 'vibe' – that elusive and ineffable quality of underground dance music events which defines a 'totally sick' night out. Yet, throughout the course of this event, many participants on the dance floor regularly disengaged themselves from dancing in order to buy drinks, go to the toilet, etc. By taking temporary reprieves, dancers were able to monitor the proceedings and reflect on their own perception of and participation in events as well as the agency of others. But because the narrative of a DJ's set is cyclical and liminality is always revisited, underground dance music events allow a fluidity of fully engaged participation and unregulated reintegration into dancing at any point. In most cases it was observed that, within the span of a single, complete mix, most participants returning to the dance floor found themselves fully incorporated into that cultural space.

During his set, beginning at 10.30.p.m. and finishing with Donald Glaude playing his first record at 1.00 a.m., Patrick played a total of 22 different records with 21 mixes connecting them. With 21 opportunities to encourage liminally located interactions between dancers, it took 90 minutes for Patrick and a particularly lethargic Toronto club crowd to find some sense of collective expression. After he dropped the bass out of the first eight bars of Harley & Feller's 'Deep Sensation' at midnight, more than 200 people were on the dance floor. For the next hour, Patrick managed to lead dancers further away from the world they left behind at the door and closer to club culture's promised land of transcendent dance. Although it was not Turbo's most successful night, Tim Patrick maintained his status as a DJ cult leader, and 600 people were well on their way to becoming 'essentially us'. Even the four college girls had broken a sweat *and* their circle.

Having participated in this rite too many times to count, I call it a night at 4.00 a.m. Donald Glaude has whipped the crowd into a frenzy with a set of progressive, funky breaks, and Stretch & Hooker have just mixed their way into their third record. Temporally, my incorporation might be somewhat premature. This party will continue until sunrise and, while other patrons will also drift out of the club before closing, many will celebrate something of a triumphant return to the world upon greeting the dawn. For some, incorporation might be prolonged at private after-parties where, over breakfast and before returning home, talk of the event serves to interpret the performance both within the framework of group and individual participation and within the context of past performances. Spatially – past security, out of the club and into the almost deserted street – my return to the everyday world is marked by the knowledge that I can always return next weekend. While less frequent and more anticipated summer events such as the World Electronic Music Festival[13] perhaps fit more neatly into van Gennep's spatialization of ritual passages (an extended pilgrimage to the site, a longer period of being sequestered in the bush, a protracted return home), the frequency of Lifeforce Fridays at Turbo suggests a less idealized version of incorporation. The reality is that the orthodox boundaries set by choice and obligation, seriousness and play, or agrarian and industrial prevent underground dance music events from being 'airbrushed' (Grimes 2000: 94) enough to match Turner's inclination for viewing activities in popular culture through the lens of tribal ethnography. Instead of efficiently returning to the mundane world as adults or other elevated social categories, participants receive their incorporative recognition as valued initiates only by returning to the ritual community itself.

Conclusion

For Turner, this recognition that the ritual event can be revisited positions rave and club performances as liminoid events. While somewhat devaluing the liminoid as a commodified leisure activity, Turner nonetheless suggests that liminoid events are 'proto-structural' (V. Turner 1979a: 39) in that they offer new cultural paradigms to the mainstream. I have argued that, foregoing Turner's distinction, liminality is the root paradigm of underground dance music. Furthermore, I have suggested that, as a recorded format and a performed activity, liminality is encoded in underground dance music as an incentive for dance. Dance, therefore, is the primary conduit for liminal, transformative experiences in the lives of ravers and clubbers. As a coordinated social action, dance transmits culture, encourages interconnectedness and reconfigures the body beyond the confines of the individual ego; as a liberatory, ecstatic experience of collective effervescence, it reveals new ways of being in the world, opens up the possibilities for transcending restrictive social categories and undoubtedly offers numerous health benefits from the spiritual to the physical (Thomas 1997). While the extent to which the value of ecstatic dance and liminality has been incorporated into the mainstream is not at issue here, it is important to note that over the last decade underground dance music events have become a global phenomenon. Perhaps this indicates a more complete and socially recognized ritual incorporation for participants in that the liminal experiences produced by the music–dance continuum are transformative not only at the micro levels of individuals to communitas, DJ to shaman and club to church, but also at a macro level, where popular culture itself has become somewhat infused with the aesthetic forms generated by rave and club cultures.[14]

Diverging from the subcultural studies agenda which theorizes them as cultures of resistance, Turner's similar view that liminoid genres offer a social critique of the mainstream, or the postmodernist assertion that they are celebrations of meaninglessness, I suggest (as do virtually all of my informants) that rave and club events occupy their present status in popular culture primarily because DJs, clubs, raves, dancing, getting high and other features of underground dance music offer multidimensional liminal experiences not found in the everyday world. The extent to which those experiences are transformative, transcendent or quasi-religious for all participants is unknown, perhaps unlikely and, for the purposes of this chapter, largely irrelevant. Whether from emic accounts or my own experiences, rather than excavating the meaning of a club event my intent has been to investigate the form of a club event and how liminality is encoded through performance. Recognizing that ritual has a 'constancy of form and variability of interpretation' (Boas, in Harrison 1991: 231), in describing the processual model as it occurs through music, dance and space, I hope to extend future inquiries into rave and club cultures beyond the metaphorical and into the actual.

That said, as I walk home along Adelaide Street beyond the rattling walls and windows of Turbo, I am struck by the decidedly emic suspicion that Victor Turner's quest for retribalization is well underway.

Notes

1 Turner maintained a distinction between the liminal as obligatory and the liminoid as optional, part of the leisure world as opposed to the religious world. See also Richard Schechner (1977) for how he contrasts the two categories in terms of efficacy and entertainment. While acknowledging the differing characteristics of both realms, I have opted for 'liminal' in recognition of the significance of rites of the leisure world in young people's lives.
2 The legal drinking age in Toronto (and the entire province of Ontario) is 19. Although Turbo had previously been an all-ages venue with a wristband giving access to roped-off bar areas, that policy changed for many events following the summer of 2000.
3 Prohibited substances at Toronto raves and clubs include all illegal drugs, weapons and food or drinks from the outside. While patrons at such events generally agree that security should confiscate weapons, the fact that many cross the entrance threshold while concealing Ecstasy, marijuana, cocaine and other illicit drugs underscores the conflicting agendas of participants and those of promoters, club owners and the police. Considering that four Ecstasy-related deaths occurred in Toronto between 1999 and 2002, one might suggest that some clubbers and ravers are notoriously prepared to flirt with substances many believe to be central to producing heightened states of liminality.
4 I refer to flyers, event phone lines, advertising, magazines, websites and other promotional tools, which are largely responsible for conveying information about the 'scene', events, DJs, etc.
5 While a number of both rave and club DJs have taken to using CD mixing technology in their sets, on the night in question only vinyl records were used.
6 Filtering refers to a method of digital production in which sound is shaped by reducing or increasing the loudness of certain frequencies by processing specific sound samples through an 18dB octave low-pass filter. The effect is rather like ascending or descending through sound. Looping refers to a process where a sample – such as a word, spoken or sung phrase, or a particular instrumental hook from a horn or guitar (most often taken from classic disco and funk records) – is edited in a repeating cycle throughout a section of the record. Both digital effects are often created by producers using an Akai S1000 stereo 16-bit linear sampler, first available in 1985.
7 EQing refers to a process through which DJs manipulate the frequency spectrum of vinyl records. Most DJ mixers feature three knobs controlling the bass, mid and treble ranges fed to the amplifier and speaker system.
8 In Toronto, circle dancing generally indicates that patrons have been schooled in clubbing primarily at Top 40 clubs, where the 'female huddle' is often employed to rebuff male advances.
9 Snug is a Toronto-based clothing label worn mainly by ravers and clubbers across North America.
10 Mixing, spinning, selecting and DJing all refer to a particular performance idiom in which DJs often seamlessly connect and combine separate records into what is recognized as a whole performance. Although being a DJ necessarily involves related activities such as buying records, practising privately and programming records for public play, mixing is the most visible activity of the DJ. Its importance in the relevant cultures cannot be understated: DJ booths at clubs and raves are often hawkishly

watched over by would-be DJs hoping to learn some tricks of the trade; the various dance music media, including the liner notes of DJ-mixed CDs, often refer to and promote the technical mixing prowess of certain DJs; and, while an impressive record collection and the skill to program records over the course of a performance are highly valued, DJs who boast the skills to perform intricate, difficult and often the longest mixes are generally hailed as the best 'bricoleurs' (Langlois 1992: 235), 'soundscape architects' (Fikentscher 2000: 8) and masters of 'a cult following' (Gore 1997: 62).

11 'Trainwrecking' is one of many terms which describe a mix gone wrong, generally a clash between two portions of separate records when the DJ has failed correctly to beat match one record to another.

12 As Simon Jones (1988: 30) defines it, this consists of the 'interruption and constant "cutting-back" of a popular record to its opening bars...to increase the sense of drama and anticipation amongst the audience', a practice which, along with 'the DJ's exhortations and interjections...help[s] to socialise the dance event as a whole, by making it "live" and turning it into a creative performance' (1988: 30).

13 The World Electronic Music Festival is a three-day event held over the second weekend in July outside of Toronto. Organized and promoted by local promotion company Destiny (in conjunction with Lifeforce and other niche music promoters), the event has been variously located in a farmer's field, on a beach and in a national park.

14 I refer here not only to the popularity of rave and club events in various countries around the world, but also to the use of underground dance music in other media (television advertising, film soundtracks, etc.), the use of images specific to underground dance music (the resurgence of the vinyl record and record players in various advertising) and the fetish-like popularization of rave and club fashion in the mainstream.

Bibliography

Bey, Hakim (1991) *TAZ: The Temporary Autonomous Zone – Ontological Anarchy and Poetic Terrorism*, New York: Autonomedia.

Bradby, Barbara (1993) 'Sampling sexuality: gender, technology and the body in dance music', *Popular Music* 2(2): 155–75.

Broadhurst, Susan (1999) *Liminal Acts: A Critical Overview of Contemporary Performance and Theory*, London: Cassell.

Fikentscher, Kai (2000) *You Better Work!: Underground Dance Music in New York City*, Hanover: Wesleyan University Press.

Foucault, Michel (1986) 'Of other spaces', *Diacritics* 16: 22–7.

Gerard, Morgan and Jack Sidnell (2000) 'Reaching out to the core: on the interactional work of the MC in drum & bass performance', *Popular Music and Society* 24(3): 23–43.

Gibson, Chris and Rebecca Pagan (1997) 'Subversive sites: rave, empowerment and the Internet', paper presented at the IASPM Conference: Sites and Sounds: Popular Music in the Age of the Internet, UTS, Sydney, 21–3 July.

Gore, Georgiana (1997) 'Trance, dance and tribalism in rave culture', in Helen Thomas (ed.) *Dance in the City*, London: Macmillan Press.

Grimes, Ronald L. (2000) *Deeply into The Bone: Re-inventing Rites of Passage*, Berkeley, CA: University of California Press.

Hall, Stuart and Tony Jefferson (eds) (1976) *Resistance through Rituals: Youth Subcultures in Postwar Britain*, London: Hutchinson & Co.

Harrison, Simon (1991) 'Ritual as intellectual property', *Man* 27: 225–44.

Hebdige, Dick (1979) *Subculture: The Meaning of Style*, London: Methuen.

—— (1987) *Cut 'n' Mix: Culture, Identity and Caribbean Music*, London: Comedia and Methuen.

Hutson, Scott R. (1999) 'Technoshamanism: spiritual healing in the rave subculture', *Popular Music and Society* 23(3): 53–76.

Jones, Simon (1988) *Black Culture, White Youth: The Reggae Tradition from JA to UK*, London: Macmillan Education.

Jordan, Timothy (1995) 'Collective bodies: raving and the politics of Gilles Deleuze and Felix Guattari', *Body and Society* 1(1): 125–44.

Kapferer, Bruce (1986) 'Performance and the structuring of meaning', in Victor Turner and Edward Bruner (eds) *The Anthropology of Experience*, Urbana, IL: University of Illinois Press.

Langlois, Tony (1992) 'Can you feel it? DJs and house music culture in the UK', *Popular Music* 11(2): 229–38.

McCall, Tara (2001) *This Is Not a Rave: In the Shadow of a Subculture*, Toronto: Insomniac Press.

Martin, Daniel (1999) 'Power play and party politics: the significance of raving', *Journal of Popular Culture* 32(4): 77–98.

May, Beverly (2000) 'Participatory theatre: the experiential construct of house and techno music events', *Contemporary Theatre Review* 103: 8–13.

Melechi, Antonio (1993) 'The ecstasy of disappearance', in S. Redhead (ed.) *Rave Off: Politics and Deviance in Contemporary Youth Cultures*, Aldershot: Avebury.

Noys, Benjamin (1995) 'Into the "jungle"', *Popular Music* 14(3): 321–31.

Pini, M. (1997) 'Cyborgs, nomads and the raving feminine', in H. Thomas (ed.) *Dance in the City*, London: Macmillan.

—— (2001) *Club Cultures and Female Subjectivity: The Move from Home to House*, New York: Palgrave.

Redhead, Steve (1993) *Rave Off: Politics and Deviance in Contemporary Youth Cultures*, Aldershot: Avebury.

Rietveld, Hillegonda (1997) 'The house sound of Chicago', in Steve Redhead (ed.) *The Club Cultures Reader*, Oxford: Blackwell.

—— (1998) *This Is Our House: House Music, Cultural Spaces and Technologies*, Popular Cultural Studies 13, Brookfield: Ashgate.

Rouget, Gilbert (1980) *Music and Trance*, Chicago: University of Chicago Press.

Schechner, Richard (1977) *Ritual, Play and Performance*, New York: Seabury Press.

Stanley, Chris (1997) 'Urban narratives of dissent in the wild zone', in Steve Redhead (ed.) *The Club Cultures Reader*, Oxford: Blackwell.

Tagg, Philip (1994) 'From refrain to rave: the decline of figure and the rise of ground', *Popular Music* 13(2): 209–23.

Thomas, Helen (ed.) (1997) *Dance in the City*, London: Macmillan Press.

Thornton, Sarah (1996) *Club Cultures: Music, Media and Subcultural Capital*, Hanover: Wesleyan University Press.

Turner, Edith (ed.) (1986) *On the Edge of the Bush: Anthropology as Experience*, Tucson, AZ: University of Arizona Press.

Turner, Victor (1969) *The Ritual Process: Structure and Anti-structure*, Chicago: Aldine Publishing.

—— (1974) *Dramas, Fields and Metaphors: Symbolic Action in Human Society*. Ithaca, NY: Cornell University Press.

—— (1977) 'Variations on a theme of liminality', in Barbara Myerhoff and Sally Moore (eds) *Secular Ritual*, Amsterdam: Van Gorcum.

—— (1979a) *Process, Performance and Pilgrimage: A Study in Comparative Symbology*, Delhi: Concept Publishing.

—— (1979b) 'Dramatic ritual/ritual drama: performance and reflexive anthropology', *The Kenyon Review* 1(3): 80–93.

—— (1982) *From Ritual to Theatre: The Human Seriousness of Play*, New York: Performing Arts Journal Publications.

—— (1984) 'Liminality and the performative genres', in John J. MacAloon (ed.) *Rite, Drama, Festival, Spectacle: Rehearsals toward a Theory of Cultural Performance*, Philadelphia: Institute for the Study of Human Issues Inc.

—— (1990) 'Are there universals of performance in myth, ritual and drama?', in Richard Schechner and Willa Appel (eds) *By Means of Performance*, Cambridge: Cambridge University Press.

van Gennep, Arnold (1960) *The Rites of Passage*, Chicago: University of Chicago Press.

9 Sounds of the London Underground

Gospel music and Baptist worship in the UK garage scene

Ciaran O'Hagan

Not everyone understands house music, it's a spiritual thing, a body thing, a soul thing.

(Eddie Amador 1998, 'House Music')

I use the term 'dance culture' throughout this chapter to describe the phenomenon originally referred to in the UK as 'acid house' then 'rave', which continues to develop, utilizing various cultural spaces, such as nightclubs, festivals and a range of unlicensed premises for the production and consumption of various forms of dance music. In this chapter, I aim to outline the process of scene fragmentation before providing an overview of the rise of the UK garage scene from an underground entity to a major element within Britain's dance culture. Particular attention will be given to tracing the scene's origins and providing insight on various practices possessing cultural significance for its members that have helped to shape the scene. I begin by examining the formation of UK garage music, highlighting the heavy influence from gospel music and religious practices within the Baptist church, in terms of both its musical structure and delivery. I will then pay particular attention to some of the unique features of UK garage, such as the importance of the Sunday scene, the constant dialogue developed between MCs, DJs and participants, and the centrality of pirate radio, which distinguish this scene from others in London. I will examine the role of the modern MC and explore its link with that of the religious preacher and consider pirate radio as the spiritual home of UK garage. The chapter intends to provide readers with an understanding of the spiritual and religious influences involved in the production and consumption of UK garage and to reveal the way in which these processes are mediated.

This chapter draws on various primary and secondary sources, and is influenced by my own experience and involvement within dance culture. I am currently a PhD candidate researching dance music, drug use and the information needs of London's UK garage and underground trance and techno scenes. I have chosen to use ethnography to examine both scenes through insider status in a similar way to previous dance culture scholars (Thornton 1995; Rietveld 1998; Malbon 1999; Bennett 2000; Fikentscher 2000). Researchers who adopt this method are encouraged to 'locate or situate' themselves within the research, establishing their relationship to their subject area (Back 2001). In doing so, I can now appreciate how my previous experience as a consumer of dance music since the late 1980s and as a DJ, promoter, drugs counsellor and dance outreach worker since the 1990s has informed my methodology and translated into my ethnographic research practice. These roles have not only provided me with crucial insights and improved my understanding of dance culture, but in addition helped me to develop networking techniques required for gaining access to specific areas of my research field. These factors, combined with living in London and being constantly exposed to the current sounds of pirate radio, have enabled me to view the constantly changing landscape of the capital's dance culture.

Scene fragmentation

To understand the development of UK garage, it is important first to consider the process of scene fragmentation which began in the early 1990s and consequently led to the formation of an array of interconnected scenes comprising Britain's wider dance culture. This process is linked to early attempts aimed at restricting the development of British dance culture through the introduction of various legal measures. These began in December 1989 when Graham Bright, Conservative MP for Luton South, sponsored a Private Member's Bill, which later became the Entertainments (Increased Penalties) Act 1990. This legislation raised the level of fines for breaching the licensing laws from £2,000 to £20,000 and introduced a maximum six months prison sentence for those organizing unlicensed parties (Collin 1997: 111–12). The act was later strengthened when the then Home secretary, Douglas Hurd, granted the police additional powers to confiscate equipment used at these unlicensed events (Push and Silcott 2000: 60). Other amendments to the Local Government Act 1963, the Private Places of Entertainment Act 1967, the Local Government (Miscellaneous Provisions) Act 1982 and the Civic Government (Scotland) Act 1982 were all clearly aimed at the early 'acid house' phase of dance culture (Redhead 1997: xi). Later, the introduction of the Criminal Justice and Public Order Act 1994 crucially shifted focus, in that it became the first Act to place restrictions on individuals attending or attempting to attend unlicensed events.

Throughout the early 1990s the British police and local authorities pursued a continual crackdown on illegal parties, which coincided with the liberalization of licensing laws, as clubs' opening hours were extended whilst promoters were encouraged to organize events under a regulated framework. This resulted in a gradual demise of 'illegal' events held in unlicensed premises that took several years to transpire, as the majority of party organizers moved their operations towards nightclubs and other licensed venues. Consequently, divisions began to emerge in the early 1990s, as dance-music participants began to fragment and mutate into smaller social groupings focused around specialized subgenre consumption (Newcombe 1992: 7–8). Many of these groups contributed new discourses to dance culture by adapting it to suit their own needs and sensibilities

(Collin 1997: 5). This ongoing process of restructuring continues to produce an array of interconnected scenes that combine to form the wider British dance culture.

Currently, throughout London, specific scenes focusing on UK garage, underground trance and techno and drum 'n' bass music have continued to adapt and adopt an array of supporting structures to encourage their development in an increasingly competitive market. This has included the creation of scene-specific niche media in the form of magazines and websites dedicated to certain genres, coinciding with an increase in specialized record shops catering for individual or related scenes. Distinct forms of visual imagery associated with these scenes have emerged and are now clearly visible in the advertising and marketing of events. When discussing flyer designs, Nathan Brett suggests that, as a medium, flyers 'boast more freedom of visual expression than almost any other area of commercial art and design' (1996: 1). Brett also asserts that, in contrast to the images of rock and pop musicians, dance music lacks an obvious visual focus. Therefore flyers are left to convey the 'spirit, emotion or vibe of a club' (*ibid.*: 1), which is why UK garage flyers have adopted slick design protocols that often incorporate sexualized imagery of female clubbers and references to champagne. Reflecting the glamorous dress code associated with UK garage events and the upwardly mobile aspirations of its participants, this design style is clearly distinguishable from the psychedelic imagery favoured by the underground trance and techno scene, which alludes to its participant's favoured repertoire of recreational drugs. More recently, flyer-distribution companies have begun to create scene-specific flyer packs, handed out at related events or distributed through associated record shops, adding to a further separation of musical scenes existing in London.

It's a London thing

Since the late 1990s, UK garage music has been a predominant feature on London's unlicensed network of pirate radio stations (Braddock 2000: 66) and the scene has up until recently dominated much of the capital's clubland. Participants at UK garage nights generally reflect London's multicultural and multi-religious diversity. Second- and third-generation Afro Caribbean, South and East Asian, Greek, Turkish and Irish youth are an integral part of the scene, and at events held in London there is usually an equal mix of white and ethnic-minority participants, the majority of whom were born in the UK. However, this can vary and will often reflect the socio-demographics of a particular area, especially if an event is heavily advertised on a local pirate radio station, as this is more likely to attract a specific local crowd. Birmingham, Manchester and Bristol have also developed sizeable UK garage scenes and many UK universities are regularly visited by touring UK garage artists. In a secular society, the UK garage scene provides participants with a sense of belonging to a wider community, which is accessed through participation at UK garage events and continually reinforced by listening to pirate radio.

The genre's crossover into mainstream popular music culture has enabled many within the UK garage scene to develop a range of successful music-industry careers whilst helping to establish it as a key element of British dance culture and a feature of the international dancescape. Since 1996, UK garage consumers have followed their favourite DJs and MCs to holiday destinations such as Ayia Napa in Cyprus, Ibiza and, more recently, Faliraki in Rhodes. This reflects the influence much of dance culture has had on the UK youth tourism market, which sees young people organizing their holidays to correspond with their musical interests (Sellars 1998: 611). Although Ayia Napa caters for other dance-music genres, it has nevertheless become an essential component in the lives of UK garage consumers. Many of London's biggest UK garage club nights, such as Twice As Nice, Smoove, Exposure and La Cosa Nostra, lead the almost quasi-religious pilgrimage to the Cypriot resort each year. Attending Ayia Napa, whether as a DJ, promoter or participant, enhances an individual's cultural capital and is regarded as a defining element of inclusion in the higher echelons of the UK garage scene.

It's a spiritual thing

Many of the spiritual and religious aspects found within contemporary UK garage can be traced to key genres instrumental in its development, such as house music, which influenced many of the early UK garage productions. Hillegonda Rietveld reveals that African-American musical traditions, including gospel, disco, soul, funk and Latin salsa, informed the musical structures and sensibilities of house music developed in Chicago and New York during the 1990s (Rietveld 1998: 6). Kai Fikentscher (2000) adds to this, suggesting that New York underground dance music, which includes house, shares several features with African-American worship. He asserts that, as institutions, both the church and underground dance clubs 'feature ritualised activities centred around music, dance, and worship, in which there are no set boundaries between secular and sacred domains' (*ibid.*: 101). Fikentscher asserts that both the consumption of underground dance music and African-American worship are equally inter-twined within processes of unification and self-affirmation. He also points to similarities in the way DJs and preachers each strategically build pace throughout their respective performances or ceremonies towards an emotional peak. In addition, Fikentscher sees parallels in the way they are equally regarded as cultural heroes who are respected and admired by their followers. He goes on to suggest that many underground dance-music producers and artists served musical apprenticeships in community church ensembles and choirs. As a result, the stylistic vocal features of gospel music were incorporated into underground dance music along with 'a variety of themes, sacred and secular, social and polit-ical, that have long been associated with the Black church tradition' (*ibid.*: 105). Furthermore, he reveals that the use of prominent gospel instruments such as the organ and acoustic piano became a common feature of house music produced in New Jersey, New York, Detroit and Chicago.

In Britain, American house productions which featured gospel-like vocals were generally known as 'US garage', referring to the seminal New York Paradise Garage club, where resident DJ Larry Levan played an eclectic mix of records including gospel-inspired disco and early house productions. The club ran from 1976 until 1987 and still 'remains the most mythologized of all the New York gay discos' (Silcott 1999: 19). Levan drew a great deal of inspiration from the idealism of David Mancuso's Loft parties held at 647 Broadway, and was undoubtedly influenced by Mancuso's musical preferences for soulful, rhythmic songs with lyrics that carried positive meaning, that were playing in a way in which each followed 'the last in a profound musical narrative' (Brewster and Broughton 1999: 253). Crucially, the majority of early UK garage productions were heavily influenced by American artists who extended Levan and Mancuso's musical aesthetics, such as Frankie Knuckles, David Morales, Todd Terry, Tommy Musto, Victor Simonelli, Marc Kitchen, Roger Sanchez, Masters At Work, Mood II Swing, Kerri Chandler, Blaze and, most importantly, Todd Edwards and Armand Van Helden. Many house-music records often feature sentiments of recognition printed on the centre label from producers to various individuals. These acknowledgements regularly mention 'thanks to God', revealing the religious beliefs present within the American house movement.

South London's Sunday scene

UK garage events emerged in the early to mid-1990s, originally as Sunday morning 'after hours' parties held in various South London pubs in and around the Elephant and Castle area. These events attracted clubbers keen to keep the party going after leaving house and garage events across London such as Garage City, Release the Pressure and events held at the Ministry of Sound. At these parties, DJs such as Mickey Simms, Justin Canter and Matt 'Jam' Lamont became renowned for pitching up house and garage records to increase their tempo to help clubbers stay alert (Bidder 2001: 223; Sawyer 2000). Subsequently, the first wave of UK garage productions by artists such as Grant Nelson, then Tuff Jam, Smokin Beats, Industrial Standards, Booker T, MJ Cole, Baffled, Ramsey and Fen, Banana Republic, Scott Garcia and R.I.P., began to increase the beat-per-minute ratio of tracks, whilst creating a distinct skippy beat and heavier bass-line sound. These new 'roughed-up' and faster UK productions were clearly distinguishable from the smoothly produced and slower US tracks (Chapman 2000). At this stage, UK garage was a relatively underground entity, reliant on the Sunday-scene and pirate radio support, which began to broaden its appeal. Events also took place at the Southwark Arches, near London Bridge and, in 1997, the most influential Sunday-scene party, Twice As Nice, opened at Club Coliseum in Vauxhall. Sunday-scene events attracted an older dressier crowd, many of whom worked in the club and wider music industry, and helped to establish a glamorous designer dress code that was to become associated with future UK garage events. Rietveld suggests that this element of the scene is infused with religiosity, in that events occur on the main church day, which is regarded as 'best-clothes-day for South London Caribbean youth, who have grown up with Gospel Sunday School experiences' (2000: 209). Rietveld goes on to point out that it is also 'a day to show off one's material achievements and upwardly mobile aspirations' (*ibid*).

Reynolds asserts that 'dancehall reggae fans originally lured into jungle by its ragga samples back in 1994' moved towards the developing UK garage scene (1998: 420). During this crossover, the MC became an integral part of UK garage events and many of the production techniques associated with jungle merged into the evolving UK garage sound. By 1997, wide music press coverage led to the term 'speed' garage being used to identify the genre; this was later replaced by 'underground' and then 'UK' garage. The Sunday scene also introduced R 'n' B to the second or backroom at events, which in turn influenced the emergence of '2 step' garage. This addition drew heavily on R 'n' B influences, especially in terms of its vocal arrangements. All of these Sunday-scene developments helped to further distinguish UK garage from its American counterpart, which continued to remain predominately DJ focused.

Rewind and come again

Drawing on Paul Gilroy's (1993) work, Rietveld suggests that in various examples of UK garage music one can hear crossovers of musical techniques that have developed in both local and imported genres, which can be said to be part of a Black Atlantic musical logic (2000: 208). Like so much of UK garage, the continuous dialogue between the MC and audience is a tradition originating in the early Jamaican sound systems. Dick Hebdige reveals that during the 1950s Jamaican sound-system DJs such as Duke Reid and Prince Buster would 'add spice to the instrumental records they were playing by shouting out their favourite catchphrases over the microphone. These talk-overs or toasts soon became a popular feature of the blues dances' (Hebdige 1997: 83). Tracing the development of reggae in *Bass Culture*, Lloyd Bradley indicates that once the DJs of these early systems 'began to chat on the mic about more than their sound systems, their records, their women or their selves, it was the ghetto's newspaper' (2000: 5). The process of 'chatting on the mic' performs a community role, which is observable within the contemporary UK garage scene.

The MCs customary function of hosting an event whilst maintaining a rapport between participants and DJ has begun to expand. Currently many MCs incorporate discussions on a wide range of issues directly or indirectly related to the UK garage scene. Some MCs make reference to political and social issues affecting young people growing up in urban environments – such as unemployment, rising crime, gun culture, drug use and social exclusion. This particular dimension, combined with other communication methods adopted by UK garage MCs, provides us with parallels to the role of the Baptist preacher. For example, discussions concerning sensitive issues that directly effect local parish communities are an integral part of Baptist church services. This aspect was reinforced during my ethnographic fieldwork at a New York Baptist church in 2001, as both the resident and visiting preacher spoke openly about issues concerning alcohol and drug use which were of relevance to their local parish communities. Both preachers integrated these sensitive and often contentious subject areas into their sermons in the same way that many UK garage MCs raise similar issues in their lyrical dialogues. Furthermore, UK garage MCs have incorporated call–response techniques to encourage vocal and physical feedback from their audience in a similar way to that in which Baptist preachers do to interact with their congregation. Baptist preachers frequently end a statement by inciting a response from parishioners to acknowledge its content, often by calling for a 'witness'. Parishioners normally respond by raising their hands and vocally agreeing with the preacher's statement. MCs often use this technique to confirm or stimulate UK garage participants' loyalty to the scene by encouraging members of an audience to respond to questions about their participation at key events. This can include whether people have or intend to support particular sound systems at the London's Notting Hill Carnival, attend a named event, visit Ayia Napa or listen to a specific radio station or show. In addition, they regularly send out 'big ups', confirm or deny rumours and, most importantly, call for 'rewinds'. Sending out a 'big up' involves an MC specifically mentioning an individual, crew, organization or particular geographical location during the course of their performance. This gesture is usually accompanied by positive comments and can be used to establish respect for particular people within the scene according to how often they are mentioned.

In London, UK garage MCs often use call–response techniques as a way of identifying local divisions within a crowd and to establish respect for certain parts of the capital. This will depend on how often an area is mentioned, but, more importantly, on the order in which areas are announced. The last area to be announced usually receives the loudest reaction and establishes where the majority of participants come from. This may be used to acknowledge local tensions, for example between areas north and south of the river Thames, which have existed for many years. When an MC feels that a particular record is favoured by the audience he or she often calls for a 'rewind', which involves the DJ dramatically stopping the record and quickly winding it back to a particular point to start it again. This often produces a screeching sound effect, which adds to the tension created by the accompanying MC and involvement of the crowd. The range of vocal acknowledgements used by UK garage participants in appreciation of the MC's and DJ's skills can include screams, shouts and whistle or horn blowing. Physical responses usually comprise raising hands, jumping in the air, waving handkerchiefs and banging on wall or tables. Although the range of physical and vocal gestures used within the UK garage arena can be seen as more intense than those employed by Baptist congregations, they follow the same ritualized procedures of interaction, which foster a sense of belonging and communion within both environments.

A contemporary UK garage MC's role requires an ability to read and direct the mood of the crowd whilst commenting on and pre-empting the DJs skills. However, it is important to point out that there are great disparities in the levels of competence displayed by various UK garage MCs, in terms of both their technical skills, such as controlling vocal levels, and their ability to interact with their audience and maintain the collective energy of the dance floor, often referred to as the vibe (Fikentscher 2000: 81). Nevertheless, there are some extremely talented MCs on the UK garage circuit, whose performances are conducted with exceptional professionalism. Many have diverse repertoires of rhymes, raps and lyrical dialogue, which can often involve dramatic stage performances including throwing microphones between MCs whilst maintaining an intense vocal tempo. Stylistically, a distinct UK garage vocal delivery has developed and been popularized by the mainstream success of MC crews such as the Masters of Ceremonies and So Solid. Many UK garage consumers attend events specifically to see their favourite MCs, in the same way that participants follow particular DJs within other scenes. Often UK garage crowds can be observed repeating an MC's lyrics word for word, in a way that resembles a congregation following a preacher's sermon.

Recently, the UK garage scene began experiencing difficulties generated by an alleged association with gun crime. This came about after a shooting at London's Astoria nightclub, which took place during a So Solid concert at the end of 2001 (Smith and Nettleton 2001). The incident resulted in the cancellation of the group's subsequent tour dates and saw the emergence of an informal ban on UK garage events taking place within London's West End. Recently comments made by the government's Culture Minister Kim Howells concerning MCs' lyrics supposedly glamourizing gun crime were criticized as racist, failing to understand that the discussion of gun culture merely reflected the society in which fans live (Gibbons 2003). Nevertheless, these remarks further compounded the issue and added to the scene's dispersal to Greater London and suburban venues. However, in other parts of Britain numerous nightclubs and promoters have become reluctant to cater for UK garage events. In response to these restrictions UK garage promoters have begun to place more significance on their R 'n' B content to reduce any negative associations. This issue has further enhanced the centrality of pirate radio to the existence and maintenance of the scene. Now, more than ever, pirate radio is viewed as the 'spiritual home' of UK garage, providing DJs, MCs and UK garage music with essential exposure. Parallels can be drawn between the way the scene has become reliant on an illegal network of radio stations to support its community and how members of 'undesirable' religions have resorted to clandestine worship to uphold their faith. One such example is the 'mass rock' services that took place in Ireland during the 18th century when Catholicism, the majority religion at the time, was outlawed by British rule. As a consequence, the faithful were forced to gather on common land, usually on high ground in order to avoid detection and subsequent prosecution. At these locations, a priest would place a hand-carved crucifix on top of a rock and perform a service to support the religious needs of the persecuted Catholic community. In a similar way, the clandestine operations of pirate radio stations are supporting the UK garage community through this problematic period, as their main places of 'worship', nightclubs in this instance, are restricted.

Locked in, locked on

Britain's relationship with unlicensed radio broadcasting, or 'pirates' as they are more commonly known, dates back almost 40 years. Throughout this period, they have given crucial exposure to new forms of music. Between 1964 and 1968, pirates began broadcasting from offshore ships located around the UK. The most famous of these was Radio Caroline, which Matthew Collin (1997) suggests was the first pirate station to play rock and R 'n' B, music that was rarely aired on national radio at the time. He also suggests that since their introduction pirates have continued to fill cultural gaps, particularly for black music such as reggae and soul. Collin (1997) argues that this process continued with house, which was noticeably absent on licensed radio stations until 1990 (*ibid.*: 130). The emergence of London's dance culture was greatly influenced by pirates such as Centreforce, which began broadcasting various forms of dance music in May 1989. They were later followed by a host of others, including Sunrise, Obsession, Fantasy and later Dance and Kool FM (Garratt 1998: 155; Belle-Fortune 1999: 57). Other stations, including Girls FM, London Underground and Freak FM, are regarded as important pirates that were amongst the first to introduce UK garage music to the London-wide audience during the early to mid-1990s. During the formative years of the UK garage scene, when the music was 'filling the clubs, but not being played on mainstream radio, the role of the pirates was fundamental' in maintaining its presence and attracting new consumers (Sawyer 2000). Drawing on Sarah Thornton's work, one can argue that as a form of communications medium they played an important part 'in the assembly, demarcation and development' of this musical scene (Thornton 1995: 160). Since 1997, the majority of the capital's pirates have focused on various elements of UK garage, and at present, there are 73 pirate stations broadcasting in London, of which 37 play UK garage (Pir8radio 2003). Throughout the late 1990s several licensed British radio stations such as BBC Radio 1, Capital Radio and Kiss FM have moved previously 'specialist' UK garage shows to primetime audience slots, making ex-pirate radio acts such as the Dreem Teem, DJ EZ, DJ Luck and MC Neat household names (Williams 2000).

Pirates help to foster a sense of community amongst UK garage participants due to their apparent openness and accessibility to listeners, who are encouraged to contact stations via telephone or text messaging so they can exchange greetings with friends and relatives, send out 'big ups' and ask for requests. It is here that the community role of the MC again comes to the fore, as they often provide and maintain an important link with disaffected youth, by regularly sending out messages of support to individuals serving custodial sentences in young offenders' institutes and prisons, a community function often overlooked by commercial stations. Many operate on a small-scale basis involving a network of friends run on a semi-professional basis, whilst others are highly organized and directly involved with the promotion of UK garage parties in and around the capital. Their daily running is fraught with dangers, mainly due to their illegal nature, as stations operating without a Radio Authority broadcasting license are liable to prosecution (Radio Communications Agency 2002). As a result, pirate stations employ a range of methods to avoid detection, including relaying signals between booster aerials in an attempt to safeguard their studio's location, and are shrouded in secrecy. Gaining access to participate as a DJ or MC requires intricate negotiations often only initiated via personal connections. Nevertheless, despite numerous complications, individuals involved with pirate radio broadcasting regularly negotiate a myriad of complex issues in order to support the cultural development of their scene.

Conclusion

This chapter has provided insight into several procedures that have been in-corporated into the UK garage scene and identified a sense of belonging or spirituality resonating within the UK garage community. Undoubtedly, gospel-music traditions were crucial in the development of house music emanating from New York, New Jersey, Chicago and Detroit. Notably, the production and consumption of house music in these regions drew on various aspects of African-American worship to inform its musical structure and delivery. The emergence of UK garage was heavily influenced by American house music and later embodied religious practices associated with the Baptist church. Similarities can be found in the way DJs and preachers approach their respective performances and also in the way they are regarded as key cultural figures. However, in the context of UK garage these parallels can be extended further to incorporate the central role of the MC, as MCs have adapted features associated with Baptist preachers, such as using call–response techniques to interact with their audience. In addition, MCs have developed a community role by raising a wide range of social issues in their vocal repertoires and maintaining essential links with disaf-fected youth and the wider UK garage community through their involvement in pirate radio broadcasting, which has recently grown in significance as a direct consequence of informal restrictions placed on UK garage events. Furthermore, the emergence of Sunday after-hours events transformed a traditional worship period into a key element of the scene and helped to establish UK garage's 'Sunday best' dress code.

Bibliography

Back, L. (2001) 'On the limits of what is said: ethnography and participatory research', paper presented at NPRA meeting, 22 October 2001, London, Institute of Education.
Bidder, S. (2001) *Pump Up the Volume*, London: Channel 4 Books.
Braddock, K. (2000) 'The 3 kings', *The Face* 3(41), June: 54–68.
Bradley, L. (2000) *Base Culture: When Reggae Was King*, London: Viking.
Belle-Fortune, B. (1999) *All Crew Muss Big Up*, Basildon: Business Community Press.
Bennett, A. (2000) *Popular Music and Youth Culture*, London: Macmillan.
Brett, N. (1996) *Fly: The Art of the Club Flyer*, London: Thames & Hudson.
Brewster, B. and F. Broughton (1999) *Last Night a DJ Saved My Life*, London: Headline.
Chapman, A. (2000) 'Two steps forward', *Guardian*, 14 April.

Collin, M. with Godfrey, S. (1997) *Altered State: The Story of Ecstasy Culture and Acid House*, London: Serpent's Tail.

Fikentscher, K. (2000) *You Better Work: Underground Dance Music in New York City*, Hanover, NH: Wesleyan University Press.

Garratt, S. (1998) *Adventures in Wonderland: A Decade of Club Culture*, London: Headline.

Gibbons, F. (2003) 'Minister labelled racist after attack on rap "idiots"', *Guardian*, 6 January.

Gilroy, P. (1993) *The Black Atlantic: Modernity and Double Consciousness*, London: Verso.

Hebdige, D. (1997) *Cut 'n' Mix: Culture, Identity and Caribbean Music*, London: Routledge.

Malbon, B. (1999) *Clubbing: Dancing, Ecstasy and Vitality*, London: Routledge.

Newcombe, R. (1992) *The Use of Ecstasy and Dance Drugs at Rave Parties and Clubs, Some Problems and Solutions*, Liverpool: 3d Research Bureau.

Pir8radio (2003) 'London FM listings', available online at http:www.pir8radio.co.uk (accessed January 2003).

Push and M. Silcott (2000) *The Book of E: All About Ecstasy*, London: Omnibus.

Radio Communications Agency (2002) *Student Information Pack*, London: Radio Communications Agency.

Redhead, S. (1997) *Subcultures to Clubcultures: An Introduction to Popular Cultural Studies*, Oxford: Blackwell.

Reynolds, S. (1998) *Energy Flash: A Journey through Rave Music and Dance Culture*, Basingstoke: Picador.

Rietveld, H. (1998) *This Is Our House: House Music, Cultural Spaces and Technologies*, Aldershot: Ashgate.

—— (2000) 'A London thing: development of garage in London', in Tony Mitchel, Peter Doyle with Bruce Johnson (eds) *Changing Sounds: New Directions and Configurations in Popular Music, Proceedings of IASPM Biannual International Conference*, University of Technology, Sydney, NSW, Australia.

Sawyer, M. (2000) 'Beat generation', *Observer*, Sunday, 2 July.

Sellars, A. (1998) 'The influence of dance music on the UK youth market', *Travel and Tourism* 19(6): 611–15.

Silcott, M. (1999) *Rave America: New School Dancescapes*, Toronto: ECW Press.

Smith, L. and P. Nettleton (2001) 'Shoot-out in West End club', *Evening Standard*, 1 November (1–2).

Thornton, S. (1995) *Club Cultures: Music, Media and Subcultural Capital*, Cambridge: Polity Press.

Williams, C. (2000) 'All about the music', available online at http:www.ukgarage.com (accessed January 2003).

Discography

Amador, E. (1998) 'House Music', Yoshitoshi Recordings YR028.

A selection of key records played during the development of the UK garage scene

Artist	Title	Label	Year
24 Hour Experience	'Together'	Nice 'N' Ripe	1994
Todd Edwards	'Saved My Life'	I!	1995
C.J. Bolland	'Sugar Is Sweeter' (Amand's Drum 'N' Bass Mix)	Internal	1996
Scott Garcia	'A London Thing'	Connected	1997
Kristine Blond	'Love Shy' (Tuff Jam Classic Vocal)	Reverb	1998
DJ Luck & MC Neat	'A Little Bit of Luck'	Red Rose	1999
So Solid	'Oh No'	Relentless	2000
Pied Piper & The Masters of Ceremonies	'Do You Really Like It'	Soul Food	2001
The Streets	Original Pirate Material	Locked On	2002

10 *Gamelan*, techno-primitivism, and the San Francisco rave scene[1]

Gina Andrea Fatone

In August of 1997, at a rave in the foothills of the Sierra mountains, a five-member Balinese *gamelan*[2] group based in Santa Cruz, California, became part of the Vibe.[3] Via a powerful performance experience that fused techno music with traditional Balinese *gamelan*, the group's participation in this alternative cultural event[4] led to subsequent invitations to perform at raves in the San Francisco area, as well as an invitation to cut a collaborative CD with a DJ in May of 1998. Gamelan Anak Swarasanti[5] has since performed repeatedly at events hosted by various Bay Area rave collectives. I find this musical appropriation illuminates two notable aspects of these local events: the value of a kind of musical structure commonly present in communal gatherings leading to altered states of consciousness[6] and the juxtaposition of a nostalgia for the "primitive" and exotic with a reverence for high technology.[7] I maintain that a paradoxical "techno-primitive" ideology comes into relief as the processes by which this Southeast Asian musical ensemble has recently been incorporated into the San Francisco rave scene are examined. This techno-primitivist construction, one amidst multiple stances performed in rave, involves the interrelated roles of cultural borrowing, homogenized "ethnic-ness," and the quest for "authenticating" experiences in the context of the technocultural present.

A return to innocence

It is evident from the growing body of literature concerning rave culture that so-called "tribal," "primitive," or "pagan" elements of raving are decidedly self-conscious amongst a prominent constituent of participants. In logging on to one of the many rave collective web pages, for example, the self-identification of ravers with "pure," unadulterated, pre-industrial society, and the romantic notion of collectively returning to "tribal" roots through the rave process is strongly apparent. The Guerillas of Harmony web page (Twist 2000: 1) includes links to essays with titles such as "Roots of Trance Dance," "Children of the Evolution," "Cybertribe Rising Revisited," and "Rave and the Rebirth of Celebration." One San Francisco raver states: "I think it's a return to innocence." Quoting him further:

It has roots in prehistory. It's like one of these big dance sessions where they would chant all night long until the sun comes up or something. That's my personal feeling…I really think they're tapping into something really deep in the psyche.

(personal interview, 21 May 1998)

As ravers often draw analogies between themselves and what they conceive of as tribal or primitive societies, rave culture has been referred to as "neo-tribal" (Gore 1997: 54) or neo-primitive. This identification with "primal" societies is not limited to the rave scene, having strong representation in other forms of alternative culture, such as New Age, Wicca, and various radical ecological reform groups. Graham St John identifies a "postcolonial primitivist" movement amongst Australian youth, "a culture variously committed to the defence of the rights of native ecology and peoples, or natural and cultural heritage," with a goal of "returning" to the "wild" themselves (1999: 164). In "approximating "nature," St John proposes, participants engage in a "quest" for authenticity (*ibid.*). Similarly, ravers' casting of all-night mass dance events as "prehistorical," along with the implication of an inherited psychological substrate for such communal performances, points to an association of certain "primitive" behaviors with "original" human experience. In imitating or recreating perceived "primal" activities, rave participants experience "pure" humaness – they are themselves authenticated.

The will of the Technology Goddess

Raving is often referred to as ritualistic by participants and scholars of performativity alike (e.g. Gore 1997; Reynolds 1998; Silcott 1999). Originally applied to premodern cultures, the classic ritual theory of Arnold van Gennep (1981), later "modernized" by Victor Turner, has been useful in the analysis of alternative cultural performances, although the model has been criticized for excluding both corporeality and competing interpretations of the ritual event among participants (see St John 1999). It may be valid to argue that raving is essentially a continuation of an ancient performative ritual behavior and nothing fundamentally new. However, core components of the rave event – the means of sensory bombardment – are produced through electronic/digital technology (e.g. computer-generated visual projections and highly amplified electronic music). Beyond this, social relations between participants are mediated by the presence of modern technology. The sheer volume of the music dictates that communication between participants is largely non-verbal.

Like other alternative cultural events, rave is a site of multivalent experience (Gore 1997: 65). For some, raving is a spiritual experience through which they feel deeply connected to other participants. Initial rave experiences often evoke in the novice a sense of enlightenment. Note the following excerpt of a "testimonial" in which a participant describes the vibe he experienced at his first rave:

It wasn't until I was 25 that I discovered the scene. It was like becoming color for the first time. I love being awake, I love having my eyes open, I love every moment that I'm alive. I've been painted by the brush of raving with a palette of vibes, people, love, music, unity, movement, peace, and together-ness. I am in color.

(posted on the sfraves discussion list, 13 June 2000)

As has been discussed elsewhere in this collection, writers and ravers have noted that a main motivation for participants is immersion in a feeling of communitas generated at the event (Somberg n.d.: 6; Saunders 1995: 1). This communitas (or even ecstatic trance), it is significant to note, is achieved through high-tech means – particularly through mass dancing to music comprised of simulated and sampled sounds, often enhanced by pharmaceutical technology. In *Generation Ecstasy*, Simon Reynolds refers to the various musics (or "hallucino-genres" of rave) as "sampladelia," or "perception-warping music" which decon-structs "the metaphysics of presence" (1998: 41, 44). Ravers, involved in what they themselves term "ecstatic trance dancing," speak of submitting themselves to the will of the DJ, often referred to as a shaman: "House music is the sound of the cultural blender running at warp speed. It's a techno-shamanic dervish" (Heley 2000).

As René Lysloff writes, "trance is actualized via the interaction of the human and the machine, implicating a postmodern "secular religion" where technology itself is worshipped" (Lysloff n.d.: 11). In fact, the credo of techno-paganism may be found at hyperreal.org, along with prayers such as "We thank the Technology Goddess for giving us the ability to rave" and "We finally wish that the Technology Goddess will receive our ecstasy while raving as an offering and a celebration of her omnipotence." This ethos of abandoning oneself to the will of the machine and dissolving into a communal mass of dancers has remained one of rave's most salient aspects, dating back to proto-rave techno music of the early 1980s.

Rave is also distinguished as a technocultural artifact in that its planning and restoration phases take place in virtual space. This forum, in scope and nature of social relationship, is not something that could be replicated in reality, due to the anonymity afforded by faceless interaction in virtual space. As the drug Ecstasy removes fear, allegedly the element which controls our behavior (Saunders 1995), for the purpose of establishing a greater communitas, I suggest that the virtual forum serves as an extension of this chemical agent for some ravers.

'I reached a nirvana/euphoric state sitting right in front of the *gamelan*...'

I have drawn attention to a nostalgia for the "primal roots" of mankind among ravers and interpreted the rave event as a technocultural practice. I will now introduce Gamelan Anak Swarasanti and discuss the ensemble's role(s) within the San Francisco rave scene.

Anak Swarasanti primarily plays a type of ceremonial orchestra known in Bali as *gamelan angklung*. It is a four-tone ensemble consisting primarily of four-keyed bronze metallophones of different sizes or registers, the keys of which are suspended over bamboo resonators. Other instruments of the *gamelan angklung* include a horizontally mounted row of knobbed gongs, two drums, a small pair of cymbals, bamboo flute, a small vertically suspended gong, and a small horizontally mounted gong used for time-keeping (Tenzer 1991: 86). In Bali, the *angklung* ensemble traditionally performs at temple ceremonies, processions, cremations, and village festivals.[8] It is one of three theoretically required ceremonial *gamelan* in village ritual life (along with the larger *gamelan gong* and the processional orchestra *gamelan beleganjur*) (McPhee 1966; Bakan 1999: 11). In Northern California, *gamelan angklung* Anak Swarasanti rehearses weekly and performs regularly in the Santa Cruz community. Most of the group's performances are purely for entertainment (e.g. summer music festivals, college performances, and local garden parties). In November 2002 the group performed at a Santa Cruz benefit for the Balinese victims of the October 2002 terrorist bombing in Kuta, Bali. The Anak Swarasanti website includes descriptions and photos of its various performance venues. The *gamelan*'s all-Western membership is mixed in gender (three females, seven males) and age (24–60). Members are either working professionals (most are in the high-tech industry) or university students. Repertoire includes traditional and contemporary compositions for *gamelan*.

Compositions for *gamelan angklung* are cyclical in form and thereby variable in performance length. At raves, where Anak Swarasanti is normally expected to play a set several hours long, the group collectively arranges extended versions of traditional ceremonial pieces. Anak always performs in what is known as the ambient space. This is a room or space set apart from the main dance location(s) where ravers can come at any point during the evening to "chill out," or take a breather from the more extreme goings-on at the event. Although some dancing does take place here, people usually use the space to be still. There are often mattresses to lie on or rugs to sit on. Music in the ambient space is generally calmer, quieter, may be rhythmic or non-rhythmic, and is meant to function in an atmospheric way.

The *gamelan*, with its seamless, minimalist, and repetitively structured sounds, fits well into this scheme. However, its presentation is almost always mediated by the addition of a layer of electronically produced music added to the texture. This is not meant to be a simple overlay of synthesized music contributing to the ethereal soundscape, but an interactive relationship between electronic musicians and the *gamelan*. This syncretic ideal is illustrated by the following email excerpt authored by a member of Anak Swarasanti planning the group's appearance at a rave in the spring of 2000:

> Use more of the big gongs. For example: have the gongs match beats with the dj, phase the dj out, bring in the *gamelan*, and reverse that at the end of the *gamelan* set. Possibly even keep the gongs (in different varieties) playing

continuously between songs, so there is no silence. Participation (like dancing or meditation) is much easier with continued sound.

(email by a member of Anak Swarasanti, spring 2000)

And this is from a DJ to the sfraves list:

I hope to be joining the Gamelan Anak Swarasanti in the ambient area for a special marathon sunset performance.... If you've been looking for music historically associated with hypnotic mental states, this is the real stuff...all presented with great reverence for the culture from which it came (and a gong that I love sitting next to 'cause it just goes BBBBAAAAAAAAAAHAHHHHHHHnnnnnHnnnHHHHHHHHHMMMM mmmmmmmmmmmnnnnnnmmmmmm...).

I'll be joining them with a notebook running some bizarre german [*sic*] sound design software and digital effects on some instruments in the ensemble...so expect a collage of audio textures that balances somewhere between futuristic electronic experimental works with the awe inspiring interlocking cyclical progressions from across the pacific [*sic*].

(DJ Andy W, posted 15 August 2000)

Comments posted to the sfraves discussion list, along with repeat invitations to perform at raves in the Bay area, underscore the successful appropriation of the *gamelan* by the San Francisco rave scene:

as I melted through the visible sound atmosphere plastic polyester neon vibrant flower piece, my soul radiating from my eyes and every other inch of my joyful physical and spiritual being...then I reached a nirvana/euphoric state sitting right in front of the gamelan orchestra, absorbing their message and sending it back with equal love.

(posted 26 March 2000)

i [*sic*] must say that it is rare these days for parties to be thrown for the right reason at all...lately the parties seem to be all about getting fucked on 3 hits of e and running around yelling PLUR (which most people don't live by to begin with)...i especially enjoyed dancing to the space of the gamelan...i hope this time is a turning point within the scene...and that the events will return to their spiritual roots.

(posted 26 March 2000)

Overall I thought the party rocked. I definitely loved the gamelan ... I danced a bit toward the end of the gamelan set, but wished more folks were dancing so I wouldn't feel so self conscious :-) But maybe ya shouldn't dance when folks is prayin :-) I also wished they had orches-trated the switch from gamelan back to dj's a bit better so that there could have been more of a connection....It just kinda felt like BAM! back from ecstatic music to THUMP THUMP THUMP.

(posted 27 March 2000)

I STRONGLY recommend that you listen to some gamelan.... The slower pieces tend to sound like trance, the faster stuff is like jungle played at twice the normal speed.

(posted 23 March 2000)

How might this appropriation be interpreted? I suggest two possibilities: the shared use and value (in both Balinese and rave contexts) of a particular kind of musical structure commonly present in communal participatory events leading to altered states of consciousness – specifically, repetitive, minimalistic, seamless cyclings of sonic patterns accompanied by a relentlessly driving or metronomic rhythm; and the self-conscious desire of ravers to associate themselves with icons of a generic "ethnic-ness."

As both a *gamelan* player[9] and a rave initiate, I am willing to consider the structural or textural similarities between much traditional *gamelan* music and music played at raves, and to speculate on the connection between the roles and contexts of each. David Roberts describes the structure of "transformational" music in rave as containing a minimum of melody and vocals, "substituting a mesmeric, repetitive beat as the central element" (in Redhead 1993: 124). Dance ethnologist Georgiana Gore describes rave music as "minimalist with a relentless 4/4 beat," reputed to drive ravers into a state of frenzy (1997: 58). Numerous sources detail the structural aspects of traditional *gamelan* music (both Balinese and Javanese), which often (though certainly not always) involve seamless repetition of rhythmic and tonal patterns over a steady beat. Ethnomusicologist Margaret Kartomi, in describing the required musical elements in Javanese *gamelan* accompaniment to folk trance, states that music must be "mesmeric in effect," and contain a steady regular pulsation with repetitive tonal patterns based on a restricted number of pitches (1973: 166). Balinese psychiatrist Luh Ketut Suryani discusses the hypnotic effect of traditional Balinese ceremonial *gamelan* music on Balinese *gamelan* players, and describes the music as having a basic, relatively unchanging pattern, repetitive, rhythmically steady, and tending toward monotony in volume and intensity (Jensen and Suryani 1993: 123). Suryani reports that Balinese ceremonial *gamelan* players feel "as though they are floating above the ground," "nearer to the gods" and "in another world" (*ibid.*). In both *gamelan angklung* (and commonly in other types of *gamelan* music) and techno, there are simultaneous layers of musical complexity playing out at different levels of tempo and "busy-ness." Although rave music is much louder than *gamelan* music, often the emphasis (in both musics) is on the creation of a kind of endless ground through minimalistic repetition of instrumental bytes which tends to entrain the mind of the listener.

Coincidentally or not, types of techno and *gamelan* music, and their respective musical textures, are both present in communal gatherings where dance and altered states of consciousness are the intention of at least a subgroup of participants. Institutionalized occasions for "entranced" dancing (with *gamelan* orchestra accompaniment) in Bali include the Kris dance (male, group trance ritual) and the Barong/Rangda ritual (protector dragon vs. monstrous witch in showdown between the forces of good and evil). A larger five-tone orchestra (*gamelan pelegongan*) accompanies these dramas involving trance. The repertoire of this *gamelan* again involves intricate, closely interlocked melodic figuration as well as complex stratified polyphony. Although the dramatic accompaniment requires sudden changes in tempo and dynamics at times, repetitive clichéd figurations over ostinatos and stretches of metronomic tempo remain characteristic of the music.

While the *gamelan angklung* is not the particular *gamelan* ensemble associated with rituals involving trance in Bali, its textural characteristics are in many ways idiosyncratic to much *gamelan* music in general, including those ensembles that are present in trance contexts. This had led me to consider possible relationships between events that employ similar musical textures and whose participants intend to achieve extraordinary consciousness. At Hyperreal's Trance List Archives the trance subgenre of techno is plainly characterized as a means to altered states of consciousness (ASC): "Through the use of repetitive and extended beat patterns and/or rhythms, this music often induces trance-like states in those who listen or dance to it."

In Rouget's often cited work *Music and Trance: A Theory of the Relations Between Music and Possession*, the author states that, although music "does play a part in triggering and maintaining the trance state, it does not owe its effect to the properties of the musical structure, or if it does, it does so only to a small degree" (1985: 96). Becker applauds Rouget for "putting to rest" the idea of a causal relationship between types of music and types of trance (Becker 1994: 41). It is generally understood that the entire trance context as a package – including all sensory stimulation, in addition to belief system and expectations of the participant – is responsible for inducing altered states of consciousness. Becker suggests that the musical component of trance, acting as a "physiological metonym," "invokes" an entire "mythology" to which certain emotions and behavior are attached (*ibid*.: 45). In Bali, deeply sensual cues such as incense, strongly scented flowers, and bright ornate costumes accompany ritual. It is likely that in the rave context the music volume, visual bombardment, physiological excitement of dance, desire for an altered state, and other elements of rave described earlier, heighten possible transportative mechanisms perceived in the music. However, the musical contribution (or "universal" relationship of music) to trance states remains debated amongst scholars. I would feel uncomfortable dismissing the commonly expressed experiences of those who feel entrained, transported, or some other hypnotic-like effect when exposed to the musical textures described above, even in a sterile concert hall. Transformative experience associated with music is highly idiosyncratic and resistant to linguistic expression. Exactly what individual ravers mean when they use the term "trance" and speak of a trance experience is a significant issue that merits further exploration.

Towards the 'electronic re-tribalization of society'

I have suggested one possibility for the appropriation of Balinese *gamelan* by the rave scene: a similarity in musical structures typically accompanying events associated with ASC in both contexts. Now I'll explore the implications of a more socially complex second possibility. I propose that it is part of the ideology of some rave participants to associate themselves with icons of a generic "ethnicness' – perceived as synonymous with "primitiveness." As an "exotic" entity, the *gamelan* affords this association. Note one raver's ideas about how the *gamelan* might function at an event:

> I think it would be REALLY cool to have a couple of Balinese dancers dance to the last gamelan piece, and then have the dj start back up with something similarly exotic, maybe Middle Eastern, that the dancers could also dance to. Then bring up the music again slowly, to help tie the different pieces of the ceremony together.
>
> (posted to sfraves, 27 March 2000)

A further exploration of this notion of interchangeable exotica will illuminate the seemingly contradictory techno-primitive "aesthetic" of the San Francisco rave scene.

Another participant states: "[w]hat the *gamelan* was doing was the same as what rave was doing. That it's all tapping into the same roots" (personal interview, 21 May 1998). This comment, alluding to "the same roots" of a common, pre-industrial ancestry, emphasizes the valued connection between raving and ancient ritual – a connection distinguishing ravers ideologically from industrialized mainstream society. What is especially interesting in this view is that high technology (the ultimate product of industrialized society) and especially electronically produced music are seen as *means to accomplish* this goal of reconnection with the primitive in us all. The following posting to hyperreal.org clearly illustrates this idea: "There are many developments in technology however, that have the potential to create an electronic re-tribalization of society and help humanity remember our place on this sacred sphere" (Amoeba 1994: 1).

Far from being contradictory, combining high technology with perceived "tribal values" is viewed as the ultimate tool of collective transcendence and self-actualization.[10] This vision is clearly expressed in Kathleen Williamson's characterization of raving:

> There is a pulsating awareness of sharing archaic understandings, reviving lost traditions…which are all invested with *new technological innovation*. The sounds are the new epic poetry of this century…. The knowledge is beyond consumerism and materialism, and associated disaffected, alienated and generally *self-destructive style of the industrial being*… The sounds and rhythms produced by tekno artists seem to be more and more profound in their ability to communicate the most…deeply resonating *primal understandings*. It's

the *re-discovered language* of transcendence…. Here is the "coming of age" ritual which Western culture has long forgotten.

(Kathleen Williamson, at hyperreal.org; italics mine)

Within techno-primitivism, it appears, technology is paradoxically *embraced* in an attempt to regain the very thing which mechanization is denigrated for taking away – our basic human-ness. Reynolds asserts that digital music "abandons all the elements of *feel*" (1998: 44). While all instrumental music makes use of technology of some kind, electronically produced sound is often viewed as particularly "artificial," "lacking warmth," "emotionless," or "removed" from the human body. While revering such a music, could ravers' concurrent attachment to "the primitive" be an unconscious effort to resist (or counterbalance) the dehumanizing aspect of the music being embraced – an effort to reclaim or hold on to the human element in the face of pervasive, ever-expanding technology while reveling in the hedonistic aspects of both? This construction within which participants worship both technology and the primitive perhaps keeps the Vibe in balance. Technology may have its way, but at the same time identification with the primitive quells anxiety produced by the threat of ever-increasing mechanization and distancing from the "authenticating" power of the "natural."

When viewed from this perspective, the appropriation of the *gamelan* by the San Francisco rave scene appears to have its own logic. In addition to proposed formal musical similarities with techno, the *gamelan* is successfully integrated into the rave event, on the basis of its perceived homogenous "ethnic-ness," "otherness," or primitive associations – in other words, for what it represents. This representation is effected through the "exotic" *gamelan* instruments – intricately carved and painted, sitting amongst carefully prepared offerings, burning incense, and other miscellaneous Balinese 'paraphernalia' – and the otherworldly sound of an orchestra of bronze gongs and metallophones. I propose that information such as where this ensemble comes from, its history, its "authentic" performance practice, who usually plays it, or even what it's called is irrelevant in the context of rave. It is not necessary to possess such in-depth knowledge. What *is* important is that the presence of the *gamelan* affirms the romantic, self-perceived identity of raving as part of something "primal" and resistant to the mainstream. In this construction, I suggest that the "exotic" equals the "primitive," associated with the roots of humankind and the sacralized lifestyle to which some ravers desire to return. More to the point, through a conflation of the ethnic/exotic and the primitive, the *gamelan* serves as an authenticating agent within the rave event.

While participants may perceive themselves as experiencing "authentic" culture in the form of the *gamelan*, the unwitting result of this borrowing process may be the eliding of cultural particularities, and the subsequent reinforcement of the concept of a generic ethnic/primitive/Other. It is likely that other "world" musics may be successfully appropriated by rave.[11]

Contrary to the intentions of alternative cultural events, in the very act of interacting with surfaces of entities in this way, ravers are perhaps engaging in a very mainstream kind of behavior. Turkle (1997) describes a current psychosocial operative mode in which *representations* – rather than transparent entities – are sufficient for interacting with the world. It is often claimed that there is an increased tendency within postmodern industrial culture for one to be satisfied with surface-only knowledge of, or relationships with, cultural items that make up one's "idioverse" and contribute to identity construction. Hopefully without appearing to accept wholesale a totalistic concept of postmodernism, I suggest that the *gamelan*'s appropriation into a context (such as rave) in which it *functions* as a more or less origin-free entity speaks to this claim.

Conclusion

My intent was to consider how and why a Balinese *gamelan* could have made its way to the foothills of the Sierra mountains in the summer of 1997 and, in doing so, contribute to the discussion of local rave culture in the U.S. via electronically produced sensory experience, community in virtual space, and attributing cosmic significance to modern technology, San Francisco rave is an alternative cultural performance firmly located in the technocultural present. In an interpretation of rave's appropriation of a *gamelan* ensemble, I considered two possibilities: a similarity in musical structure within rave music and traditional *gamelan* music, and the ensemble's absorption as a tool of authentication for rave participants. It is likely that both possibilities possess merit. Through a simultaneous embrace of the modern technological revolution and a redeeming, nostalgic identification with the "primitive," I argued, a seemingly contradictory techno-primitive ideology has been constructed. An examination of techno-primitive practice revealed how disembodied cultural entities may be mixed and matched in such a way that genuine differences are eradicated, and how a resulting generic ethnic-ness (conflated with primitive-ness) serves as an authenticating agent. The agent in this case is the Balinese *gamelan*. Additional studies of the means by which representations of homogenized ethnic-ness, in the form of live "world" musics or instruments, are incorporated into other alternative cultural events may further illuminate processes inherent in subcultural identity formation.

Notes

1 This chapter is an abridged and edited version of an article published online in *ECHO* 3, spring 2001. I thank the editors of *ECHO* for graciously allowing me to publish the abridged version that appears here. The original expanded article ("We thank the Technology Goddess for giving us the ability to rave: *gamelan*, techno-primitivism and the San Francisco rave scene"), including musical and video examples, is available at:
http://www.humnet.ucla.edu/echo/volume3-issue1/Table-of-Contents/Table-of-Contents.html.

2 An Indonesian orchestral ensemble comprised primarily of bronze-keyed metallophones, gongs, and gong-chime instruments. The predominant texture of *gamelan* music involves multiple layers of interlocked, repetitive, metronomic cycles of sound.

3 "At the heart of a true rave there's the pulse of something intangible; a positive unifying groove, an extraordinary feeling, a Vibe that transcends description" ("The Spirit of Raving Archives" at http://www.hyperreal.org/raves/spirit). The Vibe is often nostalgically referred to by ravers as a "lost" mode of experience to which human beings inwardly yearn to return.

4 In using the term "alternative cultural event" (ACE) I follow Graham St John, who defines alternative culture as "a diverse network of discourse and practice opposi-tional to perceived deficiencies in the parent culture, which is the system of values, beliefs and practices hegemonic under modernity" (1999: 6). The ACE referred to here was entitled "4x4," put on by the San Francisco-based rave collective Harmony on August 16, 1997.

5 This group is an offshoot of a larger Balinese *gamelan* ensemble (Gamelan Swarasanti) that is part of the curriculum at the University of California, Santa Cruz Music Department. "Swarasanti" is roughly translated as "the sound of peace." "Anak" means "child." Photos of various rave performances may be found at the group's website at http://www.sei.com/users/kk/swarasanti/anak.html.

6 The relationship between music and trance remains highly controversial. See the classic text on the subject by Rouget (1985). A variety of arguments appear in James Porter (1987).

7 My fieldwork has so far been limited to one regional expression of rave culture: the San Francisco rave scene between 1997 and 2000. San Francisco ravers are typically white middle-class youths between the ages of 18 and 30, often college students, and are usually interested in alternative culture (Brown 1995: para. 4) Amongst rave scenes, San Francisco is known for its psychedelic, New Age-y, idealistic ethos. This is due to the "wishful anarchist/spiritualist agenda" of the scene's British founders (Silcott 1999: 51–4), which catalyzed with San Francisco's countercultural past in the late 1980s. These themes are expressed in the titling of rave events such as Warmth, Innercense, Expansion 2.0, and Unity. For an analysis of San Francisco rave music, see Sellin (1999).

8 Nyoman Sedana, Balinese performing artist and scholar, explained in a personal communication with the author in 2001 that, although the ensemble has traditionally served a Hindu–Bali ceremonial function, performances of contemporary music or adaptations of non-ceremonial pieces for *gamelan angklung* have more recently begun to take place in secular settings. Indeed, *gamelan angklung* groups now take part in government-sponsored *gamelan* competitions (Bakan 1999: 97). And while member-ship in *gamelan angklung* groups has traditionally been confined to males, Sedana added that females currently perform this music in Balinese conservatory settings.

9 My experience with *gamelan* includes study of Balinese *gamelan angklung, gamelan gong, gamelan gendèr wayang,* and central and west Javanese *gamelan* in the U.S., Bali, and Java.

10 An opposition to this view of techno music is found within Australia's alternative cultural event ConFest (Conference/Festival), where nostalgia for the primitive and a return to "pure," earth-connected living are similarly core values (St John 2001). As described by Graham St John, the aural space of ConFest is decidedly contested. Here, techno-trance enthusiasts find themselves at odds with a significant constituent of event-goers who view loud, electronically based music as "invasive," "inappro-priate," and threatening the environment as well as the overall authenticity of the ConFest experience. Sharply contrasting with the techno-primitive view of dancing to techno as a means of building communitas, this music is regarded by many ConFest participants as mechanistic and a threat to sociality (*ibid.*: 258–66).

11 The San Francisco Bay area-based Hawaiian hula company Na Lei Hulu I Ka Wekiu recently fused traditional dance and music with techno for a performance at a Bay area rave. This performance was repeated for an audience at the downtown Los Angeles Grand Performances summer music festival in August 2002.

Bibliography

Amoeba, Mark (1994) "Why tribal future: the only thing constant is change," *Hyperreal*, posted October 28, 1994 at:
http://www.hyperreal.org/raves/spirit/vision/Tribal_Future.html (accessed February 13, 1999).

Bakan, Michael (1999) *Music of Death and New Creation: Experiences in the World of Balinese Gamelan Beleganjur*, Chicago: University of Chicago Press.

Becker, Judith (1994) "Music and trance," *Leonardo Music Journal* 4: 41–51.

Brown, David J. (1995) "Techno music and raves FAQ," *Hyperreal*, posted December 1, 1995 at http://www.hyperreal.org/mike/pub/altraveFAQ.html (accessed February 13, 1999).

Gore, Georgiana (1997) "The beat goes on: trance, dance and tribalism in rave culture," in Helen Thomas (ed.) *Dance and the City*, New York: St Martin's Press.

Heley, Mark (2000) "House music: the best techno-shamanic cultural virus so far," *Guerillas of Harmony: Communiques from the Dance Underground*, posted 2000 at http://www.wenet/donut/virus.html (accessed July 27, 2000).

Jensen, Gordon and Luh Ketut Suryani (1993) *Trance and Possession in Bali: A Window on Western Multiple Personality Disorder, and Suicide*, New York: Oxford University Press.

Kartomi, Margaret (1973) "Music and trance in central Java," *Ethnomusicology* 17(2): 163–208.

Lysloff, René (1996) "DJ shamanism and New Age technospirituality: trance and meditation in popular music," paper presented for the joint meeting of the International Association for the Study of Popular Music (U.S. Chapter) and the Society for Ethnomusicology in Pittsburgh, PA.

—— (n.d.) "DJ shamanism and New Age technospirituality: music and transcendence in American technoculture," unpublished document.

McPhee, Colin (1966) *Music in Bali: A Study in Form and Instrumental Organization in Balinese Orchestral Music*, New Haven, CT: Yale University Press.

Porter, James (moderator) (1987) "Trance, music, and music/trance relations: a symposium," *Pacific Review of Ethnomusicology* 4: 1–38.

Redhead, Steve (ed.) (1993) *Rave Off: Politics and Deviance in Contemporary Youth Culture*, Brookfield, VT: Avebury.

Reynolds, Simon (1998) *Generation Ecstasy: Into the World of Techno and Rave Culture*, Boston, MA: Little, Brown & Company.

Rouget, Gilbert (1985) *Music and Trance: A Theory of the Relations between Music and Possession*, Chicago: University of Chicago Press.

St John, Graham (1999) *Alternative Cultural Heterotopia: ConFest as Australia's Marginal Centre*, Ph.D. thesis, La Trobe University, Melbourne, available online at:
http://www.confeStorg/thesis (accessed November 15, 2002).

—— (2001) "The battle of the bands: ConFest musics and the politics of authenticity," *Perfect Beat: The Pacific Journal of Research into Contemporary Music and Popular Culture* 5(2): 69–90.

Saunders, Nicholas (1995) "The spiritual aspect of rave culture," posted 1995 at http://www.ecstasy.org/info/rave.html (accessed February 13, 1998 and October 13, 1998); first published in the *Guardian* (July 22, 1995).

Sellin, Yara (1999) "San Francisco style: rave music performance practice and analysis," M.A. thesis, University of California, Santa Cruz.

Silcott, Mireille (1999) *Rave America: New School Dancescapes*, Toronto: ECW Press.

Somberg, Eden (n.d.) "Rave as Ritual: creating community in a postmodern society," site formerly posted at http://www.nrv8.com/monthly/1-01/copy/rave.html.

Tenzer, Michael (1991) *Balinese Music*, Berkeley, CA: Periplus Editions.

Turkle, Sherry (1997) *Life on the Screen: Identity in the Age of the Internet*, New York: Touchstone.

Turner, Victor (1982) *From Ritual to Theater*, New York: Performing Arts Journal Publications.

Twist, Cinnamon (2000) *Guerillas of Harmony: Communiques from the Dance Underground*, site formerly posted at http://www.wenet.net/donut/virus.html (accessed July 27, 2000).

van Gennep, Arnold (1981) *Les Rites de passage*, Paris: Éditions A. & J. Picard; reprint of the 1909 edition.

Part IV

Global tribes

The technomadic counterculture

11 Techno millennium

Dance, ecology and future primitives

Graham St John

[O]nly a mass idealistic fashion within Youth Dance Culture, swelling up from the gene-pool itself and now planet-wide, can produce the sufficiently colossal fractal mutation in Humanity's lifestyle necessary for it to survive and go on to rave among the stars.

(Fraser Clark, from *The Book of RavElations*)[1]

Where technician meets tradition. With ancient ways and modern means; we pilot the temple, to the land of the gods.

(Gaian Mind)[2]

Throughout the 1990s, psychedelic trance accelerated the interfacing of technology, ecology and spirituality. Psytrance became a transnational context for the growth of a planetary ethos among youth, for the evolution of eco-spiritual commitments expressed and performed through dance. This chapter charts these developments, uncovering a pattern of revitalization associated with the *fin de siècle* – a period of unfettered optimism fed by cyber and digital developments adopted and championed in the cultural response to an accelerating environmental crisis. It documents an eco-millenarian dance movement rising out of global centres and marginal sites throughout the 1990s. The creative amalgamation of contemporary technologies and reconstructed religiosity is shown to have manifested in the cultural output of influential 'altered statesmen', and is communicated through the rituals and epochal events of new 'tribal' formations emerging within a global technospiritual youth network.

In the early 1990s, humanity, so the consensus seemed to be, had built up a momentous head of steam. With the implosion of the Soviet Union, the emergence of post-apartheid South Africa, and the prevalence and utility of computer-mediated communication, David Dei, founder of Cape Town's alternative magazine *Kagenna*, observed that '*the* most important social manifestation in the history of humanity' was taking shape. A complex counterculture consisting of a 'fragmented rag-tag nation of reality technicians, cyber operatives, pagan evolutionaries, trance guerrillas, and Zippies' were adopting 'African Shamanic Technology' – a hardware thought appropriate for 'recolonizing the psyche-space of the entire superstructure of society' (Dei 1994). It was time, according to Dei, 'to use our newly won tools-of-the-gods or Deity Devices as true extensions of our being...for the creation of a perfect and beautiful deep green world' (*ibid.*). This strident narrative taps into a sense of hope amidst crisis, an idealism at odds with the dominant historical trajectory of war, environmental disaster and famine. Heralding novel technological developments deemed necessary for consciousness revolution, the idealism echoed that of the techno-utopian Peter Russell, who regarded new communications media as critical in achieving inward development, triggering the shift from personal to global consciousness. In *The Global Brain Awakens* (1995/1982), Russell indicated how the history of humanity demonstrates a tendency toward greater interconnectivity. With the internet and the worldwide web, Gaia was speculated to be 'growing herself a nervous system'. Drawing upon the message of self-maintenance and responsibility in Lovelock's Gaia Hypothesis, the mounting crisis was itself considered to be 'an important evolutionary drive' pushing us into new levels of cooperation, with human cells self-organizing into 'a rapidly integrating global network, the nerve cells of an awakening global brain' (Russell 1995). And, since many of the advocates and emissaries of the IT-led global consciousness revolution were also electronic-music enthusiasts, as Rushkoff conveyed in *Cyberia* (1994), the sentiment was perhaps more accurately 'rave-olution'.

Timewave Zero and the Alien Dreamtime

Terence McKenna (1946–2000) was the principal spokesperson for the rave-olution – his body of work on technological 'ingressions into social novelty' becoming prominent amongst techno-millennialists. A student of the ontological foundations of shamanism and the ethno-pharmacology of spiritual transformation, McKenna championed psychedelic consciousness. Discovery of a complex fractal 'timewave' encoded in the I Ching, the ancient Chinese Book of Changes, led McKenna, together with his brother Dennis, to found Novelty Theory. Rooted in Chaos Dynamics and Complexity Theory, Novelty elaborated Alfred North Whitehead's notion of novelty into a mathematical speculation concerning 'the fundamental architecture of time'.[3] The ultra-novel event McKenna called 'Timewave Zero' models the world as we know it, achieving 'congrescence', the apogee of infinite complexity, on 21 December 2012.

Discovering the quantum mathematical ordering principles of the ancient Chinese oracle, the McKennas were able to plot waves of 'habit' (conservation) and 'novelty' (strangeness) transpiring over the course of history, observing that the last 1,500 years reveal an acceleration of novelty which will culminate in 'a complex attractor that exists ahead of us in time' – pulling us towards it, determining and terminating history. In Alien Dreamtime, a live spoken word performance recorded with ambient Space Time Continuum at San Francisco's Transmission Theatre on 26 February 1993,[4] McKenna stated that 'something is calling us out of nature and sculpting us in it's own image'. 'You can feel', he elaborated, 'that we're approaching the cusp of a catastrophe, and that beyond that cusp we are unrecognizable to ourselves. The wave of novelty that has rolled unbroken since the birth of the universe has now focused and coalesced itself in our species'. The statement was an iteration of an earlier performance reproduced as part of the track 'Re: Evolution' from the Shamen's 1992 album *Boss Drum*:

> History is ending. I mean, we are to be the generation that witnesses the revelation of the purpose of the cosmos. History is the shock wave of the Eschaton. History is the shock wave of eschatology, and what this means for those of us who will live through this transition into hyperspace, is that we will be privileged to see the greatest release of compressed change probably since the birth of the universe. The twentieth century is the shudder that announces the approaching cataracts of time over which our species and the destiny of this planet is about to be swept.[5]

In McKenna's framework, planetary novelty will accelerate exponentially to a point which, according to the maths, possesses a quantified value of zero – the Omega Point, the Eschaton: December 2012. In a most extraordinary development, the calculations were only much later discovered to be almost identical to the cosmic rebirth foreseen in the Tzolkin, the Mayan Sacred Calendar. According to archeoastronomer John Major Jenkins (who published his work in *Maya Cosmogenesis 2012* [1998]), over 2,300 years ago the Maya calculated that the December solstice of 2012 (6 a.m. on 21 December) will occasion an alignment of the path of the sun with the Galactic Equator of the Milky Way (which the ancient Maya recognized as 'the Sacred Tree'), an event signifying cosmogenesis in Mayan thought, the end of a great gestation period and the birth of a new world age.[6]

Corresponding with the Tzolkin, McKenna modelled an accelerating rate of change making major species change immanent. Yet, while the end of the world was nigh, it would hardly correspond to the apocalyptic scenarios of orthodox religion. According to McKenna, the 'strange attractor' lying in the future 'throws off reflections of itself, which actually ricochet into the past, illuminating this mystic, inspiring that saint or visionary'. Furthermore, 'out of these fragmentary glimpses of eternity we can build a kind of map, of not only the past of the universe, and the evolutionary egression into novelty, but a kind of map of the future'. While psilocybe mushrooms catalysed the evolution of language (and technology) in *Homo sapiens* 50,000 years ago, our species once again stands at the threshold of a major evolutionary event. McKenna felt that the understanding of 'planetary purpose' was critical for humans to become 'agents of evolution'. An advocate of the 'archaic revival', a return to 'the palaeolithic world of natural magic' and community in preparation for the coming Eschaton, McKenna was himself such a humble visionary. In the revival, humanity would experience reconnection to 'the vegetal Goddess', to the Earth Mother: 'Returning to the bosom of the planetary partnership means trading the point of view of the history-created ego for a more maternal and intuitional style.' And the use of hallucinogenic plants would enable the reawakening of traditional attitudes towards the natural world, re-establishing 'channels of direct communication with the planetary Other' (McKenna 1991: ch. 15). McKenna thus effectively promoted the role of the shaman in the contemporary world. With the dissolution of boundaries triggered by psychedelics,

> one cannot continue to close one's eyes to the ruination of the earth, the poisoning of the seas, and the consequences of two thousand years of unchallenged dominator culture, based on monotheism, hatred of nature, suppression of the female, and so forth.... So, what shamans have to do is act as exemplars, by making this cosmic journey to the domain of the Gaian ideas, and then bringing them back in the form of art in the struggle to save the world.... The message that nature sends is, transform your language through a synergy between electronic culture and the psychedelic imagination, a synergy between dance and idea, a synergy between understanding and intuition, and dissolve the boundaries that your culture has sanctioned between you, to become part of this Gaian supermind.[7]

From the early 1990s, McKenna had championed the underground dance phenomenon as an integral component in the psychedelics-led revival. Enabling one to see 'the wiring under the board...to recover the jewel lost at the beginning of time', rave would assist in conditioning humanity for the upcoming transition to 'hyperspace' from three-dimensional time and space. Psychedelic youth culture was a quantum leap in the novelty model. Again, speaking on 'Re: Evolution', he stated:

> The emphasis in house music and rave culture on physiologically compatible rhythms...is really the rediscovery of the art of natural magic with sound. That sound, properly understood, especially percussive sound, can actually change neurological states, and large groups of people getting together in the presence of this kind of music are creating a telepathic community of bonding that hopefully will be strong enough that it can carry the vision out into the mainstream of society.

Raves, and psychedelics were going to bootstrap humanity for the impending shift. This new youth culture, he stated,

> is the real new world order and it's going to carry all of us into a world of completion and caring that we have not known since the pyramids were raised.... The new rave culture is the cutting edge of the last best hope for suffering humanity.... Take back the planet – it's yours, it's yours. These are the last minutes of human history folks. The countdown is on. This is not a test. We're leaving this world behind, for a brighter, better world that has always existed; in our imagination.[8]

Like the ultimate scout leader, the message McKenna delivered to thousands of young people in his capacity as guest speaker at psychedelic trance events across the globe – from Megatripolis in London, to San Francisco's Toon Town and Australia's Transelements – was 'be prepared':

> This is not a dress rehearsal for the apocalypse....This is the last chance before things become so dissipated that there is no chance for cohesiveness. We can use the calendar as a club. We can make the millennium an occasion for establishing an authentic human civilization, overcoming the dominator paradigm, dissolving boundaries through psychedelics, recreating a sexuality not based on monotheism, monogamy and monotony.... We are the inheritors of a million years of striving for the unspeakable. And now with the engines of technology in our hands we ought to be able to reach out and actually exteriorize the human soul at the end of time, invoke it into existence like a UFO and open the violet doorway into hyperspace and walk through it, out of profane history and into the world beyond the grave, beyond shamanism, beyond the end of history, into the galactic millennium that has beckoned to us for millions of years across space and time. THIS IS THE MOMENT. A planet brings forth an opportunity like this only once in its lifetime, and we are ready, and we are poised. And as a community we are ready to move into it, to claim it, to make it our own.[9]

While it was criticized for propagating a not unfamiliar 'linear masculine eschatology' featuring a 'breakneck rush towards a crescendo of connectedness and barrier dissolution – a Cosmic Climax' (Gyrus 1999) – the predicted encounter with the 'transdimensional object at the end of time' gathered conceptual momentum. And the process enhanced McKenna's status as a heroic folk-theorist at the same time as it lent legitimacy to the preoccupations of the global underground dance community.

Post-rave psychedelic dance culture has embraced variations of Timewave Zero and the Mayan Tzolkin, granting 21 December 2012 varied significance. Indeed, what the date actually implies is open to vast interpretation, as it is taken to occasion hyperspatial breakthrough, alien contact, planetismal impact, historical explosion, quaser ignition at the Galactic Centre,[10] the 'dawning of the techno New Jerusalem or Cyber-Zion' (McDaniel and Bethel 2002), or the birth of the 'World of the Fifth Sun, the cleansing of the earth and the raising of a higher level of vibration',[11] etc. The Melbourne-based Barrelful of Monkeys (BoM) elicit a principle message. Post-2012 is regarded as a 'Dreaming Universe' and 'our very momentum of describing this event continues to concrese it into the act of becoming'. Whether the coming event is held to be 'the Eschaton, the Dreamtime, the Logos, the Imagination, the Omega Point, an AI [artificial intelligence] Virtuality or simply the momentum of history and culture reaching it's [*sic.*] zenith...we get to choose how we intepret it'. Catching glimpses of eternity, they're following McKenna's advice and preparing 'to be born into the next world'. Grafting the Hundredth Monkey syndrome, the BoM have taken on the role of 'artists and madmen and trypsters and children [and] all God's Fools', divined to 'pass on the new awareness to the rest of the race'. Just as it took 1 per cent of humanity to 'make that SHIFT in consciousness, as happened about 50,000 years ago when we fell into language and history...[w]e have to lock in the harmonic upload opportunity synchronizing through local spacetime Dec 21st 2012 and reel in the 5th dimension!'[12]

CyberTribe Rising: anarcho-spiritual techno-tribalism

The writing of anarcho-mystic Hakim Bey (a.k.a. Peter Lamborn Wilson) was heavily implicated in forging the primitivist-extropian alliance at the heart of the Alien Dreamtime. His *Temporary Autonomous Zone* (1991), or TAZ, became poetic inspiration for cooperative, consensual, non-commodified dancescapes amplifying re-enchantment and the liberation of desire. Outside the surveillance of the state and the incursions of the corporate world, the free outdoor rave-TAZ became a tech-savvy anarcho-liminal utopia wherein inhabitants claim to achieve that which resembles a peak-experience, or union, with co-liminaries and nature. As 'a means to maximize autonomy and pleasure for as many individuals and groups as possible as soon as possible', the TAZ is also an effort to 'reconcile...wilderness and cyberspace' (Bey 1995). While it accommodates efforts to attain the 'palaeolithic', the immediate insurrection is optimized and orchestrated through the internet. Hosting promiscuous utopics, the TAZ would give birth to mutant offspring carrying primitivist and extropian genes. And while gatherings became humanist laboratories hosting techno-shamanic experimentation with unpredictable results, the 'downloading [of] political expression and reverie learnt on the dancefloor and inside the webs of networked mainframes INTO the OUTSIDE geography of LIFE AS WE KNOW IT' (Dei 1994), was a practice widely assumed in the global dance community throughout the 1990s (cf. Razam 2001).

The popularity of McKenna's psychedelicism, the Mayan Sacred Calendar and the TAZ idea amongst the 'digerati' illustrated disenchantment with the conventions of radical opposition. As the idea of socialist *revolution* was eschewed, there grew an optimistic belief that 'disappearance from the grid' in the form of networked 'communities of feeling' would, with the assistance of technology and deconstructionist spirituality, stimulate the *evolution* of the Global Brain – thus giving rise to psycho-cultural transformation. This trajectory was exemplified by the social formation given character in Geoff White's influential 'CyberTribe rising' (1993). In White's view, a new horizontal 'cybernetic model', which he called 'C5I2' (or 'Community, Consensus, Cooperation, Communication, Cybernetics, Intelligence and Intuition'), and its concomitant technology, was mutating from the post-World War II vertical-control model which, he conveys, was often referred to in military circles as 'C3I' (or 'Command, Control, Communication and Intelligence'). With C5I2 technology, '[i]nformation passes from small groups to other small groups through what some call the Web, an interconnected communications network made up of mail, word-of-mouth, phone-trees, VCRs, FAX machines, audio cassettes, free software and computer networks' (*ibid.*). White promoted a decentralized social and economic paradigm, observing a network of 'CyberTribes' which were operating through autonomous, consensual and cooperative strategies, and which, while based on the cybernetic model, were being shaped by Deep Ecology, Distributed Systems Theory and Chaos Theory. As a technology of sharing and cooperation, C5I2 was heralded as 'the technology behind Temporary Autonomous Zones', and the inspired CyberTribe was 'a step towards the realization of Global TAZ networks' (*ibid.*).

Others would take up the baton and run with the 'convivial technology'. Throughout the 1990s, numerous inspired techno-tribes emerged in Europe, North America, Australia, Japan and other locations in pursuit of the desired 'revival' through the facilitation of TAZ-like enclaves. One of the earliest and perhaps most influential examples of cyber-tribalism was London's 'terra-technic' sound system Spiral Tribe. With techno as their 'folk music', the Spirals believed their free parties were techno-shamanic rites, 'reconnect[ing] urban youth to the earth with which they had lost contact, thus averting imminent ecological crisis' (Collin 1997: 203–4). While some cyber-tribals, like the Barrelful of Monkeys, build robust conceptual scaffolding heavily indebted to the likes of McKenna or Sheldrake, others, like the Midwest's Future Harmonix, emit cloying off-planet trajectories: 'together we will build a galactic network of light. And now we are issuing a call to awakening and uniting of Starry Family on this planet, so we can all Together go home into galactic oneness'.[13] Regardless of agenda, these DiY dance collectives and sound systems are sites of youth belonging and identity. As an umbrella organization in British Columbia, Tribal Harmonix, states:

> By radically rethinking the meaning and function of community, tribal dance collectives are creating a model of positive social and cultural change in society as a whole. Moreover, the experience of dancing together brings healing, understanding, and peace in an otherwise tumultuous and rapidly changing world.[14]

Like Maffesoli's 'neo-tribes' (1996), these tech-savvy organizations are voluntary, unstable and sensuous micro-cultures interconnected in a network of lifestyle nodes and centres of sociality between which individuals are known to oscillate.[15] And each node achieves its fullest expression in the festal, the DIY event, the techno-corroboree – where various new tribes gravitate to share grievances and exaltations, and to forge a recombinant culture of cyber, psychoactive and ecological concerns. Thus, in 1999 in Berlin 35 communities representing a spectrum of projects and agendas founded Sonics-Cybertribe-Network for Rhythm and Change,[16] members of which converge annually. And in more recent times an annual conference-festival, the LA-based Gathering of the Tribes (GoTT) emerged. In 2002, with Biodiversity as the event's theme, the GoTT hosted workshops and presentations on a range of issues from 'Indigenous Rituals and the Making of Sacred Space', through 'Yoga and Temple Dance', to 'Social, Environmental or Political Change through Music'.[17]

The Book of RavElations: zippy Eschaton

Speaking at the launch of the Zippy Pronoia Tour held at the Wetlands nightclub in Manhattan on 15 June 1994, Terence McKenna announced that 'every 50 years or so, society needs liberation from the forces of fascism'. Fifty years since the end of World War II 'a vanguard of liberators has secured a beach head on the east coast of America, and has begun to work its way inland along the Hudson'.[18] For a man who once wrote how he anticipated 'the great gaian dj "strange attractor" mix[ing] the end game of the second with the opening chords of the third millennium',[19] zippy imagineer Fraser Clark's association with McKenna's cosmogonic scheme had been well established. In the years approaching Z Day, Clark, the editor of *Evolution* magazine (originally *Encyclopedia Psychedelica International, Epi*) and founder of London clubs Megatripolis and the Parallel YOUniversity, had been an influential articulator of the technology/ecology/spirituality tryst. Coining the word 'zippy' (Zen-inspired pronoid pagan) to describe those who disowned hippy-like pastoralism and embraced the cyberdelic evolutionary possibilities in technology, and compiling *Sharmanarchy in the UK*, an album championing England's revitalization through a fusion of the house generation and green movement, like McKenna, Clark evangelized rave as the newest and most significant vehicle through the end-times. 'Like the old pagan festivals', Clark announced in a speech delivered at Stanford University on 2 May 1995,

> we're all in this together. This is our planet. She is indescribably beautiful, gigantic. We are atoms of that living Goddess. Personally, I can't see a better way to help people to learn a love, respect and reverence for Nature than the classical open-air all-night Rave. Can you imagine what it felt like with 20,000 people going for it and actually feeling together, and the power of a people together…and then dancing the sun up? It is awesome, it is religious, and it is life-changing.[20]

In a communiqué posted on California's WELL (Whole Earth 'Lectronic Link) conferencing system in May 1994, Clark proposed that 'any relatively conscious planeter has at least begun to suspect that the competition-based system within which human culture is currently operating is incapable of adapting, and needs to be re-coded'. And since 'the Sign' for which we all yearn is 'that WE, the relatively conscious, are a hell of a lot more numerous than even WE supposed', there was reason for optimism. Thus:

> The news is good. Very, very good. I see only one sociological phenomenon within Western Culture which has any chance of bringing about the required maximum change in the maximum number of people in the minimum period of time. UK Rave Culture has been evolving for five years now, and at its most accelerated, the tribal rave scene has united the raw young idealism and enthusiasm of Rave with the eco-wisdom of Festival Culture to produce a mix of meltdown proportions.[21]

Clark's trans-Atlantic missiology was born. 'Rave Culture' was 'the end of the word as we know it', and the cross-hemispheric zippies, harmonizing rationality and mysticism, fusing practicality with idealism, and technology with ekstasis, were the inter-subcultural intercontinental vanguard of the end-times. Emerging from the 1960s counterculture, influenced by Gurdjieff and witnessing the possibility of new technology, Clark considered 'the System' to be collapsing under its own weight of contradictions, and anticipated rave as the next and last 'breakthrough device'. In 1987 the *Epi* predicted that a cooperative cultural virus reproducing within the new dance culture would 'infect the whole planetary culture'. The coming 'renaissance of sixties idealists and end-of-the-millennium techno-shamans' was prophesized in Clark's *The Book of RavElations* to be humanity's last chance.[22] Rave was to be the final carrier of the inclusive, cooperative 'meme', constituting the critical mass necessary to get everybody 'out of their heads and purely mental processes and into…their bodies and hearts'.[23]

For the man who came to share the mantle with McKenna as 'the Timothy Leary of the 1990s', possessing distinct millenarian possibilities, the acid house phenomenon was more than a mere simulacrum of the 1960s. Indeed, in a later prediction a 'Global Summer of Love' was expected to blossom in 1997, when the 'Raver children' would continue the 'Beautiful Revolution' – the task of changing the world unfinished by hippy forebears 30 years before.[24] To this end, Clark had founded the London dance club Megatripolis. The meaning of the name can be inferred from Clark's postings on the WELL in February 1995.[25] Megatripolis was an evolved biographical concept raised from Clark's unpublished science fiction novel 'Megatripolis Forever'.[26] 'After centuries leading right across the short hairs on the very cusp of System Disaster', he wrote, 'WoMankind finally made the necessary evolutionary leap to collective consciousness long foretold, escaped the illusion of Time itself and camped permanently in the FUTURE PERFECT STATE which they named Megatripolis.' But only a few 'escaped the illusion', evolving 'beyond time' and capable of 'balling': wandering through the past, obsessed with 'researching' why things had remained wrong for so long amongst their ancestors. We also learn that the utopian dreams and visions universal to human societies are actually 'future memories' of the Megatripolitan Utopia, of 'how things already are beyond this absurdly thin veil of time'.[27] Thus, as was announced in his speech on 4 November 1993 at Megatripolis, zippies were starting to pick up the pieces of the future: by remembering it (because 'we've lived there so long in the future'), and since the citizens of the future perfect state keep dropping hints in our time as they travel through.[28] In Clark's techno-organic science-futurism, Megatripolis (which in 1995 opened for a while in San Francisco as Megatripolis West) was a this-worldly accelerated learning model for the long awaited mass mutation to the Future Perfect State. The ethno-trance club offered ambient lectures ('edutainment') in the early evening, with 'Parallel YOUniversity'[29] talks delivered by the likes of McKenna, Ram Dass, Alexander Shulgin, Rev. Ian Stang (Church of the Subgenius), Rupert Sheldrake, Francis Huxley and Robert Anton Wilson. Musicians and DJs present included Deee-Lite, Irresistible Force (Mixmaster

Morris), Mark Sinclair (Pendragon), Youth and Chris Decker. Inside, Clark claimed, you would meet time-travelling Megatripolitans amongst the residents and patrons. Were these zippy residents the immediate predecessors of Megatripolitans themselves? Perhaps – though in Clark's Gurdjieffian logic, as humans are all potentially zippies we are indeed all Megatripolitans – we just aren't conscious of it yet:

> at my highest I have sometimes seemed to glimpse that we are actually *all* Megatripolitans, in some sense, already. Whether we realise it or not. Take another look. Doesn't this present 'unfinished state' feel more like the dream, the teaser, the pale shadow of what we're meant to be?[30]

Following this narrative, at Megatripolis, patrons could get closer to their destiny, perhaps even merging with the landscape of their becoming – if only for the night. The role of future memories, remembrance of the future perfect state, are as crucial to Clark's vision as they are to McKenna's theory. Timewave Zero is the Future Perfect State is the Archaic Revival. Preparation appears to be the key. And in terms of the novelty wave chart, with Megatripolis as 'the beach head of a benign mutation in the present',[31] the tide was apparently in.

In a proclamation dated January 1995, '[t]he Final Battle for the Human Soul will be decided here in America. And you, dear Raver or Raver-to-be, are destined to be on the front line, and already are, whether you yet realise it or not'.[32] The greatest, or at least most hyped, campaign in Clark's rave-o-lutionary Millennium was the 1994 Zippy Pronoia Tour of the US. The Tour's objective was to 'bootstrap the hedonic bliss and communal vibe of the rave party into a mass movement for planetary awakening' (Ferguson 1995: 54). Accordingly, Rainbow hippies coupling with techno-freaks were destined to produce 'Rainbow Ravers'. While Clark and many of his eventually estranged team of zippies operated underground events in New York City, Boulder and San Francisco, and at the Rainbow Gathering in Wyoming, his 'Omega Rave' – envisioned to host 60,000 in the Grand Canyon in August – turned out to be a much reduced event held in Arizona's Kaibab National Forest as part of the World Unity Festival. Anticipated as 'a cultural and spiritual tsunami poised to sweep across America' (Huffstuffer 1994), hosting 55,000 short of the initial forecast the Zippy-Woodstock failed to materialize.

Yet 'zippy' was more *zeitgeist* than movement, the term being adopted by various individuals and groups whose networked activities evinced a turn of the 1990s optimism that had been fermenting within experimental formations inheriting the cultural and spiritual resources of previous countercultures (especially hippies) and holding fast against government and corporate encroachment. In response to the early commercialism of rave, young digital musicians, activists and esotericists produced their own music, built websites, published zines and held free parties. And this network of new digital, chemical and cyber-enabled artists and anarchists was held together by a hopeful view that decentralized and pirated technology can be adopted in the quest for spiritual advancement, self-development and wider cultural change: 'what we have here is a major player in the premillennial cultural meme pool, and a loose-knit movement of folks who aim to change the world – while having the best time of their lives' (Marshall 1994: 79).

While Clark believed that the zippy phenomenon would stimulate the quickening of the 'new new age', promoting the rave-millennium, he was often perceived as little more than a media-wise hustler of youth culture, little removed from other marketeers selling the millennium. As had been noted by Sarah Ferguson, 'the Zippy pitch – combining the entrepreneurial zeal of the yuppie with the spiritual indulgence of the hippie – sounded dangerously close to a Fruitopia commercial' (1995: 54). Since the approach seemed long on enthusiasm and short on efficacy – Clark was never one to spoil a grand vision with fine details – he was rebuked and dismissed by cultural radicals and anarchists. Yet, for one thing, the zippy 'programme' deviated from the tech-dependent libertarianism harboured by Extropians. As cyberpunk critic Vivian Sobchak commented, 'A zippie feels the terror and promise of the planet's situation and is prepared to use anything short of violence – magic, technology, entrepreneurial skill – to create a new age in as short a time as possible' (Sobchak, in Marshall 1994: 79). Moreover, the intentional consciousness-raising party is a lasting zippy legacy. While Megatripolis became London's edutainment capital, San Francisco's the Learning Party – where events like 'Envision the Eco-village', held in October 2001, are themed with guest speakers, DJs and VJs – may well be the US equivalent.

Global trance-formations: children of the sun and moon

With its reputation as a countercultural hotbed, San Francisco became a laboratory for the 1990s cross-pollination of techno–eco-spirituality. The Bay Area became a crucible for technospiritual trends sampling New Age and Neo-Pagan lifestyle traits using accessible and alternative technologies. Trance, trance dance or psytrance – which, at the hands of a 'digital shaman' like Goa Gill, had been incubating on the beaches of Goa between the mid-1980s and early 1990s and later percolating in domestic clubs like London's Megatripolis and Return to the Source – carried the weight of an expressive spiritualism adopted by a community harnessing new electronic media in their simultaneous return to tribal roots and ascension to the stars. Desmond Hill declared that, from 1991, San Francisco was home to 'the most vibrantly conscious House Movement in the world...[with] an energetic enthusiasm and sense of togetherness that is sadly lacking in the gray wastelands of England's dark Albion isles' (Hill 1999: 105).

In the early 1990s, buoyed by the dot-com boom, and filled with a growing awareness of the global environmental crisis, techno-millenarians seemed to be at their highest density in San Francisco. Many of the young tech-savvy populace believed they were at the head of a new information revolution, and members of the emergent San Francisco rave community set forth to emit the signals of a 'liberation theology'. Writing in 1996, Hill stated:

> Something is going down in California.... The SF [San Francisco] Rave Community are the precursors of that something.... The post-literate techno prankster is just a hint of what is promised.... The movement is gaining in strength, in numbers, in vision, in purpose. It is international in scope, and, like a strange new virus in our cultural biocomputer, it is not to be ignored.
>
> (Hill 1999: 106)

Hill went on to display the mood of possibility that pervaded this community, a network identifying with the countercultural advances made by 1960s forebears, and whose goal was to 're-adapt, re-educate, re-generate in order to face our responsibilities for the future of the Earth and all the species upon it' (*ibid.*: 99). A 1992 article by Anarchic in *Rhythmos* audaciously broadcast that 'we are the generation' (in Twist 1999: 8). Come-Unity, the early 'House Nation' crew, stated 'We Are The Planet's Future' (*ibid.*: 29). And Mission Earth, an early San Francisco rave, stated on its flier: 'always remember we have a responsibility to guide the next generation into the next millennium' (Hill 1999: 105).

As part of the WholeLife Expo, members of the SF Rave Community had converged at the SF Cyberforum on 30 April 1993, where expatriate Briton and Toon Town organizer Mark Heley stated: 'it is important that we only have one item on our agenda: Heal the Planet' (in Eisner 1994 xviii). In another statement attributed to Heley: 'When you dance you integrate your body with your mind, you integrate your individuality with the collective, and you integrate this human race with the planet' (in Hill 1999: 105). Indeed it was the intentional ritualizing of trance dance that came to feature prominently in an emergent spiritual practice developing on the periphery of the electronic dance community – itself becoming saturated with the integrated foci of person and planet. Consistent with webs of understanding manifesting in New Age and Neo-Pagan networks (St John 2001a), an eco-dance consciousness rose within the post-rave community, revealing the interdependence of self-growth and planetary-conservation among its participants. Clark had earlier pointed out that the 'local rave is the local opening point…[in] the battle to save the planet and ourselves'.[33] The integrated web of self and globe, of thinking globally and acting locally, retained a strong presence in later dance discourse and practice.

Contemplating the meaning, purpose and direction of the 'energy' or 'vibe' often stated and felt to be at the heart of the local 'tribal' party, Jason Keehn (a.k.a. Cinnamon Twist) has articulated a self-globe ethic arrived at via Gurdjieffian philosophy, eliciting an affirmative response to the enquiry about whether trance-dancing can 'save the planet'. In a self published essay, Keehn (2001) builds on Gurdjieff's doctrine of 'reciprocal maintenance' to speculate about the possible role of underground global dance culture, thus following Clark (and McKenna) in valorizing psychedelicized mass trance dances as the viable 'antidote' to the egotism at the heart of the West's ecological vandalism. We are informed that Gurdjieff draws attention to humanity's *forgotten obligation* to perform our ecological function in the web of life. That is, as opposed to serving the evolutionary process by continuing to supply the planet, the moon and the solar system with 'the particular gradient of energy' understood to be their due, human beings have largely become parasitical energy consumers, despoilers of the planet, circumstances which have resulted in the humanitarian disasters of the 20th century. As a possible mode of 'intentional suffering and conscious labour', Keehn argues that trance dance may be a Gurdjieffian 'path of return', the kind of sacrificial 'work' thought necessary for humans to regain consciousness. Perhaps a small-scale means of establishing a necessary partnership or synergy with what Gurdjieff's student J.G. Bennett (in Twist 2002: unpaginated) calls the 'invisible world', it is inferred that such activity may be a means of serving the future through meaningful human reciprocation with the planet. According to Keehn, paralleling that found at Grateful Dead concerts and Rainbow Gatherings, 'a melding of group feeling and energy into an ecstatic, orgasmic release' is experienced at trance parties 'that feels nothing less than spiritual or religious' (Keehn 2001). Performed 'by the right people in the right way with the right intentions', trance dance:

> is capable of producing that same energy Gurdjieff believed Mother Nature needs from us…[and] the use of psychedelics in conjunction with intensive dancing to certain rhythms, by a new breed of individuals, may be a way to fill our cosmic obligation without the life-long spiritual training otherwise required.
>
> (Keehn 2001)

More than self-salvation, or simply implying the salvation of community – as in the ecstatic plight of the underground gay community discussed in Chapter 1 – Keehn's trance-dance sacrifice is a 'cosmic obligation', a possible means of ensuring the survival of humanity in the planetary system. A possible answer to modern distancing from natural world rhythms, trance approximates an obligatory rite, something of a dutiful performance, for re-enchantment-seeking youth. As Kathleen Williamson indicates, such dance holds significant grounding potential: 'our experiences with sound, psychedelics and the dance ritual are the stirrings of communicating via the ebb and flow of the earth's rhythms and letting it seep into our collective emotions' (Williamson 1998). Such 'communication' is possible at events that are not only 'immediate' in Bey/Wilson's sense of convivial paroxysms, but potentiate familiarity with non-human otherness. In these experimental zones, encountering native biota and participation in natural cycles through the technologically mediated dance contextualize the dissolution of human/nature boundaries.

The immediate events implied had evolved in San Francisco from the early 1990s. At the time it was reported that 'futuristic nomads are taking music out of the clubs and back to the earth. Sitting around campfires, sharing nocturnal tales, they are recreating timeless environments and reconnecting with natural forces' (Hill 1999: 100). Influenced by Goa psychedelic full moon parties and the UK feral sound-system tradition, these gatherings are often held in open-air locations (where dance floors are positioned in bushland, forest, beach or desert), celebrate celestial events and seasonal transitions (e.g. moon cycle, solstices, solar eclipse and other planetary alignments), and are attended by a large cross-section of the dance community, including pagans, travellers and other practitioners and affiliates of a techno-Earthen spirituality who may or may not consume psychoactive alterants. Hosting intentional 'Trance Dance' rituals approximating Keehn's paean to 'transform energy into higher gradients and radiate it back out into the world', these events incorporate fluorescent décor, fractalized mandala projections, altars, chai tents, totemic installations, sacred geometry, earthworks, large speaker stacks positioned at the cardinal points and psytrance – with a seductive syncopated rhythm using 'ethnodelic' samples (e.g. didjeridu, djembe, sitar) together with an assemblage of psychotropic lights and visuals. Sonorous and sensual, sometimes opened with permission ceremonies conducted by indigenous custodians or through blessing rites, such events are celebrated as 'no spectator'-style odysseys with a celebrated climax at sunrise.

Following the first SF Full Moon party held by British expatriates Wicked sound system (incarnated from Tonka sound system) at Baker Beach in March 1991 (see Push and Silcott 2000: 54–8), new spiritual dance collectives emerged on the West Coast, and then elsewhere across North America. The most influential of these has been southern California's Moontribe, which formed in Los Angeles in 1993, holding regular full moon parties (Twist 2002). For instance, Moontribe's Gaian Mind, held in January 1997 (Perring 1999: 23–4), celebrated a 'six-pointed star' formation consisting of an alignment of all the planets, the sun and the moon. Koinonea, who have facilitated trance events called '2012' since 1996, claim they are 'dedicated to bring healing to the planet through sacred dance ceremonies [by employing]…ancient rites using modern day technology, hoping to reaffirm the bonds of connectedness with each other, the planet, and the spiralling galaxies'.[34] Having led a dance ritual at Four Quarters InterFaith Sanctuary of Earth Religion in Artemis, September 2002, Philadelphia psytrance collective Gaian Mind are proponents of a dance-based eco-spirituality:

> The energy of modern electronic dance harnessed by pagan spirituality and ceremonial settings joins the tribal traditions of our ancestors with the living tribal traditions of today. The result creates an experience of spirit that unites our common heritage as children of this planet.[35]

The Consortium of Collective Consciousness (CCC) publicize the theory of evolution proposed by Judith Anodea in *The Wheels of Life* (1987), which sees humanity currently evolving into the Fourth Chakra Age – that of Air, which means an awakening consciousness. Converging in San Francisco a year after an inspirational Goa beach experience in 1993, the CCC are definitive. 'We dance for hours and hours', they state on their website, 'encountering aspects of our own personal karma, and the karma of humanity, transcending layer after layer like an onion, until the dancer disappears altogether and only the dance remains'. This techno-mediated 'rediscovery of ancient trance tradition' represents a 'full-circle return of humanity to its primordial beginnings':

> Is it by pure coincidence that this profound, inspired, reconnection is occurring now, in the looming shadow of a world grown sick through over-population, environmental decay and corruption? Or could this be a divine manifestation, gifting the collective shaman of humanity with a vision of interconnected love consciousness at the most crucial moment...?[36]

Enabled by communication technology and cheap airfare, the CCC further speculate: 'Perhaps we are the earth's first global tribe...spread across the planet and circum-navigating it'. The key rendezvous points for this self-identifying 'fluoro-Rainbow tribe' are gatherings celebrating not only lunar cycles, but total solar eclipse – like the annual Solipse Festival held in Zambia in 2001, or Outback Eclipse in South Australia 2002. Other events include the Solstice Music Festival on the slopes of Mount Fuji and Australia's Rainbow Serpent. Such global dance tribe events are lauded as 'planetary healing communities' (Antara and Kaye 1999), where collectively generated ecstatic energy can be consciously directed into the 'planetary grid', thought positively to impact collective consciousness.

Casting the Dreamspell

A further strategy of reconnectivity is evident in the adoption by new tribes of the Mayan 13 Moon Calendar. Post-rave dance milieus are affiliating with the World 13 Moon Calendar Change Peace Movement committed to the replacement of the Gregorian calendar with what is known as the Dreamspell calendar on 25 July 2004, 'Galactic Freedom Day'. Stimulated by José Argüelles, who claims to have revealed timecodes in the classic Mayan calendar consisting of complex physical and spiritual cycles, the Dreamspell calendar forms the basis of the movement for a new Time. While the annual cycle of 13 moons falling each 28 days demonstrates 'harmony with the Earth and with the natural cycles coded into the human female biological cycle',[37] the Tzolkin records a spiritual cycle which the Maya claimed came to them from the galaxy. In this cycle, widely regarded as the '13:20', there is a 13-day galactic cycle and a 20-day solar cycle. Both cycles turn together, overlapping to form the 260-day cycle of the Tzolkin. Argüelles began interpreting the Mayan codes of time in his *The Mayan Factor* (1987); and, in conjunction with Lloydine Argüelles, a subsequent work, *The Dreamspell: Journey of Timeship Earth 2013* (1991), conveyed the mathematics of fourth-dimensional time ('the Law of Time') in the Tzolkin – a synchronic order of time distinguished from third-dimensional astronomical time. In his *Time and the Technosphere* (2002), Argüelles distinguishes the 'natural time' of the cosmos from the 'artificial mechanistic' time which humanity entered 5,000 years ago. For Argüelles, since the artificial time frequency of the 12-month Gregorian calendar and the 60-minute hour is arbitrarily imposed (a paradigm of the 'warrior hero, separation and fear'), the survival of humanity and the avoidance of an environmental catastrophe are dependent upon our adoption of a harmonic calendar based on the Mayan cycles.

For Argüelles, the end-times are chiming. On 11 September 2001, we received a signal that history is ending. Ostensibly, the collapse of the World Trade Center towers created a fissure in 'the technosphere' and opened up the noosphere: 'Earth's mental envelope'. Such a disaster is thus apparently a sign of humanity's progression 'into the love based, artist hero paradigm of natural time'. But this is not the end of the world, just the end of the world as we know it, part of a prophetic 'time release'. The approaching end-time is in fact the end of Time.[38]

In the campaign for 'the New Time' a 'major planetary consciousness shift'[39] is propagated through contemporary techno-tribal networks. In September 2002, at Portugal's Boom Festival, the Planet Art Network's 'Caravan for the New Time' created a 'Natural Time Zone': a 10.5-metre dome surrounded by a tipi village where, amongst meditations, universal ceremonies to honour the directions, Dreamspell play shops and galactic passport decodings, participants were able to discover their own 'galactic signature'. The annual Global Eyes calendar features a 'Mayan natural time calendar', and DIY 'tribes' have self-organized to spread the message of 'eco-techno-evolution' through time shift: 'We are now at the end of the Dreamspell of history and at the beginning of the Dreamspell of galactic culture'. Citing Argüelles, such is the belief of the Circle of Tribes, a Northern New Mexico dance collective who choose to align their gatherings with the full moons and the lunar Mayan calendar. Accordingly, 'we are coming to the end of the belief in the male dominant, warrior hero, fear and separation paradigm [a]nd we are preparing to move into the love based, artist hero paradigm of natural time'.[40] Furthermore, EarthTribe, a group of artists, DJs, filmmakers, 'bioneers and dreamers', have undertaken plans for a multimedia project, Journey Through the End of Time, documenting their adventures through North America and into the heart of Latin America to build a self-sustaining eco-village in the Costa Rican rainforest. Gathering knowledge and skills required to create a globally sustainable culture, the EarthTribe aim to travel through Mexico to

> investigate the message of time left behind by the ancient Maya. Visiting their modern day descendents and sacred sites, they'll engage in shamanistic rituals, where the dream world and our own collide, discovering together what the Mayans believe will happen as their calendar comes to an end in the year 2012.[41]

A transhumant collective of artists, DJs and promoters, Mycorrhiza, encourage people to create their own Eden or Shambhala by returning to 'natural time and natural living'. Apostles of the Campaign for the New Time, they have focused on establishing 'a network of sustainable, conscious, harmonious 13:20 communities'. Travelling from their base in Canada, down through the US, Mexico and Guatemala, to Costa Rica, Mycorrhiza's annual Timeship

Terra Gaia caravan is committed to 'creating a web of energy to protect and sustain Earth, aiming at increasing awareness of our interdependence with the natural world'. The collective takes its name from 'the largest living organisms in the forest'. Mycorrhizae 'act as a vast underground web to help sustain the forest. Mycorrhiza is a symbiotic association that forms protective strands around the roots of trees, forming a dense energetic network throughout the forest soil'. As 'an underground energy network that sustains', they are the 'human macrocosmic reflection'[42] of a fungus whose role in forest ecosystems was earlier valorized by Terence McKenna (see McKenna 1991).

Earthdreaming: from the Isle of Albion to the Red Desert

While North American dance tribes valorize ancient Mesoamerican culture, elements of which have been excavated and reconfigured by various popular scholars, European future primitives like the semi-nomadic Spiral Tribe revere ancient monuments – especially those at Stonehenge and Glastonbury – as sites of special significance. Yet, as earlier discovered by New Age travellers, migration by semi-nomads to these and other significant sites dotting the rural landscape was perceived by the government as an invasion, a sacrilege. Thatcher was intent on repelling the invasive hordes populating and profaning the tranquil idyll of rural England (see Sibley 1997), their wild spatial territorializations precipitating moral panics and state terrorism. Such was incarnated most famously in the 1985 'Battle of the Beanfield' (McKay 1996), where 1,000 police routed New Age travellers en route to their annual Stonehenge Free Festival on the summer solstice. Further Draconian statutes and domesticating measures followed the Castlemorton 'mega-rave' of 1992, culminating in the Criminal Justice and Public Order Act (1994), which criminalized a lifestyle and immobalized large free celebrations, including those representative of Earthen spirituality with an electronic soundtrack.

Such repressive measures have been met with intriguing tactical responses. An infamous creative manoeuvre was manifested in the series of scrap-metal 'Henge' installations built by London's 'recycladelic' industrial-sculpture collective Mutoid Waste Co (MWC). The first MWC Car-Henges were raised at Glastonbury Festival in 1987, followed by another in Amsterdam (1989), a Truck-Henge in Italy, Tank-Henge in Berlin and several fixed antipodean installations: a Car-henge at Australia's ConFest (1991), Combi-Henge in East Gippsland, Victoria (1997), and Plane-Henge, raised in May 2000 on Arabunna land near Lake Eyre in the South Australian desert. A response to English Heritage's confiscation of the 'cultural headstones' of New Age travellers, the new and diasporic Henges became 'an iconic substitute for the real thing' (Cooke 2001: 139), providing a new generation of travellers with a set design for the performance of wild abandon and rallying points for cultural and ecological struggle. While public access to the stones during summer solstice was reinitiated in 2000, under the MWC mantra 'Mutate and Survive' these sculptures have evolved into significant reference points for international technomads whose cultural logic combines the desire to dance fiercely in the present with the commitment to 'reclaim the future' (St John 2001b). Conceptually transmuted and geographically relocated by scrounger-shaman and founding member of MWC Robin Cooke, in the Australian landscape these icons became scaffolds upon which new activists were invited to hang their own flags and banners, portals through which future primitives and antipodean *terra-ists* would pass.

Plane Henge was constructed during Earthdream2000, a nomadic carnival of protest attracting hundreds of travellers (representing over 20 countries) through central Australia from May to September that year.[43] Beginning in 2000, this outback odyssey was envisioned by Cooke as a 'mega-tribal' gathering tran-spiring annually until 21 December 2012. In the lead-up to 2000, via subterranean communication channels and over the internet, crews rallied to Cooke's call. Eco-radical collectives, white sadhus and sound-system crews were ready to integrate his vision with their own, travelling the last few thousand kilo-metres of the old millennium together. Disembarking from around the globe, techno-tribes, performance artists and other parties mapped Earthdream into their itinerary. Since 2000, in cooperation with and in support of traditional owners, a series of free party events (including a major event held on the winter solstice) and intercultural anti-uranium mining protests have transpired on Aboriginal lands.

The proactive millenarian event of a technospiritual movement, Earthdream is the product of a strengthening alliance between radical environmentalism, new spirituality and dance culture. In Australia such an alliance has evidenced unique reconciliatory patterns amongst techno-tribalists. The element of sacrifice endemic to reconcilement possesses a feral legacy. Since the early 1980s, eco-radical youth formations became committed to the celebration and defence of natural and cultural heritage, forming throughout the 1990s a network of *terra-ist* collectives engaged in campaigns to blockade unethical logging, mining and road projects (St John 1999, 2000). These reclamational strategies have been assisted through the adoption and repurposing of a range of sophisticated campaign tools (laptops, digital cameras, samplers and synthesizers) by DIY techno-tribes whose appearance can be understood in the context of the deep wounds inflicted upon the natural environment and indigenous inhabitants, of which settler Australians and their descendents are increasingly aware (St John 2001b).

Opposing the nuclear industry and supporting Aboriginal sovereignty, Ohms not Bombs is a techno-tribe exemplifying this process. Largely the labour of expatriate Londoner Peter Strong, Ohms not Bombs is a Sydney-based nomadic sound system inheriting proactive and inspired agendas downstream from the confluence of DIY anarcho-punk and New Age traveller movements recom-bined within a community context influenced by Jamaican émigré reggae and rasta sound-system traditions. As the technomadic 'edutainment' capital of Australia, since 1995 the Ohms objective has been: 'tuning technology with ecology, DJing our soul force into the amazing biorhythms of nature':

[With] co-created magic...this land is returned to the ancient and magical indigenous chain of wisdom. If we unite our purpose a massive healing can be set in motion.... Help institute a sound system for all, join the Earthdream, support Aboriginal sovereignty, and help dance up the country in rave-o-lution.[44]

A reconcilement with native land and people is a frequent pattern detected in the discourse and practice of Australian techno-tribes like Ohms. Many outdoor events, or 'bush doofs', recognize the authority of traditional custodians. For example, following a ceremonial welcome from the Wardani elders, participants at Western Australia's Earth Stomp (facilitated by the Tribe of Gaia) are said to undergo 'collective awakening and unification of human consciousness to the wider interconnectedness of Gaia' (Rowe and Groves 2000: 159). According to Rowe and Groves: 'Technology can be used in the interests of the Earth. Sound is a potent force when it comes to igniting human energy fields, it has the ability to make you move. We utilized technology to synchronize Earth, Body, Mind and Spirit' (*ibid.*: 160).

Conclusion

Re-enchantment and reconciliation are pervasive tropes motivating a network of new tribes formed by Western (and Westernised) youth participating in spiritual relationships with the natural world through dance. This chapter has demonstrated how electronic dance culture became implicated in a principle of revitalization associated with ecologism. Documenting the vast terrain of techno-millennialism – an interacting compendium of influential salvific models, utopian dreams, poetic tracts and visionary art emanating from the likes of McKenna, Clark, Bey, Argüelles and Cooke variously cannibalized by trance elements within the global electronic music diaspora – it uncovered a characteristically 'shamanic technology' percolating within trance culture. The techno-futurist/revivalist attributes evoked and exploited by an emergent milieu have been mapped – from local DIY tribes and regional scenes to a global movement of technomads celebrating significant celestial events.

From the Dreamspell to Earthdream, from the Isle of Albion to the Red Desert, 'trance-formations' respond to environmental crises by acting locally. Such 'action' includes open-air dance, an intimate participation in landscape occasioning a somatic relationships with place, ostensibly enabling a meaningful connection or synergy with the Earth. Sometimes silly and sometimes sound, in revolutionary attitudes towards the self, time and one's immediate environment, in heroic doses and mega-raves, in intentional rituals and dance activism, this eco-rave consciousness champions the interdependence of person and planet.

Notes

1 http://easyweb.easynet.co.uk/fraserclark/docs/ravelations/countdown.htm
   (accessed 2 October 2002).
2 http://www.4qf.org/gaian/gaianindex.htm (accessed 14 November 2002).
3 See www.levity.com/eschaton/novelty.html (accessed 11 November 2002).
4 Alien Dreamtime was produced as a video documentary featuring live video mixing
   by Rose X.
5 From 'Re: Evolution' on the Shamen's 1992 album *Boss Drum*. Written by McKenna,
   Angus and West (Evolution Music). Published by Warner Chappell Music/Flowsound
   Ltd: http://www.deoxy.org/t—re-evo.htm (accessed 3 November 2002).
6 See http://www.dromo.com/fusionanomaly/mayacosmogenesis2012.html (accessed
   8 November 2002).
7 From 'Re: Evolution', http://www.deoxy.org/t—re-evo.htm (accessed 3 November
   2002).
8 From the live performance of 'Re: Evolution', San Francisco, 1993:
   http://www.cuttlefish.net/universalshamen/lyrics/reevolution.html   (accessed   5
   November 2002).
9 Alien Dreamtime: http://www.deoxy.org/t—adt.htm (accessed 3 November 2002).
10 See www.levity.com/eschaton/finalillusion (accessed 10 November 2002).
11 http://www.dkfoundation.co.uk/FriendsFoundation.htm (accessed 1 January 2003).
12 Barrelful   of   Monkeys: http://www.barrelfullofmonkeys.org/inphomation.html
   (accessed 2 November 2002).
13 'A call to the Starry Family', from the Future Harmonix webzine (April 1998):
   http://www.futureharmonix.com/resonance/wave1/starry.html   (accessed   8
   November 2002).
14 http://www.tribalharmonix.org/events/reconvergence/intention.php   (accessed   8
   November 2002).
15 This characterization appeals to researchers of contemporary rave and club cultures
   (see St John 2003).
16 The Mayan Dreamspell 13 moon calendar: http://www.2012.com.au/mayan.html
   (accessed 18 November 2002).
17 Thus using the name of their predecessors who converged at the Gathering of the
   Tribes For a Human Be-In on 14 January 1967 in San Francisco's Golden Gate Park.
18 http://www.pronoia.net/tour/essays/terence.html (accessed 14 October 2002).
19 From 'Countdown to chaos culture',
   http://easyweb.easynet.co.uk/fraserclark/docs/ravelations/countdown.htm
   (accessed 8 October 2002).
20 http://www.pronoia.net/tour/net/well21.html (accessed October 13 2002).
21 'The Planet Awaits a Sign': http://www.pronoia.net/tour/net/well1.html (accessed
   10 October 2002).
22 *The Book of RavElations*: http://easyweb.easynet.co.uk/fraserclark/docs/writings.htm
   (accessed 9 October 2002).
23 http://www.pronoia.net/tour/net/well13.html (accessed 12 October 2002).
24 From 'Countdown to chaos culture':
   http://easyweb.easynet.co.uk/fraserclark/docs/ravelations/countdown.htm
   (accessed 8 October 2002).
25 These were reproduced from a November 1994 flier for San Francisco's Megatripolis
   West: http://easyweb.easynet.co.uk/fraserclark/docs/ravelations/sfmeg1.htm
   (accessed 20 October 2002).
26 Excerpts of this were published in the Megatripolitan Newsletter, circa February 1994,
   and reproduced at:
   http://easyweb.easynet.co.uk/fraserclark/docs/ravelations/megat10.htm (accessed 25
   October 2002).

27 Fraser Clark, posted on the WELL, 10 February 1995:
   http://www.pronoia.net/tour/net/well17.html. (accessed 16 October 2002).
28 http://easyweb.easynet.co.uk/fraserclark/docs/ravelations/megat0.htm (accessed 16 October 2002).
29 This concept later evolved into a London club called Parallel YOUniversity.
30 Fraser Clark, posted on the WELL, February 1995:
   http://www.pronoia.net/tour/net/well17.html and
   http://www.pronoia.net/tour/net/well18.html (accessed 16 October 2002).
31 From Megatripolis West flier:
   http://easyweb.easynet.co.uk/fraserclark/docs/raveltions/sfmeg1.htm (accessed 15 October 2002).
32 http://www.pronoia.net/tour/net/well14.html (accessed 16 October 2002).
33 http://www.pronoia.net/tour/net/well12.html (accessed 12 October 2002).
34 Koinonea: http://www.club.net/koinonea (accessed 5 November 2002).
35 http://www.4qf.org/ (accessed 10 November 2002).
36 'Trance Parties' at Consortium of Collective Consciousness:
   http://www.ccc.ac/2001/index.htm (accessed 7 November 2002).
37 Email from W. Sterneck, 'Techno, trance and politics', 28 April 2002.
38 The Dreamspell Story: http://home.earthlink.net/cosmichand/dreamspell.story.html (accessed 18 November 2002).
39 http://www.tortuga.com/foundation/timeline.html (accessed 14 November 2002).
40 http://www.circleoftribes.org/ (accessed 15 November 2002).
41 The EarthTribe Foundation: http://www.earthtribefoundation.org/journey.html (accessed 6 November 2002).
42 Mycorrhiza Collective: http://www.greengrooves.org/about.htm (accessed 8 November 2002).
43 Earthdream: www.earthdream.net (accessed 20 November 2002).
44 www.ohmsnotbombs.org (accessed 13 September 2002).

Bibliography

Anodea, Judith (1987) *Wheels of Life: A User's Guide to the Chakra System*, St Paul, MN: Llewellyn Publications.

Antara, L. and N. Kaye (1999) 'Connected consciousness in motion: the power of ceremony for creating positive social change', in Cinnamon Twist (ed.) *Guerillas of Harmony: Communiques from the Dance Underground*, San Francisco: Tribal Donut.

Argüelles, J. (1987) *The Mayan Factor: Path Beyond Technology*, Santa Fe, NM: Bear & Co.

—— (2002) *Time and the Technosphere: The Law of Time in Human Affairs*, Rochester: Bear & Co.

Argüelles, J. and Lloydine Argüelles (1991) *The Dreamspell: Journey of Timeship Earth 2013*, An independent publication; see http://www.vortexmaps.com/htmlb/josebib.htm.

Bey, H. (1991) *TAZ: The Temporary Autonomous Zone – Ontological Anarchy and Poetic Terrorism*, New York: Autonomedia.

—— (1995) 'Primitives and extropians', *Anarchy* 42; available online at http://www.t0.or.at/hakimbey/primitiv.htm (accessed 29 October 2002).

Castle, R. (2000) 'Doof disco didges of the digerati', in A. Dearling and B. Handley (eds) *Alternative Australia: Celebrating Cultural Diversity*, Dorset: Enabler.

Collin, M. (1997) *Altered State: The Story of Ecstasy Culture and Acid House*, London: Serpent's Tail.

Cooke, R. (2001) 'Mutoid waste recycledelia and Earthdream', in G. St John (ed.) *FreeNRG: Notes From the Edge of the Dance Floor*, Melbourne: Common Ground.

Dei, D. (1994) 'Competing memes for a bi-millennium or an empire trance-formed', available online at:
http://www.hyperreal.org/raves/spirit/politics/Empire—Trance-Formed.html (accessed 15 October 2002).

Eisner, B. (1994) [1989] *Ecstasy: The MDMA Story*, Berkeley, CA: Ronin.

Ferguson, S. (1995) 'Raving at the edge of the world, *High Times*', February: 53–7.

Gyrus (1999) 'The end of the river', *Towards 2012*, 4; available online at http://serendipity.magnet.ch/twz/gyrus/river.htm (accessed 15 November 2002).

Hill, D. (1999) 'Mobile anarchy: the house movement, shamanism and community', in T. Lyttle (ed.) *Psychedelics ReImagined*, New York: Autonomedia.

Davis, E. (1994) 'Zippy the tech-head: British cyber-hippies invade New York', *Village Voice*, July 5: 29–30.

Huffstuffer, P. (1994) 'We're not in Woodstock any more', *LA Times*, 7 August: 78–9.

Hutson, S. (1999) 'Technoshamanism: spiritual healing in the rave subculture', *Popular Music and Society* 23(3): 53–77.

Keehn, J. (a.k.a. Cinnamon Twist) (2001) 'Can trance-dancing save the planet?', available online at http://www.duversity.org/archives/rave.html (accessed 11 November 2002).

Linstrom, D. and Schwartz, T. (1994) 'Party politics (or the politics of partying)', available online at http://www.pronoia.net/tour/essays/politics.html (accessed 27 September 2002).

McDaniel, M. and Bethel, J. (2002) 'Novelty and the wave harmonic of history', *Omegapoint.org* ezine, available online at http://www.omegapoint.org (accessed 27 December 2002).

McKay, G. (1996) *Senseless Acts of Beauty: Cultures of Resistance Since the Sixties*, London: Verso.

McKenna, T. (1991) 'Plan/plant/planet', in *The Archaic Revival*, San Francisco: Harper; available online at http://www.deoxy.org/t—ppp.htm (accessed 10 November 2002).

Maffesoli, M. (1996) [1988] *The Time of the Tribes: The Decline of Individualism in Mass Society*, London: Sage.

Major Jenkins, John (1998) *Maya Cosmogenesis 2012: The True Meaning of the Maya Calendar End-Date*, with an introduction by Terence McKenna, Santa Fe, NM: Bear & Co.

Marshall, J. (1994) 'Here come the Zippies', *Wired* May: 78–84, 130–1.

Perring, R. (1999) 'Moontribe voodoo', in Cinnamon Twist (ed.) *Guerillas of Harmony: Communiques from the Dance Underground*, San Francisco: Tribal Donut.

Push and Silcott, M. (2000) *The Book of E: All About Ecstasy*, Omnibus Press.

Razam, R. (2001) 'Directions to the game: Barrelful of Monkeys', in G. St John (ed.) *FreeNRG: Notes from the Edge of the Dance Floor*, Altona: Common Ground.

Reynolds, S. (1998) *Energy Flash: A Journey through Rave Music and Dance Culture*, London: Picador.

Rowe, K. and D. Groves (2000) 'Earthstomp 99', in A. Dearling and B. Hanley (eds) *Alternative Australia: Celebrating Cultural Diversity*, Lyme Regis, Dorset: Enabler Publications.

Rushkoff, D. (1994) *Cyberia: Life in the Trenches of Hyperspace*, London: Flamingo.

Russell, P. (1995) [1982] *The Global Brain Awakens: Our Next Evolutionary Leap*, Palo Alto, CA: Global Brain Inc.; available online at http://www.peterussell.com/GB/Chap8.html (accessed 11 November 2002).

St John, G. (1999) 'Ferality: a life of grime', *The UTS Review – Cultural Studies and New Writing* 5(2): 101–13.

—— (2000) 'Ferals: terra-ism and radical ecologism in Australia', *Journal of Australian Studies* 64: 208–16.

—— (2001a) ' "Heal thy self – thy planet": Confest eco-spirituality and the Self Earth nexus', *Australian Religion Studies Review*, 14 (1): 97–112.

—— (2001b) 'Techno terra-ism: feral systems and sound futures', in G. St John (ed.) *FreeNRG: Notes from the Edge of the Dance Floor*, Altona: Common Ground.

Sibley, D. (1997) 'Endangering the sacred: nomads, youth cultures and the English countryside', in P. Cloke and J. Little (eds) *Contested Countryside Cultures: Otherness, Marginalisation and Rurality*, London: Routledge.

Tramacchi, D. (2000) 'Field tripping: psychedelic communitas and ritual in the Australian bush', *Journal of Contemporary Religion* 15(2): 201–13.

Twist, C. (1999) (ed.) *Guerillas of Harmony: Communiques from the Dance Underground*, San Francisco: Tribal Donut.

—— (2002) 'Children of the moon', assembled by Cinnamon Twist for Moontribe's ninth anniversary gathering.

White, G. (1993) 'CyberTribe rising (Beltane communique)', *CyberTribe-5*; available online at http://www.essentia.com/book/inspire/cybertribe.htm (accessed 28 October 2002).

Williamson, K. (1998) 'Trance magick', *Octarine* 3: unpaginated.

12 Global Nomads

Techno and New Age as transnational countercultures in Ibiza and Goa

Anthony D'Andrea

> The nomad does not move.
>
> (Deleuze and Guattari 1980: 381)

The globalization of digital art-religion

Reflexive change is a leitmotif of Western modernity, progressing, modernists believe, towards universal happiness and enlightenment. This teleological claim of infinite progress has, nonetheless, been denounced by "countercultural" movements as farcical – an Enlightenment ideal of utopia to be replaced by Romantic dys/utopias. Yet, paradoxically, these cultures of resistance emerge from *within* modernity itself. They manifest cosmopolitan, expressive, and reflexive trends arising from the very modern dynamics they criticize.

Globalization complicates this counter-modern dialectic by speeding up self-reflexivity in a non-teleological way (Giddens 1989; Wallerstein 1989). Digitalism, nomadism and the acceleration of transnational flows become constitutive of emerging countercultures (Featherstone and Burrows 1995). Representative phenomena, such as Techno and New Age movements, are thus situated at the intersection of countercultural *continuity* and postmodernist *rupture* and, enmeshed with the technological, political, economic, and cultural realities of global modernity, their development is crucial for understanding the possibility of *alternative modernities*.

What constitutes a "counterculture" in the early 21st century? Can New Age and Techno movements be seen as "countercultures"? Most scholarship on the matter provides historical outlooks on 1960s "radicalism," 1970s "decline" and 1980s "cooptation" (Frank 1997; McKay 1996; Roszak 1995). However, this presumed decadence occludes the pluralization of "the 1960s" into a variety of single-issue movements and academic area studies (queer, ecological, feminist; subcultural, new religion, popular studies). Nonetheless, within a wider historical perspective all of these movements express a basic dissatisfaction with the promises, modes, and rewards of modern life.[1]

In any case, Techno and New Age embody powerful living fields of problematization of Western life. Techno[2] is ritually expressed in multimedia dance gatherings such as "raves" and "trance parties" taking place at urban "wild zones" (Stanley 1997) or secret rural areas. Techno rituals constitute temporary spaces of ecstatic and psychedelic experience induced by techniques of shattering and reshaping identities (Collin 1997; Redhead 1997; Reynolds 1998). "Rave is more than music plus drugs, it is a matrix of lifestyle, ritualized behavior and beliefs. To the participant, it feels like a religion; to the mainstream observer, it looks more like a sinister cult" (Reynolds 1998: 5). Positioned between leisure, religion, and politics, debates circulate about Techno's meanings and political content, notably its emphasis on sensorial hyper-stimulation, intense hedonism, and communitarian effervescence (Borneman and Senders 2000; Ingham *et al.* 1999; Best 1997; McKay 1996). Nevertheless, the current proliferation of Techno tends to veil its origins in the 1980s among marginalized, "underground" subcultures in global cities and utopian sites: ethnic gays in Chicago and New York (house and garage music), blacks in Detroit and London (techno and jungle music), and hippies/freaks in Ibiza (Spain) and Goa (India) (trance music). These cultures of resistance emerged during the wild times of the neo-liberal capitalism of Thatcher and Reagan, and have been rapidly disseminating throughout international circuits and "postcommunities" (Ortner 1999). In sum, "Techno" signifies the emergence of aesthetic and stylistic manifestations of digital culture, which unfolds through symbiotic interactions between a global counterculture and various national mainstream cultures.

As a movement and process, New Age queers religious, scientific, and aesthetic realms, and designates a rhizomatic "network of networks" incorporating a vast universe of subjects, practices, and groups (D'Andrea 2000; Heelas 1996; York 1995). Underlying its multiple forms, the New Age's basic premise is the cultivation of the self (*Bildung*), rendered as a precondition for a new secular and spiritual age. As an early 1970s countercultural derivation, New Age ethno-ecological, parascientific and psy-spiritual syncretisms reflect the diffusion of a *reflexive mysticism* formerly confined within erudite circles of Western Romanticism (Luckmann 1991; Bellah 1985). Thus, expressed in casual statements such as "I don't have any religion but my own spirituality," growing interest in Zen, Yoga, Sufi, Cabala, Alchemy, and Wicca indicates the psychologization of world religions and native traditions as tools for the reflexive and expressive cultivation of the "self." Techniques of the self (music, meditation, body-techniques, encounter groups, diets, etc.) are employed for attaining special subjective moods. But a dual logic of "love-wisdom" and of "power-control" evinces contradictions between expressivist and instrumentalist drives within the New Age movement, reflecting either historical trends toward individualism or neo-liberal ideologies of predatory capitalism (D'Andrea 2000; Comaroff and Comaroff 2000; Bellah 1985). New Age stimulates religious transformations in the West, particularly the emergence of a global meta-spirituality which indexes a multiplicity of equivalent spiritualities of the self.

Although studies on New Age and Techno do not usually interface, a careful comparison evinces a common horizon: alternative lifestyles informed by aesthetic, erotic, and hedonic/ist values and practices; cultivation of expressive forms of individualism; reflexive (often mystic) outlooks on reality; ritual centrality of aesthetic and transpersonal experiences (music, drugs, traveling); and, also, valorization of cosmopolitan life in special locations. Based on modes of shattering and shaping identities, Techno and New Age operate as sites of experience wherein new forms of subjectivity and community are central concerns (McKay 1996; Grof and Grof 1990; Lukoff *et al.* 1990).

These shared characteristics are intensified by global processes, such as cultural rootlessness, hyper-mobility, and new network forms, which contribute to the development of a culture of transpersonalism on a global scale. As such, countercultures express and entail a wider crisis of cultural legitimacy by problematizing dominant categories of "reason," "ego," and "objectivity" through the cultivation of non-ordinary states: "our normal rational consciousness is one special type of consciousness, whilst all about it there lie potential forms of consciousness entirely different" (James 1936: 378). Thus, the seemingly disparate practices of Techno and New Age index a globalizing *digital art-religion*.

However, this global subculture has to interact with various national cultures, institutions, and forces – markets, states, societies – which seek to regulate and appropriate New Age and Techno. It is often claimed that these movements are merely social forms of alienation and escapism, profitable economic activities exploring "naive" and "exotic" drives, or ideological expressions of a new global middle class. While not disagreeing, we must assess the accuracy of such claims since factors surrounding the implications of Techno and New Age remain largely unknown. The development of "global countercultures" across contemporary societies under global compression manifests tensions readable in multiple ways: social diffusion (from "underground" to "mainstream") and distinction (production of "new" substyles), transgression and cooptation, singularization and commodification, reflexivity and fundamentalism, utopia and dystopia.

Since global flows reterritorialize in concrete sites of experience, struggle, and signification, a critical dimension of analysis resides in the issue of space. Because of their historical, geographical, and cultural importance, this study considers the centrality of Ibiza and Goa in the shaping of global countercultures. Not only are these sites charged with "charisma" and "movement," but Goa and Ibiza are also linked through the transnational circulation of alternative subjects, practices, objects, and imaginaries. In addition, both places exhibit a similar picture: leisure industries capturing and commodifying "utopia," spirituality, and *freakness*. Alternative subjects thus navigate through turbulent spaces of mainstream labor, leisure, and law via supple strategies of material–symbolic negotiation and informal networks of support.

In sum, based on an ethnographic study of Techno and New Age experiences of nomadic subjects who live and circulate within Ibiza (Spain) and Goa (India), this project addresses the formation of transnational networks of "alternative" lifestyles in "utopian" spaces. Within global and critical studies, the emergence of global countercultures relates to three interconnected issues. First, in the context of globalization, Techno and New Age can be seen as transnational formations that suffer as well as induce the deterritorializing effects of "time–space compression" (Harvey 1990). Digitalization, migration, and media are main processes in the analysis of how globalization affects Techno and New Age, requiring new methodologies on translocality and network mapping.

Second, in the context of modernity, Techno and New Age can be seen as countercultures that critically respond to (or express) the *modern apparatus of "sexuality"* (Foucault 1976).[3] In this case, Techno and New Age operate as a politico-cultural "counter-apparatus" centered on an aesthetics-erotics of the self. Requiring detailed analysis of ritual and lifestyle, this "counter-apparatus" potentially allows new forms of subjectivity, sociability, intimacy and institutionality that depart from the biopower of the nation-state and major moralities.

Third, in contrast to postmodern studies that rely on fictional, literary, or abstract materials, this investigation of global countercultures focuses on *empirical phenomena* that instantiate seminal postmodern tropes: the nomad, the cyberpunk, and the neo-tribe (Deleuze and Guattari 1980; Featherstone and Burrows 1995; Maffesoli 1996). It seeks to demonstrate how nomadic, digital, and tribal practices are empirically articulated in a "counter-apparatus," which indexes a field of possibilities and agencies enabled by the complex nature of reflexive globalization.

Freak ethnoscape: aesthetics, nomadism and spirituality

Around April, global freaks arrive on the Mediterranean island of Ibiza (Spain), before the mass of Anglo-Saxon tourists. They live and work throughout the tourist season (May–October), after which they leave again for faraway locations. And so did I from 1998 to 2002, living with a DJ, a yoga teacher, a *neo-sannyasin*, and a couple of eco-workers in various circumstances throughout my anthropological fieldwork. I was researching Techno and New Age experiences in various sites, such as mega-clubs (Space, Privilege, Amnesia, Pacha, El Divino, Es Paradis, Eden), trendy bars (Café del Mar, Bar M, Khumaras, Dome), and trance parties, as well as alternative markets, sunset meditations, and Biodance, yoga and Reiki workshops. In terms of national cultures, I circulated within three main groups: the Spanish inhabitants and club workers; the seasonal mass of British tourists and club/bar workers; and the multinational community of cosmopolitans dedicated to the shaping of an eco-expressive "style of life."

"Ibiza" dazzles as a charismatic icon of freedom and pleasure, a golden Utopia for European youth. In addition to its 100,000 residents, each summer the tiny island hosts 2 million tourists, an impact that has left Ibiza struggling with the pattern of hotel concentration initiated in the 1960s. Consistent with the rise of tourism as the largest global industry, 80 percent of the island's wealth derives from leisure, with major clubs and bars being central to it. While Space is renowned as "the best club in the world" within the global club scene, Privilege stands out as the world's largest club, with a 10,000 capacity (see *Guinness Book of World Records*). Industry estimates indicate that around 12 percent of visitors fall directly into the "club tourism" category, while marketing strategies sell the concept of "sun, fun, and sex galore," attracting a youthful, carefree tourist clientele constituted predominantly by the British working class (40 percent of tourists), and German and Spanish middle classes (25 percent and 15 percent, respectively). As a result, after centuries of poverty and isolation, La Isla Blanca often tops Spanish, Mediterranean, and even European rankings for per-capita income, economic growth, and tourism – as well as those for divorce, AIDS, and drug consumption. These socio-economic indices demonstrate an intense and fast-changing society, and validate the claim that "Ibiza is paradigmatic to those who interrogate the development of contemporary societies" (Rozenberg 1990: 3).

Yet Ibiza projects us outward, into a complex logic interrelating global and countercultural processes. The island's foreign population is unique. While there are officially 11,000 immigrants, the real figure may double when frequent, albeit mobile, "visitors" are included. In this community of increasingly hyphenated and blurred citizenships, national origins (German, British, French, Dutch, Italian, Latin and North American) are fading references. In addition to Spanish cosmopolitans, a large number of this population are born of bohemian parents of differing nationalities, hold dual citizenships, and speak multiple languages. Having lived in three or more countries, India holds a special signification in the lives of many. Many are drawn from middle and upper social strata locally and abroad, often members of artistic, cultural, and economic elites (Institut Balear d'Estadística 1996; Rozenberg 1990).

Most have chosen the island as an ideal place for shaping an *aesthetic "style of life"*, rather than the usual economic-centered motivations of most Spanish and African immigrants. Embodying reflections of later Foucault (Foucault and Lotringer 1989), their "aesthetics of existence" is manifested in various spiritual, creative, and hedonistic practices, cultivating values of freedom, pleasure, tolerance, and self-exploration. Often, these cosmopolitan subjects have sought to break away from the stress, boredom, and meaninglessness they experience in "mainstream" society. However, despite fleeing "the mainstream," Ibiza's transnational imaginary has paradoxically placed these self-*marginalized* people at the very *center* of its creative life, a cultural elite crafting much of the seductive charm of the island.

This charisma is disseminated globally, as these cosmopolitan subjects are also global nomads who sustain alternative lifestyles by tracing nodes of freakness along transnational circuits. Typical alternative careers include luxury traders, therapists, healers, yoga teachers, fashion professionals, musicians, DJs, party promoters, drug dealers, travel agents, pack-and-go workers, rich bohemians, etc. Art and spirituality loom large on this alternative map of "utopian" sites that includes Ibiza (Spain), Goa (India), Bali (Indonesia), Bahia (Brazil), Ko Pagnan (Thailand), Byron Bay (Australia), San Francisco (U.S.A.), in addition to other varying locations. At another level, such utopian sites are interconnected and sustained by big urban centers (usually global cities) such as London, Frankfurt, Milan, Tel Aviv, Barcelona, Buenos Aires, Mumbai, and Bangkok.

Such geo-cultural formations can be represented as a *freak ethnoscape*,[4] understood as a global web of mobile subjects, practices, objects, and imaginaries correlating to an alternative lifestyle centered on expressive, hedonic, cosmopolitan, and nomadic tropes. The making of alternative formations through the trajectories and discourses of nomadic subjects indicates discontentment towards Western dominant structures, and suggests, more than the congealing of various national self-expatriations, a general *civilizational diaspora*.

Displaced souls in India: the alternative triangle of Techno and New Age

Besides multi-locality, the organizational and ideological dimensions of the "freak ethnoscape" characterize it as a truly global culture. Alternative subjects circulate within planetary regions as distant as Ibiza and Goa; nonetheless, more than mere instrumental means, their practices of displacement and connectivity are constitutive elements of a lifestyle informed by globalism. Their shared practices are co-informed by a worldview structured by core categories of "movement-and-charisma," as this study seeks to demonstrate.

In Western Romantic imaginaries, India is a referent that nurtures utopian desires for an alternative life away from the despiritualized routine of modern reality. In fact, many Ibiza "residents" have visited India, particularly Goa, Poona, and Manali, the "alternative triangle of India." In Ibiza, Indian religious, artistic, and gastronomic objects overtly circulate within tourist markets and chic boutiques, reflecting the consumerist drives of the majority (tourists and middle classes). On the other hand, an aestheticized "India" pervades the daily life of many Western subjects by means of cosmo-mystic life-orientations and body-techniques (meditation, yoga, super diets, breathing), reflecting a *"style of life"* inspired by ethical decisions (Davidson 1994; Hadot and Davidson 1995).

By late October, global nomads arrive in India, in advance of the charter tourists and vacationing backpackers from Western/ized countries. And so did I. During the pre-monsoon seasons of 2001 and 2002, I interacted with various alternatives, freaks, and bohemians, attempting to understand their lifestyles, cultural orientation, and background, as well as their socio-economic strategies in relation to native and tourist formations at the local, national, and global levels. Traveling and living in freak regions, my daily life in India consisted of attending various events in the "alternative triangle": guesthouses, underground bars, parties, hippie markets, beaches, ashrams, bus and train stations, etc. I sought to combine ethnographic methods with a nomadic sensibility in order to grasp the movement within the movement.

Consequently, I had to move in and out of Ibiza and Goa several times between 1998 and 2002 in keeping with important geo-climatic windows that complement both sites. Goa "happens" during the European winter (from November to April) while Ibiza "happens" during the Asian rainy season (from May to October). This climatic periodicity frames oscillatory patterns of nomadism traced by global freaks. As Deleuze and Guattari point out, *"nomads do not move"* (1980: 381): they are permanently trying to keep the smooth space of creativity and experimentation.

During the early 1970s, a community of hippies and *neo-sannyasins* (Osho followers, as described below) colonized the northern Goa beach areas of Anjuna and Vagator (Odzer 1995; Chapter 14 in this volume). Paradoxically, although fleeing from the West, they benefited from Goans' Christian–Westernized legacy of relative tolerance for leisure practices and individualism! In the ensuing years, "Goa" emerged as a signifier for a party-cum-drug paradise during winter seasons (Newman 2001; Odzer 1995; Saldanha 1999). By the late 1980s, the scene turned digital and tribal, with post-hippie post-punk freaks developing a new style of electronic music in rituals of psychedelic intensity: the hypnotic "Goa trance" (or "techno trance") music played in secret "trance parties" in secluded beach or jungle areas of Goa. This concept filtered back to the West and resulted in the proliferation of "Goa parties" around the world (Begrich and Muehlebach 1998), as well as in the commodification of Goa music into more docile styles such as "mainstream trance" or "Euro." As these developments reveal, the diffusion and resignification of countercultural practices, objects, and symbols can be read in a mapping of de/reterritorializing flows.

At the onset of the 21st century, the trance scene was still taking place in Anjuna and Vagator, whose villages now boast upgraded resorts, bars, cyber cafes, and other ancillary services. Nonetheless, the area still differs from the nearby charter tourist beaches of Baga and Chapora, with their chaotic hotel urbanization, and from the more relaxed beaches of Arambol and Palolem, frequented by backpackers. And new sites are gradually incorporated into the trance scene, such as the highly secluded Om beach (in Karnataka), where long and wild parties are occasionally thrown.

The global freak community is a tiny minority, probably a few thousand people in the midst of 1.1 million annual tourists visiting Goa State and its 1.5 million population (Goa Directorate of Planning, Statistics and Evaluation 1998). Although 90 percent of tourists in Goa are male Indians, the industry targets the 10th of Western tourists for their superior purchasing power. Foreigners come from the U.K., Germany, Israel, Japan, Italy, and Scandinavia, among a myriad of other nations. The majority is comprised of charter tourists, who do not travel around, but just spend a couple of weeks in beach resort areas demonstrating no real interest in local life, let alone culture and history.

Nevertheless, the freak minority plays a critical role in the development of "utopian sites." Alternative subjects are well aware that they will inevitably be succeeded by backpackers, then tourists and, gradually, all the urban and tourist structures. Utopian paradises are thus transformed into giant tourist traps, while cultures of resistance are commodified as "empty" entertainment for the vacationing populace. Inflation, land value, pollution, and resource depletion escalate as a result. For these reasons, freaks generally avoid tourists, local authorities, and natives, other than for basic income-generating exchanges (e.g. artistic and healing activities, hippie markets, drug dealing, etc.). In this context, techno-freaks perceive themselves as belonging to a marginal and vanishing culture requiring countermeasures of mobility and stealth against commodification and repression. Their postmodern melancholia stems from an awareness of the contradictions between their countercultural forms of resistance and the capturing modes of mass societies from which they (unsuccessfully) flee.

Freaks are not tourists. While tourists consume exotic places for short periods and within tightly structured labor/leisure life-cycles, alternative subjects assume remote places as "homes" for extended periods and within a holistic "style of life" that seeks to combine labor, travel, leisure, and spirituality. Moreover, although scorning the "commodification of experience" by conventional tourists (MacCannell 1989), freaks do not find anything special about most traditional cultures they engage with. They thus emulate the skeptical, romantic, and elitist gaze of the "post-tourist" (Urry 1990). For all their material and cultural particularities, it is wrong to conflate them with tourists. In Deleuzian terms, tourists belong to the striatic space of dwellers, while freaks live by the lines of flight of nomads.

Within this culture of nomadism, Goa is not only a center for the territorialization of global countercultures but also a corridor linking other main nodes in India, particularly Manali and Poona. In northern India, Manali and the villages of Parvati Valley accommodate the trance scene in the Himalayan mountains. Here, multinational freaks are outnumbered in a party population that is 90 percent Israeli. Considering the popularity of Goa trance music in Israel, most of this party crowd is formed not by nomadic freaks but rather by Israeli travelers and "part-time" freaks, i.e. subjects who consume alternative fashion, albeit devoid of the meanings that motivate countercultural resistance. In any case, these giant mountains provide a magnificent scenario for techno trance gatherings, a sublime experience of digital paganism at a 4,000-meter altitude: high-tech tribal music and young bodies, dancing and wandering within green forests of pine and grass, lit bonfires, the refreshing breeze of snowy peaks, and an absolute blue sky – a veritable experience of the Nietzschean "superhuman."

Located between Goa and Manali, Poona is a gentrified city near Mumbai hosting the world famous *Osho Commune International*. This paradise-like "meditation resort" provides a total environment for those seeking self-transformation and spiritual growth. The Osho movement is a good case for exploring the relations between New Age and Techno. Music, therapy, celebration, and meditation pervade daily life in the "Osho ashram." In the huge camp-like Buddha Hall, hundreds of practitioners (about 80 percent Westerners) do one-hour "dynamic meditations," which begin with cathartic stages of chaotic dance and gibberish, moving towards introspective stages of silent stillness and relaxation. Moreover, the commune's "Multiversity" offers a wide range of group workshops centering on creative and cathartic expression. During three-day "encounter groups," potent music is employed by therapists as transformative catalysts. Notably, predominant musical styles are techno, house, trance, ambient, and New Age music, played at specific moments throughout the workshop. Besides the Buddha Hall and Multiversity activities, once a week the ashram administration "allows" short-duration dance parties where DJs play house music, exotic world-beats and a bit of trance. Nonetheless, too emotionally derailing trance music is opposed by some therapists since many visitors are already undergoing intense therapies during the day.

During the 1970s, Osho's vision attracted many youthful, creative and wealthy converts from the Western world. Very briefly, Osho (Bhagwan Rajneesh), also known as the "Rolls-Royce Guru" or "Sex Guru," was an outrageous Nietzschean philosopher who sought to combine Buddha with Zorba, by affirming and celebrating Life ("I would only believe in a God who danced") (Osho 1967, 1987). For decades, Osho lectured and organized "meditation camps" throughout India (Osho and Neiman 2000). When he lived in America his commune in Oregon was closed by conservative political forces in 1984 due to Osho's virulent speeches against religion and politics. Osho returned to Poona, where he died in 1990. The permanence and growth of the ashram after his death depended on adaptation to legal and political structures. Internal dissent and purges took place within the movement, as more countercultural *sannyasins* disagreed with the ashram's official take on elegant marketability and social accommodation, in addition to its disapproval of trance parties and drug experiments being carried out by "rebel" *sannyasins* and freaks around Poona.

During the post-Oregon diaspora, many *sannyasins* returned to Ibiza, a special place for practices of "love and liberation." While participating in the nightclub life, they also introduced New Age techniques from the U.S.A., including the use of MDMA for meditation and body therapies. Although "ecstasy" was already known in European gay and anti-psychiatric circles, it was through the interaction between *sannyasins* and late 1980s clubbers in Ibiza that MDMA became an explosive discovery for European youth enduring the harsh times of neo-liberal capitalism on the rise. The legendary 1987 "enlightenment" of British DJ figureheads (Oakenfold, Rampling, and Holloway) upon first trying ecstasy in Ibiza was pivotal in the subsequent explosion of Loved Up 1990s rave culture. The phenomenon rapidly flowed from the underground to the mainstream, from Poona, to America, to Ibiza, to London, to the world. Within multiple flows of alternative subjects, objects, and imaginaries across East and West, Osho *sannyasins* were a bridge between the 1960s counterculture and the 1990s Techno movement.

This genealogy of flows exposes the singularity of countercultural lifestyles. While "displaced peoples" have "localized minds," such as migrants orienting melancholic identities to their homelands, alternative nomads pose a quite different picture. Techno-freaks and Osho *sannyasins* belong to a universe of displaced peoples with *displaced minds*. These Global Nomads seek to drift away from their Western homeland and, inspired by imaginations of a Romantic East, they asymptotically move towards a smooth, impossible space – "u-topia" by definition. By celebrating rootlessness and nomadism, global nomads shape cosmopolitan post-national identities that question the essentiality of the "local," and embrace the "global" as the new home and reference.

Silicon cage and post-sexualities

The emergence of transnational forms of digital art-religion must be understood in contexts of postmodern global capitalism. The "iron cage" of modernity rapidly becomes the *silicon cage* of techno-financial capitalism, while the human body is reduced to a *carbon cage*, a map of genes and rights colonized by high-tech engineering, legal intervention and commodification (in a *Robocop* scenario). At the semiotic level, fast production and circulation of signs and commodities undermine the subject's ability to make sense of reality, forcing him or her to make dramatic and uneasy decisions (Appadurai 1996; Giddens 1991; Jameson 1991).

On the other hand, the corrosion of tradition by globalization enables the emergence of post-traditional identities by means of reflexive and cosmopolitan forms, understood as "detachments from provincial identities" and "strangeness within and outside the self" (Cheah and Robbins 1998). The very *problematization* of locality-making must be seen as a resource rather than as a barrier for the production of meaning and identity (Lasch 1994). Thus, the retrieving of reflexive meaning from global chaos can contribute to overcoming the corrosive effects of global commodification (Turner 1994). It is through the interplay between local environs and global processes that such aesthetic hermeneutics reconfigures time–space notions and structures of affection and belonging. As the production of localities and of subjectivities are interrelated (Appadurai 1996; Povinelli and Chauncey 1999), the "self" becomes "the new strategic possibility," an open project of reflexive elaboration within a "life politics" (Foucault and Lotringer 1989; Giddens 1992). The question is to evince *how reflexive subjectivities are formed within deterritorialized conditions.*

In this sense, rather than agonizing chaos, reflexive globalization also provides the conditions through which New Age and Techno can rework the new cages of postmodern capitalism. Through playful moves of micro-transgression and cali-brations of "intensity-moderation," we may be witnessing exercises of emancipation, or, conversely, escapes from the pasteurized rationale of modern life. Or still, echoing Weber and Foucault, "something other we don't know what it is." All in all, the central characters of critical poststructuralism – the *mad*, the *marginal*, and the *artist* – are metonymically condensed in the "global freak," the schizo-nomad of this research.

Art therefore arises as a site of experimentation for reconstituting social life and harmonizing spheres of science and politics. If so, how to evaluate social movements of liberation? According to Foucault, they are innocuous in so far as they remain parasitic of science, rooted in the dominant apparatus of "sexu-ality" and "biopower," which constitute the modern subject of discipline, production, and self-control. Not only have liberation movements centered their struggles on questions of sex and "natural" rights of the "individual," but they have also subsumed their tactical moves under scientific modes as resources of legitimacy. Since these gestures preclude a real move away from the legal-scien-tific apparatus of "sexuality," liberation movements remain entrapped in the epistemic vectors they seek to transcend.

" 'Couldn't everyone's life become a work of art?' This was not some vapid plea for aestheticism, but a suggestion for separating our ethics, our lives, from our science, our knowledge" (Hacking 1986: 239). Liberation from and through modern arrangements (market, state, and science) will require a new ethical "morality" centered on an "aesthetics of life" in which science and morality play an informative, not a normative, role (Foucault 1984: 611). "New forms of community, co-existence and pleasure" would overcome scientific colonization and body politics centered on the "normal–pathologic" binary of confinement and exclusion. By displacing the modern apparatus of "sexuality," a new erotico-aesthetic ethics can operate as a counter-apparatus leading towards an age of *post-sexuality* (a new arrangement of bodies, selves, intimacies, sociabilities, knowledges, and institutions).

The central question is how erotico-aesthetic formations of Techno and New Age contribute to this post-sexuality age. As such, they amoralize desires by emphasizing degenitalized pleasures; they appropriate techno-scientific knowledge by transgressing their uses and disciplinary foundations; they defy the centralizing logic of legal administration of bodies and spaces by promoting rituals that celebrate marginalization; they criticize modern economic rationality by pointing out its ecological irrationality. In sum, as countercultural formations, Techno and New Age queer, transgress, and reverse dominant devices that constitute modern subjectivities.

"Limit-experiences" of digital shamanism and nomadic spirituality

Because the forging of the self is experienced at the phenomenological level, the analysis of subjectivity forms must consider lived experiences, subjective practices, and imaginaries. Devised by Foucault via Nietzsche and Bataille, "an experience is something you come out of changed" (Foucault 1978: 27). Since the macro-analysis of countercultures is important but insufficient for understanding the nature of emerging subjectivities, the transformative power of queer spiritualities must be assessed with reference to the notion of "limit-experience" (*ibid.*; Jay 1993).

At the intersection of body, power, and identity, a limit-experience happens as a traumatic or sublime event that transgresses the boundaries of coherent subjectivity, "tearing the subject from itself" at the limit of living, intensity, and impossibility. Yet, in a second stage, such events require recollection in a space outside: "an experience is, of course, something one has alone; but it cannot have its full impact unless the individual manages to escape from pure subjectivity in a way that others can at least cross paths with or retrace it" (Foucault 1978: 40). The mutual acknowledgement of something extraordinary animates a sense of sharing that bonds individuals and the world.

Oftentimes limit-experiences are induced by altering devices, grasped in Weberian terms as "intoxicating elements of orgiastic sensuality": music, drugs, dance, touch, among other techniques (Weber 1913). Alternative ways of perceiving and understanding reality thus entailed are potentially disruptive of subjective, collective, and political identities. This potential for transformation poses a menace to the legitimacy of civilizations, which depend on the control of populations and subjectivities, as particularly exemplified by the biopower mechanisms of the nation-state. However, as absolute eradication is impossible, exercises of self-transformation become marginalized while reinforcing exclusionary practices and moralities. The ritual exploration of limit-experiences is then largely confined to alternative or "underground" subcultures, for which "intoxicating elements" are rendered as catalysts of charisma and problematization.

In New Age and techno music, rhythmic and melodic features stimulate specific sensorial-affective responses, such as states of well-being, timelessness, disorientation, and intensity, often associated with imaginaries of inner utopia (or dystopia) or *unio mystica*. Whether as "narcotic," "angelic," or "plastic" sounds, the development of digital music as a "science of psychedelic sounds" seeks to mimic psychedelic or spiritual states (Erlmann 1996; Reynolds 1998). Such audio-emotional mimicry of inner states facilitates the experience of "movement" towards the "extraordinary."

Among intoxicating elements, drugs stand out for their corporeal and political implications. They amplify extraordinary experiences, whether in dance or spiritual scenes. LSD and MDMA provide two different phenomenological registers. While LSD (acid) propitiates a *psychedelic asceticism* enacted by mental states of hyper-imagination and mystical transcendence, MDMA (ecstasy) creates an *oceanic eroticism* expressed by affective states of excruciating pleasures and overflowing immanence. Notwithstanding their phenomenological complementarity, both substances greatly facilitate the setting of collective experiences of the extraordinary, such as "Temporary Autonomous Zones" ("TAZ") (Bey 1991). But as dangerous as sacred, drugs can destroy as well as enlighten the user. Drug abuse by itself quite often transforms chemical blissfulness into nightmarish despair, as the two-year cycle of MDMA indulgence repeatedly demonstrates. In Techno, it is arguable whether drugs are mandatory for "understanding" digital music or achieving group acceptance. In any case, the following maxim holds: the basic drug is the music, a music that drugs the subject and makes him or her dance.

The history of drugs congeals New Age and Techno, suggesting a single countercultural formation. Synthesized in Germany in 1910, MDMA was rediscovered by American psy-researchers by the mid-1970s and employed in experimental psychotherapy. Known as "Adam" for its effects of "Edenic rebirth" on patients, MDMA was also quickly absorbed by New Age circles as a device for creativity and self-exploration (Escohotado 1998: 1,019–33). However, the epidemic dissemination of MDMA as commercial 'ecstasy' during the 1980s led to its criminalization in most Western countries. Even so, ecstasy became the drug of choice in the club scene, reaching massive levels of consumption in Western Europe throughout the 1990s.[5] By and large, a comparison of MDMA and LSD reveals similar patterns of discovery, multiple cross-usage, dissemination, and criminalization.[6]

An overlap between Techno and New Age ritual symbolism frames digital dance events as neo-shamanic experiences. Particularly raves and trance parties, these are multimedia dance events in hidden urban or rural areas, secretly announced within informal networks of young "initiates." A tribal layout places the dance floor at the center of the venue, and technological devices are strategically positioned for altering subjects' minds: mega-speakers powered by multi-deck amplifiers; smoke machines; laser beams, ultra-violet and stroboscopic lights; and video projections of extraordinary images: kaleidoscopic fractals, dazzling angels, digital babies; ethereal gardens, crystalline waves, supernova stars; zooming spaceships, industrial plants, sex manga cartoons; or air bombardments, atomic mushrooms, and slavery; wastelands, destruction, cyber monsters, etc. As a postmodernist art genre, these videos are set on *iterable* mode: images unfold for a few seconds and are instantaneously repeated; the next sequence, though, extends shortly, and is looped again, and so on: repetition with difference. At a deeper level, iterability dramatizes modern routine and neurosis in a clash of boredom and excitement, hugely intensified by psychoactive substances. Likewise, rave décor draws on tribal, military, psychedelic, and utopian elements: colorful drapes, tents and banners, psychedelic paintings, aromatic candles, incense, religious symbols (Om, Shiva's Trident) and statues (Buddha, Nataraj, Ganesh). Enveloped in kaleidoscopic mystery, a rave or trance party is felt as a pulsating organism that engenders extraordinary experiences.

By combining art, technology, and religion, the DJ is the new *digital shaman*, responsible for creating and maintaining an atmosphere of excitement and communion in the crowd. As a witchdoctor healing the sick, divining the hidden, and controlling events (Mauss and Hubert 1902), the DJ plays music with techniques of continuous beat matching, planning, and improvisation of "tracks" (records) in direct, albeit intuitive, interaction with the dancing and non-dancing crowds. The music is extremely loud and its multi-rhythmic layers unfold through iterable and restless refrains: repetitive beats and loops of sound with minor alterations of tones and insertion/removal of layers and staccatos. This endless pattern of repetition-cum-difference pumps untiringly for many hours, often days, as DJs alternate without interruption. Rather than circular, digital music is spiral, if not fractal. As intensity sets in, iterable sounds transform music into a meta-music of derailing sounds, altering people's sense of mind, body, feeling, time, and reality. The dance floor gradually becomes a powerful zone of *psychic fields*.

While "raving," "when the dancer becomes the dance" (Osho 1988: 55), sounds and lights acquire tangible textures and are felt to merge with the dancer's soul. It is Neo mastering *The Matrix*. Induced naturally or chemically, states of perception are altered, and the self disintegrates; the ordinary sense of a bounded atom melts into waves of flows: flows of pleasures and imaginations, synchronizing with other bouncing bodies, merging with the crowd into an ocean of light, sound, warmth, and dance. The Judeo-Christian individual is replaced by a Confucian experiencing of a cosmic self. Or, in the Zen acceptance of paradox, raving sensations are as orgiastic as ascetic, as private as collective, as inner as outer – a dismantling organism, a Body-without-Organs.

This explains why a rave (or trance party) never really climaxes but remains looping, spiraling in a crescendo, into higher plateaus of intensity (Deleuze and

Guattari 1980). Good digital music and gatherings keep creativity at the edge of experimentation: the Body-without-Organs of Techno, which unfolds like a nomadic desiring-machine, an assemblage of lines of flight moving into and through the realms of the "extraordinary."

This phenomenology of ecstasy corresponds to "limit-experiences," as, both in Techno and New Age rituals, subjects repeatedly report sublime and traumatic experiences. Pleasure, pain, catharsis, awareness, despair, and happiness underlie such accounts of non-ordinary sensations and states. Telepathy, mystical visions, paranoia, ego dissolution, excruciating pleasures, deep insight, serenity, and cosmic love are not uncommon. It is not that the experience awakens a particular feeling, but rather that amplified feelings are the source of a limit-experience. As an exercise of intensity and impossibility, these transpersonal practices engender experiences of personal derailment – deterritorializing asignification – sacred madness with rewards and dangers.

Nonetheless, the tribal features of Techno and New Age rituals should not be seen as revivals of primitive, premodern forms of life, as is often claimed by insiders and some scholars. Countercultural neo-tribalism is structured by meanings and functions centered on the question of subjectivity, sensed sacredly by the subject as a matter of "utmost individuality" (Heelas 1996; cf. Dumont 1983; Maffesoli 1996). Such ritual spaces emulate dilemmas of postmodern subjectivity: the constitution of flexible and reflexive identities within digital, mobile, and neo-capitalist environs. The Durkheimian notion of "collective effervescence" must be reassessed within these parameters: through the group – as a necessary condition – but because of the individual.

In global countercultures, horizontal (spatial) displacements are accompanied by vertical displacements (self-identity). Global nomads (bohemians, New Agers, freaks, ravers) enjoy their condition as long-distance travelers, spiritual pilgrims, regarding the whole planet as a space for moving, if not a "home" in itself. Significantly, these peoples are familiar with "limit-experiences," seen as "trips" into and out of the self (as vertical displacements). Poles of mystic contemplation and ascetic action are reconfigured at this point as "tripping" indexes hedonic/ist and erotic forms of innerworldly redemption (*"innerweltliche Erlösung"*) (Weber 1913; Corsten 1998). New Agers and techno-freaks refer to their explorations with music, dance, and drugs as spiritual experiences, a "deep trip." DJs describe their central task as "taking the crowd on a journey." When taking acid or ecstasy, the consumer is wished a "nice trip." "Spaceships" and "intergalactic voyages" are common representations of the psychedelic "journey" into non-ordinary dimensions. Significantly, the word "hallucinogen" comes from the ancient Greek *alyein*, which means "to wander," and relates to the distracted gaze of trancing shamans. A drive for something not ordinary underlies all of these examples, a drive for movement as an extraordinary experience.

Ibiza and Goa are as intoxicating as music and drugs. On the one hand, it is obvious that limit-experiences and countercultures may occur anywhere in the world and without recourse to "intoxicating elements." On the other, there is a general belief that emphasizes the importance of "being there" (in India, in Ibiza – in the "Otherland") in order to experience life and Being. Travel-talk endows as much meaning as prestige upon those who have "been there," to extraordinary places *and* dimensions. Yet, as the world shrinks, Ibiza and Goa become global icons for the expression as well as for the commodification of alternative lifestyles: Goa parties, New Age Orientalisms, and Ibiza fashion have become signifiers with a global circulation. Paradoxically, the more countercultures capture the desire for alternative charisma, the more they serve consumptive capital (Povinelli 2000; Best 1997). Nevertheless, Ibiza and Goa still hold as global references for an alternative way of life animated by a cultivation of nomadism and spirituality. How countercultures prompt social transformation through the very capitalist forms they criticize remains a critical question.

Counter-conclusions: flexible economies and subjectivities

In the capitalist stage of flexible accumulation (Harvey 1990), alternative subjects live within interstitial spaces of leisure, alternative or informal economies and welfare systems. Nomadic strategies include autonomous, seasonal, or part-time jobs, artistic, tourist, and "health" careers, or illegal activities. They frequently count on parental allowances, inheritance, or state-based unemployment support. Quite often these strategies involve a combination of all of these possibilities. In Ibiza and Goa, typical locations for income-generation and socialization are night-clubs, ashrams, tourist markets, sunset bars, alternative centers, eco-cooperatives, among others. In India, Global Nomads purchase exotic luxuries from local producers (handicrafts, clothing, jewelry, psychoactive substances) in mutually bene-ficial, albeit unequal, exchanges. In the West, these commodities will be sold in boutiques, markets, and streets at highly inflated prices, exemplifying how alterna-tive strategies are materially reproduced.

The geo-economic territorialization of global countercultures in "freak" sites impacts on the lives of local communities, as perceived by natives and analysts. The presence of big hotel chains in Goa and Ibiza has led to environmental degradation, capital alienation, and social conflict (Dantas 1999; Rozenberg 1990). On the other hand, the presence of freak communities represents decon-centrated income for local villagers in addition to the queer charisma that they convey to visited places, inadvertently paving the way for tourism. However, local populations disagree with alternative lifestyles (dressing, parties, sociability, nudity, drugs, music, noise). In Ibiza, despite their role in promoting the island's utopian imaginary since the 1930s, alternative subjects had to adapt to the conditions and opportunities of a rapidly modernizing society or leave the island for "more primitive" sites in Mexico, India, or Brazil. As the old hippie complains, "Then they loved us, now they blame us!"

In India, Techno and New Age activities became sources of income for local communities. Besides the ancillary activities of taxing, lodging, restaurants, and the pervasive "*chai* economy," trance parties in Goa became complex joint-ventures of Goan gangs and Western DJs, the former seeking profit through sound-system rentals, bar sales, and police bribes, and the latter aiming at shamanic excitement and prestige. Although drug consumption abounds in the clubs, bars, and parties of Ibiza and Goa, in most cases there is no basic economic motivation linking party organization and drug dealing, as commonly suspected regarding trance gatherings. It is well known that party promoters often lose money on their parties. Nonetheless, they allow drugs as a way of creating a "nice atmosphere" among friends and the crowd. In Ibiza, trance parties are organized by non-profit gangs of youngsters, and the underground scene unfolds secretly through the agonistic motivations of sociability, excitement, and transgression of global and Spanish freaks.

On a larger scale, transnational flows of nomadic countercultures and the resulting circuits, networks, and ethnoscapes are affected by various agencies and structures operating at the local and global levels. By the early 1990s, legal repression of raves in the U.K. contributed to the dissemination and commodification of parties and drug consumption in Ibiza and Goa. Conversely, in 2000, north Goan villagers protested the tough repression of trance parties by authorities and police, as it stifled their main source of subsistence by scaring freaks, backpackers, and party-tourists away. Goan authorities had to respond by recalibrating their actions in order to accommodate different interests. This meant that a certain degree of freak activity had to be allowed. As we have seen, a complex dynamic of conflict and accommodation also underlies the development of the Osho meditation resort in Poona. In sum, the interconnectedness of global flows develops through tensions and disjunctures among social, political, and economic domains, and characterizes the turbulent environments through which global nomads navigate.

As evinced, the co-presence of multinational backgrounds, nomadic practices, and transpersonal experiences among global nomads is central to their identity. By exploring "limit-experiences" (Foucault) in transgressive cults of "orgiastic sensuality" (Weber), Techno and New Age provide sites for the cultivation of a cosmopolitan nomadism, by which alternative subjects attempt to make sense of their lives in contexts of high mobility and instability. As a matter of fact, countercultures have been comfortably exploring strangeness, rootlessness, and displacement much before these qualities became considered by media and academia as core predicaments of contemporary social life. The familiarity of countercultures with such predicaments illustrates the richness of Techno and New Age as advanced sites for the investigation of emerging realities.

Hence, theories claiming that alternative subjects have "dropped out" of neoliberal capitalism are unable to explain why and how they make critical decisions regarding their life strategies. Certainly, material contexts introduce powerful conditions, but, as this study has sought to demonstrate, away from the alienation and routine of modern life, alternative subjects seek to rearticulate labor, leisure, and spirituality in an exquisitely meaningful way, irreducible to economic explanation. Above all, global nomads attempt to engender holistic charisma in a fragmented and disenchanted world.

By assembling nomadic, digital, and spiritual apparatuses, New Age and Techno constitute a common semiotic space of subjectivity formation and social critique. Their practical strategies may diverge, as New Agers cultivate the Romantic shaping of the self as an unfolding inner substance, while techno-freaks celebrate the self-shattering shamanism of "machines for freedom." Nevertheless, both movements congeal in the deployment of material–symbolic devices to foster alternative forms of self-identity, life strategy, and post-community. Such life experiments seek to drift away from the Western regimenting apparatuses of the nation-state and sexuality; and as long as their lines of flight – desire and creativity – are kept, Techno and New Age will remain as sites for such life experiments, notably cosmopolitan post-identities and holistic post-sexualities.

Notes

1   It is in this context that "subculture," "counterculture," and "alternative culture" are differentiated. A subculture refers to the shared values, symbols, and practices of a group whose members also adhere to and function in wider societies. The notion of "alternative" implies subcultures that seek autonomy from or replacement of such major social models. "Alternative" is broader and looser than "counterculture," which is marked by high levels of dissatisfaction, critical stance, and refusal of Western major institutions and values, and the cultivation of transgressive practices and lifestyles. A counterculture thus is a type of radicalized subculture, and analytically operates as a powerful ideological referent for practices of resistance in times of cultural crisis. In the scope of this study, my interest lies in alternative formations with countercultural drives and background, i.e. those relating genealogically to the 1960s upheaval and, further back, to 19th-century Romanticism. In this chapter, "alternative" and "countercultural" are used interchangeably unless noted otherwise.

2   In this chapter, "Techno" is employed as a broad umbrella term for the whole movement and history of digital music. It refers to all dance styles born from the new technologies and forms of musical production, diffusion, and consumption that emerged during the late 1980s: house, techno, jungle, trance, ambient, etc.

3   "Sexuality" is a sociocultural apparatus of practices, institutions, and knowledge (*scientia sexualis*) that constitutes the modern subject. It reflects control mechanisms of the nation-state and related institutions (science, family, church, workplace) in controlling populations and individuals (*biopower*). "Sexuality" is thus constructed as a category and a domain of obscure causalities, pathologies, external intervention, and deciphering of the subject, to whom categories of "sin" or "desire" are rendered central in the formation of modern self-identities (Foucault 1976; Davidson 1988; Dreyfus *et al.* 1983).

4   In the anthropology of globalization, the suffix "-scape" signifies transnational distributions of correlated elements whose display can be represented as landscapes. For example, transnational arrangements of technological, financial, media, and political resources can be seen, respectively, as technoscapes, financescapes, mediascapes, and ideoscapes (Appadurai 1996: 33). The prefix "ethno-" refers to "people" rather than strictly to "ethnicity."

5   It is estimated that 1–2 million people consume ecstasy every weekend in the U.K. (Reynolds 1998).

6   In addition, shamanic substances traditionally ministered within "primitive" societies have been appropriated by Techno and New Age under similar patterns of re-usage and resignification, as analyzed in this study.

Bibliography

Appadurai, A. (1996) *Modernity at Large: Cultural Dimensions of Globalization*, Minneapolis: University of Minnesota Press.

Begrich, R. and A. Muehlebach (1998) *Trancenational Goa: Travelling People, Parties, Images*, Basel, Switzerland: University of Basel.

Bellah, R. (1985) *Habits of the Heart: Individualism and Commitment in American Life*, Berkeley, CA: University of California Press.

Best, B. (1997) "Over-the-counter-culture: retheorizing resistance in popular culture," in S. Redhead (ed.) *The Clubcultures Reader: Readings in Popular Cultural Studies*, Oxford: Blackwell.

Bey, H. (1991) *The Temporary Autonomous Zone: Ontological Anarchy, Poetic Terrorism*, New York: Autonomedia.

Borneman, J. and S. Senders (2000) "Politics without a head: is the 'Love Parade' a new form of political identification?," *Cultural Anthropology* 15: 294–317.

Cheah, P. and B. Robbins (1998) *Cosmopolitics: Thinking and Feeling beyond the Nation*, Minneapolis: University of Minnesota Press.

Collin, M. (1997) *Altered State: The Story of Ecstasy Culture and Acid House*, London; New York: Serpent's Tail.

Comaroff, J.L. and J. Comaroff (2000) "Millennial capitalism: first thoughts on a second coming," *Public Culture: Millennial Capitalism and the Culture of Neoliberalism* 12: 291–343.

Corsten, Michael (1998) "Ecstasy as 'this-wordly path to salvation': the techno youth scene as a proto-religious collective," in L. Tomasi (ed.) *Alternative Religions among European Youth*, Aldershot: Ashgate.

D'Andrea, A. (2000) *O Self Perfeito e a Nova Era: individualismo e reflexividade em religiosidades pós-tradicionais*, São Paulo: Ed. Loyola.

Dantas, N. (ed.) (1999) *The Transforming of Goa*, Mapusa, Goa: The Other India.

Davidson, A.I. (1988) "Closing up the corpses: diseases of sexuality and the emergence of the psychiatric style of reasoning," in George Boolos (ed.) *Meaning and Method: Essays in Honor of Hilary Putnam*, Cambridge: Cambridge University Press.

—— (1994) "Ethics as ascetics: Foucault, the history of ethics and ancient thought," in G. Gutting (ed.) *The Cambridge Companion to Foucault*, Cambridge: Cambridge University Press.

Deleuze, G. and F. Guattari (1980) *A Thousand Plateaus: Capitalism and Schizophrenia*, Minneapolis: University of Minnesota Press.

Dreyfus, H.L., P. Rabinow and M. Foucault (1983) *Michel Foucault: Beyond Structuralism and Hermeneutics*, Chicago: University of Chicago Press.

Dumont, L. (1983) *Essais sur l'individualisme: une perspective anthropologique sur l'idéologie moderne*, Paris: Éditions du Seuil.

Erlmann, V. (1996) "The aesthetics of the global imagination: reflections on world music in the 1990s," *Public Culture* 8: 467–87.

Escohotado, A. (1998) *Historia General de las Drogas*, Madrid: Espasa.

Featherstone, M. and R. Burrows (eds.) (1995) *Cyberspace, Cyberbodies, Cyberpunks: Cultures of Technological Embodiment*, London: Sage.

Foucault, M. (1976) *Histoire de la sexualité I: la volonté de savoir*, Paris: Gallimard.

—— (1978) *Remarks on Marx*, New York: Semiotext(e).

—— (1984) "À Propos de la généalogie de l'éthique: un aperçu du travail en cours" (trans. from "On the genealogy of ethics: an overview of work in progress" and reviewed by Foucault), in *Dits et écrits IV: (1980–1988)*, ed. D. Defert and F. Ewald, Paris: Gallimard.

Foucault, M. and S. Lotringer (1989) *Foucault Live (Interviews, 1961–1984)*, New York: Semiotext(e).

Frank, T. (1997) *The Conquest of Cool: Business Culture, Counterculture and the Rise of Hip Consumerism*, Chicago: University of Chicago Press.

Giddens, A. (1989) *The Consequences of Modernity*, Stanford: Stanford University Press.

—— (1991) *Modernity and Self-Identity: Self and Society in the Late Modern Age*, Cambridge: Blackwell.

—— (1992) *The Transformation of Intimacy: Love, Sexuality and Eroticism in Modern Societies*, Oxford and Cambridge: Polity Press in association with Basil Blackwell.

Goa Directorate of Planning, Statistics and Evaluation (1998) *Statistical Handbook of Goa*, Panaji: Government of Goa.

Grof, S. and C. Grof (1990) *The Stormy Search for the Self: A Guide to Personal Growth through Transformational Crisis*, New York: Tarcher-Putnam.

Hacking, I. (1986) "Self-improvement," in D. Hoy (ed.) *Foucault: A Critical Reader*, Oxford: Blackwell.

Hadot, P. and A.I. Davidson (1995) *Philosophy as a Way of Life: Spiritual Exercises from Socrates to Foucault*, Oxford: Blackwell.

Harvey, D. (1990) *The Condition of Postmodernity: An Inquiry into the Origins of Social Change*, Cambridge: Blackwell.

Heelas, P. (1996) *The New Age Movement: The Celebration of the Self and the Sacralization of Modernity*, Oxford: Blackwell.

Ingham, J., M. Purvis and D. Clarke (1999) "Hearing places, making spaces: sonorous geographies, ephemeral rhythms and the Blackburn warehouse parties," *Society and Space (Environment and Planning)* 17: 283–305.

Institut Balear d'Estadística i Demografia (1996) Presentación "Padró Municipal d'habitants 1996" Eivissa-Formentera: Govern Balear – Conselleria de Economia i Hisienda.

James, W. (1936) *The Varieties of Religious Experience*, New York: Modern Library.

Jameson, F. (1991) *Postmodernism; or, The Cultural Logic of Late Capitalism*, Durham, NC: Duke University Press.

Jay, M. (1993) *The Limits of Limit-experience: Bataille and Foucault*, Berkeley, CA: Center for German and European Studies, University of California.

Lasch, S. (1994) "Reflexivity and its doubles: structure, aesthetics, community," in U. Beck, A. Giddens and S. Lasch (eds.) *Reflexive Modernization: Politics, Tradition and Aesthetics in the Modern Social Order*, Stanford: Stanford University Press.

Luckmann, T. (1991) "The new and the old in religion," in P. Bourdieu and L. Coleman (eds.) *Social Theory for a Changing Society*, San Francisco: Westview.

Lukoff, D., R. Zanger and F. Lu (1990) "Transpersonal psychology research review – psychoactive substances and transpersonal states," *Journal of Transpersonal Psychology* 22: 107–48.

MacCannell, D. (1989) *The Tourist: A New Theory of the Leisure Class*, Berkeley, CA: University of California Press.

McKay, G. (1996) *Senseless Acts of Beauty: Cultures of Resistance since the Sixties*, London: Verso.

Maffesoli, M. (1996) [1988] *The Time of Tribes: The Decline of Individualism in Mass Society*, London: Sage.

Mauss, M. and R. Hubert (1902) "Esquisse d'une theorie generale de la magie," in M. Mauss (ed.) *Sociologie et Antropologie*, Paris: Presses Universitaires de France.

Newman, R. (2001) "Western tourists and Goan pilgrims: a comparison of two ritual dramas," in *Of Umbrellas, Goddesses and Dreams: Essays on Goan Culture and Society*, Mapusa, Goa: The Other India.

Odzer, C. (1995) *Goa Freaks: My Hippie Years in India*, New York: Blue Moon Books.

Ortner, S. (1999) "Fieldwork in the postcommunity," *Anthropology and Humanism* 22: 61–80.

Osho (1967) *From Sex to Superconsciousness*, Poona: The Rebel.

—— (1987) *Zarathustra: A God that Can Dance*, Poona: The Rebel.

—— (1988) *Meditation: The First and Last Freedom*, Poona: The Rebel.

Osho and S. Neiman (eds.) (2000) *Autobiography of a Spiritually Incorrect Mystic*, Poona: The Rebel.

Povinelli, E. (2000) "Consuming *Geist*: popontology and the spirit of capital in indigenous Australia," *Public Culture: Millenial Capitalism and the Culture of Neoliberalism* 12: 501–28.

Povinelli, E. and G. Chauncey (1999) "Thinking sexuality transnationally," *GLQ: A Journal of Gay and Lesbian Studies* 5: 1–11.

Redhead, S. (ed.) (1997) *The Clubcultures Reader*, Oxford: Blackwell.

Reynolds, S. (1998) *Generation Ecstasy: Into the World of Techno and Rave Culture*, Boston, MA: Little, Brown.

Roszak, T. (1995) *The Making of a Counterculture: Reflections on the Technocratic Society and its Youthful Opposition*, Berkeley, CA: University of California Press.

Rozenberg, D. (1990) *Ibiza, una isla para otra vida: inmigrantes utópicos, turismo y cambio cultural*, Madrid: Centro de Investigaciones Sociológicas: Siglo XXI de España.

Saldanha, A. (1999) "Goa trance in Goa: globalization, musical practice and the politics of place," paper presented to the Annual IASPM International Conference, Sydney, 1999.

Stanley, C. (1997) "Not drowning but waving: urban narratives of dissent in the wild zone," in S. Redhead (ed.) *The Clubcultures Reader*, Oxford: Blackwell.

Turner, B.S. (1994) *Orientalism, Postmodernism and Globalism*, London and New York: Routledge.

Urry, J. (1990) *The Tourist Gaze: Leisure and Travel in Contemporary Societies*, London: Sage.

Wallerstein, I. (1989) [1968] "Revolution in the world-system: theses and queries," *Theory and Society* 18: 431–48.

Weber, M. (1913) "Religious groups (the sociology of religion)," in G. Roth (ed.) *Economy and Society*, Berkeley, CA: University of California Press.

York, M. (1995) *The Emerging Network: A Sociology of the New Age and Neo-Pagan Movements*, Lanham, MD: Rowman & Littlefield.

13 Hedonic tantra

Golden Goa's trance transmission[1]

Erik Davis

In the early 1990s, I started tapping into the growing psychedelic undertow of dance and electronic music. With the exception of the Bay Area, the United States was largely out of step with this dimension of the techno scene, and it was only through stray clues – a boast by a British backpacker, liner notes on an import ambient CD – that I first heard about Goa. When I interviewed Orbital for *Spin*, Paul Hartnoll confirmed the rumors: on the west coast of India, in the ex-Portuguese state of Goa, an old hippie haven hosted raves every winter, massive techno freak-outs that were less parties than rites of passage. These parties rode the cutting edge of psychedelic techno music – what we now call psy-trance – and they attracted New Age traveler types as well as the raver elite. Some suggested that Goa was the true source of raves, or at least of their spiritual essence, that ineffable gnostic intoxication whose articulation usually leaves outsiders in the dark.

Techno historians already know that English working-class kids brought raves back from Ibiza, the cheap vacation island off Spain whose weather, mellowness, and lack of extradition treaties made it a Goa-style hippie colony decades ago. The original Ibizan DJs were certainly freaks, mixing Tangerine Dream in with their disco. But the holders of bohemian lore will tell you that the authentic esoteric lineage of electronic trance dance lay further east, in Goa. When I spoke to Genesis P-Orridge, the leader of the magickal techno/industrial outfit Psychic TV, he said that "the music from Ibiza was more horny disco, while Goa was more psychedelic and tribal. In Goa, the music was the facilitator of devotional experience. It was just functional, just to make that other state happen."[2]

Contemporary attempts to characterize underground dance culture's experience of this "state" often turn to the French philosophers Deleuze and Guattari, whose writings have helped us wrestle with non-ordinary states of consciousness and perception without recourse to either religious or reductivist languages (see Reynolds 1998: 245–6; and Chapter 14 in this volume). The notion of a plateau, derived from cybernetic philosopher Gregory Bateson's studies of Balinese aesthetics, helps characterize a state of becoming whose intensities are realized without climax or resolution. Similarly, the famous "Body-without-Organs," a phrase cribbed from Artaud, can be said to describe an immanent and literally dis-organized field of animate matter, at once a pure virtuality and a synthetic bundle of molecular affects.

Though Deleuze and Guattari take great pains to avoid any taint of the transcendent, the Body-without-Organs, or BwO, veers ineluctably towards sacred forces. In "How to Build a Body without Organs," the authors explore the BwO in the context of drugs and somatic spiritual praxis (Deleuze and Guattari 1987: 149–66). There is mention of Taoist arts, of Artaud's peyote experiences in Mexico, of a Castaneda-like "egg." The most important parallel, however, is one that they do not explicitly draw, and that is between the BwO and Hindu tantra. Loosely speaking, tantra aims, not to suppress or transcend the emotional and physical energies of the body, but to embrace and transmute those energies through a kind of internalized, psycho-ritual alchemy.[3] Over and against study and reflection, tantra emphasizes *procedures*: mantra, visualization, hatha yoga, ritual, all geared toward the transmutation of a fundamental cosmic energy called *shakti*. A serpentine store of this stuff, known as *Kundalini*, lies coiled at the base of the spine. This energy, which some claim is artificially stimulated by certain drugs, can be coaxed up the various etheric centers – or *chakras* – that lie along the central channel, or *sushamna*, associated with the spine. As metaphor and sometimes as practice, sexuality is key to this process, and the most paradigmatic tantric sexual procedure is the retention of orgasm in the male, an ascesis which helps transmute sexual energy into rarer and more potent elixirs.

I apologize for this almost offensively oversimplified account, though at the very least it reflects notions of tantra circulating within the popular discourse of bohemian or alternative spirituality. At the moment, though, I want us to hear the tantric echoes in Deleuze and Guattari, echoes that in turn will help us understand the alchemical dynamics of the rave. Here is Deleuze himself on courtly love:

> Now, it is well known that courtly love implies tests which postpone pleasure, or at least postpone the ending of coitus. This is certainly not a method of deprivation. It is the constitution of a field of immanence, where desire constructs its own plane and lacks nothing.... Courtly love has two enemies which merge into one: a religious transcendence of lack and a hedonistic interruption which introduces pleasure as discharge. It is the immanent process of desire which fills itself up, the continuum of intensities, the combination of fluxes, which replace both the law-authority and the pleasure-interruption.... Ascesis, why not? Ascesis has always been the condition of desire, not its disciplining or prohibition.
>
> (Deleuze 1993: 139–40)

The process whereby desire "constructs its own plane and lacks nothing" is intimately allied with the emergence of the BwO. And if one replaces the term "desire" with "energy" or "*shakti*," one can sense the continuity of this construction with tantric procedures – operations that, on an admittedly crude and ad-hoc level, inform both Goan trance parties and the "spiritual hedonism" of the freak subculture that gave these fetes their shape.

I want to make one more initial point. Despite the anti-authoritarianism shared by Deleuzians and underground ravers alike, it is crucial to emphasize that the BwO is, in many cases, a product of *tradition*. Perhaps better characterized as transmission, tradition is a consistent feature of spiritual claims: even the most anarchic and disruptive spiritual dynamics are often couched in terms of teachers, sacred texts, and initiations. This is certainly the case for the Taoists, for the Tarahumaras Artaud met, for the Sufi masters who may have inspired the tradition of courtly love, and even for Castaneda's simulated studies in sorcery. The BwO is certainly constructed, but that construction itself participates in transmission. Prophets of religious transcendence may proclaim novel revelations, but the closer one sticks to the powers of the earth – and that is what we are talking about here – the more likely it is that your line of flight emerges from an abiding spiritual matrix, however mutant.

One might legitimately argue that within the contemporary spiritual subcultures of the West – postcolonial, technologized, thoroughly disrupted by modernity – traditions of practice are either unavailable as such or hopelessly fabricated out of problematic and commodified desires for continuity and "authentic wisdom." In general, that may be true. But this condition does not obviate the fact that *procedural elements* of these traditions – the "algorithms" that drive the praxis of Taoist energetics, yoga, tantra, and even alchemy – have been transmitted by individual teacher-bodies into bohemian, psychedelic, New Age, and "alternative" subcultures. In addition, these subcultures, despite their provisional and open-ended character, invariably fabricate their own lineages, traditions, and networks of transmission. In other words, the contemporary production of the BwO, at least in the context of exotic mystical practices, drugs, sacred sex, and trance dancing, constitutes a "tradition" *within* the West, one that, while essentially anti-authoritarian, is passed on and refined as much as it is constantly reinvented.

The question of tradition interests me because Goa has become the site, both mythical and historical, for a sort of tantric hand-off between an earlier generation of Western trance dancers and today's psychedelic ravers. Whether or not Goa is the core source of rave spirituality – and we are right to resist such origin stories – the freak colony has *emerged* as a sacred birthplace, a font. The fact that this story is partly a construction of desire does not make it a mere myth. In a roundabout way, the narrative surrounding Goa in itself affirms the spiritual aspirations and tantric power of today's global psy-trance scene – because, for all its rhizomatic multiplicities and cyberdelic futurism, the scene demands a backstory for its embodied illuminations, a context-building tale about initiation and transmission. For it is in invoking such a tale that tonight's BwO can encompass the eternal return of its progenitors, and that something rather ancient can find its dancing feet again.

Profane illumination

At the tail end of 1993 I took a one-stop hop from New York to Bombay, before transferring to one of India's recently deregulated flights to Goa. At the airport I caught a taxi up to Anjuna Beach, which my Lonely Planet guidebook told me was one of the last hippie holdouts. We drove through broad rice patties and thick palm groves, and then into Anjuna, where the taxi dumped me onto one of the village's countless sandy paths.

After scoring a room in a local villager's house for two bucks a day, I was ready to ring in the New Year. Though I didn't know the location of the party, the auto-rickshaw driver did, and I hopped into his sputtering three-wheeled machine. The waning moon filtered through the cracked window, only a few days past the full. Soon we arrived at the party site: a tree-lined hill about a mile inland from Vagator beach.

The dance area was still quiet when I wandered in, nothing but a clearing lined with black lights. A few yards away, scores of *chai* ladies from nearby villages had laid out rows of straw mats and piled them high with fruit and cookies and bubbling pots of syrupy brew. People flopped out on the mats by the light of kerosene, smoking, sipping *chai* from scalding hot glasses, awaiting the dance. The international crowd was pretty evenly divided between furry freak brothers and hip clubbers strutting their cyberdelic stuff: incandescent sneakers, flared fractal jeans, floppy Dr. Seuss hats stitched with the bright mirrored cloth of Rajasthan.

Then an ambient raga began: the bubbling tablas and droning sitar of an Orb remix. A crowd of young Indian men in dress shirts and slacks set off fire-works. Then the beats bubbled into an insistent digital pulse soon punctuated with kicking bass thumps. Computer bleeps, digital winds, and melancholic arpeggios gradually layered the incessant beat, which approached the 150 bpm mark, where dancing breaks down into jitters and tics. The freaky dancers rode that edge, keeping the flow in their hips as they chased the looping liquid melodies with their hands. Occasionally a disembodied voice floated through the mix, triggering mindfucks left and right: "Music from the brain;" "There are doors;" "Everybody online?"

I made my way to the DJ booth, squeezing between dancers spinning in exotic rags and local children begging in filthy ones. Behind the mixing table stood an old-school hippie: long dreads, black jacket, and leathery, sunburned face. The man was slapping tapes into two DAT players run through a pint-size mixer. Alongside his stacks of black-matte cassettes stood a candle, a few sticks of Nag Champa incense, and a small devotional portrait of Shiva Shankar, sitting in *ardha-padmasana* on a tiger skin.

"That's Gil, one of the best," one of the Indians mobbing the booth tells me. What luck. Genesis had told me about Gil: an old psychedelic warrior from the Haight Ashbury, an intense being, a heavy-set bear of a DJ. "You have to find him," Genesis had said. "He's one of the links." But Gil was too lost in his craft to talk.

By 3 a.m. or so, the music grew heavier and the so-called "power dancers" took the floor: utterly absorbed, ceaselessly flowing, totally dedicated to the beat. Their bodies sought to express every oscillating pulse, every twisting melody and waveform, like Deadheads bonedancing in overdrive. Many shut their eyes, plunging through some private and glittering darkness while unsettling voices shot through the mix: "The last generation..." These people were surfing the psychedelic bardo, that liminal zone that variously evokes dreamtime and death, primal rites and apocalypse. My own limbs had first plumbed that zone during Grateful Dead shows in California in the early 1980s, especially during the legendary second sets. But in contrast to the Dead's notoriously loose if often resplendent noodling, Goan trance seemed more economically engineered for psychedelic journeying.

Let's be clear: most of the psychedelic characteristics of psy-trance are *functional* rather than simply representational. That is, they trigger and extend psychedelic perception as much as they signify it with characteristically "trippy" cues. Just as the combination of Fluoro-lite dyes and black lights seems to virtualize visible objects to suitably tweaked nervous systems, the music's sonic after-images and timbre trails disintegrate conventional spacetime and allow shimmering micro-perceptions to emerge on the melting border between soundwaves and internal sensations. Portals appear, resonating geometries that seed further cognitive and somatic shifts, while the relentless and essentially invariant rhythm – what the Australian-Goan DJ Ray Castle calls "quantum quick step" (ENRG 2001: 165) – at once anchors and fuels the voyage. Repetition becomes a carrier wave, the audible beats seemingly dissolving into pulsing nervous systems whose mutual entrainment brings on a collective intensity which transcends – yes, *transcends* – the usual dance-floor heat.

Enough of this. Seeking relaxation and discourse, I wandered over to *chai* land and plopped down next to a crowd of Brits. Pete was in pajama pants and an open vest, his aristocratic features oddly framed by long scraggly hair. Hunched next to him was Steve, a skinny blond rolling a spliff.

"Have you seen *The Time Machine*?" Steve asked me. "There's this noise that the Morlocks use to call the Eloi underground. That's exactly how it was five years ago when my friends and I first came to Goa. We heard this booming rhythm in the distance. We didn't know where the fuck we were, but we just crashed through the jungle with our torches. The sound was calling us. I got real paranoid that there was some alien intelligence directing the computers, like the Morlocks, summoning us to a place where they were gonna eat our souls."

Pete nodded as if nothing his friend says could surprise him. "My first party, I just got the feeling I was in some spiritual Jane Fonda gymnasium," he says. "Boom, boom, boom, and everyone going into trance. It was quite alienating actually."

I asked them how Goa parties differed from the raves in England. "Here people know about the history of freakdom, of free-form living," said Steve as he passed the smoke. "That vibe is carried forward with the music. In England it's not really freaky anymore. It's too organized. People are wearing the right kind of T-shirts, whereas here people will rip their T-shirts apart and run down the beach."

Steve and Pete's comments showed how Goa functioned as a locus of tradition. How "spiritual" you consider this tradition depends on your definition of the term. "Free-form living" implies sensual practices and low-commitment lifestyles at least as much as it implies supernatural notions of the Tao or spiritual practices of, say, choiceless awareness. But it is precisely this "pseudo-spiritual" mix, incoherent or even repugnant to observers but rather delicious to participants, which characterizes bohemian or freak religiosity – what I am calling its *spiritual hedonism*.

Steve's reference to *The Time Machine* also reminded me of the almost sinister edge to psy-trance's science-fictional imaginary, an edge most visible in the thankfully fading images and lore of the Grey aliens. Such images should curb any easy attempt to sacralize the dance floor as either a utopian site or an essentially archaic one. This is a music, a consciousness, ghosted by futurity, which for contemporary (post-)humans has become a great abyss, however full of marvels. In other ways, this consciousness is a testament to the seriousness of the scene's psychedelia, because serious psychedelia plumbs many spaces far outside conventional markers of the spiritual. If more mainstream clubbers are willing to sacralize the Teletubby bliss of MDMA, then psy-trance dancers tip their hats to the cosmic reptiles that snicker eternally from the inky depths of psilocybin or DMT. Shamanspace is no walk in the park.

But Steve's technological paranoia also reflects the trickiness of freak transmission, with its anti-authoritarian and free-form biases. Instead of formalized rites of passage, it relies on happenstance, personal contacts, the vagaries of underground media, and pure synchronicity. A defining element of this anti-traditional tradition is the emphasis on the individual's personal experience with various techniques of ecstasy, from meditation to drugs to unconventional sex. Decoupled from the cultural constraints that characterize most traditions, ecstatic technologies carry a powerful Promethean – dare we say Faustian? – ambivalence, and provide few safety nets.

In rave culture, these techniques also include the technologies and technologists (DJs, musician-programmers, blinky lights) that collectively engineer the dance. Submitting one's altered consciousness to such powerful electronic assemblages is nontrivial, because technology's great question – the question of control – is always left open. As with psychoactive substances themselves, our spiritual relation to technologies often takes on the character of a pact, an uncertain alliance. Bohemians have long recognized that such pacts imply a certain diabolism. In its very sonic logic, psy-trance suggests that the West's colossal pact with electronic and digital technology is driving us towards a radically post-human future. The fundamental paradox of this music is that in its path towards the ancient trance and a life beyond Babylon it must march straight through the manic machines of the *datapocalypse.*

Enough of this. As the first hints of sunlight streaked the night sky, it was time to return to the dance. Dawn, I discovered that day, was Goa's sweetest moment, both antithesis and reward for the night's long darkness. The bpms slowed, and the bracing attacks gave way to a smoother, more euphoric vibe. According to Goa's more self-consciously shamanic DJs, the change of pace had a ritual function: after "destroying the ego" with hardcore sounds, "morning music" fills the void with light.

As the dawn rays floated through the dusty clearing, a crazy quilt of beautiful people slowly emerged from the gloom: Australians, Italians, Indians; Africans in designer sweatshirts, Japanese in kimonos, Israelis in polka-dot overalls. A crowd of old-time Goan hippies ringed the clearing, gray-haired and beaded creatures who dragged themselves out of bed just to taste this moment. Eyes met, and flush bodies drank in the pleasure of their mutual moves. Eros charged the air, but I felt none of the sleazy, late-night vibes common to urban clubs. I recalled something Genesis had said on the phone, when he traced Goa's mode of ecstatic dancing back to 1960s London clubs like UFO and Middle Earth. "Unlike most popular dance, trance-dances aren't about sexual encounter," he said. "Instead, you dance like a dervish to accentuate your artificially induced mental state to a point that's equal to and integrated with an ecstatic religious state. You're seeking illumination, not copulation."

Now I knew what Genesis had been talking about. Gil's set was a story about illumination: after the initial hook compels you to get up and go, a gradual intensification of psychedelic effects brings the bodymind into a space at once heavy and incorporeal, an exquisite dark night of the soul that more or less matches the splintering plateaus of a drug peak. Dawn proclaims a sweet return, as the rising heat and light reconnect you to the human family, to nature and the faces of all your fellow travelers, radiating feelings at once loving and impersonal. However deterritorialized the core of the evening, its flights were mobilized inside an essentially narrative frame – a frame that, if not fixed in the archetypal basement of human consciousness, is at least hardwired by the metabolism of psychoactive substances.[4]

Genesis' comment also helped me realize something about the Goan beat, which to outsiders can seem inexcusably monotonous and unfunky. By minimizing syncopation and flattening any potential sinuousness in the grooves, Goan trance releases energy from the gravity well of the hips. This redirects the pelvic undulations that anchor the more sexual energies of dance, deterritorializing them across the entire frame, and especially the upper body.

Such displacement has been explained in part by the action of MDMA, which is notorious for generating libidinal attractions that cannot, for men anyway, be genitally fulfilled (Reynolds 1998: 246–8). But MDMA is a secondary drug within psy-trance, and even psychedelic phenomenology only takes us so far. Perhaps we need to invoke tantra's esoteric physiology. As Ray Castle noted, Goa's "sound frequency alchemy" revolves around "raising the kundalini serpent energy in the body's chakra system" (ENRG 2001: 162). In addition to the frequent use of ascending arpeggios and digitized glissandi, psy-trance's quintessentially impersonal and non-copulating beats might help trigger such ascendant energies. At the very least, these highly directed vibrations serve as immediate, functional analogs for the secret life of *shakti*.

Castle's rhetoric may simply be another example of freak appropriation of the East, alongside the Ganesha tapestries, Rajasthani handbags, and pervasive stink of Nag Champa. But I think not. In the midst of his morning mix, Gil introduced the mantra "Om Namah Shivaya," intoned over sitars and a bubbly beat. Spinning far outside of orthodoxy, East or West, Gil knew who he was invoking:

> Shiva, dread-headed lord of destruction and transformation, your electric drum heralds the close of the world.
> You dance with Shakti, refusing climax, among bands of wild youths and sneaky gnomes.
> Your blue throat holds the world's poisons, its toxins and psychoactive drugs. Shiva, you are stoned.
> Your serpents tongue our spines, fuck inside our cells. They proffer amines, the gnostic fruits that taste like
> no
> turning
> back.[5]

Freak transmission

Shiva, of course, is Dionysus' Eastern twin, giving Goa's patron saint an East–West doubleness that also marks the psycho-geography of the Indian state. As an Indian stoner I met in Mysore put it, "Goa isn't India." And Goa hasn't exactly been India since the Portuguese first colonized the area in the 1600s. Then, "Golden Goa" provided the kind of oriental luxury that allowed an already waning imperialist power to really go to seed. Miscegenation was encouraged, and some adulterous native wives reportedly took to dosing their husbands with datura weed, rendering the men, as one early account put it, "giddy and insensible" (Collis 1943: 38).

Goa remained in Portuguese hands until India seized the region back in 1961, and the largely Catholic area was still deeply syncretic when beatniks like Eight-Finger Eddie discovered its beautiful beaches a few years later. By the end of the 1960s, hundreds of thousands of European and American freaks were streaming overland into South Asia. Though Goan beaches like Calangute and Baga did not offer electricity, restaurants, or much shelter, they did provide sweet relief from the overwhelming grind of travel in the East. The impoverished locals, most of whom practiced a Western religion and were already used to Europeans, were largely accepting. Every winter a motley tribe of yoga freaks, hash-heads and art smugglers would gather, until the growing heat and the threat of the summer monsoon pushed them further on. Going to Goa was like going home for the holidays, and the freaks celebrated: Christmas, New Year's, and especially full moons.

Many of these transients were seekers, willing to weather the rigors of Indian music, meditation, and yoga in order to taste sacred forces. But, as heirs to bohemia, their desires for exploration also encompassed drugs, orgies, and general freakiness. This mixed mode is what I characterize as *spiritual hedonism*. Here the West's secular affirmation of the body and its pleasures, most certainly including aesthetic experiences, is no longer strictly contrasted with religious forces. Instead, pleasure itself is refined beyond mere sensuality, ramping up into an *outré* spirituality hungry for immediacy, energy, weirdness, and unchurched gnosis. Because of its taste for intensities, spiritual hedonism even includes room for strict asceticism alongside indulgence and a variety of "middle paths."[6]

Gil the DJ – who goes by Goa Gil in the West – was one of Goa's original spiritual hedonists. Gil grew up in Marin County in the 1960s, and fell in with Family Dog, the loose freak collective that helped spawn the San Francisco concert scene's heady sound and light shows before Bill Graham moved in. In 1969, fed up with "rip-offs and junkies and speed freaks," Gil made his way to India, where he encountered the *sadhus*, Hinduism's wandering holy men.

Hymns in the ancient Vedas describe these "long-haired sages," living in the forest, covered in ash and drinking *soma*, the ancient holy brew that some scholars believe was psychedelic. Today, millions of *sadhus* still drift about the land, gathering at huge holy festivals, or holing up in the Himalayas to practice yoga. Some are strict ascetics, some are simply beggars, while a select group, the followers of Shiva, resemble nothing so much as Hindu Rastafarians. These Shaivite *sadhus* wear their hair in long dreads and find spiritual sustenance in *charas*, India's yummy mountain hash. Before they inhale, the Shaivites cry out "Bomm Shiva!" the way Rastas bark "Jah!" They identify the force of the herb with *shakti*, the immanent power of creation the *sadhu* seeks to transmute back into essence.

Not surprisingly, the freaks took to the *sadhus*. Gil went whole-hog, living in caves, wearing orange robes, and coaxing the *Kundalini* up his spine. But he still found his way to Goa every winter, where he banged on acoustic guitars at the firelit drum circles. When Alan Zion smuggled a Fender PA in overland, live electric jams and pre-recorded rock became their yearly soundtrack.

According to Gil, these parties were the direct ancestors of raves. The crucial transition – from guitars to electronic dance music – occurred at the impressively early date of 1983, when two French DJs named Fred and Laurent got sick of rock music and reggae. About the same time that Derrick May and Juan Atkins created the futuristic disco-funk first called "techno," Fred and Laurent used far more primitive tech – two cassette decks – to cut-and-paste a nightlong aural journey out of industrial music, electronic rock, Euro-disco and experimental bands like Cabaret Voltaire and the Residents. Stripping out all the vocals, they designed their mixes to amplify the bacchanalia of hard-traveling psychedelic partiers, and it worked. Soon hipsters started slipping them underground tapes from the West. When the German trance maestro Sven Väth first showed up in Goa, he was amazed to discover that Laurent admired his earliest and most obscure 16-bit recordings.

Gil and his friend Swiss Ruedi quickly followed the Frenchmen, but the techno transition was not smooth. The freaks were attached to their Bob Marley, their Santana, their Stones. Once Ruedi had to enlist a bodyguard to ward off some rocker's blows. But eventually Goa's DJs managed to plug the functional needs of heavy psychedelic trance dancers into the emerging electronic land-scape of machine beats and trippy instrumental remixes. Within a few years, a distinct sound emerged.

When I interviewed Gil, he was adamant about the spiritual core of the Goan parties. "When I was fifteen, I'd burn certain colored candles and certain incense and invoke spirits. Now I'm basically just using this whole party situation as a medium to do magic, to remake the tribal pagan ritual for the twenty-first century. It's not just a disco under the coconut trees." He paused to light up a Dunhill. "It's an initiation."

At the core of this initiation, according to Gil, is trance, an experience of psychoactive grace. Here is the description he gave to the San Francisco writer and trance DJ Michael Gosney:

> When there's no problem, and everything's set up right, and the music just flows, then it can come to the point where you go into the trance, and everybody's going in a trance. And it builds and builds. When it's just perfect, and it's a perfect song for the moment, perfection opens up in that moment, and it keeps sustaining itself. Then it becomes so perfect in the moment, with the trance, magic starts to happen. Everybody all at once will start to get tingling up their spinal column, and outside of their skin, like your hair's standing on end. Everybody will be getting it all at once. It will be so perfect in the moment that that feeling just sustains....It can build and build and build 'til it comes to a point where it goes *sssssssshhhh* through everybody all at once, like a bolt of lightning.[7]

Gil's language lends itself equally to a Deleuzian or tantric gloss, but the real strength of his claims lies in their core appeal to experience. Besides a certain inherent ineffability, such experiences emerge as largely unspoken intensities within a cultural context that eludes and even actively undermines the usual anthropological markers of religion. The psy-trance party allows the commingling of age-old ecstatic techniques with attitudes and technologies that reject tradition in the name of an open-ended, novelty-seeking alternative technoculture. This mixed quality helps explain how and why the pagan primitivism of psy-trance's gnosis is also wedded to apocalyptic expectations. We return to move forward, accelerated.

As if on cue, Gil slapped on two remixes he had made while visiting San Francisco the previous summer. The original tracks were made by Kode IV, a German duo who bragged in interviews about producing techno tracks in five minutes. Gil blasted the tunes at ear-splitting volume, the first of which sampled Pope John XXIII, Aleister Crowley dropping Enochian science, and a *sadhu* shouting "Bum!" Then Gil played his "Anjuna" mix of "Accelerate." He towered over me as he repeated word for word the sample he cribbed from some flying-saucer movie: "People of the earth, attention." Gil's eyes bored into mine, as if he was channeling the message directly from the aliens. "This is a voice speaking to you from thousands of miles beyond your planet. This could be the beginning of the end of the human race." For a moment, I could hear the Morlocks call.

Spy in the *chai* shop

"Goa Gil" self-consciously presented himself as a carrier of tradition, and he slagged a number of Goa's younger DJs for being on ego trips instead of cultivating the proper devotional attitude. The idea that DJs carried the burden of the tradition made me even more intrigued to speak to Laurent, the French DJ who had pioneered the electronic parties back in 1983 but, to my knowledge, didn't spin at parties anymore. Gil hadn't been too encouraging: "He probably won't talk to you. He's very mysterious." He told me where Laurent could be found every day: in the last *chai* shop on little Vagator beach, playing backgammon.

I was not and never will be cool enough to ride an Enfield bike,[8] so I puttered my lame moped towards the cliffs north of Anjuna. Clamoring down bluffs packed with coconut trees and tall, pale teepees, I bumped into a Belgian I had met on New Year's Eve. He lived in one of the teepees and loved it. I told him how ironic it was that the temporary shelters of the nomads mistakenly called "Indians" by Europeans were now housing European nomads in India. This confused him.

The last *chai* shop on the beach was a grimy hut filled with folks as weather-beaten as the long wooden tables they hunched over. Some played backgammon, others sipped orange juice and *chai*, and everyone smoked. A sour-faced Indian girl serving up a bowl of porridge and honey pointed to Laurent: a scrawny guy in a Japanese print T-shirt, tossing a pair of dice. The man was gaunt and blood-shot, and his teeth were in bad shape. He looked like a hungry ghost.

Laurent gave a caustic laugh when I asked to interview him. But I took his lack of an obvious refusal for a go-ahead. He kept slapping the tiles with his partner Lenny, a balding, washed-out middle-aged Brit. "Art does not pay so I am forced to gamble," Laurent explained in a throaty Parisian accent thickened with sarcasm. He fiddled with my Sony mini-tape recorder, clearly bent on soaking this little episode for all the humor it was worth.

"The spy in the *chai* shop," mused Lenny as he drew heavily on a cigarette. Laurent cracked up, his laugh degenerating into an asthmatic coughing fit.

"You know, it used to be very bad here for spies," Laurent said, with mocking concern.

Despite his sarcasm and creepy laughs, I took a liking to Laurent. He also proclaimed Goa's fundamental contribution to rave culture – "This is the source of the source" – but he was low-key about it all. No mysticism, no nostalgia. "I am a simple person," he said. He gave his friend Fred the credit for first mixing electronic tapes at the parties, but said it was too experimental for the crowds. "Nobody liked it. Then I played and made it so people liked it. And now people like it all over the world." Laurent then let slip that he had some of his early party tapes, and I pressed to hear them. "Ah, this would be very, very expensive," he mocked. "We must draw up a contract."

Laurent told me he played the Residents, Cabaret Voltaire, Front 242 – but only after cutting out the vocals, which irritated him. I kept pressing him about his style. He paused, and looked me in the eye. "Here you make parties for very heavy tripping people who have been traveling everywhere. You have to take drugs to understand the scene here, what people are thinking."

Laurent's comment raises a vital point: how we address the spirituality of psy-trance turns significantly on how we assess the spirituality of psychedelic use, not in some half-imagined Neolithic or shamanic context, but inside Western subculture.[9] This is not the place to hash out this question, but it is important to note that the distrust of psychedelic spirituality partly turns on the *technological* dimension of drugs. As Goan parties prove, some of the most exalted states of the human spirit – cosmic communion, the integration of self and other, the sense of timelessness – can be triggered with molecules, programmed beats, and electronic effects. Even if you sacralize these elements, couching their technical power in supernatural over-beliefs or the performative power of the rave's *Gestalt*, there is still the problem of *the morning after* – which, given the psy-trance emphasis on dancing well into the next day, is more of a metaphor than usual. Think of it as a metaphysical morning after, a period of deflation, drift, and potential despair. It is during this period, which is rarely given much focused attention, that the merely hedonistic or "druggy" character of the psychedelic experience becomes most evident. Leaving the question of somatic costs aside, bohemian scenes still fall short because they rarely provide the cultural mechanisms that, in traditional psychoactive societies, allow people to integrate their experiences into everyday life.

In many ways, this resistance to over-beliefs or strict communal rituals is a good thing. Such "psychedelic agnosticism" goes a long way toward squelching authoritarian tendencies or religious delusions. Moreover, many looser and more ad-hoc quasi-spiritual contexts have emerged in the psychedelic and psy-trance community, as individuals and groups seek to deepen their experiences through art, environmental activism, meditation, yoga, group processing, or any number of occult techniques and interpersonal therapies. Also, the increasing popularity of *ayahuasca* sessions has focused attention on the spiritual intentionality surrounding serious psychedelic use. Because without the long-term transformation of the psyche and its network of embodied relationships the ecstatic trance may do little more than stage its own repetition – no longer as a meta-erotic ritual of rhythmic return, but as habit and jaded escape.

Holy Hampi

Towards the end of the 1980s, when Goa's electronic dance music had already become a distinct style, the tracks played at parties were produced in the West with the colony in mind. But some trance cuts were homemade. I met one German producer named Johan, a handsome fellow who had released tracks under the name Mandra Gora and lived in a huge house in a small inland village. His room contained little more than a bed, a batik print, and his gear: Macintosh PowerBook, Akai sampler, keyboard, DAT deck.

Johan arrived in Goa in 1988, when the trance scene was totally underground. "It was like a poker game no one could follow," he told me. Johan was not into DJing – he was one of those power dancers who treated the night as one long track. "With a combination of good music, a good spot, and good dancing, it's like a cosmic trigger goes off," he said of Goa's greatest rites. After a night's ride, Johan would return to his home studio, mix his vibes into new tracks, dump the bytes onto DAT, and pass the tape on to his DJ friends. "It was like a perfect feedback loop."

Unlike most music-makers or DJs in Goa, Johan didn't care about talking to a writer like me, because he knew that, in some sense, it was already too late. Goa trance was just beginning to emerge as a genre in the West, and he was prepared to take advantage of the future he accurately saw coming, a future of packaged tours, label hype, and marketed identities. As he saw it, the obscurity necessary for a genuinely esoteric underground was no more. "Soon we'll have a global digital network where everyone will know where everybody is all the time." He looked at me impassively. "What you're here to write about is already dead and gone."

It's a common story in subcultural scenes, especially musical ones: the better days were before. But in Goa this familiar hepcat tale directly recalled the religious paradigm that lurks beneath it. Though generally focused around a charismatic leader, the early days of a religious movement are typically characterized as possessing a directness and spontaneity later lost as the movement's forms and dogmas become routinized while spreading into larger populations. In its need to generate images of Goa's spiritual authenticity, the psy-trance scene has partly transformed the object of its desires into a simulacrum.

Johan's comment brought on the predictable melancholy of belatedness. Anjuna now seemed to me like a freak Club Med, with yummy restaurants, "authentic" primitive digs, and a currency that might as well have been monopoly money. I grew tired of interviewing DJs, most of whom displayed the same snotty power games endemic to Western club scenes, although here they were supercharged with the esoteric withholds of a gnostic elite. And the superficiality of the scene's purported relationship with India, either its culture or its people, grew more and more dispiriting. I began to sympathize with one gray-haired Frenchman I met, who first came to India in the early 1970s and had become a master of *sarod*. "These new people have no idea," he complained. "They didn't come overland, they didn't have to find their own food, and they never really got lost."

But the trance transmission was not done with me. One hazy, hot afternoon, I was hanging around the Speedy Travel agency waiting for a fax. A steady stream of freaks bought tickets for Hampi, in the neighboring state of Karnataka. "It is a very ancient place," a bronzed Dutchman rolling a Drum told me, describing what sounded like a Hindu Stonehenge 300 kilometers to the east. "I hear some German with a bus will throw a full moon party in the temple there."

That was all I needed. A week later, a creaking local bus spat me out at Hampi bazaar. Named after Shiva's consort Parvati, Hampi is not exactly an "ancient" place – the Hindu city fell to rampaging Moslems during Queen Elizabeth's reign. But the ruins that spread out for miles around the small, freak-filled village exuded a haunting, archaic calm. Green parakeets roosted in silent temples encrusted with jesters and monkey gods. Rice paddies lined the nearby Tunghabhadra River, which snaked past huge mounds of desert boulders. Across the river, a number of *sadhus* tended Shiva shrines and passed the pipe with hearty Caucasians who had turned their backs on the minimal comforts of the village.

I spent the days poking through ruins, munching cashew curry, or dozing on the mats at the Mango Tree, a simple and peaceful outdoor hash cafe on the banks of the lazy river. Local tourist regulations insisted they post an anti-drug sign, but the staff kept slipping their "Smoking Psychotropic Drugs Not Allowed" announcement behind a poster, so all you could see was the word "Smoking." Sometimes the white *sadhus* from across the river would show up, with their orange robes and mala beads and ancient, fading biker tattoos. They were no joke, these white *sadhus*, however eccentric they may have been. I heard a marvelous tale about one fellow who vowed to spend a month sitting in one of the caves that peppered the landscape. After beginning his vigil, he was so pestered by other freaks coming to gape at his feat that he wound up letting a room in the village in order to fulfill his vow.

Gil had criticized the whole idea of a Hampi rave before I left. Hampi was where you hung with *sadhus*, he said, not where you threw parties. His comment reminded me that, despite the supposed spirituality of a good Goan fete, their hedonic logic did not exhaust one's spiritual life. Nor did it fit the psychogeography of "real" India, whose spiritual possibilities far outshone a mere rave.

In the week leading up to the full moon, I could understand Gil's reservations. A noticeably trendier crowd moved into Hampi: nattier threads, better cheekbones, more cash. Rooms filled to capacity, kids slept on roofs or in temples. Finally a huge tour bus drove up and parked in the dusty bazaar. Slogans blazed across the side: Techno Tourgon, LSD 25, Shiva Space Age Technology. Jörg the DJ had arrived.

I finally caught up with Jörg on the day of the full moon. The BBC had just finished interviewing him, and the man was beaming, his blue eyes glowing with a mad lucidity. A huge bronze Shiva Nataraj danced on the dashboard, an image echoed in the Shankar tattoo on Jörg's taut naked belly.

Jörg was pure freak, too maniacally enthusiastic to cop a snobbish DJ attitude. "I used to be a typical heavy-metal rock 'n' roller. Now I am addicted to techno," he said. "For five years time now I listen to nothing else. Except meditation songs in the morning." Like many techno-freaks, Jörg's first Goa party was nothing less than a conversion experience. "You can laugh, but it was like seeing a keyhole to God," he said in a hoarse voice. He'd been back and forth to India ever since, selling Landcruiser parts at the Chinese border, DJing parties around Kathmandu, dipping in the Ganges with the *sadhus* at the holy city of Haridwar.

"I'm a little bit extremist," he admitted, grabbing a cigarette from a pack lying next to a crumpled photo of Bhagwan Shree Rajneesh. The previous year, after a month in Goa packed with drugs and dancing, and with hardly any DJ experience, Jörg set up his gear in Hampi's underground Shiva temple and threw the archaeological area's first rave. "After that party I feel like this big hole. I sat for another month under a tree. Nothing inside anymore." He fiddled with the five-inch Sony mini-discs he uses instead of DATs. "But believe me, to be empty and open to everything is exactly the right position when you come to India. You have to improvise."

Only hours before moonrise, Jörg was still improvising. After spending days finding the right official to bribe in order to throw a party, he made his case. "We talked for hours. We got to know each other very well. Then he said no."

So in the fading sunlight Jörg decided to cross the river into another district. He and his crew lugged their gear down the river's edge, and loaded the equipment into the same round, leather-covered basket boats the Portuguese explorer Paes noted when he passed through Hampi in the 16th century. Darkness descended, and they had no idea where they were going.

Hours later, hundreds of us ferried across the river in the same leaky boats. We threaded our way past crumbling walls and along paths lined with ominous palms, following a trail of lanterns a mile or so on to a treeless plateau of moony rock. We glimpsed black lights in the distance, hear the dull thud of techno. No *chai* ladies tonight. We were partying in Bedrock.

Jörg crouched over his machines beside a large boulder dry-painted with the appropriate icons for the night: peace, Om, anarchy. Though his music was old, his mixing rough and his generator tepid, Jörg soon sank the dancers into the groove. I started taking snapshots. Unlike Goa, where blissed-out hippies transformed into ferocious assholes at the sight of a camera, nobody here cared. An Indian *sadhu* passed through the crowd, joshing with a grizzled Italian in orange robes who occasionally whipped out a conch shell and blew. "Who is the holy man?" I wondered. "Who is the pothead?"

After a bug-eyed Jörg led us careening through an eon's worth of cartoon wormholes, dawn arrived, dusting the rocks with pale purples and rusty reds. Fairytale temples emerged in the distant mist, but it was no hallucination. Jörg climbed up on a rock and pumped his fist, exhorting us into a supreme embrace of the moment. The shivers came, the lightning flash, the exquisite plateau: it was nighttime, daytime, alltime. As the rising sun and the setting moon touched the horizons on either side of us, the heavenly bodies seemed momentarily to align and balance the fragile, fantastic orb on which we danced.

What follows such moments of pop gnosis is, as they say, another story. The great problem with experiential spirituality is that experiences pass. As I mentioned above, if there is no context or tradition of integration to work with the energies generated, then it's tough to say what will follow. We do not live by intensities alone, and destratification, particularly involving psychoactive substances, can leave quite a mess in its wake. Given the spectacle of the 1960s counterculture, we should be wary of any claims, spiritual or otherwise, that place an ineffable electronic gnosis at the heart of its global aspirations.

But it's easy to grow pessimistic at this hour, and so I'll leave the final words to Gil, whose hopes about Goa's initiatic trance-dance frisson are nothing short of religious sentiment:

That's when the seed is being planted in everybody's consciousness at the same time. The spirit has come and given that grace, and they've gotten something. Hopefully, they'll go home, and they'll live in truth, and improve their life…. They'll start to be more spiritually oriented, and hopefully that seed will flower and bloom. Light a light of love in their heart and mind. Make them more sensitive and aware of themselves, their surroundings, the crossroads of humanity, and the needs of the planet.

Notes

1 In late 1993, on assignment from *Details* magazine, I visited Goa in order to write about the psychedelic techno scene there. The piece eventually ran as "Sampling Paradise" in *Option* magazine. The present chapter is a reflective remix of the original article.
2 Interview with the author, December 1993.
3 A good popular introduction to tantra can be found in Feuerstein (1998), while Gopi Krishna's personal account (1967) is fascinating for its first-person and profoundly somatic account of *shakti*. For a scholarly analysis of the somatic side of traditional Hindu tantra, see White's (1996) excellent book.
4 This is a problem with the usual routine of dividing the night between various DJs, each of whom focuses on his or her own individual set: the overarching development of the night is usually lost. In this case, a little more "master narrative" may not be such a bad thing.
5 Daybreak (n.d.: 23).
6 See Bhagavan Das's freak autobiography, *It's Here Now (Are You?)* (1997) for an exemplary expression of profound spiritual hedonism.
7 Interview with Michael Gosney: http://www.radio-v.com/main/beam/innerviews/goagil/ (accessed August 10, 2002).
8 See Chapter 14.
9 For an interesting discussion of this question inside rave culture, see Tramacchi (2001). For a general overview, see Forte (1997).

Bibliography

Collis, M. (1943) *The Land of the Great Image*, New York: New Directions.
Das, B. (1997) *It's Here Now (Are You?)*, New York: Broadway Books.
Daybreak, L. (n.d.) "Shiva," in *Shards of the Diamond Matrix* (Katmandhu offset printing, privately circulated).
Deleuze, G. (1993) "What is desire?," in Constantin Boundas (ed.) *The Deleuze Reader*, Columbia: Columbia University Press.
Deleuze, G. and F. Guattari (1987) *A Thousand Plateaus: Capitalism and Schizophrenia*, trans. B. Massumi, Minneapolis: University of Minnesota Press; first published in French in 1980.
ENRG, E. (2001) "Psychic sonics: tribadelic dance trance-formation," in G. St. John (ed.) *FreeNRG: Notes from the Edge of the Dance Floor*, Melbourne: Common Ground Publishing.
Feuerstein, G. (1998) *Tantra: The Path of Ecstasy*, Boston, MA, and London: Shambhala.
Forte, R. (ed.) (1997) *Entheogens and the Future of Religion*, San Francisco: Council on Spiritual Practices.
Krishna, G. (1967) *Kundalini: The Evolutionary Energy in Man*, Boston, MA, and London: Shambhala.

Reynolds, S. (1998) *Generation Ecstasy: Into the World of Techno and Rave Culture*, New York: Little, Brown & Co.

Tramacchi, D. (2001) "Chaos engines: doofs, psychedelics and religious experience," in G. St John (ed.) *FreeNRG: Notes from the Edge of the Dance Floor*, Melbourne: Common Ground Publishing.

White, D.G. (1996) *The Alchemical Body*, Chicago: University of Chicago Press.

14 Goa trance and trance in Goa

Smooth striations

Arun Saldanha

Let us admit that we have attended parties where for one brief night a republic of gratified desires was attained. Shall we not confess that the politics of that night have more reality and force for us than those of, say, the entire US government?

(Bey 1991: 134)

Rave studies, poststructuralism and spirituality

The 1990s witnessed the consolidation of "rave studies" in academia. Research into electronic dance culture was from the beginning heavily influenced by cultural studies, as opposed to other possible theoretical trajectories such as symbolic interactionism or cultural anthropology (see Gilbert and Pearson 1999). Rave studies then inherited cultural studies' reliance on poststructuralist and postmodernist philosophers to formulate not only its objects of inquiry (the deaths of the subject, the sign, identity, reality, modernity, marketing, memory, and place), but also its evaluation of rave as a subversive phenomenon.

Generally speaking, this academic evaluation has been on the positive side. For most commentators, rave and club culture embodies one of the few sites in contemporary society where the cultural industry, patriarchy, bureaucracy, Oedipal family, heterosexism, surveillance, and the pettiness of community and traditional morality are effectively resisted.[1] They then largely reproduce rave culture's own discourse of transcendence of social difference, a discourse of absolute newness and exteriority to both systems of domination and everyday life. Let me call this transcendence a question of *spirituality*.

In rave studies, the usual lessons learned from poststructuralist and postmodernist analyses of Western power relations seem to be, first, that power is quasi-total and, second, that resistance only exists where power is perfectly absent; that is, resistance is self-sufficient, related to power only in terms of opposition instead of reciprocity, circularity, and ambivalence. The take on domination and resistance in this chapter will attempt to be more complicated than that, following recent work in critical geography (e.g. Atkinson 2000) to account for the possibility of resistance breeding power, and power breeding resistance.

Poststructuralism and postmodernism lend themselves quite well to an adoption in rave studies. The Nietzschean celebrations of desire, micropolitics, art, music, spontaneity, marginality, chaos, indulgence, and undecidability implicit or explicit in the work of Barthes, Baudrillard, Foucault, Irigaray, Lyotard, and especially Deleuze and Guattari, as Todd May (1994) has contended, betray a flirtation with older tropes of anarchism (see Bey 1991). We cannot, of course, conflate anarchism or the avant-garde with spirituality, but what is common to both is the self-proclaimed position *outside* of social reality. Poststructuralism avoids completely nihilistic conclusions from analyses of total power by exalting experiment to spiritual degrees. The close congruence of 1960s counterculture and poststructuralism in the events of 1968 and their aftermath suggests that it might not be too far off the mark to state that a certain structure of feeling of reinvented spirituality informed them both.

Now, this chapter won't deny that there is something "spiritual" present in rave. Neither will it impede the creative possibilities for secular philosophy and cultural theory of an engagement with some sort of spirituality. Instead, it makes quite a simple point: that spirituality can never be thought of and evaluated outside its situatedness in assemblages of power. Transcendence, peace, love, resistance just aren't the whole story. Although there are debates in religious studies about the social and cultural contexts of mystical experience (e.g. Rothberg 1990), power relations hardly ever come into the picture. Any engagement with spirituality, practical or theoretical, needs to connect to political analysis and a sense of responsibility or its claims of transcendence remain hollow, possibly hypocritical. The case study through which I will reach this conclusion is the rave scene in Goa, India, which might seem an extreme case, but I hope similar arguments about the dynamics of spirituality and power can be made elsewhere.[2]

Goa trance

The former Portuguese enclave of Goa, 400 kilometers to the south of Bombay, with a third of its population Catholic, started attracting white travelers at the end of the 1960s (see Chapters 12 and 13). The palm-fringed beaches and simple fisher villages of Calangute and Colva soon harbored small communities of hippies. Soon, when more and more "straight" Western and domestic tourists flooded in, some hippies left for the northern villages of Anjuna and Vagator, where to this day the tourism sector is largely in the hands of local people and many foreigners stay for a few months. The hippies' lives centered around nude bathing, smoking hash in copious quantities, and holding full moon parties on the beach. Electricity arrived in 1975, and the amplification of music became possible. The late Cleo Odzer's unique account of Anjuna's hedonistic heydays in the 1970s, *Goa Freaks: My Hippie Years in India* (1995), has to be read with caution, as her experience, say many generational survivors, cannot be transposed to all foreigners then present. Indeed, Anjuna has always had close connections with the Osho Commune in Poona (see Chapter 12), *sadhus* (wandering Hindu holy men), yoga, Ayurveda, meditation and New Age practices such as Reiki and palm-reading. Karma, mandalas, auras, and chakras figure in everyday conversations. Anjuna's hedonism and spiritualism have therefore always existed, not side by side, but implicated in each other, thereby together propelling the scene forward.

By the early 1980s, despite the heroin deaths, smuggling scandals, and widespread paranoia, Anjuna had become a must-see place for all sorts of punks, New Agers, musicians, bohemians, Rastafaris, and globetrotters from Europe, North America, Latin America, and Oceania. Thousands attended full moon and end-of-the-year parties on the beach and in the forests. By this time, the urban middle classes of Bombay, Poona, Delhi, and Bangalore had heard of not only the naked or semi-naked white women on the beach, but also the fun to be had at the huge parties, and domestic tourism to Goa was institutionalized, with much of the marketing firmly confirming Indian sexist stereotypes of white women. The supply of all sorts of narcotics was secure, the sound systems were powerful, the Goan cops and politicians were routinely bribed, the locals made money through selling *chai* (tea) and snacks at parties and on the beach, and some of the newest dance music from Europe and the U.S. was played at the parties, which are traditionally free. It was this fertile ground that lead to *Goa trance*.

Between 1982 and 1985, Goa's DJs were gradually abandoning psychedelic rock music and reggae and started playing exclusively electronic sets, taking a strong liking to industrial new wave, electro pop, and proto-techno like Front 242. DJs like Goa Gil looked for the weirdest bits of the tracks and looped them. Music lovers would bring back tapes from Goa and try to recreate the exciting LSD-induced atmosphere of Anjuna's open-air parties in their studio. The resulting tracks would become Goa hits during the following season. Thus "Goa trance" was born by the closing of the decade, in a circuit of tapes, acid, and travelers. Neither techno nor house, Goa trance meticulously simulates the neurological effects of LSD with the help of a steady kick drum, swirling layers of staccato sounds often in Eastern scales, outworldly samples and hypnotic alterations in timbre. By 1994 or so, the distinct sound and fluorescent Hindu-kitsch-meets-fractals imagery of the genre was consolidated and available on CD.

Goa trance raves subsequently spread all over the world, not only to Germany, France, Britain, and Sweden, but also Israel, Thailand, Japan, Australia, Portugal, South Africa, Brazil, Hungary, and Russia (see Chaishop 2002). Meanwhile in Anjuna there were regular outbursts in the local press about the decadence and profound corruption of the trance scene, and often the police would crack down on the parties (cf. Saldanha 2002a). The season of 1999–2000 saw the definite commercialization of Anjuna's party scene, with Rupert Murdoch's Channel V hosting the last of a series of cosmopolitan parties for the Indian rich in the tiny village. Sponsorship, entry charge, magazine and documentary reports, London club hosts, and growing numbers of charter and domestic tourists are now increasingly turning Goa into a new sort of Ibiza (see Chapter 12).

Faces and bodies

To offer a sense of how poststructuralism relates to spirituality, let me focus on the collaborative work of Gilles Deleuze and Félix Guattari. In Plateau 7 of their

A Thousand Plateaus (1987: 167–91) they introduce the concept of faciality. In brief, it refers to the machinic, as opposed to ideological, phenomenological, or psychoanalytical system whereby bodies become differentiated in (Western) social formations. "Machinic" means that we have to look at how bodies *work*. We can then see that bodes are "facialized" through the material connections that they make with environments, signs, sounds, and objects such as clothes, all of which become facialized themselves. But calling this process "facialization" points to the fact that identification occurs primarily though vision and emotion. The "black hole" of subjectivity libinally invests in a grid of social identities (man *or* woman, rich *or* poor, white *or* black, etc.); the "white wall" of significa-tion imposes limits to what can be represented. The black hole/white wall system of faciality, Deleuze and Guattari say, is particularly vehement in the Judeo-Christian and colonial structures of Europe. This is because it succeeds in abstracting itself from concrete bodies and places, lending itself the possibility of becoming actualized elsewhere. More and more bodies and places can then be accommodated in a grid which becomes increasingly fine. The white European faciality machine is therefore self-replicating and expanding.

René ten Bos and Ruud Kaulingfreks (2002) rightly assert that the concept of faciality is rather determinist and isolationist, as if faces are fixed once and for all and do not interact with each other. If we compare Plateau 7 with Erving Goffman's writing on the face (1972), we see that while subjectivity and signification do reproduce power relations, is it not that bodies remain passive when they are facialized. Bodies are simultaneously capable of supporting faces *and* reworking them in the improvisatory mutual involve-ments of everyday life. If Deleuze and Guattari choose to think about the social in "cybernetic" terms (1987: 177, 179), the only "way out" for them seems to be necessarily crypto-anarchic: all facialization is bad, and all corpo-reality good.

Thus, face and body in Plateau 7 are dichotomously positioned in relation to each other. There is a homology with other well-known Deleuzo–Guattarian bina-ries: the "arborescent" thought of "state philosophy" against the "rhizomatic" thought of "nomadology"; "reterritorialization" versus "deterritorialization," "molar" versus "molecular," "majoritarian" versus "minoritarian," and "organism" versus "Body-without-Organs." Deleuze and Guattari say that an organism is only one way of organizing the organs of a body (limbs, mouth, skin, genitals, eyes), making them function in relation to each other, to other bodies, and to spacetime in particularly fixed ways. What they call (after Artaud) the Body-without-Organs, or BwO is, instead, the entire immanent range of potential actions a body is capable of, *prior* to any social organization (see Plateau 6). While faciality is only possible by tapping from the BwO, Deleuze and Guattari feel that certain bodies, like artists, sadomasochists, musicians, drug-takers, and anorexics, are more "in tune" with the BwO than others (provided they go about their experimentation in a careful manner). Witness the blend of spiritualism and anarchism in the following passage:

To the point that if human beings have a destiny, it is rather to escape face, to dismantle the face and facializations, to become imperceptible, to become clandestine, not by returning to animality, nor even returning to the head [of "primitive" society], but by quite spiritual and special becomings-animal, by strange true becomings that get past the wall and get out of the black holes, that make *faciality traits* themselves finally elude the organization of the face – freckles dashing toward the horizon, hair carried off by the wind, eyes you traverse instead of seeing yourself in or gazing into in those glum face-to-face encounters between signifying subjectivities....BwO. Yes, the face has a great future, but only if it is destroyed, dismantled. On the road to the asignifiying and asubjective.

(Deleuze and Guattari 1987: 171)

The bodies which are freed from faciality are called "probe-heads" (*ibid.*: 190). Probe-heads then exist in spaces where bodies intermingle but the faciality machine does not operate, as is claimed about dance floors. A concept sometimes used in rave and club culture discourse is PLUR (peace, love, unity, respect), self-consciously tapping into the legacy of 1960s ideologies (see Chaishop 2002). Tim Jordan writes:

The BwO of raving is the undifferentiated state that supports the connections that the rave-machine makes between its different elements. This undifferentiated state is a collective delirium produced by thousands of people jointly making the connections of drugs to dance, music to dance, dance to drugs, drugs to time, time to music and so on, and thereby gradually constructing the state of raving and so the BwO of raving. The delirium is non-subjective and smooth, as all the connections and functions of the machine give way to simple intensities of feeling.

(Jordan 1995: 130)

In Anjuna, participants are often exuberant about how nationality, skin color, class, and language cease to matter once everyone is dancing in unison to the forces of music and psychotropic drugs; all are in trance, become one with music, beach, ocean, palm trees, moon, stars, and sun.

Of course, Goa freaks aren't the first to decry the mystical force of music (especially repetitious music) and drugs (especially LSD). Alan Watts has described his experiences on LSD as properly Zen-Buddhist – on LSD, he understood that he and his surroundings were essentially made of the same stuff:

I was no longer a detached observer, a little man inside my own head, *having* sensations. I was the sensations, so much so that there was nothing left of me, the observing ego, except the series of sensations which happened – not to me, but just happened – moment by moment, one after another.

(Watts 1960: 138)

It is striking to see how many points connect Watts' philosophy to that of Deleuze and Guattari: against duality, against representation, against social conditioning, and for the pure "eventness" of the event.

> When, therefore, our selection of sense-impression is not organized with respect to any particular purpose, all the surrounding details of the world must appear to be equally meaningful or equally meaningless. Logically, these are two ways of saying the same thing, but the overwhelming feeling of my own LSD experiences is that all aspects of the world become meaningful rather than meaningless. This is not to say that they acquire meaning in the sense of signs, by virtue of pointing to something else, but that all things appear to be their own point....A chicken is one egg's way of producing others. In our normal experience something of the same kind takes place in music and the dance, where the point of the action is each moment of its unfolding and not just the temporal end of the performance.
>
> (Watts 1960: 135)

Timothy Leary (1980) famously researched the psychedelic experience and concludes not only that it meets all requirements of a truly religious revelation, but that revelation is also comparable to any scientific discovery of cosmic, biological, and sociological order. Slightly more sober than Leary's is Dan Merkur's Freudian view (1998) of the self-actualization process through the intake of psychoactive drugs. Gilbert Rouget (1980) provides a survey of the anthropology of shamanism and ecstasy. It does seem that rock concerts and raves share certain musical, psychical, technical, and social aspects with trance situations in non-Western cultures. And Régis Airault (2000) uses Jung's concept of "oceanic feeling" to explain why young people wish to "lose it" and prolong their infancy in Goa's "never-neverland."

The dance floor, the LSD trip, globetrotting, trance, and meditation then acquire the characteristics of what Deleuze and Guattari call "smooth space," the space of truly creative connections, fractalization, and flight. The space of faciality is by contrast "striated," the quantified and segregated spaces of capitalism, colonialism, the city, and the state (see Plateau 14). Following Watts, Leary, Merkur, and Airault, we'd think Goa trance and trance in Goa a particularly intense instantiation of smooth space. Well, it is. As said, I do not question the existence of smooth spaces and the truly religious aspect of rave, but their ontological primacy and oppositionality to domination, faciality, striation. Tim Jordan warns that "[t]here is nothing in the BwO of raving that would prevent rave-events incorporating, for example, sexism or racism" (1995: 139), and Maria Pini (1998) is one of the few who have empirically shown that ravers can be inconsiderate, feel pain, feel fear, be broke. Although Plateau 14 is at pains to show that the smooth and the striated presuppose each other and can only exist in their concrete combinations, the feeling remains that Deleuze and Guattari, a little like Timothy Leary, unduly celebrate *any* smoothness above any striation. What if probe-heads are the ones striating? What if dance floors are themselves segregated? What if PLUR becomes exclusionary? What if tripping doesn't take you further from, but closer into politics?

Smooth striations

In the remainder of this chapter, I will use some ethnographic evidence from Anjuna to show how mystical experience can be connected to exclusionary politics (see also Saldanha 2002b). It is important to know that there are many individual differences amongst the hippies and ravers of Goa. I will be making generalizing statements about *tendencies* inherent in the psychedelic trance scene as a whole. Those that are familiar with Goa's rave scene may find my reading idiosyncratic, but during my fieldwork I have found many participants themselves formulating similar critiques.

Chillum ritual and clique formation

A practice which has been central to the culture of Western travelers in India since the end of the 1960s is the smoking of *chillums*. The chillum is a simple cylindrical terracotta pipe which has been used for thousands of years by Hindu *sadhus* for smoking *charas* (hashish) and *ganja* (marijuana) and is now a central object in psy-trance culture. In Anjuna, an arrival at a rave or bar, a good track, a sunset or a sunrise is rarely unmarked by a chillum. It is practically impossible to smoke alone. Circles of smokers lighting or receiving the chillum often mutter praises to Shiva like "Bom Shankar." The smoking itself is a little more tricky than smoking a joint. Richard Neville instructs, back in 1970:

> Hold between thumb and four fingers (pointing straight up and bunched together at tips) of left hand. Wrap right hand around the back of left hand, leaving a hole for mouth between thumb and first finger on left hand, closing any other gaps by holding more tightly and adjusting grip. Test by drawing strongly before lighting. Keep chillum upright, head to one side and get someone else to light it. Beware of hair going up in flames. Constant strong drawing is necessary to keep it alight.
>
> (Neville 1970: 248–9)

A similar purposeful attention to ritual detail characterizes chillum preparation and cleaning. Cigarette tobacco is dry-heated and emptied in a mixing bowl, often a shaved piece of coconut shell; hash is added and the mixture is kneaded while maintaining conversation, staring, or dancing. During chillum-making, friends, and friends of friends, eagerly appear around the chillum-maker. There are only six to ten hits from a chillum, and not every psy-trancer assumes the role of chillum-maker. There can be irritation about "chillum hoppers" who use their popularity to grab hits everywhere around the rave or bar without making any chillums themselves. After the last smoldering bits are skillfully blown out of the top, the stone inside is removed, and a friend holds one end of a *safi*[3] as it is pulled and rubbed through the chillum to clean it. By peeping through the hole in the direction of a light source, the smoothness of the shaft is checked; if the chillum is sufficiently expensive not a particle should remain. Then the whole process starts anew. Goa freaks can do this the whole day long: heating, mixing, filling, lighting, smoking, cleaning, peeping.

The amount of smoke one obtains from a chillum is much tougher for the lungs to digest than is the case with joints. The idea is, moreover, to impress with the sheer volume of smoke ingested. If the first smoker's head is clouded by fumes, one can hear encouraging laughs and cries of "Bom Shankar!" No wonder, then, that one can hear coughing everywhere in Anjuna, especially during the morning. The thicker the cough, the cooler. But no matter how frequent the smoking or how potent the hash, you're not supposed to get stoned in Anjuna. The giggles, talking bullshit or philosophy, sleepiness, sluggishness, munchies, and staring into space that are often associated with cannabis are very much avoided amongst Goa's regulars. One is to keep one's cool, manage the THC (tetrahydrocannabinol) in the blood, keep talking and walking straight.

The practical knowledge of coordinating hands, lungs, mouth, brain, legs, and eyes necessary successfully to smoke the chillum has to be acquired, of course. And those who have acquired it tend to stick together. This is what Sarah Thornton (1995), following Bourdieu, calls "subcultural capital." She argues that subcultural capital leads to hipness as an exclusionary identification. If a somewhat naive tourist at a rave attempts to open up a chillum circle and asks for a hit, it will be only with the greatest reluctance that the thing is shared. Being admitted into the most privileged of chillum circles – the "posse" around the DJ and organizers of raves (restaurant owners, drug dealers, and some local men) – is little short of a blessing.

And so, the chillum produces cliques of Italians and Israelis, French speakers and English speakers, old-timers and newcomers. Within the cliques, there is a certain degree of smooth space, communion, spiritual becomings-smoke, becomings-*sadhu*, becomings-Shiva. But every organ still does what it does in other situations. In fact, effectively denying the chemical impact on the brain, there is even more organization required than if one didn't smoke; it is the discipline which makes chillum space hermetic. And outside the chillum circle there roam the package deal tourists, domestic tourists, and backpackers passing through Anjuna who can't manage the hash, don't even know where to buy it, and might find all the ritualism quite silly or else intimidating.

Sunrise politics

Since about 1997, Goa trance music has become progressively darker and more minimal. The old type of multi-layered, twinkling, and spiraling trance gave way to a predominance of a frighteningly deep kick drum and industrial percussive noises, sometimes getting very close to some Detroit techno and hard electro, with the only reminder of the old Goa sound located in the bass riff and some weird pad sweeps. Many no longer speak of "Goa" but psychedelic trance (abbreviated to psy-trance), "progressive" trance, psy-tech, or acid techno (cf. Chaishop 2002). In Anjuna, this musical evolution had a strange impact. Many of the older hippies and local boys prefer the older, happier Goa trance, while the younger generation of ravers now finds Goa trance tacky, "too hippie." Most of the charter and domestic tourists, too, find the new minimal trance too heavy and depressing. As I will argue, this fissure in tastes has made the striation of smooth dance-floor space possible.

At parties, especially those of late December, the presence of charter and domestic tourists was always resented by the hard core of hippies and ravers. It is felt that especially Indians are dressed stupidly, can't dance, become drunk, and constantly ask for chillum hits and harass white women. Freaks always tended to arrive a bit later to ensure that domestic tourists wouldn't be too plentiful. Moreover, already in the 1970s, *sunrise* had attained intense subcultural significance in Anjuna's party culture, inciting, through its warmth and light, the feeling of being visible again, alive again. Still, to get as much out of the acid and music trip as possible, most freaks in Goa's early rave scene would get to the party by midnight and often start dancing straightaway.

In 1998, I visited Goa for my first research trip. While it was already apparent that the hard core were arriving later, at 4 or 5 a.m., nighttime was still populated by a mixed crowd, and the music was still enveloping and invigorating enough to convey a lively atmosphere. By 2000, however, all DJs had quite abruptly switched to darker trance, and nighttime at parties had become a rather dead affair. Raves in Anjuna hardly ever have more than a few blacklights, so if there are few people dancing, there is hardly any visible movement. The darkness of the music coincides with the darkness of the dance floor. At night, the majority of the dancers are middle-class males from Bombay, plus a handful of local boys and some white package-deal tourists. The hippies and ravers who stay in Anjuna for much longer periods of time sit patiently, smoke chillums, and drink *chai*. "Too many Indians" was by then a much-heard justification for going through such pains.

This was even more apparent during the 2001–2 season: a few dozen domestic tourists trying to make the best of it until the party would properly take off at dawn, when the freaks started streaming in, most of whom had just awoken. It is a self-replicating process: the *thinner* the presence of the freaks at night, the more *massive* the Indian presence, the duller the party, the later other freaks arrive. Under the sun, the reverse: the sheer visibility of the few domestic tourists left on a dance floor full of whites makes them uncomfortable enough to leave.

When prompted about it, a DJ admitted he intentionally plays the very dark trance at night to make "the Indians" leave. The hardest tracks are reserved for the period just before dawn. Then, epic "morning trance" is played, after which DJs will switch back to progressive and psychedelic trance till noon or later. By this time, however, the dance floor is full of spirit, smiles, togetherness, sociability, and mystical connections with sun, music, earth, hash, and acid. And thus the music, so monotonous before, makes sense now. But all this smoothness is only achieved by a subtly concerted form of excluding others from the primary moment of the party – the morning session. During the night, the whole village of Anjuna is kept awake just for the build-up of the party – and this, in high season, several times a week.

Noise pollution

In Anjuna, there is an enormous difference between the sonic landscape during winter and during summer and monsoon. Goan villages of comparable size serve as a test case. There, life is rather slow, traffic consists of a few motorbikes an hour, perhaps one can hear TVs and Bollywood music, and most of the noise is made by crows and dogs. But from November to March Anjuna is completely transformed, doubling or tripling its population, and harboring hundreds of rented motorbikes and scooters, domestic tourism buses, taxi vans, auto-rickshaws, private cars, jeeps, and Land Rovers. On Wednesdays, with Anjuna's flea market, and during high season in the end of December, there are veritable traffic jams, with all the four-wheelers and their car stereos and horns – even at night.

The favorite bike amongst Goa freaks is the Enfield 350cc (some are 500cc), an old-fashioned, heavy motorcycle whose exhaust pipes produce a distinct thud discernible from up to a kilometer away. There is a hierarchy in the hipness to be attained by riding specific bikes – from the rare TVS moped, through the popular Honda Kinetic scooter and the Yamaha 100, to the Enfield (only diehard health freaks cycle). The worst thing for one's cool in Anjuna is walking – only backpackers who stay for a few days do that. The warm sea breeze (the helmet law is not yet implemented in Goa), the narrow roads through paddy fields, the palm-tree shadows, the dodging of cows and buffaloes and potholes and schoolchildren, perpetually stoned: all add to the smooth-space experience of riding. The Goa freaks sit proudly saddled, shirtless (if they're men), looking straight ahead through their sunglasses as they ride through the coastal villages. Given the charming stubbornness of its engine, many males who have bought an Enfield for the season learn the art of motorcycle maintenance – spending days or weeks in the garage. Amongst all the object-signs of India incorporated in Anjuna's hippie and rave scene, the Enfield must be the one most spiritualized.

Then there are the hazards. Every year in Goa there are at least a dozen road deaths and many more minor injuries to riders (often due to LSD and/or Ecstasy), pedestrians and cattle. The air pollution may be slight, but yet so are most distances covered. I have mentioned the racket Enfields create. When a bar like Ninebar in Vagator closes, there is a cacophony of exhaust pipes. Some Goa freaks enjoy the thud so much they get their exhaust altered to increase the volume. It seems as if they want to trace their ego in thuds wherever they go.

So the smoothness of the experience of riding goes hand in hand with the striations of noise, accidents, ego, and sleeplessness. This is of course more so with the raves themselves, which are always open air and never far from houses. The older inhabitants complain about the noise of Goa trance, carried all the way to the surrounding villages. The big New Year raves go on for days. It would be impossible to mount raves of this scale in the home countries of the Goa freaks. But most of Anjuna's inhabitants are tourism dependent and therefore co-organizers of the scene, at least in the indirect way of providing rooms, food, bikes, internet access, drugs, etc. Only sometimes will they lobby to cancel a rave, for example when school exams are due. Those Goans who do not make any money from tourism, mostly middle-class Catholics, have vehemently opposed Anjuna's hippie and rave scene. Following successive moral panics in the press (e.g. "Beach parties raise a rumpus," *Goa Today*, February 1996; theme issue on the rave scene), the Goan government and High Court imposed a ban on loud music in 2000. Though quite consistently implemented during the first months of 2001 and 2002, the ban is often breached – bribes reach government officials too. Anjuna without loud music (in bars, at raves, in restaurants) agitates Goa freaks. Frustration increases as nearly every day there are rumors of parties, which are then inexplicably cancelled. Many foreigners feel they have an indisputable right to party, justifying their presence with the income the parties bring to Goa.

Over the last few years many disappointed ravers have stopped coming to Goa, going instead to Koh Phangan in Thailand, or Bahia in Brazil, or Madagascar, or trying to organize parties elsewhere in India. Any place in the sun where living is relatively cheap would do for psy-trancers. Ultimately, it is not exotic Indian spirituality (for some people I spoke to, not even the beach) but the psychotropic chemicals and trance music which attracted them to Goa. While Goa remains, of course, the "mother scene," psy-trance's smooth space could be created in any Third World village. However, it seems that at least for another decade or so no other place on earth will be able to boast as many eager DJs, dealers, and locals, and a legal and economic infrastructure corrupt and dependent enough to supply psy-trance parties for foreigners at the scale and frequency of Anjuna. It remains to be seen whether the party bans imposed by the courts and police manage to stop new freaks from coming to reconstitute the scene.

Conclusion

Poststructuralists in general, and Deleuze and Guattari in particular, seem to be the "natural" theorists for the study of the spiritualities of rave. This is because there is a strong correspondence between, on the one hand, the self-proclaimed freedom and transcendence of social difference in rave and club discourse and, on the other, the anarchic celebration of desire, disorder, and flight evident in poststructuralism. But what many ravers and poststructuralists do not realize is that power and desire, domination and resistance, regulation and freedom, discipline and trance, habit and transcendence cannot be so easily disentangled in social reality. Even if there are real mystical connections through music and drugs, there is a flipside to *any* "smooth space." The point of coining the term "smooth striations" was to show that many practices and spaces in rave can actually reproduce striations (of capitalism, state regulation, patriarchy, heterosexism, classism, nationalism, and racism) precisely *because* they center around music and drugs – because they are smooth.

In Goa, the trance state, the Enfield experience, ritual togetherness through smoking chillums, enjoying loud music, being cool, PLUR on the dance floor, and reverence for the sun all entailed exclusions or at least some sort of arrogance towards others. Due to the specific subcultural dynamics of the rave scene, those who feel they belong least to the rave scene are ultimately the Indian tourists. And, finally, when moral panics lead the Goan government and police to crack down on the parties, mainly for electoral or ideological purposes, the tourism-dependent inhabitants of Anjuna become the dupes. The 2001–2 season was a bad season for business. While this was connected to the events of September 11, 2001, it had far more to do with the erosion of Anjuna's reputation as a party Mecca through word-of-mouth and email reports about the zero-tolerance noise-pollution policy. The simple solution – legalize the parties but have them regulated in between villages or on the beach – is increasingly difficult to realize as corruption becomes more profound, venue owners and drug dealers greedier, competition fiercer, ravers more arrogant, and Goans more conservative about their local identity.

My criticisms of Deleuze and Guattari attended to their dichotomizing of the smooth and the striated. However, their materialist philosophy of social identification, revolving around the concept of faciality (amongst others), remains preferable to psychoanalytical, Marxist, or existentialist alternatives. In fact, their materialism might not be materialist enough: by adding a bit more flesh, a bit more terracotta, sunlight, exhaust pipes, and sleeplessness to my ethnography, I was able to argue that spiritual becomings and power relations are not so diametrically opposed as Deleuze and Guattari's cybernetic model suggests. If there is something to be done about things going awry in rave (as is obviously happening in Goa), we will need quite sophisticated methods of imagining the smooth and the striated. This will consist of admitting to the spiritual force of music and drugs, but also to their less benign effects, and, crucially, the empirical relations between the two.

Notes

1   See, especially, Steve Redhead's edited collection *Rave Off* (1993). See also Collin (1997), Currid (1995), Gilbert and Pearson (1999), Malbon (1999), McRobbie (1994), Redhead (1990), Richard and Kruger (1998), Rietveld (1997). Compare the more nuanced or critical perspectives of Gibson and Pagan (1997), Hesmondhalgh (1997), Ingham *et al.* (1999), Pini (1998), Reynolds (1998), and Thornton (1995). I am here deliberately conflating the categories of "raves," "dance music," and "club culture," as most of the methodology and evaluative schemes are common to the study of each.

2   The evidence presented here derives from an on-going Ph.D. project. I have been to Goa over the winter four times for ethnographic fieldwork: about five weeks in 1998, 1999, and 2000, and four months in 2001–2. The main method I used was participant observation and informal interviewing, inspired by microsociologies such as that of Goffman. Additional information came from press and magazine archives, emails, websites, novels, and interviews/conversations with local villagers, DJs, journalists, lawyers, activists, police officers, doctors, and academics.

3   A thin cloth used to prevent burning particles from entering the mouth.

Bibliography

Airault, Régis (2000) *Fous de l'Inde: Délires d'occidentaux et sentiment océanique*, Paris: Payot.

Atkinson, David (2000) "Nomadic strategies and colonial governance: domination and resistance in Cyernaica, 1923–1932," in Joanne P. Sharp, Paul Routledge, Chris Philo and Ronan Paddison (eds.) *Entanglements of Power: Geographies of Domination/Resistance*, London: Routledge.

Bey, Hakim (1991) *The Temporary Autonomous Zone: Ontological Anarchy, Poetic Terrorism*, New York: Autonomedia.

Chaishop (2002) "The psychedelic chaishop," http://www.chaishop.com (accessed June 27, 2002).

Collin, Matthew (1997) *Altered State: The Story of Ecstasy Culture and Acid House*, London: Serpent's Tail.

Currid, Brian (1995) "'We are family': house music and queer performativity," in Sue-Ellen Case, Philip Brett and Susan Leigh Foster (eds.) *Cruising the Performative: Interventions into the Representations of Ethnicity, Nationality, and Sexuality*, Bloomington, IN: Indiana University Press.

Deleuze, Gilles and Félix Guattari (1987) *A Thousand Plateaus: Capitalism and Schizophrenia*, trans. Brian Massumi, Minneapolis: University of Minnesota Press; first published in 1980.

Gibson, Chris and Rebecca Pagan (1997) "Rave culture in Sydney, Australia: mapping youth spaces in media discourse," unpublished paper, Division of Geography, University of Sydney.

Gilbert, Jeremy and Ewan Pearson (1999) *Discographies: Dance Music, Culture and the Politics of Sound*, London: Routledge.

Goffman, Erving (1972) "On face-work," in *Interaction Ritual: Essays on Face to Face Behaviour*, London: Penguin; first published in 1957.

Hesmondhalgh, Dave (1997) "The cultural politics of dance music," *Soundings* 5 (spring): 167–78.

Ingham, J., M. Purvis and D.B. Clarke (1999) "Hearing places, making spaces: sonorous geographies, ephemeral rhythms and the Blackburn warehouse parties," *Society and Space* 17(3): 283–305.

Jordan, Tim (1995) "Collective bodies: raving and the politics of Gilles Deleuze and Felix Guattari," *Body and Society* 1(1): 125–44.

Leary, T. (1980) "The seven tongues of God", in *The Politics of Ecstasy*, Berkeley, CA: Ronin; first published in 1963.

McRobbie, Angela (1994) "Shut up and dance: youth culture and changing modes of femininity," in *Postmodernism and Popular Culture*, London: Routledge.

Malbon, Ben (1999) *Clubbing: Dancing, Ecstasy and Vitality*, London: Routledge.

May, Todd (1994) *The Political Philosophy of Poststructuralist Anarchism*, Pennsylvania: Pennsylvania State University Press.

Merkur, Dan (1998) *The Ecstatic Imagination: Psychedelic Experiences and the Psychoanalysis of Self-actualization*, New York: SUNY Press.

Neville, Richard (1970) *Play Power*, London: Paladin.

Odzer, Cleo (1995) *Goa Freaks: My Hippie Years in India*, New York: Blue Moon.

Pini, Maria (1998) "'Peak practices': the production and regulation of ecstatic bodies," in John Wood (ed.) *The Virtual Embodied: Embodiment/Practice/Technology*, London: Routledge.

Redhead, Steve (1990) *The End of the Century Party: Youth and Pop towards 2000*, Manchester: Manchester University Press.

—— (ed.) (1993) *Rave Off: Politics and Deviance in Contemporary Youth Culture*, Aldershot: Avebury.

Reynolds, Simon (1998) *Energy Flash: A Journey through Rave Music and Dance Culture*, London: Picador.

Richard, Birgit and Heinz Hermann Kruger (1998) "Ravers' paradise? German youth cultures in the 1990s," in Tracey Skelton and Gill Valentine (eds.) *Cool Places: Geographies of Youth Cultures*, London: Routledge.

Rietveld, Hillegonda C. (1997) *This Is Our House: House Music, Cultural Spaces and Technologies*, Aldershot: Ashgate.

Rothberg, Donald (1990) "Contemporary epistemology and the study of mysticism," in Robert K.C. Forman (ed.) *The Problem of Pure Consciousness: Mysticism and Philosophy*, New York: Oxford University Press.

Rouget, Gilbert (1980) *Music and Trance: A Theory of the Relations between Music and Possession*, trans. Brunhilde Biebuyck with Gilbert Rouget, Chicago: University of Chicago Press.

Saldanha, Arun (2002a) "Power, spatiality and postcolonial resistance: geographies of the tourism critique in Goa," *Current Issues in Tourism* 5(2): 94–111.

—— (2002b) "Music tourism and factions of bodies in Goa," *Tourist Studies* 2(1): 43–62.

ten Bos, René and Ruud Kaulingfreks (2002) "Life between faces," *Ephemera: Critical Dialogues on Organization* 2(1): 6–27.

Thornton, Sarah (1995) *Club Cultures: Music, Media and Subcultural Capital*, Cambridge: Polity.

Watts, Alan (1960) "The new alchemy," in *This is it and Other Essays on Zen and Spiritual Experience*, New York: Vintage.

15 Dancing on common ground

Exploring the sacred at Burning Man

Robert V. Kozinets and John F. Sherry, Jr

Where on Earth can you find tens of thousands of people gathering in a gigantic festival intended to provide a huge variety of entertainment? Where can you find people costumed, covered in glitter, or in feathers, riding unicycles, wearing funny hats, body paint of every color, or nothing at all? Hundreds of art cars and extraordinary vehicles, from starlit UFO taxi cabs to mobile taxidermied horses, giant glowing lobsters, Viking ships, or enormous flame-belching dragons? Endless miles of participatory "theme camps" – with names like Astral Headwash, Lingerie Planet, Mad Cow Country Club, Technofartz Camp, Porn Star Lounge, and the Temple of Atonement – where festival-goers artfully offer up to one another a bizarre concatenation of spiritual and carnal sustenance and smart, regressive, pop-culture-inundated, ironic fun? Dozens of radio stations? An immense range of art, from massive sculptures made of books to digital kaleidoscopes? Where? You can find them about 120 miles east of the city of Reno, in the middle of the desert near the center of the state of Nevada, in the United States of America. For one week every year, you can find this combination of unparalleled weirdness and breathtaking inspiration at Burning Man, and at no place else on Earth.

While it began in 1985 in San Francisco with Larry Harvey, Jerry James, and a small group of effigy-burning bohemians, Burning Man now hosts over 29,000 people, temporarily becoming Nevada's fourth largest city. In colonizing fashion, for one week the event's participants inhabit the bleak Black Rock Desert, transforming it into "Black Rock City." Burning Man also transforms social space, blending a "no spectators" experiential ethos with a variety of other important rules, such as "no vending" and "radical self-expression." For one week, participants come to live, celebrate, and co-create a utopian play space on the blank canvas of the desert floor, which is called the "playa." With its pioneering, endlessly experimental, libertarian, individualist, flag-flying, diversity-seeking, hardworking ethos, Burning Man could be considered a quintessentially American event.

Burning Man shares common ground with rave and post-rave phenomena, and with other contemporary events like neo-pagan festivals, women's music festivals such as the Lilith Fair, Oregon's Country Fair, and Rainbow Family gatherings. A variety of commonalities between these events can be ascertained.

Burning Man shares ideologies drawn from the human potential movement and New Age philosophies, invoking primitivist, techno-shamanic and neo-pagan myths, ideologies, and literatures. Although not exclusively a neo-pagan event (or any other distinctive or exclusive kind of event), it contains many neo-pagan and sacred elements that we will explore within this chapter. It is a temporary spatial phenomenon that its participants construct as sacred and even utopian. Burning Man focuses on the ecstatic creation of community. It urges participants to celebrate embodiment and features radical inversions of social norms. It embraces the exploration and use of ritual. It is deeply entwined with the participative ethos of DIY (do-it-yourself) culture and politics (McKay 1998). It embraces contemporary technology, extensively using the internet as a recruitment, organizational, and communication medium (Gibson 1999). Like the "doof" – an important post-rave manifestation (see St. John 2001; Tramacchi 2000) – it is opposed to commercialism and commercial sponsorship, seeks a participative ethos, and follows an environmental "leave no trace" ethic.[1] Finally, music (electronic and otherwise) plays a key role within the event. Due to its importance within this volume, we will introduce the role of music before turning to our central exploration. To demonstrate how a Burning Man participant's experience of the event is shaped by music, we will begin by considering and analyzing "Alexander's" recounting of his experiences after he entered Burning Man for the first time.[2]

> We stopped at another gate for info on where to set-up camp. Apparently there was a "quiet" side (South) and a "loud" side (North). We picked the "loud" side…. There weren't many signs of people, just a million tents and wisps of smoke slowly rising in the distance. In contrast, the spacey sounds of techno music were pounding the desert sky. It added to the surreal ambiance of this strange new world we had entered…Burning Man had lots of music. Yeah there was plenty of electronica in the air, but I also saw rock and reggae bands. One afternoon, I grooved for hours to a Latin band in the neighboring camp. Some complained of the constant techno dance music. The techno did seem to play 24/7 here.[3]

There are several important points to note in Alexander's account that link our examination of Burning Man to the investigation of post-rave techno culture. First, Alexander begins by telling us how, from the very first moments of their Burning Man experience, the sound of music spatially orients participants within Burning Man. The volume of music unites and divides Burning Man communities, as people arrange themselves preferentially in response to it. Alexander's experience of his social reality is also shaped by his interpretation of sonic reality at the event. Diversity in music can be seen as an expression of tolerance for diversity in culture and way of life. Grooving for hours to Latin music can be construed in some sense as an accepting experience of another culture, a signal of the expansive inclusiveness of Burning Man's culture. The ubiquity of the beat seems to signal a different type of social space, and perhaps the phase-shifting to a different timing for everyday life. The presence of 24/7 techno, rather than signaling a rave, therefore signals a liminal space (Turner 1967), a place that is betwixt and between, a site where the party is intense and ongoing. The techno beats also signify a sonic transcendence, a uniting of primal drumming with digital waveforms. Drum-dominated music therefore plays an important ritual role in Burning Man, as it does in post-rave. It grounds techno in the primitive, energizing the modern by rooting it in a tribal past.

In another part of his online recounting, Alexander describes the music as the "spacey sound of techno music" which adds to "the surreal ambiance of this strange new world." His use of the term "spacey" is doubly fitting. For music, by its sonic nature, defines a particular space. Multiple musics demarcate, blend, and merge on geographic boundaries, spilling into one another. At Burning Man, music defines and is owned, pooling into pure concentrations near encamped banks of speakers. Techno music's drum and bass heavy pulsing also has reputed abilities to induce altered states in listeners, creating a sensation of floating in space. Adding to the vastness of Burning Man's desert setting, dominated by sand, wind, and sky, the loud, pulsating music can seem to push the horizon – communal, geographical, and personal – to infinity.

The "techno" culture explored in this volume relates directly to the meanings and rituals of youth milieus orbiting around styles of music often referred to as "techno" or "electronica," manifesting in, for example, house, hard house, trip hop, trance, happy hardcore, drum 'n' bass, big beat and speed garage. This music is as unavoidable at Burning Man as it is at any dance party. Techno is the soundtrack to many Burning Man experiences, the unifying soundscape auguring the breakdown of old divisions and ringing in new forms of communality. Music is a key element in the expression of identity, and in the intensification of ecstatic sacred moments at Burning Man – as it is at neo-pagan festivals (Pike 2001: 5) and raves.

As with these other gatherings, Burning Man participants – especially those in the many drum circles and at the multitudinous dance camps – often "immerse themselves in the performance of dancing and drumming, releasing their bodies in ways unique to the festival setting" (*ibid.*: 191). Music also has deep ties to the sacred, existing in a timeless biocultural nexus where popular culture, emotion, and bio-basic responses collide. It is from this position in the ancient, embodied, and transcendent realm of music that we launch into an exploration of Burning Man's sacred elements, the commonalities with post-rave, and what these might illuminate about other events. Throughout the chapter we explore the common elements of Burning Man and rave culture, in particular focusing on the construction of the sacred, its therapeutics, and its relation to neo-pagan, New Age, and techno-pagan practices and discourses.[4]

Spirit healing

Let's begin this analysis as good folklorists and ethnographers would, by listening to a story of an inhabitant of this place. The place that we refer to is a little problematic here, since Burning Man is not a permanent location, its residents are not permanent citizens, and pseudonymous-but-expressive names are used through the event as a form of decoration or expression. In addition, this story was reported through email, another anonymous and uncertain medium. However, the story we present is typical of many other types of tale we heard while at Burning Man about the event's transformative properties. It was also chosen by the Burning Man organizers as laudable and worthy of distribution in their mass email newsletter. While many people consider Burning Man to be nothing more than a terrific place to celebrate, gawk or meet people, an undeniable quest for self-transformation also transpires. In interviews, some informants compared Burning Man with other ritual therapeutic events they experienced – such as personal growth seminars, dream quests, and sweat lodges. Others seemed drawn to the event by a sense that it was a place they could go to learn more about themselves. Friends also played a major role, often serving as the source of urging that culminated in the desert adventure: "you just have to go; it would be so *good* for you." Whatever the source, a range of different participants end up telling tales of Burning Man that are variations on the themes raised in the official Burning Man organization's website "Burning dreams" file and then shared with all the members of the Burning Man mailing list.

> For 11 or so years I've been in vague anticipation of The Event. First hearing of it on one of the variety shows that comes on late nite [*sic.*] Saturday nite, so many years ago. It took me so long because I really didn't know what I could have – what exactly was missing in me. On the playa, 2001 my first time, like the first time in my life I felt a freedom and a sense of being alive so intense that I never felt before, overwhelmed and strong. For an entire week I had goose bumps. And I realized many, many things that week. The meaning of life, and how it's not the same for everyone. That there are places that people can truly be happy and free. That I exist, I just need to know where to look. And beauty. Pleasure and beauty, the two most important things in Living. Beauty in all things. My dream for re-entry is my reality. To live for personal freedom and excavate all the bindings that for a while, I thought I needed in life to be happy. My entire life I've felt a sadness within me. A constant non-existence of meaning. Fearful of any good feelings, fearful that they may end. I've been in search of something I couldn't quite put my finger on. Organized religion always made me gag, and people in general arrrrgghh-ed me. But now, things are different. It's been over a month since The Event and there exists in me a constant of a dust-covered happiness. I found myself in the desert. My dream, is of living freedom. I'm a little new at it, but in my dream, I get better. My dream is of beauty and experience, my dream is of the outrageous and chaotic, my dream is of opening my eyes, and waking up.[5]

In this tale, Zelga articulates a kind of nomadic archaeology of self-realization, a kind of ceramic theory of the vision quest, wherein the dust of the journey (and the absent inventory of binding things) bears witness to one's trans-figuration. She hints to us that one may see truly only with playa dust in the eyes. She gains holism. But most important of all is the nature of this story as a tale of healing. For Zelga, Burning Man was therapy of the highest order. She was sick, sad, depressed, mentally ill by most standards. There was an emptiness, a hollowness that she couldn't fill. Religion didn't help. Even people in general could not help with the ailment. "The Event" – blessed, perhaps, as in rebirth or resurrection – is attended, and Zelga is cured. In terms that sound as if they describe a cure or a remission, Zelga notes that it has been a month and she is still well. She sees the vast web of connections, the beauty of all things in life. She dreams of being permanently healed: of getting better.

Zelga's sense of spiritual therapeutics is crucial to our understanding of Burning Man and many other contemporary festivals. Whether it is loneliness, inhibitions, repressions, guilt, pyromania, or any of a vast number of obsessions, participants view these events as places where healing happens. In 1999 we witnessed an obese and hirsute middle-aged man lying naked and outstretched in his tent while crowds walked by. Someone remarked as we walked by that his behavior was healthy. "Imagine," they said to us, "what this guy might do in the outside world if he didn't have this place." Thinking about this gave us a shiver – the thought echoed with wider social ramifications and responsibilities. At festivals such as Burning Man, healing is emplaced in permissive events that allow the expression of bottled-up desires. They may seek to cure an emptiness and sense of lack of meaning in life, replacing it with a holistic emphasis on vast and important connections between the personal, the social, and the transcendent.

Healing and holism are central concerns within the New Age and Neo-Pagan movements. According to York (1995: 8), it is in their healing and holistic emphases that these movements are in part outgrowths from the broader human potential movement. Viewed as part of a broader alternative spiritual move-ment, events like Burning Man, post-raves, and many other festivals might be seen to contribute to personal and collective development. They offer particular, dynamic, contemporary, sacralized, therapeutic, holistic flavors to their utopias. For instance, Hutson concludes that

> raves increase self-esteem, release fears and anxieties, bring inner peace and improve consciousness, among other things. Raves don't cure disease, but when someone claims that "last night a DJ saved my life", it is reasonable to suspect that at least some form of healing takes place.
>
> (Hutson 1999: 71)

Beckford (1984) recognizes the way in which groups and events involved in healing tend to relativize the institutional boundaries around practices usually confined to religion and psychiatry. In the discourse and practice of many New Age groups, spiritual belief and psychotherapy commingle. Yet, despite this commonality, we should acknowledge the immense pluralism and diversity existing within the New Age movement. As York (1995) indicates, New Age is an

umbrella term, which overlaps in places with Neo-Paganism, itself highly pluralistic and diverse. Both movements exhibit what is often called the "American
metaphysical tradition" (*ibid.*: 33), but Neo-Pagans tend to place greater
emphasis on embodiment, earth religions, ecology, and magic. While there are
other differences and similarities, Neo-Pagans tend to stress ceremony and ritual.
It is thus in their ceremonialism that post-raves and Burning Man relate most
closely to Neo-Paganism.

An important link between New Age and Neo-Pagan discourse and practices
and those of Burning Man and other post-raves is the centrality of ritual within
the healing practices of these groups and gatherings. York contends that "self-
improvement and self-growth orientations" constitute the *raison d'être* behind the
rituals of New Age and Neo-Pagan practitioners (*ibid.*: 11). To this, we would add
many of the various rituals performed at festivals and post-rave affairs, from ritual
drug use, dance, trance-invocation, to ceremonial social bonding. Outside critics
often decry the Bacchanalian aspects of these events as mindless intoxication. Yet
the institutional equivalents of many festival actions are recognized to be therapeutic: confessions, group therapies, exercise, prescription drugs. Regarding the
latter, altered states of consciousness are widely understood within the New Age
movement as legitimate forms of questing for meaning and spiritual experience
(see Ferguson 1987: 31). For participants at events like raves and Burning Man,
New Age and Neo-Pagan philosophies provide an ideological wedge allowing
them to insert rituals into a sophisticated and individually (rather than institution-
ally) driven process of healing the self. In the next section, we explore the specific
role that Neo-Pagan rituals and discourses play in this process.

Neo-Pagan connections

The central and culminating event of Burning Man has probably done the most
to give the event a pagan profile – although we, along with the erudite organizers
of the event, would contest singular and constricting assignments of meaning to
the ritual or the event itself (see Black 1998). A Neo-Pagan reading is only one
potential interpretation among many. Yet it is also important to realize that this
open-endedness is an important hallmark of New Age and Neo-Pagan philosophies, and indeed of many American religious movements that followed the
countercultural period of the 1960s. "With no central authority, New Age is not
doctrinaire and consequently means many things to many people" (York 1995:
35). Communications on Burning Man's website emphasize the open-endedness
and individualism of the event. Here is a small section from an article entitled
"What is Burning Man" that blends this open-endedness of ritual interpretation
with distinct promises of sacred, transformational experience:

> On Saturday night, we'll burn the Man. As the procession starts, the circle
> forms, and the man ignites, you experience something personal, something
> new to yourself, something you've never felt before. It's an epiphany, it's
> primal, it's newborn. And it's completely individual.[6]

One of the most interesting aspects of Burning Man's open-endedness is the ways in which it has allowed participants to hybridize new and ancient forms of technique, technology, or ritual. The effigy of the Man blends past and future, science and religion, high technology and the primal: a gigantic 50-foot tall figure, reminiscent of the statuary and sanctuary of old times, a symbol of humanity raised up from the ground to reach the sky. He is constructed of wood, of trees, of ground, of nature, combined with technological contraptions harnessing fire and electronics, with two brilliant colors of neon tubing. The Man hums with electricity and is in this sense alive. Before being burned, he will raise his hands skyward, exhorting the crowd, possessing motion. He is duplicated every year. Like the seasons, like the sun, like life itself, he returns from the fire and dust, resurrected. The ritual and the ritualists vivify him.

As the time for the burning draws closer, a wild spectacle is enacted. The stage is filled with fire-twirlers. Masses of drummers unite in a thrumming, pounding, amplified throb of rhythm. Glowing decorations and desert-wear finery abound as the onlookers gather to celebrate the epiphanic and eponymous moment of the gathering. Orbs of fire and gigantic flamethrowers pour heat into the quickly cooling night air. Screams of joy and thrills of awe ring out. Dozens upon dozens of twirlers and drummers perform their hearts out, and the effects are nothing short of hypnotic. The exuberant crowd presses in upon you from every side. Just like it does at a rock concert, the scent of ritual burnings and smoking fills the air. Cameras are everywhere. Documentaries are filmed. Radio shows and webcasts broadcast the event live.

As the crowd gasps, the Man's arms are raised skyward. He is readied to be burned. As the tension mounts, the Man is set ablaze. Filled with pyrotechnics, he blasts from inside and shoots out flame, expressing (for us) his mortality, his sacrificial power, the value of the moment, of this moment, of all moments. Fire becomes the central all-consuming symbol of the moment, a symbol that stands for both the technological and the primitive, heavily invested with linkages to central social concepts, from community to technology. The Man falls, his essence rising finally to the sky in a heaving puff of smoke. He is a tired idol, a toppled god. After the crashing descent of his remains, the audience is then free to rush around his fire, to throw their own artworks and creations into it, to circle it and drum, sing, and dance orgiastically until the dawn – and, of course, to debate the ever changing meaning of it all, as they await the rising of the Man from these ashes in the coming year.

Like many elements of post-rave, the burning of the Man opens up opportunities to embody a popular dance orgiasm facilitated by modern technologies. It also stands as a fiery experiential canvas on which new ideologies and new selves are written, perhaps to be blown away like dust, perhaps to be sealed in stone. For the purposes of this exploration, the giant Man burning ritual opens up opportunities to discuss the relevance of Neo-Pagan interpretation of the events, and to use these to open up discussions of techno-paganism.

What exactly are Neo-Pagans and how do they relate to festivals such as Burning Man? Pike considers "Neo-Pagans" to be people who are "reinventing ancient pagan traditions or creating new ones," shaping those traditions "to meet the needs of contemporary Americans and Europeans" (2001: 27). Pearson *et al.* similarly define "contemporary Paganism" as

> a general and inclusive category for a range of specific traditions, all of which may in varying degrees be described as *nature religions* in the sense that they involve a reorientation towards, and a resacralization of, both external nature and our own physical embodiment.
>
> (Pearson *et al.* 1998: 1; italics mine)

York offers a more detailed definition. He sees Neo-Paganism as

> comprising an animistic, pantheistic, and pluralistic religious orientation that is non-[d]octrinaire but employs traditional pagan metaphors (myths, foci, and rituals) or modern reconstructions of them as a means of celebrating a this-wordly emphasis. Neopagans stress self-responsibility, self-development, individual exegesis and full freedom of self-determination, the experience of ritual and ecstasy, and an ecological preoccupation.
>
> (York 1995: 136)

In the next section, we continue to explore these Neo-Pagan aspects of Burning Man and related events, and relate these aspects to the incorporation and utilization of modern technologies.

Invasion of the techno-pagans

The idea of building an anthropomorphic figure, animating it with electricity, pyrotechnics, and wire, referring to it as "the Man," allowing multiple interpretations of the event, and offering it as a central sacrificial rite for celebrants resonates with ineluctably pagan, especially animist, implications. As well as a call for community and an invocation of ecstasy, it expresses a need to fashion the natural world into images of living things, ensouling or reanimating the world of nature. The urge is both primal – widely ascribed to children and to non-industrial cultures – and postmodern. A complaint about contemporary society holds that "the common urban and suburban experience of our [American and Western] culture as 'impersonal', 'neutral', or 'dead'" (Adler 1986: 25). Re-enchanting the world of things is the common ground of advertising agencies and Neo-Pagan rituals which, despite their different motives and foci, seek to make material things seem alive and filled with delight.

Some of the practices and performances at Burning Man have elements that evoke Neo-Pagan rituals. The form of the circle is central and sacred in Neo-Pagan rituals, with Burning Man's enormous campsite laid out as a series of named concentric circles which act as streets, for example. Later in this chapter we will also explore the common elements of fire rituals and drum-dominated music and dance. We can also see ritual, ideological, and discursive elements of

Neo-Paganism in practice in many "theme camps" constructed by participants. Theme camps are group campsites that are organized around a guiding, organizing theme and through which Burning Man participants co-create the Burning Man experience. Similar to the "villages" at ConFest (St. John 1997), Burning Man provides theme camps, community, and a set of widely distributed rules to support participants' experimentation with a vast range of personal forms of expression. Theme camps provide an entertaining and enlightening experience for other participants. Many of them play with notions of the sacred and seek, with varying levels of seriousness and satire, to pierce fundamental mysteries of human and social existence. Indeed, on the central Burning Man website theme camps are described in playful, but distinctly religious, terms, as "your chance to be a god or a worshiper."[7]

Although there are major differences in motivation for participation in the event and for the construction of theme camps, we can definitely see many connections to Neo-Paganism in the descriptions participants provide of their theme camps. Consider a group that calls itself TOTEM: Temple of the Eternal Mysteries. TOTEM is "an organization dedicated to community, philosophical inquiry, the arts, and celebrating the joy of life." This group of friends from San Francisco has created several different kinds of theme camp at Burning Man. They began with a simple, but popular, mud-pit. They created a larger mud-pit, then a party room, followed by a large "sound-art" system that played "non-rave" music. In 2001 they changed their theme into a large-scale massage tent. The TOTEM group is apparently motivated by some of the same philosophies and ideologies that animate Neo-Pagan gatherings. Consider the relationship between Neo-Pagan discourse and ritual and Burning Man in TOTEM's web-page descriptions:

> The mysteries and our fascination with them [the eternal mysteries] are built into us at a very deep level. If we were to strip away all one-god ideology, all religious institutions and religious literature, and return to our tribal primitivism, the eternal mysteries would remain, to burn like the brightest sun above us all. Thus the Burning Man connection. Each year at Burning Man, we leave behind the baffling bureaucracies of Babylon, and return to our primal state. Stripped of our usual sources of institutionalized inspiration, we must search within ourselves for ultimate meaning. Only the truth and relevance of the eternal mysteries are stunning enough to command the attention of our modern primitive culture, newly arisen from the mud. We are at Burning Man because our participation in the festival restores our awareness of our tribal roots, of the mysteries within.[8]

The emphasis in this description is on the tribal, the primal, the primitive – on the regaining of the lost. Appearances must be stripped away, roots must be restored, mysteries must be returned to, people must be reborn from the mud. These inclinations are present in many other theme camps besides TOTEM. For example, consider the Sacred Playground theme camp, which provides "a sacred, grounding dome, sunset healing circles, and elemental rituals to give Burners the opportunity to recharge their energy and come back to their centers."[9]

Just as the key definitions of Neo-Paganism stress its adaptation to modern contexts, rather than dogmatically attempting to remain faithful to specific ancient religions (Pike 2001: 227), some contemporary pagan groups or adherents also attempt to reinvent pagan traditions that utilize, to varying degrees, contemporary technology. At Burning Man, it is easy to observe that the search for the sacred is often colored by a blending of aboriginal sensibilities with the high-tech leanings of Silicon Valley dotcommers. As in tales of old, stilted giants walk the Earth. As in the Garden (and *National Geographic* pictures of authentic, distant cultures), nudity beckons. A mountain of television screens showing digital art glows in the distance like a midnight desert oasis. Trees made of bones shamble about on motorized bases. Carefully coiffed and sun-screened people shove bones through their noses, and are branded en masse. Computerized pyrotechnics explode a postmodern Wicker Man, ending in fitful fire dancing, drumming and the wild shrieks of huddled digerati.

The cultural critic Erik Davis calls Burning Man an "avant-garde Neo-Pagan flame-bake" (1997: unpaginated) but also captures the important distinction between the event and more ecologically centered events like the Rainbow Gathering or many Neo-Pagan festivals. "The tweaked video, the cellular modems spitting digits to a router back in Gerlach [Nevada, the nearest permanent town to Black Rock City], the fiber-optic special effects – out here they speak the truth of our condition far more than any drum circle" (*ibid.*). Putting the rituals in context, combining the drum circles with techno music, the body paint with digital art, is what Davis suggests gives the Burning Man experience much of its originality and (sub)cultural power. It speaks of a potent polytheism – a long-sought fusing and collective embrace of techno-science, art, and the sacred. Bubbling in Burning Man's endlessly diverse cauldron (as in the subcultures of post-rave), the spirit of shamanism and paganism is refracted by the cyborgasms of techno-fetishism and digital lust.

Some participants and cultural observers, eager to identify and partake in new, differentiating trends, have used the term "techno-pagan" to describe those Neo-Pagan practitioners who embrace technology as a core element of their ritual life. Dery defines techno-paganism as "the convergence of Neo-Paganism (the umbrella term for a host of contemporary polytheistic nature religions) and the New Age with digital technology and fringe computer culture" (1996: 50). He considers techno-paganism to be an existential response to the "widespread yearning to find a place for the sacred in our ever more secular, technological society" (*ibid.*: 50). These are very similar motives indeed to those often ascribed to the growth of Neo-Paganism and New Age groups and philosophies.

According to Dery, techno-paganism also "surfaces in the electro-bacchanalian urges that animate raves" (*ibid.*: 52), where social norms are suspended in the context of dancing to loud, pounding techno music and psychedelics. The culture of rave also adopts terms and figures from Neo-Pagan literature, referencing influential high priests of modern chaos magick such as Aleister Crowley, along with psychedelic shamanic philosophers like Terence McKenna (*ibid.*; Tramacchi 2000). So although the "techno" in "techno-pagan" is widely considered to refer to technology, it might also (for the purposes of this volume at least) index post-rave techno culture, which appears to be important in incubating a nascent Neo-Paganism. As Hutson explains, "'techno' is a catch-all term for any type of 'electronic music' dominated by percussion rhythms" (1999: 53). The "electronic" element of techno "refers to the fact that most techno (in the catch-all sense) is produced synthetically by mixing beats from drum machines with other pre-recorded sounds" (*ibid.*: 53).

Providing a key link between all of these gatherings, music and dance are important to the rites of Neo-Pagans as well. As Pike notes, "Neopagan identity is primarily expressed at festivals through music and dance" (2001: 5). Drumming defines festival space at Neo-Pagan events, inspiring festal dance and movement as techno music does during raves. Burning Man, stubbornly pluralistic, inclusive, and diverse, summons all of these forms of musical expression to coexistence and interpenetration. The result is a music oeuvre that is ineffably diverse, but in which strong beats (percussive sounds) predominate. These strong beats, located in important meeting places like the Center Camp, barrel fires, dance camps, and at the burning of the Man, successfully signal ritual occasions when people gather and a more auto-expressive, improvisational, and uninhibited style of dance can take shape. The form of the music and the context of the dance both provide elements that can contribute to our understanding of the modern contradiction between the material world and the spiritual, between science and the sacred, between faith and reason. Hutson suggests that the DJ can be seen as a "techno-shaman" who is a "mixed symbol of human and machine" (1999: 71). The techno-shamanic DJ spins "tribal" beats on sophisticated equipment, and this

> synthesizes our desire to be spiritual with our rootedness and dependence on the material. The DJ thus serves as a model of the place of machines in the world and a model for how the soul can be integrated with them.
>
> (Hutson 1999: 71)

This emphasis on the DJ as role model is overly institutional and authoritarian considering the self-directed and idiosyncratic types of experiences emerging at Burning Man and Neo-Pagan gatherings. Nonetheless, Hutson's analysis begins to suggest the type of interesting explorations that can be germinated from a closer analysis of the energetic and creative outcomes resulting from the interplay of culturally charged opposite categories such as natural and artificial, human and machine, animal and human, and science and religion.

The fact that these cultural paradoxes – and the resultant need to negotiate or somehow resolve them – are in some sense widespread or even universal points to an important realization about techno-paganism as it has previously been defined. Dery's (1996) use of the term infers that technology is only or mainly important to a certain subsect of Neo-Pagans. Yet this inference that other Neo-Pagans avoid modern contrivances needs to be dispelled. Davis (1998) assumes what we consider to be a more supportable position *vis-à-vis* the relation of technology to contemporary paganism. In contrast with Dery's more exclusive definition, Davis notes how technology has become intertwined with the lives and identities of Neo-Pagans. For instance, he cites studies suggesting that an "amazingly" high percentage of Neo-Pagans are employed in technical and technological fields (*ibid.*: 180). Their "experimental spiritual pragmatism" has enabled Neo-Pagans to embrace new technologies that relate to their practices and rituals, such as astrological or Tarot card software, and the online community that enables them to communicate and plan gatherings (*ibid.*: 186). Pike (2001: 2–3) also notes the central role of email and websites in planning Neo-Pagan events, which relates them yet again to Burning Man[10] and raves (e.g. Gibson 1999).

While revealing some very interesting developments in contemporary Neo-Paganism, the term "techno-pagan" may not necessarily distinguish between different groups and practices for, as we argue here, many groups utilize and embrace technology in their organization, communication, and rites. We might, therefore, consider that Burning Man and post-raves share elements in common with Neo-Paganism, and resist the oversimplification that these events are technology-embracing "techno-pagan" events, casting other Neo-Pagans in the inaccurate role of dogmatic, electricity-shunning purists, akin to some sort of Wiccan Amish. Instead, we must recognize the technology-savvy consumer who stands behind many contemporary pagan altars. While we are doing this, we might also recognize the premodern, born-to-be-wild spirit that lies, perhaps tightly coiled, like a pre-strike rattlesnake, within the computer-using, cell phone-toting, high-tech contemporary Western consumer (Davis 1998).

Common ground: post-raves, Burning Man, and Neo-Pagan festivals

There are many important elements shared by Burning Man, post-raves like the Australian outdoor doof, and Neo-Pagan festivals. Many of these commonalities are rooted in the Neo-Pagan emphasis on embodiment and the Earth, and enhanced by an ethos of anti-authoritarian, spontaneous participation. Evocative of the role of the doof dance floor and the burning of the Man, Pike (2001) describes the centrality and importance of the frenetic drumming and dancing that surround the Neo-Pagan "festival fire" at such gatherings as the Starwood festival. She describes dancers dressed in dark capes and gauze gowns, wearing costumes or masks, naked and "adorned only with jewelry or tattoos" or feathers, holding fluorescent wands, candles, or sparklers (*ibid.*: 182). Although the site is carefully prepared, the fire event planned and beginning with a choreographed dance and procession, "once the fire is lit there is no leader, no orchestration, no focus of attention, and the ritual develops its own organic forms" (*ibid.*: 183). Exactly the same is true of the burning of the Man.

Describing the Australian post-rave doof phenomenon, Tramacchi (2000: 207, 210) regards fire, music, nature, and a mystical worldview to be central:

> Fire provides an appropriate symbol for the psychedelic movement: powerfully transformative, and most beautiful and useful as a tool when it is handled with care and respect. The music and the cycles of fire-twirling seem to draw out the moments of sunrise, golden beams dragging their way through the branches of the rainforest trees. The music complemented the sense of a single sacred moment being replayed again and again, eternity on display.
>
> (Tramacchi 2000: 207)

All of these events – doofs, Neo-Pagan fire festivals, Burning Man's central burn – proceed in a spontaneous manner. "Emerging structures and patterns are unplanned and unspoken, taking shape in the interplay of drums and movement" (Pike 2001: 183). It is in this sense that drum and dance become recognized at Neo-Pagan events, as they are at raves, as the heart of these gatherings. The ritual fire, like the secret dance floor, is a place to transport participants to a higher state of consciousness, a place that is particularly sacred, a place where self-transformation can occur. Music, drumming, lights, fire – these are places where participants at these events and festivals gain an experience, and a bodily knowing of loss of control and freedom. With an ancient language, the percussive beats tell the body what to do. The sensual and erotic surroundings of writhing human beings (dressed or undressed in enchanting and enticing wear) and the flashing lights or fire siphon off the distractions of the past and the future and root the mind in the moment. The dancers become less inhibited, more comfortable with their bodies, with the dance, with others, with the idea of others watching them dance. In the self-reflection of social performance, they learn something about who they are, what they want, what their place is. They gain momentary glimpses of a better world for themselves, the potentiality of a personally better place, that which Kozinets (2002b) has called a "youtopia."

The creation of a sense of sacred space is, we assert, vitally important to this transformational ability. For participants will only agree to loss of control and freedom in a space that they feel is safe and special. Neo-Pagans define a ritual space as a safe place "when they are able to identify their personal boundaries in a collective context" (Pike 2001: 190). The ritual fire becomes one important context for self-expression. At ConFest, St. John (1997) described the ludic spaces which provided a safe place for celebrants to experiment with the primitivity discovered on site, for example in "feral" practices like going nude, covering one's body with mud, or body-painting. The desert environment plays an important role here, just as the forest or rainforest does for forest raves and Neo-Pagan festivals. Emphasizing place refocuses the mind upon the body. In the Black Rock desert, the daytime heat can easily surpass 100° Fahrenheit during the day, and plunge to 40° in the evening. Constant rehydration is required: "piss clear" is a maxim of the event. Sunlight and desert dryness expose the body's needs and its fluids become suddenly (and literally) salient. These realities of daily existence are often related in informant interview and dialog to a more primitive state articulated as "back to nature" or more "authentic" than ordinary lived experience.

A number of scholars have focused on the commercialized and commodification-ridden elements of modern raves. In a popular statement on this perspective, Thornton locates rave "subculture" within commercial industries such as publishing and recording which "specialize in the manufacture and promotion of 'anti-commercial' culture" (1996: 157). Her study traces multiple instances of the commercial co-creation of the rave subculture to argue the important involvement of culture industries in subcultures such as rave and to critique the popular notion that raves are subversive acts of resistance (see *ibid.*: 116–62). The commodification rap is perhaps the main reason Burning Man's organizers and participants tend to distance their community from rave, for they seek to position their event as unsponsored, uncommodified and non-commercial.

Yet it is in this critique that our study of Burning Man can add much to our understanding of the qualities of raves or, most accurately, post-rave phenomena. For, as St. John (2001: 14–16) emphasizes, doof culture in Australia emphasizes volunteerism and freedom from corporate influences. As Kozinets (2002b) details, through its rules (such as "no vending"), Burning Man attempts ideologically and ritually to distance itself from the mainstream marketplace, offering consumers a place they can imagine they have suspended authoritarian market logics. The result is the freedom from social distancing in which participants build community, and the freedom from passivity in which they express and transform themselves. As Belk *et al.* (1989) and Kozinets (2001) have pointed out, the sacred and the commercial exist in an uneasy cultural tension with one another throughout contemporary Western society.

The anti-market and anti-organized religious elements are classic characteristics of festivals and other carnivalesque events, with their ritual inversions and anti-authoritarian discourses and themes (Duvignaud 1976; Falassi 1987). Festivals provide ritual power for inverting, temporarily overturning, and denying currently dominant social orders. In this exploration we begin to discover the way in which sacred experiences at events such as doofs, Neo-Pagan festivals, and Burning Man carve out sacred times and spaces for participants to define themselves in commercial society.

Conclusions

This chapter stands as a teaser to substantial explorations of the theme of the sacred at Burning Man. We can only hint at the future possibilities of exploring this stance further. We suggest as a provisional conclusion that Neo-Pagan sensibilities and discourse, and the cultural imperatives that underlie them, can contribute much to our understanding of many contemporary festivals, such as post-rave events and Burning Man. We further suggest that these spaces are rich sites from which scholars and students can formulate important new ideas about identity and society in the early 21st century.

Consider some questions. What is the role of commercial culture and the marketplace in these sacred spaces? What is the role of organized religion? Why do so many of these adherents feel that they need to suspend the logics of the market and of their inherited religion in order to engage in self-transformative practices? How do Neo-Pagan rituals and New Age philosophies relate to these anti-market and anti-religion connections? How do the psychotherapeutics of these events help to inform our understanding of contemporary consumer society and the deficiencies that it might have? What changes – if any – do these events make in people's lives outside of the events? What shapes and forms of utopia do events such as Burning Man portend? What are the wider implications of movements such as the spiritual-ecological elaboration of "techno-pagan" beliefs and its trickledown into multifarious festivals? We believe that this research suggests that these are important questions that may be investigated at places such as forest raves, doofs, other rave-derived events, Neo-Pagan festivals, and Burning Man.

On a deeply personal level, these events call on us to burn within ancient and ever-new fires. The fire and the drumming, the lights and the music, they urge us to sacrifice what we were for what we can be, to burn in the glory of seeking better ways, new realizations, intimations of infinite being. As contemporary sacred spaces, they hold fascinating promise for the ongoing and positive transformation of our selves and our society.

Notes

1 It is worth noting that, not unlike other contemporary events (e.g. forest raves, Rainbow Gatherings, and some Neo-Pagan festivals), even Burning Man is not fundamentalist in its adherence to the "no vending" rule. The Center Camp sells coffee and some other beverages. Ice is also sold and the proceeds donated to local charities. Year round, the website offers branded merchandise such as Burning Man posters, videos, T-shirts, and baseball caps. So much for ideological purity.

2 To preserve confidentiality, and following the guidelines of online anthropology, or "netnography" (Kozinets 2002a), informant pseudonyms have been used throughout this chapter.

3 Posted by "Alexander" on his Burning Man 1999 experience website, available online at http://www.ideamatic.com/burning/html/words/words2.html (accessed June 2002).

4 This chapter is based on ethnographic fieldwork at Burning Man during 1999 and 2000, and on yearlong online participation in the community that surrounds it. Our investigation of Burning Man and its community began in October 1996 with observation of the very active Internet community of Burning Man participants (first author). We followed this observation with six days of participant observation at the weeklong Burning Man 1999 event (first author). This was followed by a further six days of participation–observation at Burning Man 2000 (both authors). Prior to, during, and subsequent to our immersion in the events, we kept detailed written field notes. We also recorded events and interviews with a digital video camcorder. We took over 500 photographs. We conducted semi-structured interviews with over 120 informants (in one-on-one and group formations). Between interviews, and particularly during the evenings, we abandoned our cameras and participated in the event: wearing a variety of outlandish costumes, being initiated into new religions, drumming,

meeting new people, riding on strange vehicles. Our videotapes, field notes, Internet downloads, and transcribed interviews were coded and analyzed using constant comparative analytic techniques (e.g. Glaser and Strauss 1967). In all, our ethnography encompassed interviews and interactions with several hundred Burning Man participants. Much of this material was not used here, but is present in other work on the topic (see Kozinets 2002b and forthcoming; Sherry and Kozinets forthcoming).

5 This account by "Zelga" was published in the Burning Man update, version 6 #4, which was distributed to subscribers on November 14, 2001.

6 "What is Burning Man?," by Molly Steenson, posted on:
http://www.burningman.com/whatisburningman/about—burningman/
experience.html (accessed August 2002).

7 Posted on http://www.burningman.com/first—timers (accessed July 2002).

8 From the TOTEM homepage, TOTEM: Temple Of The Eternal Mysteries, posted on http://www.eternal-mysteries.org/Philosophy.htm (accessed June 2002).

9 Posted on: http://www.burningman.com/themecamps—installations/
themecamps/02—camp—vill—mz.html (accessed June 2002).

10 Burning Man uses email and websites extensively; see http://www.burningman.com

Bibliography

Adler, Margot (1986) *Drawing Down the Moon: Witches, Druids, Goddess-worshippers and Other Pagans in American Today*, Boston, MA: Beacon Press.

Beckford, James A. (1984) "Holistic imagery and ethics in new religious and healing movements," *Social Compass* 31.2–3:, 259–272.

Belk, Russell W., Melanie Wallendorf and John F. Sherry, Jr. (1989) "The sacred and the profane: theodicy on the odyssey," *Journal of Consumer Research* 16 (June):, 1–38.

Black, D.S. (1998) "Burning Man as ephemeropolis and the refusal of meaning," paper presented at the North American Interdisciplinary Conference on Environment and Community, University of Nevada, Reno, February 20, 1998; available online at http://www.spiralgirl.com/ARCHIVE/dsBlackEssay.html (accessed December 1999).

Davis, Erik (1997) "Here is postmodern space," in John Plunkett and Brad Wieners (eds.) *Burning Man*, San Francisco: HardWired (unpaginated).

—— (1998) *Techgnosis: Magic, Myth and Mysticism in the Age of Information*, New York: Harmony.

Dery, Mark (1996) *Escape Velocity: Cyberculture at the End of the Century*, New York: Grove.

Duvignaud, Jean (1976) "Festivals: a sociological approach," *Cultures* 3(1): 13–25.

Falassi, Alessandro (ed.) (1987) *Time Out of Time: Essays on the Festival*, Albuquerque, NM: University of New Mexico.

Ferguson, Marilyn (1987) *The Aquarian Conspiracy: Personal and Social Transformation in Our Time*, Los Angeles, CA: J.P. Tarcher.

Gibson, Chris (1999) "Subversive sites: rave cultures, spatial politics and the Internet in Sydney, Australia," *Area* 31(1): 19–33.

Glaser, Barney G. and Anselm L. Strauss (1967) *The Discovery of Grounded Theory*, Chicago: Aldine.

Hutson, Scott R. (1999) "Technoshamanism: spiritual healing in the rave subculture," *Popular Music and Society* 23(3): 53–77.

Kozinets, Robert V. (2001) "Utopian enterprise: articulating the meanings of Star Trek's culture of consumption," *Journal of Consumer Research* 28 (June): 67–88.

—— (2002a) "The field behind the screen: using netnography for marketing research in online communities," *Journal of Marketing Research* 39 (February): 61–72.

Kozinetis, Robert V. (2002b) "Can consumers escape the market? Emancipatory illuminations from Burning Man," *Journal of Consumer Research* 29 (June): 20–38.

—— (forthcoming) "The moment of infinite fire," in Stephen Brown and John F. Sherry,
Jr. (eds.) *Time and the Market: Ecumenical Essays on the Rise of Retroscapes*, New York:
M.E. Sharpe.

McKay, George (ed.) (1998) *DiY Culture: Party and Protest in Nineties Britain*, London: Verso.

Pearson, Joanne, Richard H. Roberts and Geoffrey Samuel (eds.) (1998) *Nature Religion
Today: Paganism in the Modern World*, Edinburgh: Edinburgh University Press.

Pike, Sarah M. (2001) *Earthly Bodies, Magical Selves: Contemporary Pagans and the Search for
Community*, Berkeley, CA: University of California Press.

St. John, Graham (1997) "Going feral: authentica on the edge of Australian culture,"
Australian Journal of Anthropology 8(2): 167–89.

—— (2001) "Doof! Australian post-rave culture," in Graham St. John (ed.) *FreeNRG: Notes
from the Edge of the Dance Floor*, Melbourne: Common Ground.

Sherry, John F., Jr., and Robert V. Kozinets (forthcoming) "Sacred iconography in secular
space: altars, alters and alterity at the Burning Man project," in Cele Otnes and Tina
Lowry (eds.) *Contemporary Consumption Rituals: An Interdisciplinary Anthology*, Mahwah, NJ:
Lawrence Erlbaum.

Thornton, Sarah (1996) *Club Cultures: Music, Media and Subcultural Capital*, Hanover, NH:
University Press of New England.

Tramacchi, Des (2000) "Field tripping: psychedelic communitas and ritual in the
Australian bush," *Journal of Contemporary Religion* 15(2): 201–13.

Turner, Victor (1967) *The Forest of Symbols: Aspects of Ndembu Ritual*, Ithaca, NY, and
London: Cornell University.

York, Michael (1995) *The Emerging Network: A Sociology of the New Age and Neopagan
Movements*, Lanham, MD: Rowman & Littlefield.

Index

Lightning Source UK Ltd.
Milton Keynes UK
UKOW03f0917070914

238186UK00006B/142/P

9 780415 552509